# THE BEATLES LIVE!

'A NIGHT TO REMEMBER'

FRIDAY 6th APRIL 7·30 P.M. - 10.0

ER BALLROOM N BRIGHTON

k again by Public Demand...the Fabulou

EMILE FORD AND THE CHECKMATES WITH THE BEETLES

(THEIR FAREWELL PERFORMANCE PRIOR TO A TWO MONTHS SEASON IN GERMANY)

ALSO MERSEYSIDE'S TOP 4 GROUPS

GERRY AND THE PACEMAKERS

HOWIE CASEY AND THE SENIORS

RORY STORM AND THE HURRICANES

THE BIG THREE

AND THE ORIGINAL KINGTWISTERS

Tickets 6/.

FROM · RUSHWORTHS · NEMS LEWIS'S · STROTHERS and TOWER BALLROOM

LICENSED BARS LATE TRANSPORT ALL AREAS LIVERPOOL AND WIRRAL

NEMS ENTERPRISES PRESENT AT NEW BRIGHTON TOWER FOR ONE NIGHT ONLY 7·30 to 11·30 FRIDAY. JUNE 14th.

"Merseysides Greatest...

"THE BEATLES AND GERRY and the PACEMAKERS

TICKETS 6/. AT DOOR ON NIGHT 7/.

IN ADVANCE

A BOB WOOLER PRODUCTION

PLUS 5 GRE SUPPORTIN GROUPS

DON'T MISS FRIDAY, JUNE 28th. JET HARRIS & TONY M

'HERE THEY COME THE FABULOUS

BEATLES

American Tour 1964

Aug 19 San Francisco Cow Palace

Sept 4 Milwaukee Auditorium
Sept 5 Chicago International Amphitheat
Sept 6 Detroit Olympia Stadium

LEACH ENTERTAINMENTS pre

The BEATLE

# THE BEATLES LIVE!

## MARK LEWISOHN

An Owl Book
HENRY HOLT AND COMPANY
NEW YORK

Published in the United States by
Henry Holt and Company, Inc., 521 Fifth Avenue,
New York, New York 10175.

Originally published in Great Britain

Library of Congress Cataloging-in-Publication Data

Lewisohn, Mark.
    The Beatles live!
    "An Owl book."
    1. Beatles—Chronology.    2. Rock musicians—
England—Miscellanea.    I. Title.
    ML421.B4L48    1986    784.5′4′00922 [B]    86–9915
    ISBN 0-8050-0158-1 (pbk.)

First American Edition

Designed by Lawrence Edwards and Madeline Serre
Printed in Great Britain
10 9 8 7 6 5 4 3 2 1

ISBN 0-8050-0158-1

# CONTENTS

# ACKNOWLEDGEMENTS

In the course of researching a book like this, one must inevitably confer with a great many people. Indeed this book would not have been possible without the input from those relevant to the story. All of the following – plus one or two others doubtless omitted out of forgetfulness – have given valuable help and support and I thank them warmly.

John Askew (Johnny Gentle), Neil Aspinall, Tony Barrow, Art Barry, Mona Best, Rod Bleackley, Albert Bonici, Brian Bowman, Johnny 'Guitar' Byrne, Roy Carr, John Cochrane, Ray Coleman, Joe Collins, Pat Daniels, Rod Davis, Harry Dickinson, Peter Doggett, Tony Elwood and Richard Wootton at Telecom Technology Showcase, Walter Eymond, Jack Fallon and Bill Fraser Reid of the late lamented Jaybee Clubs, Stan Fishman at Rank Leisure, Dave Forshaw, Danny Friedman at the V & A Museum, Bob Gannon, Nigel Greenberg and Debbie Geoghegan, Jim Gretty, Johnny Gustafson, Maurice Haigh, Colin Hanton, Roger Howell at the Woolwich Granada, Liz and Jim Hughes, Douglas Jenkins, Hilary Kay at Sotheby's, Leslie Kearney, Fred Keight, Brian Kelly, Charlie McBain Jr, Mike McCartney, Eric MacKenzie at the *Birkenhead News*, Tony Meehan, David Moores, Chas Newby, Jos Nicholl at the Old Stoic Society, Jimmy Nicol, Jos Remmerswaal, Geoff Rhind, Mike and Elizabeth Robbins, Charles Roberts, Brian Roylance, Eileen Ruane, Jimmy Savile, Helen Simpson at Beatle City, David J. Smith, John Smith, Peter and Coral Stringfellow, Derek Taylor, Chas. Tranter, Bob Woodward.

Special thanks to my parents for putting up with me, my noisy typing and the memorabilia towers that grew ever upwards from the bedroom and attic floors.

Sincere thanks too to Colin Webb, Vivien Bowler, Charis Adam and all at Pavilion for their professional but always friendly and hospitable manner, guidance, great efficiency and timely encouragement.
I truly could not have wished for a better publisher. Thanks too to my agent, Peter Hogan, for getting us together and for not giving up.

I am enormously indebted to Mark Cousins and John Walker, two very good friends and fellow enthusiasts. Without them a part-time hobby would not have become full-time slavery, for both were responsible for suggesting that my initial research had the makings of a book, much to my own great doubt. Once persuaded, both continued to offer invaluable and unstinting encouragement and suggestions.

Grateful thanks go to Spencer Leigh, ever generous with gems of information and details from his very full address book; to Monty Lister, for having the wisdom to record an interview with the Beatles in 1962 and then hang on to the precious tape for three decades; and to Roger Scott, the great disc-jockey, for remixing that tape for the free disc and for also supplying vital illustrations.

Last but most certainly not least, my thanks go to Tarja for everything past, present and for *aina*.

Mark Lewisohn

# FOREWORD

There are Beatles books and Beatles books. This one is indispensable.

Mark Lewisohn has made an enormous contribution to the history of British popular music with this volume. In compiling an accurate, detailed and entertaining record of every live Beatles and embryo Beatles performance, from the Quarry Men's audition for Carroll Levis on 9 June 1957 to the final concert in San Francisco just over nine years later, he has produced a document that illustrates the extraordinary pace, excitement and exhaustion of those years better than any ordinary biography or discography has yet done.

The Beatles on record, film, television and videotape will always be with us—the Beatles as a live act can never be experienced again. And it is good news indeed that somebody of Lewisohn's integrity and intelligence has written a book like this before the facts, figures and first-hand memories of the world's greatest group of popular musicians on stage fade away.

As a rock historian, publisher and Beatles fan, I am delighted to have a modest connection with this remarkable book.

Tim Rice
Great Milton, February, 1986

The Beatles on stage at the newly opened
Star-Club in Hamburg, May 1962.

# 'Didn't the Beatles give everything on God's earth for ten years?'

JOHN LENNON, 1980

Beatles books, these days, are hardly a rarity. But whether written by ex-lovers, ex-assistants, ex-confidants, or extremists they almost all share in a fundamental lack of care in the Accuracy department, and often show little or no research beyond the borrowing of 'facts' from other incorrect books. It brings to mind the old proverb, 'Give a lie twenty-four hours' start and you can never overtake it': if a lie/half-truth/fabrication is not refuted immediately, it will pass from mouth to mouth (or, in this case, from book to book) until it is accepted as the gospel truth by everybody. And never has this moral been more sorely tested than in the now almost-legendary tales of the Beatles. Reportage of the group's background and success began to go awry in the very early days of the Beatles' fame, often – with reason – fuelled by the Beatles or their aides themselves, and it has not stopped to this day. These inaccuracies litter what we presently know as The Beatles Story.

This book is different. Firstly, it is not an opinionated biography but a reference work, the result of almost seven years' painstaking research. Secondly, it unfolds – in meticulous detail – the one remaining untold major facet of the Beatles' career – their live performances. That it should be untold until now is strange, for their stage career was perhaps the most important ingredient of all in the make-up of their unprecedented fame. The Beatles, as this book amply illustrates, absolutely *slogged* for their success. So, beyond one or two brave but vastly incomplete efforts to remedy this situation by Beatles fan magazines, why has the whole story remained unreported until now? Several reasons. No one in, or close to, the group appears to have kept diaries during the key years of 1957–66; no magazine or newspaper ever detailed, previewed, pursued or reported the Beatles' live gigs in any great depth; and that it took almost seven years to uncover exactly what went on twenty or more years ago.

I started work on this project almost inadvertently, in January 1979, when I was approached by Philip Norman, in the middle of his writing the Beatles' biography *Shout!*, to undertake a little research. He was chiefly puzzled by three particularly cloudy, and vital facts relating to the group: the date John Lennon first met Paul McCartney (variously reported elsewhere as 1954, 1955, 1956, 1957 and 1958); the details of the Beatles' first professional tour, in Scotland, as backing group to a singer called Johnny Gentle (venues and dates previously guessed at by 'researchers'); and the Beatles' first live broadcast on BBC radio (a particularly hazy detail). Boldly I began to dig where – incredibly – no man had dug before, and it wasn't long before I came up with all the goods. As a result, *Shout!* became the first-ever book to contain the true date Lennon met McCartney – 6 July 1957 – together with a full account of that meeting, and the first book to reveal (though Norman chose not to go into detail) the time and places of the Johnny Gentle tour. Intrigued by my other findings I soon began to research the entire story of the Beatles' BBC radio career, which I presented in the March and April 1980 issues of *The Beatles Monthly Book* (since gratifyingly hailed as the most important slice of Beatles research work ever). And I also began to assemble a complete catalogue of the group's live performances, little knowing the mammoth task I was taking on.

The information for this book had to come not from a fading memory or the fertile mind of a ghost-writer but from, literally, more than a thousand sources. It has been a gradual piecing together of a myriad fragments of recollections, contemporaneous newspaper reports and memorabilia. No effort has been spared to verify every scrap of information with independent witnesses, and only reluctantly have I had to be satisfied with anything less. Where I encountered two or three conflicting accounts of the same story I have carefully tried to sift the facts from the fiction.

Memories alone are dangerous things indeed for a researcher to rely upon, and I have run across scores of instances where individuals may have been 100 per cent certain that they were right – but were, in fact, wrong. And then there's the inevitable exaggeration one encounters arising from the constant re-telling of an old story. A good example of this is an obscure 1983 newspaper report which stated that Peter Stringfellow, the now-famous London night-club owner, had once booked the Beatles for a dance in

St Aidan's Church Hall for £20 in 1961. After furious digging and many telephone calls, including interrogations with, of all people, Stringfellow's scoutmaster (!) and the vicar of St Aidan's (who kindly asked his congregation after his Sunday sermon if anyone remembered the Beatles' pop music combo blasting the rafters of the adjoining church hall twenty-two years earlier), I eventually sleuthed the real story. Stringfellow booked the Beatles in 1963, not 1961, and for £85, not £20. And the dance wasn't even held at St Aidan's church hall but at a large Sheffield ballroom!

So while this book will undoubtedly provide a great many new facts, it will also *disprove* an equal number of what are best described as 'fabricated facts'. Indeed even the most knowledgeable Beatles students, on reading it, will regularly confront details contrary to their previous beliefs. For anyone reading this who was in any way connected to the Beatles story, or with the British pop scene in the late fifties and early sixties, it should also revive happy memories of an equally happy era. Finally, the contents of this book are, in essence, an intensely detailed chronological account of the Beatle years, 1957–66, something never before compiled in such depth.

I have already written that no engagements diary for the period 1957–66, kept by a person closely connected with the Beatles, has survived the years. As a consequence, there is no comprehensive, existing catalogue of the group's live performances other than the one contained in this book. This is something of which I have been constantly aware, since I have been unable to 'compare notes' or to plug any possible holes in the chronological listing. If any person should have reason to believe that they know of a Beatles live performance not included in this book please write to me, stating as many details as possible, care of Pavilion Books, 196 Shaftesbury Avenue, London WC2H 8JL, England.

Mark Lewisohn
London, January 1986

## Author's Notes

This book is divided into eight chapters (1957–9; 1960; 1961; 1962; 1963; 1964; 1965; 1966) each of which has two main components; a commentary on the events in the Beatles' career and a complete listing – in chronological order – of their live engagements for that period. Also included in each chapter are Other Engagements Played and Engagements Not Played. These sections cover live gigs believed to have taken place for which details were impossible to locate, and aim to dispel previously reported 'facts' (rumours) about Beatles' gigs – now proven to be non-existent. Each chapter concludes with a listing of the music included in the Beatles' stage repertoire at that time.

When reading the illustrated original newspaper reports, one should remember that, in most instances, throughout their history, provincial journals – from Merseyside to Madagascar – have tended to exaggerate local stories out of all proportion. Thus 'average' becomes 'good', and 'good' 'sensational'; 'a half-full' venue becomes 'a capacity house', and any sort of national mention, however brief, or appearance in an important situation, means that the local 'artistes' are 'stars'.

One should also bear firmly in mind that comparatively few of the Beatles' 1400 live performances detailed in this book could be classified as 'concerts'. Before the inception of the discothèque in the mid-sixties the music for dancing came not from records, but from a live group, solo artist or band. Virtually all of the Beatles' pre-1963 gigs were therefore dances, mostly held in ballrooms or public halls, not concerts performed in venues with seating. In 1963 the ratio of the Beatles' dances to concerts was about 50:50. In 1964, 1965 and 1966 they gave concerts only.

Where possible the first mention in the book of a venue played by the Beatles carries its full address (written – for nostalgic purposes – exactly as it appeared in the fifties and sixties) to assist anyone wishing to visit them today. It should be remembered though that a large proportion, particularly those relics of the bygone dance era, the ballrooms, have since been demolished. All venues are in England and in Liverpool unless otherwise stated.

The discerning reader may notice some minor discrepancies between the listing of the Beatles' Cavern Club, Liverpool, performances given here, and the club's occasional bill-of-fare advertisements in the fort-nightly newspaper *Mersey Beat*. Most of the information for the Cavern Club gigs in this book came from the club's up-to-the-minute listings in the nightly *Liverpool Echo*, as opposed to the *Mersey Beat* adverts which were printed up to one month before the gigs and were therefore subject to change. Details of totally unadvertised Cavern Club performances have been compiled from numerous sources.

# 1957-59

JAZZ

CAVERN TO-NIGHT

SKIFFLE SESSION
DIRECT FROM TRIUMPHANT TOUR
RON McKAY
Plus Dark Town, Deltones, Quarry Men
and the Demon Five.

*Above: The Quarry Men's first visiting card. The address is that of Nigel Whalley, who acted as manager. Opposite: A rare glimpse of the Quarry Men at the Rosebery Street party on 22 June, John Lennon at the makeshift microphone.*

**Skiffle:** [A] Kind of folk music played by group, mainly with rhythmic accompaniment to singing guitarist.(Perhaps imitative.)

OXFORD ENGLISH DICTIONARY

When twenty-four-year-old Lonnie Donegan suddenly burst into the limelight in January 1956 he could scarcely have imagined the dramatic and spiralling effect he would have on British youth and culture. After all, his version of the old Huddie (Leadbelly) Ledbetter song 'Rock Island Line' was not *that* different from the original, aeons-old black blues version. And besides, Donegan's recording was already eighteen months old.

Yet this very record, credited to the Lonnie Donegan Skiffle Group, started a craze among (predominantly male) teenagers that swept throughout Britain in 1956 and 1957. In reality, skiffle was not really a new fad at all, since its roots were embedded in negro jazz and folk music of the twenties American depression. Even in Britain, Ken Colyer had incorporated a special skiffle section within his jazz band as early as 1949.

But what made skiffle so attractive to teenagers was not its history but its very structure. It was basic and easy to play. Literally anyone without even much imagination, talent or money could form a group. All one needed was a cheap, often Spanish, acoustic guitar, a household washboard (an implement which has long since disappeared from our homes) and an inspirational invention – the tea-chest bass. This was a crude copy of a stand-up bass, made by poking a broom handle through a hole in an upturned tea-chest and tensing a piece of cord to form a sounding string. Other instruments could be added of course if one was particularly flush with money – a banjo, or a set of drums – but these were largely superfluous to the core of the group.

It would not be an exaggeration to say that in the wake of Donegan's success and, to a lesser degree, the success of others like Tommy Steele, the Vipers, Chas McDevitt and Nancy Whiskey, and Johnny

Duncan, there were upwards of five thousand skiffle combos in existence around Britain during 1956–7. In Liverpool alone there were, quite literally, many hundreds of them.

John Winston Lennon, a bright but unruly sixteen-year-old living in Woolton, a comfortable, middle-class village bordering Liverpool city centre, had been particularly smitten with 'teenagers' music' since May 1956 when he had been overawed by the power, grace and rawness of Elvis Presley singing 'Heartbreak Hotel'. In March 1957,[1] having finally persuaded his guardian, Aunt Mimi, to buy him a £17 guitar, he decided to form a skiffle group. Fun and laughter were the chief aims of this group, with the prospect of subsequent money and fame, although not entirely unconsidered, by no means the overriding concern.

Initially (for just one week) Lennon named the group – consisting at this point of just himself and his crony Pete Shotton – the Black Jacks, but since they both attended the Quarry Bank High School for Boys, and its school song contained the line 'Quarry

1 This is the true date of the formation of the group.

13

*Bottom: The Quarry Men at the Woolton fête, taken by Geoff Rhind, a Quarry Bank schoolboy, with a Box Brownie camera and shown here for the first time directly from the negative and uncropped. Left to right: Eric Griffiths, Colin Hanton, Rod Davis, John Lennon, Pete Shotton, Len Garry.*

**Woolton Parish Church**
# Garden Fete
and
## Crowning of Rose Queen
### Saturday, July 6th, 1957

To be opened at 3 p.m. by Dr. Thelwall Jones

**PROCESSION AT 2 p.m.**

LIVERPOOL POLICE DOGS DISPLAY
FANCY DRESS PARADE
SIDESHOWS            REFRESHMENTS
BAND OF THE CHESHIRE YEOMANRY
THE QUARRY MEN SKIFFLE GROUP

**ADULTS 6d., CHILDREN 3d.**        OR BY PROGRAMME

## GRAND DANCE
at 8 p.m. in the Church Hall

GEORGE EDWARDS' BAND
THE QUARRY MEN SKIFFLE GROUP
Tickets 2/-

Men, old before our birth . . .', it was decided that they should rename the group the Quarry Men instead.

Band members – friends and various spectators – were quickly recruited, although a *full* list of them all over the years is impossible to document since some lasted for just one rehearsal or performance, and the line-up was in a continual state of flux. Certainly John and Pete's Quarry Bank class mate Bill Smith was the first new member, playing tea-chest bass. Other early personnel included Rod Davis (banjo), Eric Griffiths (guitar), Len Garry, Ivan Vaughan and Nigel Whalley (all bass) and Colin Hanton (drums). John Lennon was guitarist and, since it was his group, the vocalist, while Pete Shotton briefly played the washboard.

Early, undocumented, engagements consisted mainly of friends' parties and the ten-a-penny skiffle contests which sprang up at almost every dance hall or ballroom during the skiffle craze. They even entered a talent contest run by Mr Star-Maker himself, Carroll Levis, at the Liverpool Empire theatre,

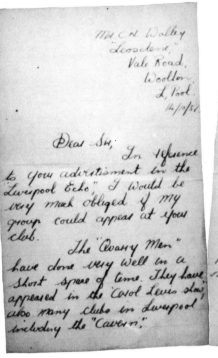

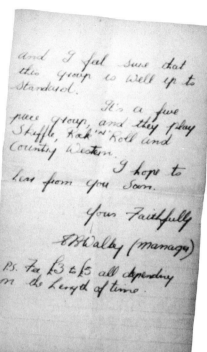

*Left: Former tea-chest bass man, now 'manager', Nigel Whalley, wrote these letters in the hope of securing engagements for the Quarry Men. Despite the grandiose claims, he was unsuccessful. (Note: Whalley occasionally dropped the 'h' from his surname.) Below: Newspaper advert for the Quarry Men's 24 January 1958 Cavern Club gig.*

**JAZZ**

JAZZ AT CHESTER

The Embassy Stompers Jazz Band
The Brian Newman Skiffle Group of
Liverpool
FRIDAY 24th JANUARY, 8 p.m.
THE PIED BULL HOTEL,
NORTHGATE, CHESTER

JAZZ AT THE CAVERN

* TONIGHT
  THE NEW:—
  BASIL KIRCHIN BAND.
* FRIDAY
  THE MERSEYSIPPI !
  QUARRYMEN SKIFFLE
* SATURDAY
  THE ZENITH SIX !
  CAVENDISH SKIFFLE
* SUNDAY
  THE MERSEYSIPPI !
  DRUIDS JAZZ BAND
  BLUE GENES SKIFFLE

(LUNCHTIME JAZZ FRIDAY)

but failed miserably, not getting through the initial audition.

On Saturday 6 July 1957, while playing at the summer fête of St Peter's Parish Church in Woolton – a booking secured by Pete Shotton's mother – the Quarry Men were watched by a chubby fifteen-year-old lad from nearby Allerton, James Paul McCartney. That day the seed of a relationship which would rock the entertainment world was sown: the partnership of Lennon and McCartney. Paul had been brought up in a musical family, his father Jim having led Jim Mac's Jazz Band in the early twenties. Paul initially learnt the trumpet and piano before he saw Lonnie Donegan in concert at the Liverpool Empire on 11 November 1956 and became besotted with the guitar. He was certainly a quick learner for legend has it that after the Quarry Men came off the outdoor stage that day at the fête, and were setting up for the evening, post-fête dance in the church hall, Paul grabbed a guitar and displayed his talents to the group with versions of Eddie Cochran's recently released 'Twenty Flight Rock' and Gene Vincent's 'Be-Bop-A-Lula'. Both were great favourites of John's but he was dreadful at remembering their lyrics, often resorting to making up his own on the spur of the moment. This was one of Paul's strong points, and he obligingly jotted down the words and handed them to the young Lennon. As if this wasn't impressive enough, Paul then showed John and Eric Griffiths his most recent accomplishment, the art of tuning a guitar. Unable to perform this difficult feat the two Quarry Men had previously taken their instruments to a man in Kings Drive, Woolton, who did it for them for a small fee.

After Paul had left to cycle home John was left with a tough decision to make. Should he strengthen and improve the group, *his* group, by inviting this comparatively talented new lad to join up – thus challenging his own undoubted superiority – or should the group plough on into eventual oblivion without him, but with his own supremacy intact? After much careful consideration he chose the first option.

Two weeks later Pete Shotton chanced upon McCartney while cycling in Woolton, and on behalf of John and the group, invited him to join up. Paul thought for a while and agreed that he would. But although he rehearsed with them regularly thereafter he didn't make his public debut with the Quarry Men until 18 October 1957 at the New Clubmoor Hall (Conservative Club) in the back of Broadway, Liverpool. He missed the group's first-ever engagement at the Cavern Club on 7 August because he was away at summer scout camp in Hathersage in the Peak District with his brother Michael (later Mike McGear of Scaffold fame).

Paul's arrival in the Quarry Men coincided with the death throes of skiffle, departing almost as suddenly as it had seemingly arrived, and the career embarkation of several Quarry Men members. While John had left Quarry Bank school for Liverpool College of Art, other group members began to drift away slowly to full-time employment. By early 1958 the group was down to a hard core of five members – John, Paul, Len Garry, Eric Griffiths and Colin Hanton, although they were supplemented by others on occasions, like pianist John Lowe, nicknamed 'Duff'. In March 1958 Paul wrote a letter to a family contact, Mike Robbins, at a Butlin's holiday camp, asking for work for the group during the long school summer vacation. It was signed on behalf of himself, John and Len Garry – Hanton and Griffiths clearly having no intention of giving up possible well-paid jobs for the vagaries of such an engagement. Although the request proved unsuccessful the letter also mentioned a young guitarist they had recently met. His name was George Harrison.

George was even younger than his school buddy Paul McCartney, having just turned fifteen years old. So despite his ability as a guitarist – formed only after hour upon hour of continual finger-tearing graft – John, in particular, felt that George was nothing more than a kid, the two-and-a-half-year age gap being a huge gulf in one's early teens. But George was persistent, following the group around a couple of party engagements and eventually ingratiating himself sufficiently, much to John's reported disdain, to become a fully fledged member of the Quarry Men.

Despite their newly strengthened line-up, bookings became extremely few and far between through the remainder of 1958 and all of 1959, and the group became restricted to playing at private parties, working men's clubs and youth clubs. It was around this time that John and Paul began to write songs together, gradually filling a school exercise book with such ditties as 'I Lost my Little Girl', 'That's my Woman', 'Thinking of Linking', 'Years Roll Along', 'Keep Looking that Way', 'Just Fun' and 'Too Bad About Sorrows', as well as instrumentals like 'Looking Glass' and 'Winston's Walk'. Several other tunes from this period were later to emerge: 'Love Me Do', 'The One after 909', 'Hello Little Girl', 'When I'm Sixty-Four', 'Hot as Sun', 'Catswalk' and others. The Quarry Men even made a demonstration record in mid-1958, recorded in the back room of a house at 53 Kensington, Liverpool, owned by an old gentleman called Percy Phillips. The five lads – John, Paul, George, Colin Hanton and John Lowe – all put up 3s 6d each, and for 17s 6d made a two-sided shellac disc. On the top side they recorded Buddy Holly's 'That'll Be the Day', with John on lead vocals, while Paul took over the B-side with a Harrison–McCartney composition 'In Spite of all the Danger', sung in fifties 'doo-wop' style. Sadly, Phillips wiped the tape soon afterwards and the only known copy

*Above: George Harrison, in the days before every house had a television set, watching the FA Cup Final in his local church hall, 4 May 1957. With him are brother Peter and friend Arthur Kelly.*

*Opposite: The opening of the Casbah Coffee Club (mis-spelt here as Kasbah) made front-page news in the* West Derby Reporter. *The girl seated closest to John in the centre photograph is his wife-to-be Cynthia Powell.*

of the disc is now in the possession of Paul McCartney who prised it from the clutches of Lowe in return for a generous cheque twenty-three years later, in July 1981.

Incidentally, several Quarry Men rehearsal sessions were also commited to tape to enable the group to hear how they sounded. Good Grundig recordings were made by Geraldine and Colette Davis (no relation to the group's banjoist, Rod) and a dedicated Quarry Men follower called Arthur Wong. All such recordings have long since been lost or wiped.

By early 1959 the group was drifting, aimlessly. Drummer Colin Hanton had a furious row with the other three after an engagement at a bus depot near Prescot. The night had turned into drunken chaos when there was a slim chance that a good perfor-

# KASBAH HAS A NEW MEANING FOR LOCAL TEENAGERS

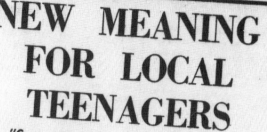

**"Come with me to the Kasbah," is a sentence familiar to Charles Boyer fans, but for teenagers in West Derby it has taken on a new meaning.**

The Kasbah is a club which was opened recently by an enterprising mother, Mrs. Mona Best, Haymans Green, West Derby, in the cellars of her home.

Two of the teenagers chat with Rory Best. (B1565/1)

"The house was like a railway station," Mrs. Best told the Reporter, "then my sons had the idea of turning the cellars into a 'den' for their friends. They began by papering the walls, but of course with it being a cellar it wouldn't stay up, so they became downhearted."

Mrs. Best decided that the job should be done properly so, after a conference with 18-years-old Peter, Rory (aged 15) and some of their friends, they decided to form a club. For two months Mrs. Best helped the boys to paint the walls and stain the boards that now give the club its Eastern atmosphere. Their pride and joy is a large dragon which is painted along the length of one wall.

## GUITAR GROUP

Three of the boys, Kenneth Brown, 149, Storrington Avenue, Norris Green, David Hughes, 119, Blackmoor Drive, West Derby, and Douglas Jenkins, 28, Cottesbrook Road, Norris Green, went to the cellars from their jobs each evening and helped with the conversion at weekends.

Kenneth Brown is also a member of a guitar group which entertains the club members on Saturday nights. The other members of the group, who call themselves "The Quarrymen," travel from the south end of the city to play.

They are: John Lennon, Menlove Avenue, Woolton; Paul McCartney, Forthlin Road, Allerton, and George Harrison, Upton Green, Speke. During the week members take their own records or play those provided by Mrs. Best. There is even room for the energetic who wish to dance.

The club has only been open a few weeks but already membership has exceeded 280. "I enjoy having them here," said Mrs. Best. And although her husband was sceptic about the idea at first he now admits that it is a great success.

## MISSIONARY WORK

The speaker at last week's meeting of the Church of the Good Shepherd Mothers' Union, West Derby, was Miss J. Troughton, who took as her subject "Missionary work."

Three "cool cats" listen to "The Quarrymen." (B1565)

## Golfers up in arms

A suggestion that Liverpool City Council may turn golf courses into housing estates— starting with the 100-acre West Derby course — has Liverpool golfers up in arms.

Ald. John Braddock, Labour leader of the council, said: "We have huge land estates and golf courses at the disposal of a few people, and, on the other hand, we have scores of dozens of ordinary men and women who have nowhere to live."

Replied Mr. Eric Dixon (secretary of the West Derby Club): "Even for people who do not play golf, a golf course is an amenity, for it provides

## IS THIS PRESTON

Is Melwood Drive another ? the Deysbrook estate think so, an Tenants Association it was one o

Mr. J. V. Woollam, M.P. for West Derby attended. Present were Mesdames Young, Baldwin, Edwards Reid and Fagil, and Messrs. F Marsh (chairman), J. Jones, G the and G. Fowler, secretary.

On the subject of Melwood Drive it was stated that the amount o clay in the soil had caused the foundations to shift and the surface was breaking up to such an exten as to be unsafe.

The transport service was also "under fire" and it was unanimously decided to ask Mr. Woollam to contact Liverpool Corporation transpor dept. with a view to the resumptio of the 12E bus service.

## BUSES OFTEN FULL

Present bus services pass alon the fringe of the estate and ar

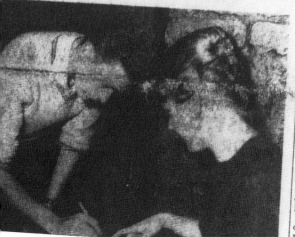

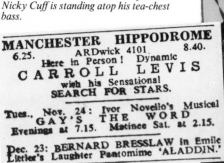

*Below: The advert for Johnny and the Moondogs' unfortunate Manchester audition for Carroll Levis. Right: The Sunnyside Skiffle Group, who often beat them in these contests, pictured at the Wilson Hall, Garston, on 23 May 1957. Nicky Cuff is standing atop his tea-chest bass.*

mance might impress the manager of a local cinema in attendance, and provide future interval bookings. On the way home, still in an alcoholic haze, Hanton – inexplicably though somewhat symbolically – hauled himself and his drums off the bus before his usual stop. He neither saw nor heard from the Quarry Men again.

Even George Harrison began occasionally to play with other groups, particularly the Les Stewart Quartet, and for several months in 1959 the Quarry Men seem to have ceased existence altogether. But on Saturday 29 August fate intervened. The Les Stewart Quartet had been promised an engagement at the opening night of a new youth venue, the Casbah Coffee Club, located in the cellar of a large Victorian house in West Derby, Liverpool, owned by one Mona Best. On the day of the opening Stewart and the quartet's bass player, Ken Brown, had a fierce argument which ended with Stewart vowing not to fulfil the engagement. In desperation Brown asked George Harrison if he knew of any mates who could help out. George duly rounded up Paul and John. The Quarry Men played at the Casbah Coffee Club that night, and every Saturday night thereafter. They had been rescued from the brink of oblivion, and Ken Brown was immediately invited to leave Stewart's group and become a part of the revitalized Quarry Men. He was to last no more than six weeks,[2] leaving after a row developed following one Saturday-night Casbah appearance, probably on 10 October 1959, when he was suffering from a heavy

cold and was consequently too ill to perform. At the end of the evening, when Mona Best gave Brown his 15-shilling share of the group's customary £3 fee, Paul McCartney could see no earthly reason why Brown should receive the dividend if he hadn't played. After a brief discussion John, Paul and George closed ranks and walked out on him and the club.

Although the run of Casbah engagements had dried up, the group still felt sufficiently buoyant to have another crack at Carroll Levis's visiting talent contest, temporarily ditching the Quarry Men moniker and christening themselves Johnny and the Moondogs in the process. (This was the era when groups had to boast a leader: Johnny Kidd and the Pirates, Cliff Richard and the Shadows, Johnny and the Hurricanes etc.) They successfully came through two Liverpool auditions and were invited to contest a further heat in Manchester. Success there would guarantee Johnny and the Moondogs a two-minute spot on Levis's ATV show, *Discoveries*. But although George was in proper employment, John and Paul were still at school and had no more than their meagre pocket money allowance to spend. So having safely got to Manchester and performed their stage stint, when the evening ran over time they simply could not afford to stay in town for the night. Before the audience came to vote for the winning act (measured by their applause), Johnny and the Moondogs were half way back to Lime Street station, Liverpool, aboard the last train.

Their one glimmer of success faded, the future of the group looked particularly bleak at the end of 1959. But though they certainly couldn't have known it then, the embryo Beatles had come to the end of the first phase of their long and arduous apprenticeship. The tough times were by no means over but from 1960 they were never to look back.

---

**2** Brown's recollection in a late-sixties interview that he played with the Quarry Men for nine months is clearly an enormous exaggeration since he didn't join them until 29 August 1959 and by mid-October, when they entered the Carroll Levis audition, he had gone.

# LIVE ENGAGEMENTS

## 1957

**9 June**
(3 p.m.)

Empire Theatre,
Lime Street,
Liverpool

The local qualifying audition for the famous Mr Star-Maker, Carroll Levis, marked the first official engagement of the Quarry Men. Levis ran these *TV Star Search* shows all over Britain, providing not only low-budget theatre entertainment (artistes, grateful for the opportunity, did not generally receive a fee) but also a steady source of acts for his season of television shows on ATV. Performers were normally a mixed bag of ventriloquists, trained budgerigars, jugglers, musical-saw players and, in 1957, of course, skiffle hopefuls.

The Quarry Men did not even qualify from this preliminary audition, won by the Sunnyside Skiffle Group, a Speke combo which featured a nineteen-year-old four-foot six-inch midget called Nicky Cuff on vocals and tea-chest bass. Literally. Cuff stood on the tea-chest while playing it!

The finals were held, without the Quarry Men, at the Empire, twice nightly, between 17 and 23 June.

---

**22 June**

Outdoor Party,
Rosebery Street,
Liverpool

An unusual engagement, even by Quarry Men standards, playing from the back of a stationary coal lorry in the afternoon and evening during street celebrations for the 550th anniversary of King John issuing a Royal Charter 'inviting settlers to take up burgages or building plots in Liverpool, and promising them all the privileges enjoyed by free boroughs on the sea'.

The party was a typical community effort. Mrs Marjorie Roberts, at number 84, was principal organizer, and her son Charles, who was a friend of Colin Hanton (it was Roberts who designed the group's logo on Hanton's bass drum), invited the Quarry Men along to play, though they did not live locally. The lorry from which they played was supplied by the man at number 76, who also ran the microphone lead through his front-room window.

The only blemish on the occasion was when a group of louts from neighbouring Hatherley Street threatened to beat the group up, and in particular 'that Lennon'. As soon

as their spot finished the group consequently wasted little time in diving for the sanctuary of Mrs Roberts' house, where she served them tea until the danger had passed.

The *Liverpool Post and Echo* newspaper group awarded Rosebery Street the prize for the best-decorated street outside of the city centre, so the residents duly celebrated with a second party, at which the more prestigious Merseysippi Jazz Band performed. The Quarry Men were not invited back.

## ALL THE FUN OF THE FAIR AT WOOLTON

Gatekeeper Mr. John Moorst and his assistant, Mr. Toakley, were kept extremely busy at the annual garden fete of St. Peter's Church, Woolton, on Saturday. Hundreds of people passed through the gates into the church field to see the crowning of this year's Rose Queen, Miss Sally Wright.

Sally and her retinue, and the retiring queen, Miss Susan Dixon, arrived on decorated lorries, accompanied by children in fancy dress, Girl Guides, Boy Scouts, Brownies and Cubs, members of the Discoverers, the Youth Club and the popular Quarry Men Skiffle Group.

The procession, headed by the band of the Cheshire (Earl of Chester) Yeomanry, made its way from Church Road, along Allerton Road, King's Drive, Saints Cross Avenue, and back to the church field for the crowning.

sented to Mrs. Thelwall Jones by Felicity Clegg, Mr. Thelwall Jones declared the fete open.

The queen's retinue included Jane Cuthbertson, Elizabeth Metcalfe, Elizabeth Rimmer, Jennifer Jones, Ann Dowell and Joyce Wright, who is the new queen's sister. The crown bearer was Harold Earp.

The retiring queen, 14-years-old Susan Dixon, was accompanied by her attendants, Marian Dobson, Edna Ward, Beryl Goodwin, Rosemary Ashton, Mary Gee and Pat Mason. Other small attendants were Pamela Cottrell, Alison Millett, Elizabeth Thompson and Anne Burgess. Soldiers were Anthony Pietka, Dennis Sowler, James Sowler, John Radford, Christopher Jones, Kenneth Edge, Brian Hall and John Dennis. The retinues were arranged by Mrs. O. Holdsworth, Mrs. A. Clegg, Mrs. C. E. Chappelle and Mrs. M. Ross.

[crowning], the fancy [decorat]ion was judged by [Mrs.] Thelwall Jones. [Th]ree groups in the [field a]nd all had quite [a lot] of entries.

[Th]e visitors were at[t]he balloon stall, [who] could send up a

hydrogen-filled balloon with their names and address attached. The sender of the balloon which is returned from the furthest place will receive a prize. A special children's attraction was the aerial car set up by the Scouts, and until early in the evening the children were queueing for rides.

Always a popular feature is a display by the dogs of the Liverpool City Police, and the people of Woolton showed their appreciation of the demonstrations by the dogs of obedience training and obstacle training.

Throughout the afternoon, musical selections were provided by the Band of the Cheshire (Earl of Chester) Yeomanry under their bandmaster, H. Abraham.

An entirely different type of music was provided by the "Quarry Men Skiffle Group." These five boys are members of the youth club, and some of them are pupils of Quarry Bank High School. Recently they appeared in the Carroll Levis Discoveries show at a Liverpool theatre, but unfortunately did not quite qualify for the finals. They are John Lennon, who plays the guitar and is the popular vocalist, Peter Shotton (washboard), Eric Griffiths (guitar), Len Garry (bass) and Rodney Davis (banjo). Colin Hanton, who is the drummer, did not appear on Saturday. Their songs included "Cumberland Gap," "Maggie May" and "Railroad Bill."

*Above: A typically detailed local paper report on the Woolton fête. Colin Hanton did play that day, but in the afternoon only. Left: Charles Roberts outside 84 Rosebery Street, a poster for the street party, naming the Quarry Men, in his front-room window.*

---

**6 July**

Garden Fête,
St Peter's Church,
Church Road,
Woolton, Liverpool

A truly historic date in the annals of entertainment but one which has been a constant source of confusion over the years – 15 June 1956, 15 June 1955, even 15 June 1954 have all been erroneously reported as the date of this fête, even in official biographies.

As can be seen from the unique newspaper report illustrated, the Quarry Men played during the afternoon from a makeshift stage in the field behind the church, and also – with the exception of Colin Hanton – at the evening dance in the church hall over the road (commencing at 8 p.m. sharp, admission 2s!), alternating with a more traditional combo, the George Edwards Band. It was while the Quarry Men were setting up their instruments in the hall during the early evening that occasional tea-chest bass Quarry Man Ivan Vaughan introduced to them his classmate from the Liverpool Institute. His name was Paul McCartney.

JAZZ
CAVERN TO-NIGHT
SKIFFLE SESSION
DIRECT FROM TRIUMPHANT TOUR
RON McKAY
Plus Dark Town, Deltones, Quarry Men and the Demon Five.
RIVERBOAT SHUFFLE !
FRIDAY AUGUST 16
THE MERSEYSIPPI
WALL CITY JAZZ BAND
GIN MILL SKIFFLE GROUP, &c.
MISS CAVERN BATHING BEAUTY FINAL.
Licensed Bars Till 11 p.m.
TICKETS 5/-. Lewis's and Rushworth's
GET YOURS NOW !
CLUB PERDIDO. THURSDAY
ALAN BRANSCOMBE
QUINTETTE
& THE DARRYL DUGDALE TRIO
The Cavern 10 Mathew Street.
NEW CLUBMOOR HALL
Back Broadway, Friday, Saxon Skiffle.
Saturday, Resident Rockers & Skiffle.
WILSON HALL THURSDAY

**7 August**
Night                     Cavern Club,
                          10a Mathew Street,
                          Liverpool

Another historic date. It has, until now, always been believed that the Beatles made their debut at this now-legendary venue on 21 March 1961. But new evidence on page 72, and here, proves that this was *not* the case.

The Cavern Club, named after Le Caveau Français Jazz Club in Paris, had been officially opened by the Earl of Wharncliffe on 16 January 1957. The owner, Alan Sytner, was the son of a doctor who played at the same golf club, Lee Park, as Nigel Whalley who was now an apprentice golf professional. Thus, via this labyrinthine route, the Quarry Men booking was made. Despite its being a jazz stronghold, skiffle, with its jazz origins, was just about acceptable in the Cavern Club, though mostly as nothing more than an interval attraction. But having performed the most acceptable 'Come Go with Me', John Lennon's brash attempt to then sing Elvis Presley's 'Hound Dog' and 'Blue Suede Shoes' was met with much disdain by the Quarry Men's folk purist Rod Davis, and Sytner, who promptly despatched a terse note to the stage

saying, 'Cut out the bloody rock!'
Note: Paul McCartney did not play with the Quarry Men on this occasion as he was away at scout camp.

JAZZ
WILSON HALL THURSDAY
Darktown Skiffle. Rockers. Before 8, 2/6.
Saturday: Eagles Skiffle, Roughley Band.
NEW CLUBMOOR HALL
Back Broadway. Friday; Members, 3/-.
Quarry Men Skiffle. Resident Rockers.
JAZZ AT THE CAVERN
TO-NIGHT:
RALPH WATMOUGH BAND
DARKTOWN SKIFFLE GROUP.
THURSDAY:
MODERN JAZZ
ALAN BRANSCOMBE QUINTET
DARYL DUGDALE.

**18 October**     New Clubmoor Hall
                   (Conservative Club),
                   (Back) Broadway,
                   Liverpool

South Liverpool dance promoter Charlie McBain, known as Charlie Mac, ran – in addition to his 'strict tempo' evenings – regular rock and skiffle nights at his venues, including Wilson Hall, Garston; the Garston Swimming Baths (known locally as the Blood Baths because of the fierce gang fights which took place there); Wavertree Town Hall and the Holyoake Hall. This one, at the Conservative Club's New Clubmoor Hall, marked the inauspicious debut of Paul McCartney with John Lennon and the Quarry Men.

Playing publicly on lead guitar for the only time in his career, Paul's first-night nerves proved far too great and he made an unqualified abortion of his long-awaited solo during a version of Arthur Smith's 1946 hit 'Guitar Boogie'. McBain's only recorded comment on the Quarry Men that evening was a rather ambiguous 'Good & Bad' written on the group's visiting card.

**7 November**     Wilson Hall,
                   Speke Road,
                   Garston, Liverpool

This programme is devoted to main-stream jazz in the best tradition with top jazz musicians.
Box Office: 10 a.m. to 8 p.m.
Tel. North 0036.
WILSON HALL. THURSDAY
QUARRYMEN Rock 'N Skiffle Group.
Saturday: Ray Ennis with Bluegenes.
DANCING
RIALTO LUXURY BALLROOM
—Royal 4576—
WEDNESDAY AFTERNOON JAZZ

The first of four known Quarry Men performances at this rough, tough venue, built by Francis Wilson opposite the Garston bus depot. Charlie Mac ran Rhythm Nights here every Thursday. Coincidentally, years later, when the hall was sold, it was

*The Quarry Men at the New Clubmoor Hall on 23 November 1957, taken by Leslie Kearney. Left to right: Colin Hanton, Paul McCartney, Len Garry, John Lennon, Eric Griffiths. Note Paul's guitar, which is upside down because he didn't know how to re-string it for a left-handed player.*

razed and rebuilt as a branch of the Lennons supermarket chain.

**16 November**     Stanley Abattoir
                    Social Club,
                    East Prescot Road,
                    Old Swan, Liverpool

Undoubtedly the most peculiar Quarry Men engagement ever – a Saturday-night dance for the social club members of the massive Stanley abattoir. Various slaughter-house personnel, meat porters and their wives, saw two – allegedly cacophonous – sets by the combo either side of an interval. They were not re-booked.

**23 November**     New Clubmoor Hall,
                    (Back) Broadway

A return visit to the Conservative Club.

this aptly named club, situated in the cellar of an enormous Victorian house, latterly a home for retired nurses. It held 100 people and had no facilities. A single bare blue bulb and one white fluorescent strip light provided the only of illumination, and one electric fan supplied the only 'fresh' air.

Because of the illegality and danger in holding meetings in such an apparently decrepit environment, its existence was, understandably, short lived. On 1 April the police 'invaded' the proceedings and on 22 April it closed down for good. Club nights at the Morgue cellar took place on Tuesdays and Thursdays, though no records exist to indicate which groups played. One can safely presume though that the Quarry Men attended on at least a handful of occasions.

Note: Caldwell, an athletic youth, travelled to London on 11 April 1958 for a cross-country running competition. Whilst in the city he played an impromptu jam session in Chas McDevitt's Skiffle Cellar, soliciting an appearance for himself and his Texans on Radio Luxembourg in the process. They duly became the first-ever Merseyside pop combo to broadcast when they played 'Midnight Special (Prisoner's Song)' on the programme *Amateur Skiffle Club* on 30 April 1958.

| | |
|---|---|
| **20 December** | Wedding Reception, 25 Upton Green, Speke, Liverpool |

If regular, paid, bookings were beginning to dry up the Quarry Men could always be called upon to provide free, and willing, entertainment at family functions. Between 1957 and 1959 they played at several such affairs, although only one date – this, at the wedding reception of George Harrison's brother, Harry, and his bride, Irene McCann, at the Harrison household – can be positively identified.

## 1959

| | |
|---|---|
| **1 January** | Wilson Hall, Garston |

Not a Charlie McBain promotion but the rather belated Christmas 1958 party of the Speke Bus Depot Social Club. Harry Harrison, George's father, was the chairman of the club, hence the booking of the Quarry Men for this afternoon affair. Fortunately the lads were all on school holidays so there was no need for truancy.

| | |
|---|---|
| **24 January** | Woolton Village Club, Allerton Road, Woolton, Liverpool |

Yet another, even later, Christmas party. The Quarry Men, chosen because of their local availability, played a ten-minute selection of skiffle numbers.

| | |
|---|---|
| **7 December** | Wilson Hall, Garston |

A slightly more prestigious Saturday-night booking.

## 1958

| | |
|---|---|
| **9 January** ~~CANCELLED~~ | Wilson Hall, Garston |

After advertising them for this date, promoter Charlie McBain switched the booking to his dance on the following night at the New Clubmoor Hall.

| | |
|---|---|
| **10 January** | New Clubmoor Hall, (Back) Broadway |

| | |
|---|---|
| **24 January** Night | Cavern Club |

| | |
|---|---|
| **6 February** | Wilson Hall, Garston |

Although disputed by several interested parties, this date almost certainly marked the first meeting of 14-year-old George Harrison with the Quarry Men. George himself remembers seeing them for the first time at this venue although Colin Hanton recalls that George was introduced to them one night at the Morgue Cellar (see 13 March 1958), and Louise Harrison, George's late mother, remembered that they met in a local chip shop. Pete Shotton who, it should be said, had long since left the Quarry Men, reckons that the lads, led by George's school friend Paul McCartney, trooped over to the Harrisons' council house at 25 Upton Green, Speke, and met him there.

| | |
|---|---|
| **13 March** | The Morgue Skiffle Cellar, 'Balgownie', 25 Oakhill Park, Broadgreen, Liverpool |

The opening night of a club run by eighteen-year-old Alan Caldwell who had his own group, Al Caldwell's Texans, later to become the Raving Texans (with, from 25 March 1959, Ringo Starr on drums) and, eventually, Rory Storm and the Hurricanes.

Several local groups, including the Texans and the Quarry Men, played from 7:30 p.m. on the opening night of

*The Quarry Men at the Casbah Coffee Club in September 1959, in a picture taken by club member David Hughes. Left to right: George, Paul, Ken Brown, John.*

## DANCE CLUB IN HOUSE CELLARS

Four young men making a name for themselves in the world of skiffle and 'pop' music are the Quarrymen, who played for many teenagers to dance at the opening of West Derby's "Kasbah" Club on Saturday evening.

The club where teenagers can meet their friends, dance and drink coffee, has been opened in the cellars of a house in Heyman's Green, West Derby. The Quarrymen, complete with a varied repertoire and their electric guitars, will play at the club each Saturday in the future.

They are John Lennan, 251 Menlove Avenue, Woolton; Paul McCartney, 20 Forthlin Road, Allerton; George Harrison, 25 Upton Green, Speke; and Kenny Brown, 148 Storrington Avenue, Norris Green.

| 29 August | Casbah Coffee Club, 8 Hayman's Green, West Derby, Liverpool |
|---|---|

The opening night of a new teenagers' social club in the extensive cellars of a large Victorian house owned by Mrs Mona Best. The Quarry Men played at the Casbah Coffee Club every Saturday night thereafter until, probably, 10 October, when they had the disagreement with Ken Brown – a total of seven engagements in all. They were not to play the club again until – as the Beatles – they returned from Hamburg, on 17 December 1960. After that they played there regularly on weekends until June 1962, when the club closed.

| 5 September | Casbah Coffee Club, West Derby |
|---|---|

| 12 September | Casbah Coffee Club, West Derby |
|---|---|
| 19 September | Casbah Coffee Club, West Derby |
| 26 September | Casbah Coffee Club, West Derby |
| 3 October | Casbah Coffee Club, West Derby |
| 10 October | Casbah Coffee Club, West Derby |
| 11, 18 or 25 October | Empire Theatre, Liverpool |

More than two years after the Quarry Men's dismal failure in 1957, the group – John, Paul and George (but without Ken Brown who had left after the disagreement at the Casbah Coffee Club) – again performed an audition for Mr Star-Maker, Carroll Levis, re-christening themselves Johnny and the Moondogs specially for the event.

These preliminary rounds were held over three consecutive Sundays, dates listed above, although the Moondogs would have appeared only once, probably on 18 October. One qualifier from the 11 October audition was Jett (later Rory) Storm and the Hurricanes, with Ringo Starr on drums.

This time Lennon and co. were more successful, and qualified for the finals.

| 26, 27, 28, 29, 30 or 31 October | Empire Theatre, Liverpool |
|---|---|

The finals of the Carroll Levis *TV Star Search* were held throughout the week at the Empire, and Johnny and the Moondogs appeared on at least two occasions. They did not win the contest (that prize went to a group called the Connaughts, ironically the same combo, albeit with a new name, as the group which won the 1957 round, the Sunnyside Skiffle Group, with midget Nicky Cuff) but were placed sufficiently high to qualify for the final hurdle of auditions, to be held at the Hippodrome Theatre in Manchester. Qualification from that would guarantee the trio a brief but prestigious spot on Levis's ATV show, with resultant 'fame' just around the corner.

| 15 November | Hippodrome Theatre, Hyde Road, Ardwick Green, Ardwick, Manchester, Lancashire |
|---|---|

The final round of Levis's north-west *Star Search* for 1959, marking the first-ever non-Merseyside appearance of the group later to become the Beatles.

Despite putting in a reasonable performance the actual judging of the contest was based mostly on the strength of audience applause after a brief on-stage reappearance by each act in the finale. Unfortunately this took place very late in the evening and the three poor Liverpool lads, with drastically insufficient funds to stay in town overnight, were long gone – as was their chance of fame – back to Merseyside by the time the MC came to announce their turn.

Notes: The suggestion by authors of several Beatles books that the group actually appeared on television in the Carroll Levis show is totally absurd, and the work of pure journalistic inventiveness.

Colin Hanton was certainly no longer with the Quarry Men/Johnny and the Moondogs at the time of the 1959 Carroll Levis auditions, as stated in *Shout!*, Philip Norman's Beatles biography. The Manchester adventure referred to by Hanton in *Shout!* was an occasion in late 1958 when the Quarry Men failed an audition for ABC television at their studios in Didsbury, South Manchester.

## Other engagements played

One should never lose sight of the fact that the Quarry Men was virtually nothing more than a fun group, formed by schoolboys. As such they were total amateurs with very little big-time aspirations. Almost all of their engagements were arranged through friends and contacts, not through promoters and contracts, and as a consequence the greater proportion of their live dates are lost for ever, since they were not advertised or noted down at the time.

It is only natural too that memories of the combo's activities have become blurred and confused with the passing of almost thirty years, to the point where even the personal recollections of the group's members themselves have become inexorably distorted. Affable Quarry Men drummer Colin Hanton would, for example, virtually stake all his possessions on his belief that the Woolton Church fête took place *before* the Carroll Levis audition or the Rosebery Street party. With this book we now have illustrated, infallible documentary evidence from the time to prove otherwise.

What follows is a list of some of the other venues, not previously detailed, but known to have been played by the Quarry Men during 1957–9. Where possible they have been ratified by the author.

From mid-1956 until early 1958 regular skiffle group contests were held as interval attractions at the larger ballrooms and theatres on Merseyside, providing not just 'an opportunity to become known' (to whom?) but, more importantly, free entertainment for promoters. Keen combos, from April 1957 often including the Quarry Men, eagerly queued up for their big chance. These venues included the Pavilion Theatre, Aintree; the Grafton and Locarno ballrooms, both in West Derby Road, Liverpool; the Pavilion Theatre, Lodge Lane, Liverpool, and the Rialto Ballrom, Upper Parliament Street/Stanhope Street, Liverpool – a venue burnt down during the 1981 Toxteth riots.

Other regular audition venues for the Quarry Men, based in South Liverpool, included the Wilson Hall, Garston and the Winter Gardens Ballroom, Heald Street, Garston. In September 1958 one winner at this latter venue was a 'rock 'n' roll comedian' called Jimmy Tarbuck, while two months later another contest was won by Ronald Wycherley, later to achieve fame as Billy Fury. The Winter Gardens Ballroom also opened up for regular Tuesday rock and roll nights on 30 April 1957, though it rarely advertised who was playing.

The Quarry Men almost certainly played at the Cavern Club on more than the two occasions listed, but since the venue's advertisements often gave nothing more than 'plus skiffle interval', 'plus mystery skiffle group' or other such nondescript statements, precise dates are impossible to discover.

One or two of its line-up being members of the St Peter's Parish Church Youth Club, Woolton, the Quarry Men undoubtedly secured a few engagements there, in addition to playing at the church's 1957 garden fête. More than one source remembers John Lennon walking out one particular evening at the club because his microphone repeatedly broke down.

St Barnabas Church Hall, Penny Lane and Holyoake Hall, Smithdown Road, Wavertree held regular unadvertised Saturday-night skiffle sessions and interval attractions. The Quarry Men attended on a handful of occasions.

The group played one Friday night in November 1957 (either 1, 8, 15, 22 or 29) at the Haig Dance Club, Haig Avenue, Moreton, Wirral, Cheshire.

Closer to their roots, the Quarry Men played during the sixth-formers' dance at the Quarry Bank High School, Harthill Road, Woolton, in July 1957.

The Quarry Men undoubtedly played at the Morgue Skiffle Cellar on several occasions after it opened on 13 March 1958.

In mid-1958 the Quarry Men had an unsuccessful Saturday-night audition at the Lowlands Club, Hayman's Green, West Derby, Liverpool. This was situated about fifty yards to the right, over the road, from the Casbah Coffee Club which opened more than a year later.

George Harrison's father, Harry, was a bus driver and chairman of several social committees. Naturally he booked the Quarry Men whenever an opportunity arose. In addition to the party listed for 1 January 1959 the group also played at busmen's social clubs in Picton Road, Wavertree; Finch Lane, near Huyton and in Prescot.

Other known miscellaneous engagements: several family celebrations; one ten-minute interval appearance in the club house at Lee Park Golf Course, off Childwall Valley Road, arranged by Ivan Vaughan; Childwall Labour Club; Gateacre Labour Club; various working men's clubs; the youth club of St Luke's Church, Stanley Road, Bootle, and birthday parties in Ford, North Liverpool, and Smithdown Lane, Edge Hill.

## Engagements not played

The author has proved, conclusively, that the Quarry Men did not play at the following events/venues mentioned in other publications during this period:

Although they attempted to secure bookings at the Attic Skiffle Club in Islington, Liverpool city centre, in early 1958, the Quarry Men were never booked and made no appearances there.

St Peters Parish Church Fête, Woolton, other than on 6 July 1957. Entertainment at the 1956 fête, held on 30 June, and the 1958 event, held on 5 July, was supplied solely by the Band of the Cheshire Yeomanry.

The Jacaranda Coffee Bar in Slater Street, Liverpool, and the Plaza Ballroom, Duke Street, St Helens, Lancashire. They did not play these venues until May 1960 and June 1962 respectively.

John and Paul's appearance 'in Reading' as the Nerk Twins took place in 1960, not, variously, from 1955 to 1959.

# THE MUSIC

Although the Lennon–McCartney songwriting partnership was to become probably the most celebrated and successful in the history of popular music, they and the other members of the Quarry Men/Beatles had their influences like anyone else. After the brief flourish of skiffle the music of Elvis Presley, Eddie Cochran, Carl Perkins, Chuck Berry, Little Richard, Buddy Holly and Jerry Lee Lewis became the staple diet of the group, although they would often perversely sandwich their songs with new arrangements of old standards to maintain an all-round appeal, something of which the group was particularly proud.

What follows is an attempt to detail the live per-formance repertoire of the Quarry Men from 1957 to 1959, showing – where possible – the group's vocalist, the composer(s) of the song and the name of the artist/group who recorded the version which particularly influenced the group. It is, in all likeli-hood, an incomplete guide.

Note: Throughout the Musical Repertoire sections of the book, the composer credits for songs written by John Lennon or Paul McCartney appear as they would on a record label; that is, mostly as a team, since the two writers had an agreement to show their songs in this fashion even if they were written by just one of them. In such cases, the name of the principal composer appears here in small capitals.

| Song title | Main vocalist(s) | Composer(s) | Influential version (year) |
|---|---|---|---|
| Ain't She Sweet[1] | John | Yellen/Ager | — |
| All Shook Up | Paul | Blackwell/Presley | Elvis Presley (1957) |
| Be-Bop-A-Lula | John | Vincent/Davis | Gene Vincent and his Blue Caps (1956) |
| Blue Moon of Kentucky | Paul | Monroe | Elvis Presley (1954) |
| Blue Suede Shoes[2] | John | Perkins | Carl Perkins (1956) and Elvis Presley (1956) |
| Bony Moronie | John | Williams | Larry Williams (1957) |
| Catswalk[3] | (Instrumental) | McCartney | — |
| C'mon Everybody | ? | Cochran/Capehart | Eddie Cochran (1959) |
| Come Go with Me | John | Quick | The Del-Vikings (1957) |
| The Cumberland Gap | John | Traditional | Lonnie Donegan and his Skiffle Group (1957) |
| Freight Train | John | Trad. arr. Cotten or trad. arr. James/Williams | Chas McDevitt Skiffle Group featuring Nancy Whiskey (1957) |
| Guitar Boogie | (Instrumental) | Smith | Arthur Smith and his Crackerjacks (1946) |
| Hello Little Girl | John | LENNON/McCartney | — |
| High School Confidential | Paul | Lewis/Hargrave | Jerry Lee Lewis (1958) |
| Home[4] | ? | Van Steeden/Clarkson/Clarkson | ? |

1 The version most likely to have prompted the Quarry Men to perform this song would be Gene Vincent's 1956 rock recording. But since John Lennon's vocal rendition sounds quite different to Vincent's it seems apparent that John arranged his own, unique, version.

2 The Quarry Men mostly performed the composer Carl Perkins' version.

3 When this tune was released on record by the Chris Barber Band in 1967 it was re-titled 'Catcall'.

| Song title | Main vocalist(s) | Composer(s) | Influential version (year) |
|---|---|---|---|
| Hot as Sun | (Instrumental) | McCartney | — |
| Hound Dog | John | Leiber/Stoller | Elvis Presley (1956) |
| I Lost my Little Girl | Paul | Lennon/McCARTNEY | — |
| In Spite of all the Danger | Paul/George | McCartney/Harrison | — |
| ✓ It's so Easy | ? | Holly/Petty | Buddy Holly and the Crickets (1958) |
| Jailhouse Rock | John | Leiber/Stoller | Elvis Presley (1958) |
| Johnny B. Goode | John | Berry | Chuck Berry (1958) |
| Just Fun | ? | Lennon/McCartney | — |
| Keep Looking that Way | ? | Lennon/McCartney | — |
| Lawdy Miss Clawdy | ? | Price | Lloyd Price (1952) |
| Lend Me your Comb | John/Paul | Twomey/Wise/Weisman | Carl Perkins (1957) |
| Like Dreamers Do | Paul | Lennon/McCARTNEY | — |
| Long Black Train[5] | John | Lennon? | — |
| Long Tall Sally | Paul | Johnson/Penniman/Blackwell | Little Richard (1956) |
| Looking Glass | (Instrumental) | Lennon/McCartney | — |
| Love of the Loved | Paul | Lennon/McCARTNEY | — |
| Lucille | Paul | Penniman/Collins | Little Richard (1957) |
| Maggie May | John | Traditional | The Vipers Skiffle Group (1957) |
| Mailman Blues | ? | Price | Lloyd Price (1954) |
| Maybe Baby | ? | Holly/Petty | Buddy Holly and the Crickets (1958) |
| Mean Woman Blues | ? | Demetrius | Jerry Lee Lewis (1957) or Elvis Presley (1957) |
| Midnight Special (Prisoner's Song)[6] | ? | Traditional | Lonnie Donegan and his Skiffle Group (1956) |
| Moonglow and the theme from *Picnic* | ? | Hudson/De Lange/Mills/Duning/Allen | The McGuire Sisters (1956) |
| No other Baby | John | Bishop/Watson | The Vipers Skiffle Group (1958) |
| The One after 909 | John | Lennon/McCartney | — |
| ✓ Peggy Sue | John | Holly/Allison/Petty | Buddy Holly (1957) |
| Railroad Bill | John | Traditional | Lonnie Donegan and his Skiffle Group (1956) |

**4** The Mills Brothers recorded a version of this song in June 1960 which may have influenced the Beatles thereafter. It is not known who influenced them to perform it before then.

**5** Rod Davis, one-time banjoist with the Quarry Men, recollects this being a very early John Lennon composition. This would seem to be verified by the fact that no song with that title has been copyrighted to date.

**6** Duane Eddy recorded a version of this song in November 1960 which may have influenced the Beatles thereafter.

| Song title | Main vocalist(s) | Composer(s) | Influential version (year) |
| --- | --- | --- | --- |
| Ramrod | (Instrumental) | Casey | Duane Eddy with the Rebels (1958) |
| Raunchy | (Instrumental) | Justis/Manker | Bill Justis and his Orchestra (1957) |
| Rock Island Line | John | Ledbetter | Lonnie Donegan and his Skiffle Group (1954) |
| Roll over Beethoven[7] | John | Berry | Chuck Berry (1956) |
| Searchin' | Paul | Leiber/Stoller | The Coasters (1957) |
| Short Fat Fanny | John | Williams | Larry Williams (1957) |
| Summertime | ? | Gershwin | Sam Cooke (1957) or Ray Charles (1958) |
| Sure to Fall (in Love with You) | Paul | Perkins/Claunch/Cantrell | Carl Perkins (1956) |
| Sweet Little Sixteen | John | Berry | Chuck Berry (1958) |
| Tennessee | John | Perkins | Carl Perkins (1956) |
| That'll be the Day | John | Holly/Allison/Petty | Buddy Holly and the Crickets (1957) |
| That's all Right (Mama) | Paul | Crudup | Elvis Presley (1954) |
| That's my Woman | ? | Lennon/McCartney | — |
| Think It Over | ? | Holly/Allison/Petty | Buddy Holly and the Crickets (1958) |
| Thinking of Linking | ? | Lennon/McCartney | — |
| Three Cool Cats | George | Leiber/Stoller | The Coasters (1959) |
| Too Bad About Sorrows | ? | Lennon/McCartney | — |
| Twenty Flight Rock | Paul | Cochran/Fairchild | Eddie Cochran (1957) |
| When the Saints Go Marching In[8] | ? | Traditional | Jerry Lee Lewis (1958) or Fats Domino (1959) |
| Whole Lotta Shakin' Goin' On | ? | Williams/David | Jerry Lee Lewis (1957) |
| Winston's Walk | (Instrumental) | Lennon/McCartney | — |
| Words of Love | John/George | Holly | Buddy Holly (1957) |
| Worried Man Blues[9] | John | Traditional | Lonnie Donegan and his Skiffle Group (1955) or the Vipers Skiffle Group (1957) |
| Years Roll Along | ? | Lennon/McCartney | — |
| You Were Meant for Me | ? | Freed/Brown | ? |
| You Win Again | John | Williams | Hank Williams (1952) or Jerry Lee Lewis (1958) |
| Youngblood | George | Leiber/Stoller/Pomus | The Coasters (1957) |
| Your True Love | George | Perkins | Carl Perkins (1957) |

7 In later years George Harrison assumed the lead vocal.

8 The Beatles may also have been influenced by the first-ever rock version of this song, by Bill Haley and the Comets in 1956. (They titled it 'The Saints Rock 'n' Roll'.)

9 This song is also known as 'It Takes a Worried Man to Sing a Worried Song'.

# COMMENTARY

If, for the members of the Quarry Men, 1960 started with the same mood of despondency evident at the end of 1959, it certainly ended with their career at its highest point so far. The twelve months of 1960 saw many major career developments: the invention and christening of the names Beatals, Silver Beats, Silver Beetles, Silver Beatles, and eventually, by the middle of August, Beatles; it saw the group's first tour, their first fully professional engagements, their first and probably most beneficial trip to Hamburg, West Germany, the realization that they might be able to earn a living from rock music, and the first, embryonic, Beatlemania, three years before Britain and the rest of the world caught on.

The man responsible for most, though certainly not all, of these occurrences was twenty-nine-year-old Welsh-born Liverpudlian Allan Richard Williams, a stockily-built opportunist who, from May 1960 until April 1961, became the group's occasional booking agent or, as he still claims, 'their first manager'. (Even now, more than twenty years on, the Beatles strongly dispute Williams's claim.) Williams ran the Jacaranda, a small coffee bar typical of the era, at 23 Slater Street in the centre of Liverpool. The Quarry Men were often to be found there, idling away their lunch hours and evenings and, in true coffee-bar style, making a single sixpenny espresso last at least two hours.

In January 1960 the Quarry Men's ranks had been swollen to four by yet another guitarist, John's close friend from art college, Stuart Fergusson Victor Sutcliffe. Although a brilliant and original artist, the nineteen-year-old Scottish-born Sutcliffe held no musical ambition or talent whatsoever but simply saw the life of a musician as a vital counterpoint to his brooding artistic persona. Between 17 November 1959 and 17 January 1960 the second, biennial, John Moores Exhibition had taken place at the illustrious Walker Art Gallery in Liverpool, and one of Sutcliffe's canvases had been selected to hang. Indeed, Moores himself was so impressed with the work that at the end of the two-month exhibition he bought the painting for £65, a huge sum of money – then and now – to an art student struggling along on a meagre grant. But instead of ploughing the money back into

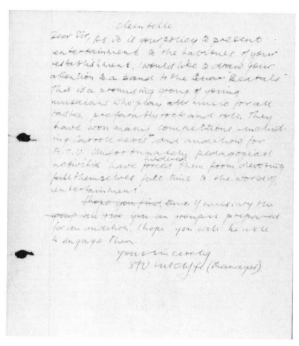

*Above: Draft of a richly worded letter from Stuart Sutcliffe to the manager of a club, seeking work for the group. Their name was in the throes of changing from Quarry Men to Beatals.*

his artistic career, as his parents wished, Sutcliffe – with a great deal of enthusiastic encouragement from John Lennon – bought himself a Hofner President bass guitar and joined the Quarry Men. He was never to learn even the basic, rudimentary skills of playing though, and would very often stand with his back to the audience to hide his inadequacies.

During the week of 14–20 March 1960 Eddie Cochran and Gene Vincent spearheaded a pop package show at the Liverpool Empire, promoted by top impresario of the day Larry Parnes. It was a huge success and Allan Williams, to use his own words, 'could smell money ... lots of it'. After the shows he wrote to, and then telephoned, Parnes and arranged for the two headlining stars and some of the support artists to return to Liverpool on 3 May for a joint Parnes–Williams one-night promotion at Liverpool Stadium, a venue behind the city's Exchange Station long famous for its boxing and

## Unlucky 13?
## It is for me
## says Allan

Bad luck has dogged the footsteps of Liverpool coffee club owner Alan Williams since he planned the city's second arts ball for FRIDAY, MAY 13th.

Superstition in fancy dress is to be one of the competitions of the event, to be held in St. George's Hall, in aid of the Cancer Research Fund.

But for Allan, Huskisson Street, Princes Park, the old superstition—unlucky 13—has come true.

Out of between 30 and 50 firms he has approached for prizes for the event only a couple have agreed; the Corporation turned down his request for a mile of silver somewhere in the city; a 'rock' show he is staging in connection with his coffee club next Tuesday was nearly called off when top-of-the-bill Eddie Cochran was killed and co-star Gene Vincent was seriously injured; and his wife Beryl, a Liverpool schoolteacher, has fallen ill during the Easter holidays.

Consolation note is that Gene Vincent has agreed to carry on with the show to be held at the Liverpool Stadium.

Said Allan: "I'm not usually superstitious. But after this . . ."

Others on the bill of Tuesday's show include Davy Jones, The Viscounts, Mal, Perry and the Cassanovas.

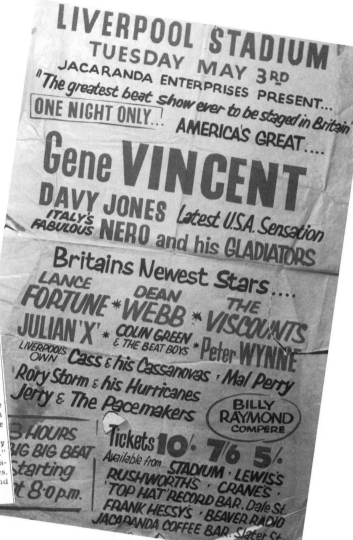

wrestling bouts. On the extensive bill were Cochran, Vincent, Davy Jones (not the Monkee-to-be but a black American rock and roll singer), the Viscounts, Colin Green and the Beat Boys (including Georgie Fame), Peter Wynne, Lance Fortune, Nero and his Gladiators, and Liverpool groups Cass and the Cassanovas[1] and Rory Storm and the Hurricanes.

Tickets began to sell and all was running smoothly when disaster struck. On 17 April, bound for London Airport from a concert in Bristol, Cochran was killed in a road crash just outside of Chippenham, Wiltshire. Vincent, already deformed from a motorcycle accident in his youth, suffered considerable additional injuries, including a broken collar bone. The Liverpool concert was scheduled for just sixteen days later yet there was no talk of a cancellation from Parnes. Instead, clinging desperately to the old show-business maxim 'the show must go on', Williams – upon receiving word from Parnes that Vincent would

still be able to fulfil the engagement – set about padding the already crowded bill even further with other Parnes artistes: Julian 'X' and Dean Webb, and more local replacements, Gerry and the Pacemakers, Wallasey group Bob Evans and his Five Shillings, Mal Perry, and the Connaughts, featuring midget Nicky Cuff. The Quarry Men, now renamed Beatals by Stuart Sutcliffe, were drummerless as always and were not invited to play, though they did attend the lengthy show, sitting quietly in the audience amid scenes of mayhem which were a strange foretaste of the years to come. At this time the only occasion Williams had engaged the group was to decorate the inglorious ladies' lavatory at the Jacaranda Coffee Bar.

Parnes was impressed by the prowess of the Merseyside rock and rollers and realized that he had stumbled upon a large array of untapped talent. Back

---

1 Cassanovas deliberately mis-spelt after the name of the group's leader, Brian Cassar.

at the Jacaranda after the show he explained to Williams that he needed groups to back his 'stable' of solo artistes on tour, all re-christened by Parnes with tempestuous stage names: Billy Fury, Duffy Power, Tommy Steele, Dickie Pride, Georgie Fame, Johnny Gentle, Nelson Keene, Lance Fortune, Marty Wilde and Vince Eager. Fury, in particular, was on the eve of a nationwide tour and was in desperate need of a backing group, so it was arranged that exactly one week later Parnes would return to Liverpool with Fury and audition a few hopefuls. Some time during that week, around 5 May, Williams, acting on advice from Brian Cassar, twenty-four-year-old diminutive leader of Cass and the Cassanovas, managed to secure the Beatals a drummer, Tommy Moore, who lived at 49 Fern Grove, Toxteth. Moore was considerably older than the others, being thirty-six, but a drummer was a drummer they reasoned, so he was welcomed into the group. Cassar also opined, in rather strong terms, that the group name they had been toying with, the Beatals (a play on their favourite group, Buddy Holly's Crickets) was 'ridiculous'. Cassar suggested they call themselves Long John and

the Silver Beetles instead, and although John Lennon refused to be called Long John, for want of anything better they stuck with the name Silver Beetles.

The audition before Parnes and Fury was held on 10 May at the Wyvern Social Club at 108 Seel Street, in premises recently acquired by Williams for a new venture, a night club he was to call the Blue Angel. Several of Liverpool's top beat groups turned out to perform before the star and The Big Man From London, among them Derry and the Seniors, Bob Evans and his Five Shillings, Gerry and the Pacemakers and Cass and the Cassanovas. The Silver Beetles were there too, more or less making up the numbers, or so it was thought. When it came to their turn to play Tommy Moore had yet to arrive as he was still across town collecting his drum equipment from a club, so burly twenty-year-old Maltese-born Johnny Hutchinson from the Cassanovas sat in with the Silver Beetles until Moore appeared half way through their ten-minute spot. Precisely what happened that day is open to conjecture. According to Williams, both Parnes and Fury loved the Silver Beetles but were put off by Stuart Sutcliffe's awk-

*Opposite: The Silver Beetles, with a bored Johnny Hutchinson guesting on drums, auditioning for Larry Parnes and Billy Fury on 10 May. Stuart Sutcliffe is standing only half-facing the front, to hide his inability to play the guitar. This photo is one of 36 existing shots taken at the audition by a Mr Kressley who had a studio close to the Jacaranda Coffee Bar. Right: The newspaper advert for the Silver Beats' 21 May gig, for which they failed to appear.*

**BEEKAY presents**

# JIVE AT LATHOM HALL

## Every SATURDAY

THIS WEEK — SILVER BEATS, DOMINOES, DELTONES.
7-30 — 11-30.                           Admission 4/-.   Members 3/6

**FRIDAY** TO-NIGHT — Transferred to ALEXANDRA HALL
(L1, L3, L30 to door).   7-30—11 p.m.   Admission 3/-

**EVERY MONDAY** 7-30 — 11 p.m.   Admission 2/6
THIS MONDAY — CLUBMEN

ward, amateurish fumblings on bass guitar; he says that Parnes' attempt to prise Stuart out of the group by dangling the offer of the tour before the four remaining members was met by a flat, loyal refusal. Parnes himself remembers nothing of the sort, only that he was slightly discouraged by the sight of the group's rather elderly drummer, Tommy Moore, who arrived late and more than a little hot under the collar.

A backing group for Billy Fury was not found that day, but Parnes did offer to use two of Williams' groups to support other, less important, artistes on various ballroom tours of north-east England and Scotland. The Silver Beetles were the first in line[2] and on Wednesday 18 May they were offered a nine-day (not two weeks as has thus far been recorded) seven-engagements tour to back twenty-year-old Liverpudlian and one-time apprentice carpenter, Johnny Gentle, in Scotland, at £18 per man per week, part expenses paid.[3] The group had just two days to prepare themselves. Proof of how suddenly the tour was sprung on the Silver Beetles can be seen by the fact that on 14 May, after an engagement as the Silver Beats at the Lathom Hall in Seaforth, they had informed the promoter, Brian Kelly, that they were also free on the following Saturday, 21 May. Yet by

20 May they had not only received notice of the tour but George and Tommy Moore had arranged time away from work (John and Stuart cut college and Paul somehow persuaded his father that the rest away from home would make it easier to revise for his forthcoming A-level examinations), they had spent a day travelling to Scotland, and were on stage in Alloa backing Gentle.

In his book[4] Williams suggests that there was a two-month period between the Vincent show, the audition and the tour. Clearly this was not the case. And his statement that the Silver Beetles helped to design floats for the one and only Liverpool Arts Ball, which he organized, held at the grand St George's Hall in 1959, is also incorrect. There were *two* such events, in 1959 and 1960, and it was only at the second one that the Silver Beetles – notably John and Stuart – helped out. This was held on Friday 13 May, slap in the middle of the aforementioned hectic activity with Parnes, and after, not before, the Gene Vincent show.

Before hurriedly setting out for their first-ever tour, three members of the Silver Beetles decided to adopt stage names. Paul became Paul Ramon, 'because it sounded really glamorous, sort of Valentino-ish', George became Carl Harrison, after his idol, American rockabilly musician Carl Perkins, and Stuart became Stuart de Staël, after the Russian artist Nicholas de Staël. So, with visions of their name in lights, money, fame, and girls chasing them, the group set out from Lime Street station on the long journey north to Alloa.

As can be seen from the 1960 Live Engagements list, the tour was not only dismally disappointing but it was poorly planned too. After Alloa, the six remaining dates were all scheduled along the north-east coast, from Inverness to Peterhead, a distance of 112 miles. But Parnes and his Scottish intermediary, Duncan McKinnon, an elderly chicken farmer

---

**2** Cass and the Cassanovas were not the first group to be used, as Williams maintains. Their turn did not come until June and July to back Johnny Gentle, and mid-August to back Duffy Power.

**3** During an appearance on the BBC radio programme *Desert Island Discs* in January 1982 Paul McCartney, with tongue firmly set in cheek, fondly recalled that he had never actually received the money from Parnes. Parnes' reply was to sue him for slander. The case was finally settled in July 1984, with an on-air apology to Parnes.

**4** *The Man who Gave the Beatles Away*, Elm Tree, 1975.

from Dumfries, had arranged the gigs without much care for geography so the group spent the week unnecessarily ferrying back and forth along the Highland roads, clocking up 300 miles in the process. On 23 May Johnny Gentle himself was driving the van from Inverness across to Fraserburgh, having relieved the regular driver, Gerry Scott, who wanted a rest. Tired, and perhaps a little the worse for alcohol, Gentle drove straight into the rear of a stationary Ford Popular at a crossroads outside of Banff. Although two old women sitting in the car were badly shaken, and Gentle later received an endorsement on his licence, the worst casualty was Tommy Moore, who felt the full impact of a flying guitar in his face. That evening, as he lay sedated in hospital, with concussion but without several front teeth, the manager of the Dalrymple Hall in Fraserburgh, led by John Lennon, arrived at Moore's side, hauled him out of bed, and insisted that he take his place on stage behind the drum kit.

Today Johnny Gentle (or John Askew as he really is) is becomingly modest about the time when he had the Beatles as his anonymous backing group, and he deliberately maintains a low profile. But he does refute any suggestion that he thought the Beatles were not much good on that tour, and – during the course of an interview with the author in March 1984 – he fondly recalled his attempts to smarten the group's appearance by making them wear uniform black shirts to match his own. 'George already possessed one,' he says, 'and I lent my spare shirt to Paul while John and Stuart bought one each at a local market. Only Tommy Moore missed out, but since he had a dark green shirt, and sat right at the back, well away from the spotlight, no one noticed.'

As the week dragged on so the tour disintegrated. In the claustrophobic van tempers easily frayed, especially those of Tommy and Stuart who were both on the receiving end of a reportedly continual barrage of acerbic and often downright nasty wit from John Lennon. To make matters worse, funds were running out fast. Meals became infrequent, and cadged from anyone foolish enough to admit to having money. Parnes recalls receiving a frantic reversed charges telephone call from John Lennon – 'Where's the bloody money?' – on 23 May, just three days after they had been paid. On one occasion the group even managed to slip out of their overnight hotel, the Royal in Forres, without settling their bill.

Although Gentle stayed on in Scotland, the Silver Beetles arrived back in Liverpool on 29 May, bedraggled, poor, hungry and desperately disappointed, though certainly a little wiser about the 'glamorous' rock and roll business. For a while there remained

a notion that they would return to Scotland in mid-July to back Dickie Pride around the same north-east ballroom circuit but this failed to materialize. While they were away Williams had secured them their first fully professional local engagements at £10 a time (£2 each) with a Wallasey promoter called Les Dodd. Dodd ran dances at the Grosvenor Ballroom in Liscard, Wallasey and the Institute Hall in Neston, venues renowed more for their terrifying, bloody violence than for entertainment. On one particular evening in Neston a boy was almost booted to death while the Beatles were playing on stage.

In return for a Coke, and beans on toast – but no money – Williams also put the group on in the minute downstairs area at his Jacaranda Coffee Bar on Mondays, when his resident steel band, the Royal Caribbean, had their night off. The cellar had no microphone stands so the Beatles' girlfriends had to sit at the group's feet holding upside-down broomsticks and mops with microphones crudely tied to the tops. It was on one of these occasions, probably 13 June, that Tommy Moore played his last date with the group. Under constant, but undoubtedly valid, criticism from his girlfriend for wasting his time with the group when he could be out earning proper money, he had also endured far more of John Lennon than any man could stand. Besides, at the age of thirty-six, he had precious little of common interest with any of the four rumbustious, ambitious and enthusiastic teenagers.

Moore intended to leave the Silver Beetles in the lurch after their 9 June date at the Neston Institute, and duly failed to turn up at the Jacaranda Coffee Bar on 11 June, as arranged, before setting out for a date at the Grosvenor Ballroom in Liscard. In a BBC radio interview in 1972 Williams recalled the group piling into his car and screeching their way round to Moore's house in Fern Grove only to find his girlfriend leaning out of an upstairs window shouting, 'You can go and piss off! He's not playing with you any more; he's got a job at the Garston bottle works on the night shift!' Back they climbed into the car and sped off to the works, to find a sullen Moore in white overalls, perched high aboard a fork-lift truck. Despite the group's vehement pleas Moore would not climb down, neither mentally nor physically, so the group had to go on at the Grosvenor with a drum kit but no drummer. To try to assuage the tough Grosvenor patrons who had been known to launch into full, unbridled attack for much lesser reasons, John stepped up to the microphone, half-facetiously explained the situation and rhetorically enquired if there was a drummer in the audience who could help out. The joke misfired disastrously when,

*Mementos from the Silver Beetles' tour with Johnny Gentle. Below: An advert for the first gig, in Alloa (Alex Harvey found fame a decade later with the Sensational Alex Harvey Band). Right: A photo taken that same night by local lensman Ken Beaton. Bottom: An advert for the dance in far-off Forres the following Thursday. The Silver Beetles' name was not mentioned in any adverts for the tour.*

# LATE NIGHT DANCE

## BEAT BALLAD SHOW
Presenting
Star of TV and Decca Recording Fame—
JOHNNY GENTLE and HIS GROUP,
Supported by Scotland's Own Tommy Steele—
ALEX. HARVEY and HIS BEAT BAND,
With Ballad Singer—Babby Rankine.

To Entertain and Play For

### DANCING

in the

## TOWN HALL, ALLOA,

on

## FRIDAY, 20th MAY,

9.30 — 1.30.

ADMISSION—Before 10 p.m., 4/-: after 10 p.m., 5/-.

Buses After Dance to the HILLFOOTS DISTRICT.

NEXT FRIDAY, 27th MAY — JOHNNY DOUGLAS and HIS NEW BEAT COMBO with Happy Jackie Benson and Andy Cook of S.T.V.

Another winner from Northern Border Dances :-

**The Beat Ballad Show,** presenting Star of T.V. and Decca recording fame, **Johnny Gentle** and his Group, supported by **Rikki Barnes** and his All Stars with Lena and Stevie, to entertain and play for dancing in the **Town Hall, Forres,** on THURSDAY, 26th MAY, 9 p.m. to 1 a.m.

**Admission 5/-**

**Please Note** Free Buses will leave Farraline Park Bus Station at 8 p.m. via Ardersier, Gollanfield, Regal Car Park, Nairn, to Forres. Returning after dance

DANCING
THE BIG BEAT!
THE INSTITUTE, NESTON,
EVERY THURSDAY
Rock & Jive to the fabulous
SILVER BEETLES
8 p.m. — 11.30 p.m.     Adm. 3/-.
Come Early & Avoid Disappointment

PARAMOUNT'S
**21**
PLUS NIGHT

WHIT
MONDAY
6th JUNE.

GROSVENOR BALLROOM
EVERY TUESDAY
NO Jiving!    NO Rock 'n' Roll!    NO Teenagers!
**DANCERS' NIGHT**
THE HIGNETT QUARTET,
Plus THE PARADANCE with TOP PRIZES.
8 - 11-30 p.m.    ★ ADMISSION 2/6 ★    Come Early

THE BIG BEAT BOYS! 2 STAR BANDS
Direct from their Tour with Johnny Gentle:
**THE FABULOUS SILVER BEETLES**
— also —
**GERRY & THE PACE-MAKERS**

*Mementos from the Silver Beetles'
first gigs for promoter Les Dodd.*

reportedly, a huge hulking Teddy Boy called Ronnie, who led the local gang but had clearly never been within a hundred yards of a drum kit in his life, clambered up on to the stage and sat, beaming at his new-found mates, from behind Moore's precious hire-purchase kit. A frantic, though surreptitious, phone call from John Lennon during the interval brought Williams across to the Grosvenor. Although not exactly renowned, either then or now, for his diplomacy, Williams nevertheless managed to extricate the group and their equipment from the alarming predicament before ruthless Ronnie 'volunteered' to join up on a permanent basis – or else.

With Moore's brief membership over the group were in the same state they had been since Colin Hanton had left the Quarry Men in early 1959: they badly needed a drummer. For a short while they again played without one, though they were especially careful not to get themselves into such a dangerous situation as the episode with Ronnie had proven. But, apart from a season of Saturday-night dates at the Grosvenor Ballroom, no one else would book them.

Around this time, probably in early July, Williams provided the by-now-renamed Silver Beatles with their oddest engagement ever. Along with a West-Indian-born gentleman known as Lord Woodbine, so nicknamed because of the cigarette always dangling from his lower lip, Williams opened up a dingy, illegal strip club, the New Cabaret Artistes, in the cellar of a terraced Victorian house at 174a Upper Parliament Street, in the heart of Liverpool 8, the so-called vice area of town, where the brothels and shebeens operated under cover of darkness. One particular week Williams was sent a girl from a Manchester club, Janice, who was quite spectacularly endowed in the bust department. Janice promised to bring in good business but, she insisted to a saddened Williams, she would only strip to order if she was

★

# Big 'beat' night

Paramount Enterprises, in complete contrast to their Tuesday "Plus 21" Night, are presenting two of the star 'Rock' groups in the North West, at the Grosvenor Ballroom on Whit Monday.

Pride of place goes to the Silver Beetles, who are returning to Merseyside after a successful tour with Johnny Gentle. Supporting them on the same programme will be another new group to Wallasey —Gerry and the Pace-Makers. Both these groups are jive and rock specialists.

★

## GROSVENOR BALLROOM

The Grosvenor Ballroom to-night introduces a new series of summer Saturday evening dances for youthful patrons, when the all-star outfit The Silver Beetles will be playing.

★

backed by a live band. Records, she made very clear, were insufficient. But since she was certain to send Williams' profits booming he reluctantly agreed, and – because they were the only group without day-time jobs – approached the Silver Beatles. At first they were incredulous and flatly refused to do it, but eventually the promise of 10 shillings per man per night proved just too irresistible and, grudgingly, they accepted. So for one week, four Silver Beatles, all with guitars and amplifiers, and Janice, crowded

*Adverts for the Silver Beetles' 11 June gig at the Grosvenor. Note their toying with the name Beatles, though they were not to change permanently until August.*

on to a stage just seven foot square and performed their act before assorted groaning men in grimy raincoats. The stripper carefully gave her backing group printed sheet music of Beethoven and Khachaturian but that was futile since they couldn't read notation. So instead they played new arrangements of old standards like 'Harry Lime (*Third Man* Theme)', 'Summertime', 'Moonglow and the theme from *Picnic*', 'September Song', 'It's a Long Way to Tipperary' and 'Begin the Beguine'. It was, quite simply, the nadir of their career.

Shortly after the strip club débâcle the group acquired another drummer, Norman Chapman, a six-foot two-inch gentle giant of a man. A picture-frame maker and renovator by trade, Chapman's interest in drums was purely a hobby, and he used to practise his skills on his hire-purchase kit kept in an office in Slater Street, virtually opposite the Jacaranda, after work, when everyone else had gone home. One summer evening, as dusk was slowly falling, Williams and the Beatles heard this mystery drumming sound drifting through the streets and were so impressed, and desperate, that they set about trying to locate where it was coming from. It took quite some time but eventually they found Chapman and offered him the vacant drummer's position in the group. Although he accepted he certainly fulfilled no

more than three Saturday engagements with them at the Grosvenor Ballroom before he was conscripted for two years' national service in Kenya and Kuwait – his career with the Silver Beatles at an end.[5]

In late June the four-man Royal Caribbean Steel Band, the resident group at the Jacaranda Coffee Bar, were – unbeknown to Williams – lured far away, kettle drums and all, to a dockside club in Hamburg by a visiting West German businessman. But colourful characters that they were, and feeling absolutely no sense of remorse over their moonlight flit, one or two members of the band guilelessly wrote back to Williams exclaiming about the high life, the fast money and the even faster women to be found in Hamburg, and particularly on the notorious and wickedly naughty Reeperbahn, the city's red-light area. 'Why don't you come over,' they said, 'have a look, and maybe bring some groups to play?' So Williams, ever on the look-out for an enterprising scheme, made the journey across, together with his business associate, the ennobled Lord Woodbine (and a party of local businessmen out for a dirty weekend) flying to Amsterdam on a rickety Dakota plane chartered by Williams. The duo, rather characteristically, then donned top hats as they drunkenly weaved their way by rail on to Hamburg.[6]

Before they had left Liverpool, Williams had got the Silver Beatles, Gerry and the Pacemakers, Cass and the Cassanovas, the Spinners folk group, and Noel Walker's Stompers, a local trad jazz outfit, to record some songs into a tape recorder which he would use to try to sell their music. But when he produced the $7\frac{1}{2}$ i/p/s, two-track tape mid-way through his hard-sell act before Bruno Koschmider, the owner

---

**5** Williams' recollection that Chapman played with the group for three months is clearly a gross exaggeration. Tommy Moore quit in mid-June, they then had several weeks without a drummer, and by early August, after Chapman, they acquired Pete Best.

**6** There is an alternative and equally plausible, though much overlooked, story about how Allan Williams first came to visit Hamburg and export groups there. Brian Cassar, Geordie-born leader of Cass and the Cassanovas, would often sleep overnight on the floor of the Jacaranda Coffee Bar. He, too, was something of an opportunist and claims that he had been using Williams' telephone to make long-distance calls to Bruno Koschmider in Hamburg, after a London intermediary had informed Cassar that Koschmider was looking for rock groups. Cassar was trying to book his own group there. One day, Cassar says, when he was out of the Jacaranda, a call came through for him from Germany and was answered by Williams. Williams quickly realized what was going on and promised the caller that, for a small commission, he rather than Cassar could supply all the groups that were required.

of a night club called the Kaiserkeller on the Grosse Freiheit, the only sound to emanate from it was unintelligible gibberish. Somehow, somewhere, along Williams' highly eventful journey from England to West Germany, the tape had become de-magnetized.

Williams returned to Liverpool downhearted, his plan of exporting rock groups to Hamburg in tatters. But fate, in the shape of Larry Parnes, intervened. Parnes had promised Williams that he could provide a group or two with work, backing his artistes during summer seasons at Blackpool and Great Yarmouth. With this offer in mind the members of one group, Derry and the Seniors, had quit their jobs in readiness. Then, out of the blue, Parnes wrote cancelling the engagement. The group were understandably livid, and their saxophonist, a rather large youth named Howie Casey, was threatening extensive bodily damage to all and sundry. Especially Parnes. Williams, out of sheer desperation, took the group down in his van to the Two I's Coffee Bar in Old Compton Street, London, in the heart of the Soho area. This was the place where Tommy Steele and many others had been discovered, and it was run by Tommy Littlewood, an acquaintance of Williams. On arrival at the club, after the long journey, Littlewood put the group on his famous stage to run through their set. By sheer, remarkable, coincidence, who else should happen to be sitting in the club at that precise moment, quietly sipping coffee, than Bruno Koschmider, owner of the Kaiserkeller in far-off Hamburg.

Koschmider had evidently been impressed by Williams' visit to him a few weeks previously, boasting that his groups were the best in the world, and playing garbled tapes. So when he didn't hear from him again he decided to take a trip to England to see these wonder groups for himself. Not unnaturally, his travels had taken him to London, the pop music capital, not Liverpool. Koschmider being unable to speak English, an interpreter, Herr Steiner – an Austrian – was fetched from a nearby coffee bar, the Heaven and Hell, to act as translator. Through the mouthpiece a booking for the evidently impressive Derry and the Seniors was drawn up there and then, with Koschmider offering 30 DM (Deutsche Marks) each man per day. This was 24 July. By 31 July the boys were on stage at the Kaiserkeller.

Like the Royal Caribbean Steel Band before them, Derry and the Seniors quickly wrote exuberant and enthusiastic letters to Williams about Hamburg. After just two days Koschmider wrote too. Business at the Kaiserkeller was booming and he intended to open a second venue nearby, the Indra, in a newly acquired strip club. Could Williams send across a second group? Williams could, but wasn't sure whom. Mindful of the Silver Beatles' drummerless state he thought first of Rory Storm and the Hurricanes, but they were mid-way through a prestigious summer season at Butlin's in Pwllheli, North Wales. And Cass and the Cassanovas were up in Scotland backing Duffy Power. He then offered the opportunity to Gerry and the Pacemakers but Gerry wasn't mad on the idea at the time. (Although he was to go a few months later, on 3 December.) Reluctantly, Williams concluded that the Silver Beatles would have to go, but only – he insisted – if they first found themselves a drummer. Around this time Williams wrote Derry and the Seniors a courtesy letter informing them of the Silver Beatles' impending arrival. Howie Casey – with signatures from all the Seniors except Derry Wilkie – wasted little time in returning a none-too-subtle howl of protest, adding that it would spoil the scene for everyone if Williams sent over a bum group like the Beatles!

It just so happened that on 6 August 1960 the Silver Beatles' regular Saturday-night engagement at the Grosvenor Ballroom in Liscard had been cancelled by the Wallasey Corporation, finally bowing to the mounting protests from local residents about the deplorable noise and hooliganism from the more vociferous members of the ballroom's teenage clientele. At a loss for somewhere to play, the four guitar-playing Silver Beatles trooped over to the West Derby area of town and presented themselves at the door of the Casbah Coffee Club, a place they hadn't visited for some months. They found the club thriving, and a quartet called the Blackjacks in residence. Guitarist in the group was none other than Ken Brown who, less than a year previously, had been unceremoniously dumped from the Quarry Men over the £3 booking-fee squabble. And on drums, sitting proudly behind his gleaming new kit, was club owner Mona Best's eighteen-year-old son, Peter. (Actually Randolph Peter.) The other members of the group were Chas Newby and Bill Barlow. A shy, retiring boy, Pete had just two weeks previously left the Collegiate grammar school and was planning a full-time, professional career as a drummer. Exactly with whom he wasn't too sure since the Blackjacks were on the verge of breaking up, its members having reached that age where careers beckon greater than playing 'silly music'. Brown, for example, moved down to London that summer and was never heard from again. Newby, after taking a job in Harlow, Essex, returned north to pursue a course of further education at a college in St Helens.

Shrewdly eyeing the imminently unemployed drummer and, moreover, his beautiful new kit, and

*Above: A rare off-stage break, with a drinking partner, in Hamburg, autumn 1960. Stuart Sutcliffe looks distinctly out of place. Left: Extract from John Lennon's travel visa for the August 1960 trip to Hamburg. It was completed rather belatedly, after the group had arrived at their destination.*

being mindful of the Hamburg offer, the Silver Beatles swiftly offered Pete the chance to join their group. On Friday 12 August, after a simple and almost superfluous audition at the Wyvern Social Club which he could hardly fail to pass (the group, after all, did not *want* him to fail) Pete was in and Hamburg was beckoning.

Four days later, on 16 August, after hastily arranging passports and visas, though conveniently forgetting to apply for time-consuming work permits (this was left to Koschmider, who also 'forgot'), the five Silver Beatles, now renamed simply the Beatles, along with their equipment, Allan Williams and his wife Beryl, her brother Barry Chang, and Lord Wood-

bine, all set out in Williams' old green Austin van for Hamburg. After stopping briefly in London to pick up yet another passenger, the interpreting Herr Steiner from the Heaven and Hell, they sauntered onward to Newhaven and caught the ferry over to the Hook of Holland. From there the overcrowded van slowly but surely made its way across country and over the border into West Germany.

They pulled into the Grosse Freiheit in Hamburg on 17 August, just as dusk was evaporating – the time when the red-light area truly comes to life. On both sides of the *strasse* and even over their heads, flashing neon lights screamed out the various entertainments on offer, while scantily clad women sat unabashed in shop windows waiting for business opportunities to arise. At the Kaiserkeller Derry and the Seniors, about to go on stage for the night, gave the Beatles a decidedly cool reception, hardly bothering to mask their patent disrespect for the group.

But whereas the Kaiserkeller was a fairly plush nighterie, with an unusual nautical theme and good lighting, the Indra, where the Beatles were due to play, was quite the opposite. Koschmider had clearly spent little or no money adapting the until-recently tatty strip club into a bar for music and dancing. The place was small, poky and threadbare, and it still boasted typical strip club décor, with its minute stage, heavy drapes, carpeted floors and small tables with little red lampshades. The Beatles' living quarters were to prove even gloomier, as Koschmider led them out of the Indra and across to a grubby little cinema he also owned, the Bambi-Filmkunsttheater at 33 Paul-Roosen Strasse. Unaware of quite why they were being led around a deserted cinema which specialized in old American westerns, the Beatles blithely followed Koschmider past rows of sparsely occupied stalls to a small, filthy room behind the yellowing screen. 'This,' he explained through the interpreter, amid the noise of gun-totin' heroes and wagon trails, 'is where you will sleep. And there,' he said, pointing back behind him to the cinema toilet, 'is where you can wash.' It was of only little consolation to the group to later discover that despite the Kaiserkeller's luxury compared to the Indra, even Derry and the Seniors were having to endure similarly awful living conditions.

Before the Beatles went on stage at the Indra one trifling business matter had to be concluded. A con-

tract. It was drawn up to run for two months, from 17 August to 16 October, at 30 DM per person per day, payable every Thursday. In addition to this, Koschmider was to deposit a weekly German equivalent of £10 agents' commission in Williams' newly opened account with the Commerzbank in St Pauli, Hamburg. In return, the Beatles would play for four and a half hours every weekday night (8:00–9:30, 10:00–11:00, 11:30–12:30, 1:00–2:00) and for six hours a night on Saturdays (7:00–8:30, 9:00–10:00, 10:30–11:30, 12:00–1:00, 1:30–3:00) and Sundays (5:00–6:00, 6:30–7:30, 8:00–9:00, 9:30–10:30, 11:00–12:00, 12:30–1:30). An additional clause, part of 'the small print', forbade the group to play at any other place of entertainment within a radius of 25 miles (40 kilometres) unless they had the written consent of Koschmider's *Betriebe* (agency).

When the five Beatles eventually took to the stage in Hamburg on 17 August, without much food or sleep since leaving Liverpool the previous day, they were so exhausted that they could barely move. Just a handful of customers turned up. And it wasn't too long before trouble reared its head in the shape of an old woman who lived in a flat above the club. She was prepared to put up with a strip club beneath her, it seems, but not noisy rock and roll music. She complained to Koschmider and she complained to the police. Their solution, to decrease the volume of the Beatles' already feeble and battered amplifiers, was

*A newspaper article on Rory Storm and the Hurricanes, 22 January 1960. Ringo Starr's marriage never materialized and his time spent making plans was wasted.*

a disaster: 'Long Tall Sally' clearly wasn't written to be whispered. On 4 October, just 48 nights after Koschmider had opened the Indra to beat music, he closed it down and moved the Beatles on to the bustling Kaiserkeller.

The only problem the Beatles faced at the Kaiserkeller was caused by the huge – though rotting – stage. Aside from John, Paul and George's four five-minute Carroll Levis auditions in Liverpool and Manchester a year previously, the group hadn't played on such a large podium in their lives. It made the Indra's platform look like a matchbox by comparison. The Beatles' stage movements froze, until on their seventh night, 10 October, Allan Williams – making a return visit to Hamburg and sitting in his familiar seat at the bar – could stand it no longer. 'Make a show boys!' he exhorted at the top of his voice. Koschmider and the club regulars soon took up the chant in their best pidgin-English. 'Mak show,' they would shout whenever the group looked like flagging during the long nights.

The Beatles' reply to this encouragement was, reportedly, quite incredible to see, with the four guitarists – though particularly John Lennon – all launching themselves into exaggerated contortions and writhings, strongly resembling Gene Vincent's unintentionally crippled movements at the Liverpool Stadium. Virtually overnight the Beatles began to go down very big with the rumbustious Hamburg club audiences. Very often a crate or two of beer, bought by customers, would be sent on to the stage for the group to drink, compulsorily, while playing. It would have been an unwise move not to oblige. One typical cry from a man in the audience might be 'Two crates if you sing "Hound Dog"!' The effect of the alcohol was devastating, especially when combined with the variety of multi-coloured pills the group – except Pete Best who never participated – were liberally swallowing just to keep themselves awake and maintain their energy during the long nights on stage. If the customers wanted the Beatles to 'mak show' there seemed no limit to which they wouldn't go to please. Soon, John Lennon, safe behind the language barrier, was calling everybody 'fucking nazis', wearing swastikas and performing *Sieg Heil*s and goose-steps on stage – all highly illegal in Germany just fifteen years after the end of the war.

On 2 October Derry and the Seniors' contract with Koschmider expired, and after hanging around town for a while they slowly returned to England. In their place, on 1 October, came Rory Storm and the Hurricanes, fresh from their summer season at Butlin's. The drummer with the Hurricanes was none other than Ringo Starr. From 4 October the Beatles and

Rory's group played welcome split shifts at the Kaiserkeller, and for a short while the two groups enjoyed a fierce contest to see which of them would be the first to demolish the club's rotten and increasingly precarious stage. Eventually Rory managed it, executing one final, deliberately heavy-footed, crash landing after an athletic leap during a version of 'Blue Suede Shoes'. Rory was severely chastised by Koschmider and had 65 DM docked from his wages to pay for the damage.

The Beatles made another record in 1960. On Saturday 15 October, while Allan Williams was in Hamburg, they got together with two members of Rory Storm's Hurricanes, drummer Ringo Starr and bespectacled vocalist/bassist Walter Eymond (stage name Lou Walters, nickname Wally), in a small studio – the Akustik, at 57 Kirchenallee, situated behind Hamburg's central railway station. Pete Best was not present at the time so, excluding Eymond, for one brief moment the four Beatles were together for the first time. They recorded one song, a version of the George Gershwin composition 'Summertime',[7] and it was initially cut on to a 78-rpm disc, the other side of which comprised a salesman's message about leather handbags and shoes. In his book, Allan Williams recalls that four 45-rpm discs were eventually cut, although this is somewhat contradicted by an article on 'Lou Walters' in *Mersey Beat* in December 1963 which stated that the song was being 'regularly played at dance halls in Liverpool'. Eymond himself remembers that nine discs were cut altogether, only one copy of which is known to have survived the years – and that is in Australia.

On 16 October the Beatles' contract with Koschmider was extended until 31 December and there was even talk of the group moving on to West Berlin on 7 January 1961 for a month's work there. At the end of October 1960 a new club, the Top Ten, opened at 136 Reeperbahn, situated in the Hippodrome, a building which had until then operated as a sex-oriented circus. The new owner, Peter Eckhorn, clearly intended to hit the Kaiserkeller hard, and immediately wooed away Koschmider's chief bouncer – an absolute necessity in Hamburg's tough clubland – former boxing champion Horst Fascher, and contracted artiste Tony Sheridan (born Anthony

---

7 Exaggerated stories in other Beatles books to the effect that they recorded *three* songs, 'Summertime' plus 'Fever' and 'September Song', can be totally discounted according to Walter Eymond in an interview with the author in July 1984. Those other two songs *were* recorded but they featured the backing of Ringo with Ty Brian and Johnny Guitar from Rory Storm's Hurricanes, not the Beatles.

Hamburg,
November 1st, 1960

Notice

I the undersigned, hereby give notice to Mr. GEORGE HARRISON
and to BEATLES' BAND to leave on November 30th 1960.

The notice is given to the above by order of the Public
Authorities who have discovered that Mr. GEORGE HARRISON is
only 17 (seventeen) years of age.

Tanzpalast der Jugend

(Bruno Koschmider)
Managing Director
KAISERKELLER.

«KAISERKELLER»
Inh. Bruno Koschmider
HAMBURG-ST. PAULI
Große Freiheit 36 · Tel. 31 07 63

Vertrag mit den BEATLES für
den Monat April 1961.
Paul Mc. Carthey, John Lennon,
Peter Best, George Harrison,
Stuart Sutcliffe.
Tagesgage pro Tag per Mann
beträgt 35.- DM. Gefällt die Band
wird der Vertrag den weiteren
Monat verlängert.
Arbeitszeit:
Von Montag bis Freitag, von 8⁰⁰-2⁰⁰
am Wochenende von 7⁰⁰-3⁰⁰.
Nach jeder Stunde 15 Min. Pause
Orig. Vertrag wird vorgelegt.
Top Ten
Hamburg
30.11.60

Above : The classic early Beatles, taken by Astrid Kirchherr at Der Dom, a Hamburg fair. Left : The hastily scribbled contract between Peter Eckhorn and the Beatles which so angered Allan Williams four months later. Translation: Agreement with the Beatles for the month of April 1961. Paul McCartney, John Lennon, Peter Best, George Harrison, Stuart Sutcliffe. Daily salary per day per member stands at 35 DM. If the Beatles give satisfaction, the agreement will be extended for another month. Working hours: on Mondays to Fridays from 19.00–2.00. On weekends from 19.00–3.00. After each hour a 15-minute break. Original contract yet to be made. Top Ten, Peter Eckhorn, 30.11.60.

Esmond Sheridan McGinnity), an accomplished English singer/guitarist who actually had several UK record releases and television appearances to his credit. The Beatles held Sheridan in very high esteem indeed, and would often take the opportunity to use their frequent half-hour breaks at the Kaiserkeller to nip across to the Top Ten. Naturally it was only a matter of time before they were up on stage jamming with Sheridan and his London group, the Jets.

News of this defection soon drifted back to an angry Koschmider who, already livid with the Beatles and Rory Storm over the broken stage incident, decided that enough was enough. Citing the clause in their agreement which stipulated that they could not play elsewhere within a radius of 25 miles without his permission, he handed the Beatles a month's cessation of contract notice. Somehow, word also found its way to the police authorities that George Harrison was under 18 and, therefore, under West German law, was not even allowed to frequent – let alone work in – a night club after midnight.

The Beatles played out their notice period under a pall of gloom, while – on 21 November – George was deported by the authorities for deliberately flouting the law. He returned home alone, a perilous 24-hour journey, spending all his savings on train fares, porters' tips, and taxis. The remaining Beatles struggled on without him, spending only the barest minimum of time in the Kaiserkeller, preferring to socialize and play their music at the Top Ten whenever possible. Peter Eckhorn offered them bunk-bed accommodation in the attic above the club. Not exactly luxurious accommodation admittedly, but a five-star hotel when compared with their atrocious and filthy quarters behind the screen at the Bambi-Filmkunsttheater. One day at the end of November, probably around the 29th, Paul McCartney and Pete Best were back at the Bambi surreptitiously packing their belongings. The cinema was closed and as there were no torches or candles to hand the two Beatles fiendishly decided to set light to the rotting, peeling tapestry hanging from the wall in order to see their way around. A dull glow soon appeared and Paul and Pete packed their clothes and left, deliberately ignoring, in their contempt for Koschmider, their makeshift lighting arrangement. The glowing tapestry was eventually extinguished by the dampness in the wall.

Within the hour, Koschmider received word from an aide that the two Beatles 'had attempted to set fire to the Bambi' and he vengefully decided that it was a matter for the police. Paul McCartney was swiftly arrested and thrown into jail at St Pauli police station on a charge of suspected arson, and very soon

Pete Best was with him in the cell too. Both were held overnight and released the following morning. Feeling tired after their detention they went to their new lodgings above the Top Ten to sleep, but a few hours later, early in the afternoon, they were rudely awakened by a heavy and constant banging on the door. When Pete Best sleepily slid back the bolt and opened the door he was greeted by two huge plain-clothes policemen. The two Beatles were ordered to dress without delay and were then bundled into a car and sped to the Hamburg detective headquarters where the officer in charge announced that they were being deported on the midnight aeroplane back to London. The police escorted Best and McCartney back to the Top Ten and gave them precisely five minutes to repack their belongings. Pete had to leave his drums behind, Paul carried his guitar over his shoulder. Then it was back to the jail until nightfall and an escort to the airport. Bemused by the language difficulties, and therefore not entirely comprehending the situation, the two Beatles asked for permission to telephone the British Consul. This was refused, and a few hours later they were touching down at London Airport. They had just enough money for an early-morning bus to Euston station and the train home to Liverpool. It was 1 December.

One other thing happened on 30 November: before Best and McCartney were deported the Beatles provisionally negotiated with Peter Eckhorn for a one-month booking at the Top Ten club for the following April, subject to them lifting their various deportation bans. Allan Williams, in far-off Liverpool, was oblivious to these dealings, dealings which would eventually sever his link with the group for ever.

Three of the five Beatles were now back in Britain, deported, and the West German police were soon after John Lennon and Stuart Sutcliffe too. On the morning of 10 December John set out on the long train journey back to England, with his precious amplifier strapped to his back in case someone tried to steal it. Stuart meanwhile had gone into temporary hiding, aided by a Hamburg girl called Astrid Kirchherr with whom he had fallen in love and become engaged. (Astrid was to prove a major influence on the Beatles between 1960 and 1962, particularly on their physical appearance, more of which later.) Stuart eventually flew home to Liverpool in late February 1961.

For a short while George Harrison, Pete Best and Paul McCartney remained unaware that John Lennon had also made it home. Indeed they didn't see or hear from him until 15 December. But once reunited, the group decided to try to find some local

gigs, though their first priority, in Sutcliffe's absence, was to find a new bass player. Pete Best thought of the Blackjacks' bassist Ken Brown, but he was now living in London, and besides, the Beatles didn't want him back in the group after his short spell as a Quarry Man had ended in disharmony. Best then remembered Chas Newby, rhythm guitarist with the Blackjacks, and phoned him at his home in Everton. As it was mid-December Newby was on Christmas holiday from his college course and he agreed to help out. Chas Newby shared two things in common with Paul McCartney: both were born on 18 June (Newby in 1941, McCartney in 1942) and both were left-handed. What Newby didn't have was a bass guitar and a leather jacket to match the Beatles' uniform. He borrowed both (though the jacket's soppy fur hood caused him some embarrassment) and became a Beatle. He was to play only four gigs with the group before returning to his college course early in January, and henceforth into obscurity in the Midlands. Speaking in an interview with the author in November 1984, Newby vividly remembered his short stint as a temporary Beatle and is in no way embittered about 'what might have been' had he stayed with the group. 'John Lennon did semi-seriously ask me if I wanted to go to Hamburg with them,' he recalls, 'if, that is, they could get permission to go back, but it was out of the question.'

On 17 December the five-man group gave their first post-Hamburg performance, at the Casbah Coffee Club in Hayman's Green, the home – literally – of Pete Best, and they played a return booking there on 31 December. Meanwhile, on 19 December Allan Williams had booked the group, for a ten-guinea fee, into the Christmas Eve dance at their old stamping ground, the Grosvenor Ballrom in Liscard. But it was on 27 December, at the Town Hall ballroom in Litherland, when it all came together, when the Beatles truly became rock and roll kingpins of Merseyside in one fell swoop.

The man responsible for getting them this date was Bob Wooler, a 28-year-old erudite figure who, until recently, had been a railway office clerk. He had resigned from his steady job to become disc jockey and compere at a new, unlicensed, cabaret-type venue opened by Allan Williams on Thursday 1 December, the Top Ten club, situated at 100 Soho Street near the centre of Liverpool. Williams had evidently returned from Hamburg with grandiose ideas. Pop luminaries Terry Dene and Garry Mills were there for the opening week, supported by prominent Mersey beat bands, and bookings for the following four weeks included Davy Jones, Danny Rivers, Michael Cox and Don Fox. But at 11:30 p.m. on

# Tonight's big night at the Grosvenor

Tonight is the big night at the Grosvenor, when for the holiday attraction two top grade bands have been engaged, Derry and the Seniors and The Silver Beetles. Both these bands have recently returned from a successful tour of Germany. Admission is 5/- with continuous dancing from 8 to 11-45.

The North Wirral Velo R.R.C. take over the ballroom on Monday next (Boxing Night) for a dance from 8 to midnight featuring the Ernie Hignett Quartet.

Next Tuesday afternoon Mrs Shaw's regular old time and modern sequence dance takes the floor at 2-30 p.m. followed at 8 p.m. by Paramount's special grand holiday dance.

BEEKAY'S
Holiday JIVE Dances

Fri. 23rd—LATHOM. Over 17's. 7-30 — 11. 3/-

Sat. 24th—CHRISTMAS EVE CARNIVALS
LATHOM. 7-30—11-45.
CLIFF, SEARCHERS, RAVENS Tickets 5/-
ALEXANDRA HALL. 7-45—11-45.
TORNADOES, RED STREAKS, RAVENS.
Tickets 5/6

Mon. 26th—BOXING NIGHT GALA at LATHOM HALL
CLIFF ROBERTS, DELTONES, RAVENS.
7-30 — 12-30. Door 5/-

Tues. 27th—LITHERLAND TOWN HALL
7-30—12-0. Door 3/-
BIG BEAT EXTRA.
DEL RENAS, SEARCHERS, DELTONES.

Thurs. 29th—LITHERLAND TOWN HALL
FARON, REMO 4, CLIFF 7-30—11. Door 3/-

Fri. 30th—LATHOM. Over 17's. 7-30 — 11. 3/-

at 31st—NEW YEAR'S EVE GALA at LATHOM. 7-30—11-45.
FARON, CLIFF, RIKKI. Tickets 6/-

Tickets for Ticket Dances from Any Beekay Dance or 15, Coronation Drive, Crosby.

★
BEEKAY PROMOTIONS

*The Beatles' Christmas activities. The group was a late addition to the bill at the Litherland gig on 27 December, hence their omission from the advert.*

Tuesday 6 December the club mysteriously burnt down, almost certainly – although nothing was ever proved – the result of arson. It was totally destroyed and much group equipment was lost in the blaze, including all of Derry and the Seniors' guitars and amplifiers. Williams received just £1086 in insurance compensation.

Suddenly out of a day-to-day job, Wooler was kicking his heels around the Jacaranda when he got talking to the Beatles. Could he find them any engagements, they wondered. Wooler said yes, he would try to find them a date with promoter Brian Kelly, for whom he was an occasional MC/compere. He duly telephoned Kelly then and there from the Jacaranda. Kelly was loath to book the Beatles again, remembering the occasion just seven months previously when, as the Silver Beats, they had let him down by dashing off to Scotland, unannounced, after he had booked them for a dance at the Lathom Hall in Seaforth. Kelly was even more disgruntled when, through Wooler, the Beatles asked for an £8 fee. Kelly offered £4 and, after protracted haggling, they settled on £6. The booking was, more than anything else, a special favour to Wooler, since Kelly already had three groups booked for the evening – the Del Renas, the Searchers, and the Deltones.

As the Beatles' addition to the night's fare was too late for Kelly to include their name in his standard advertisement in the *Bootle Times*, promotion of the

Beatles' appearance was restricted to routine stage announcements at Kelly's three other dances over the Christmas period – at the Lathom Hall and at the Alexandra Hall, Crosby – and on the hastily redesigned amateur posters which were now emblazoned with an extra legend, stuck on with flour and water: 'Direct from Hamburg, The Beatles!' So few people in North Liverpool had heard of the group, bearing in mind that they had performed only one gig in the area up to that time (their unadvertised spot at the Lathom Hall on 14 May), that most of the Litherland Town Hall clientele, upon looking at the poster, concluded that the Beatles were a German group.

As the curtains shuffled open and Paul McCartney launched himself into Little Richard's 'Long Tall Sally', everyone suddenly – and spontaneously – crushed forward to the front of the stage, swept away by the group's sheer magnetism. Five hundred hours on stage in Hamburg had forged the style that would conquer the world. The five-man Beatles – John, Paul, George, Chas Newby, and Pete – were an absolute powerhouse, creating an unprecedented and inexplicable frenzy among the teenagers, for whom all thoughts of dancing were quickly forgotten. They were, quite simply, spellbound. As the Beatles blasted out their Hamburg night-club repertoire they too were bewildered by the incredible scene they were invoking. Beatlemania was enjoying its birth pangs.

**23 April**      The Fox and Hounds, Gosbrook Road, Caversham, Berkshire

During the college/school Easter holidays, John and Paul took off for a short break in the south of England, staying for a few days with Paul's cousin Bett (Elizabeth) Robbins and her husband Mike, both of whom had recently left their employment as Butlins' Red-coats and were the new tenants of the Fox and Hounds public house.

In return for working behind the bar during the week, Mike Robbins gave John and Paul the opportunity to perform live on the Saturday night. Desperate for a name, Robbins decided to call them The Nerk Twins, and drew up hand-made posters which were duly pinned on the saloon bar door.

The Nerk Twins played in the newly decorated tap room, perched high on two bar stools, acoustic guitars in hand, without microphones. They were stuck for an opening number, and Robbins suggested 'The World Is Waiting for the Sunrise', an old variety number, and Butlin's favourite. Amid much laughter the Nerk Twins somehow managed to struggle through and complete the song, before continuing with numbers in the country and western/rock vein.

Note: This peculiar engagement has been a constant source of confusion to writers over the years. Haphazard guesses as to the precise date have varied from 1955 through to 1959, while none has ever located the correct venue beyond nearby 'Reading'. One particularly inventive American author wrote that 'The Nerk Twins played in a Bending [sic] Variety Show in 1958. The promoter was thoroughly delighted with them and tried to re-book them at a later date.' Palpable, pulpable rubbish.

---

**24 April**      The Fox and Hounds, Caversham

Before setting off on the long trek north to Liverpool, the Nerk Twins made their second, and last-ever, appearance during the Sunday lunchtime pub session, 12:00–2:00 p.m.

---

**14 May**      Lathom Hall, Lathom Avenue, Seaforth, Liverpool

The Silver Beetles' (or Silver Beats as they were called on this occasion) first-ever proper engagement was for Crosby-based promoter Brian Kelly, who ran dances at forbidding-looking halls and institutes in North Liverpool. Kelly was one of the first to spot the surging beat boom on Merseyside, promoting his first live dance/jive session at the Savoy Hall in Bath Street, Waterloo on 11 May 1959, and quickly adding such illustrious venues as Lathom Hall, Seaforth; Town Hall, Litherland; Institute, Aintree; and Alexandra Hall, Crosby, to his roster.

The Silver Beats were not advertised for this date, featuring Cliff Roberts and the Rockers, the Deltones and King Size Taylor and the Dominoes, but played a few songs in the interval by way of an audition before Kelly. Two reports on how they fared differ enormously. In *Shout!*, author Philip Norman, from interviews with Kelly and Taylor, suggests that they were so bad that Kelly ordered them off stage after their second song. But the local newspaper, the *Bootle Times* (see illustration) reported that they were 'sensational'. The truth probably lies somewhere in between, though they must have shown sufficient promise for Kelly to book them for the following Saturday's dance, on 21 May, actually headlining over King Size Taylor. For reasons that became apparent halfway through the week preceding 21 May, the Silver Beats/Beetles were unable to fulfil the engagement. Rather typically, they omitted to inform Kelly of this, who was left cold without his advertised attraction.

---

**21 May** CANCELLED      Lathom Hall, Seaforth

The Silver Beetles' first-ever official, advertised engagement, and they weren't even there to see it. For when the curtains rose at the Lathom Hall they were 367 miles away in Inverness, enjoying a taste of the Big Time.

---

**TOUR OF SCOTLAND WITH JOHNNY GENTLE**

**20 May**      Town Hall, Alloa, Clackmannanshire

The first night of the tour, and the only date fixed for the south of Scotland. The remaining six all took place along the north-east coast, well into the Highlands. The Silver Beetles and Gentle had their first, and only, rehearsal – lasting just thirty minutes – before they took to the stage at the town hall.

---

**21 May**      Northern Meeting Ballroom, Church Street, Inverness, Inverness-shire

The tour moved on 152 miles north to Inverness, the 'capital of the Highlands'. As the travelling musicians were quickly discovering, the tour was by no means 'the big time' they had hoped for. Indeed, on this occasion, as can be seen from the advertisement illustrated, they had the ignominious task of playing in an upstairs hall while below them the more traditional Lindsay Ross Band kept the older

**BEEKAY DANCES**

This week Beekay dances continue with their policy of all-jive for teenagers, tonight's dance being transfered to Alexandra Hall. The Silver Beats return to Lathom Hall on Saturday after their sensational appearance last week.

Patrons are in for another lively session at Lathom Hall on Monday and at Aintree Institute on Wednesday.

Once again, Thursday night is Big Beat Night at Litherland Town Hall

## NORTHERN BORDER DANCES PROUDLY PRESENT

**To-morrow (Saturday), 21st MAY, 7.30 to 11.30 p.m.**

**UPSTAIRS** — Modern Dancing to **THE BEAT BALLAD SHOW** introducing another TV and Decca Recording Star, **JOHNNY GENTLE and his Group**, and **RONNIE WATT** and the **CHEKKERS** Rock Dance Band.

**DOWNSTAIRS** — Old tyme Dancing to **LINDSAY ROSS** and his Famous Broadcasting Band

**ADMISSION - Before 8 p.m. 3/-     After 8 p.m. 5/-**
(Limited Numbers — Right of Admission Reserved)

---

townsfolk happy with old-tyme dancing!

| 23 May | Dalrymple Hall, Fraserburgh, Aberdeenshire |

| 25 May | St Thomas' Hall, Keith, Banffshire |

| 26 May | Town Hall, Forres, Morayshire |

Despite the fact that the Silver Beetles played here the town may well be a little more proud of its mention in Shakespeare's *Macbeth*.

| 27 May | Regal Ballroom, Leopold Street, Nairn, Nairnshire |

| 28 May | Rescue Hall, Peterhead, Aberdeenshire |

END OF TOUR

| 30 May | Jacaranda Coffee Bar, 23 Slater Street, Liverpool |

The first of several Silver Beetles engagements at this city centre venue owned by Allan Williams. When they weren't otherwise engaged the group played here on Mondays, when the club's resident Royal Caribbean Steel Band had their night off.

Note : A full listing of the Beatles' performances at this venue cannot be compiled since they were not noted down or advertised at the time. They are unlikely to number more than twelve.

| 2 June | The Institute, Hinderton Road, Neston, Wirral, Cheshire |

The first of six consecutive Thursday-night engagements at this venue, situated on the west side of the Wirral, close to North Wales. Paramount Enterprises, alias promoter Les Dodd, had been running 'strict tempo' ballroom evenings at this venue, and at the Grosvenor in Liscard, Wallasey since 1936, but had, rather grudgingly, come to the conclusion that rock and roll/jive sessions were perhaps more lucrative. On this evening Dodd paid the Silver Beetles £10, out of which they gave £1 to Allan Williams.

| 4 June | Grosvenor Ballroom, Grosvenor Road, Liscard, Wallasey, Cheshire |

Saturday night became 'big beat' night at Dodd's other venue, the lugubrious-looking Grosvenor Ballroom. But while Dodd invited youthful patrons at both venues to 'see this new all-star outfit in a swing session', the nights were little more than an excuse for a terrifying display of excessive thuggery and sheer, unadulterated violence by local louts. The scenes were watched with increasing horror by the group on stage, valiantly playing on despite the bloody mêlée beneath them.

| 6 June | Grosvenor Ballroom, Liscard |

To celebrate the Whitsun Bank Holiday, Dodd presented a special Monday jive and rock session, billing the two groups who would eventually become Liverpool's most successful, 'the Silver Beetles and Gerry and the Pace-makers'. This was the first of many occasions that they would appear on a bill together.

| 9 June | The Institute, Neston |

## 'Rock' group at Neston Institute

A LIVERPOOL rhythm group "The Beatles," made their debut at Neston Institute on Thursday night when north-west promoter, Mr. Les Dodd, presented three and a half hours of rock 'n' roll.

The five strong group, which has been pulling in capacity houses on Merseyside, comprises three guitars, bass and drums.

John Lennon, the leader, plays one of the three rhythm guitars, the other guitarists being Paul Ramon and Carl Harrison. Stuart Da Stael plays the bass, and the drummer is Thomas Moore. They all sing, either together, or as soloists.

Recently they returned from a Scottish tour, starring John Gentle, and are looking forward to a return visit in a months' time.

Among the theatres they played at are the Hippodrome, Manchester; the Empire, Liverpool and the Pavilion, Aintree.

| | |
|---|---|
| **11 June** | Grosvenor Ballroom, Liscard |

Almost certainly the night of the infamous 'Ronnie' episode.

| | |
|---|---|
| **13 June** | Jacaranda Coffee Bar |

After letting down the Silver Beetles on 11 June, Tommy Moore made one last appearance with the group on this occasion.

| | |
|---|---|
| **16 June** | The Institute, Neston |

## "DEESIDERS" AT NESTON
### Big beat night

"THE Big Beat" featured a double bill at Neston Institute on Thursday evening when the resident "Beatles" from Liverpool were supported by Keith Rowlands and the Deesiders, from Heswall.

Well known locally for their performances at the "Glee Club," the "? Jazz Club" and "le macabre," the Deesiders are Ronnie Aston, on drums, guitarists Pete Bolt and John Sanders, and guitar playing vocalist Keith Rowlands, who has also been singing as a guest artiste with the "Beatles" on Thursday nights.

Next month the "Beatles" are leaving Neston to go on tour with teenage idol Dickie Pride.

| | |
|---|---|
| **18 June** | Grosvenor Ballroom, Liscard |

Paul McCartney's eighteenth-birthday night.

| | |
|---|---|
| **23 June** | The Institute, Neston |

| | |
|---|---|
| **25 June** | Grosvenor Ballroom, Liscard |

| | |
|---|---|
| **30 June** | The Institute, Neston |

| | |
|---|---|
| **2 July** | Grosvenor Ballroom, Liscard |

What looked like being just another run-of-the-mill Saturday-night performance was considerably brightened by the sudden, unannounced, arrival at the Grosvenor of Johnny Gentle, making the most of a rare weekend without engagements to return to his home in Litherland, north Liverpool. Keen to look up his recent

# DANCE OFF AT GROSVENOR TO-NIGHT

## Bid to stop teenage gangs' 'disgraceful behaviour'

ROCK 'n' roll rows, hooliganism and complaints from residents living nearby have caused the cancellation of tonight's swing-session dance at the Corporation's Grosvenor Ballroom, Liscard. The decision has been taken after reports of fights and rowdyism among groups of teenagers.

"The trouble makers are small gangs determined to spoil the enjoyment of others." Mr A. W. Micklewright, Wallasey's Publicity and Entertainments Manager, told the *News* yesterday.

"Their behaviour during the past two or three weeks has been disgraceful. Members of the staff have been threatened by them. We are determined to stamp out the menace and maintain the good reputation of the ballroom."

Residents of Grosvenor Street and other roads in the area have forwarded to the Council a 21-signature petition complaining about "hooliganism and unreasonable noise at Saturday rock 'n' roll sessions."

backing group, Gentle and his father arrived at Williams' Jacaranda Coffee Bar, was informed of the Silver Beetles' date in Liscard, and went across to surprise them. The reunion was a good one, with Gentle leaping up on stage to sing a few numbers.

| | |
|---|---|
| **7 July** | The Institute, Neston |

| | |
|---|---|
| **9 July** | Grosvenor Ballroom, Liscard |

| | |
|---|---|
| **16 July** | Grosvenor Ballroom, Liscard |

| | |
|---|---|
| **23 July** | Grosvenor Ballroom, Liscard |

| | |
|---|---|
| **30 July** | Grosvenor Ballroom, Liscard |

| | |
|---|---|
| **6 August** ~~CANCELLED~~ | Grosvenor Ballroom, Liscard |

The Silver Beetles' run of Saturday-night performances at the Grosvenor came to a grinding halt before this, the tenth occasion. By the end of July the violence and rowdiness before, during, and after each dance had grown so bad that the local residents lodged a complaint with Grosvenor's lessors the Wallasey Corporation, giving them little alternative but to cancel the season forthwith. Strict-tempo dances resumed thereafter.

Later in the year the Grosvenor did re-open for rock sessions but the Corporation itself assumed control of the proceedings, thus relieving (albeit temporarily) Les Dodd/Paramount Enterprises of the dubious, though certainly remunerative, pleasure.

*The Silver Beatles' run of Grosvenor gigs came to an abrupt end.*

## VISIT TO HAMBURG

| | |
|---|---|
| **17 August – 3 October (48 nights)** | Indra Club, 34 Grosse Freiheit |

The first 200-plus hours the Beatles played in Hamburg.

| | |
|---|---|
| **4 October – 30 November (58 nights)** | The Kaiserkeller, 36 Grosse Freiheit |

After a constant barrage of complaints over the noise and commotion at the Indra, Koschmider's solution was to move the Beatles into his other club, the Kaiserkeller. Here they shared the bill with fellow Liverpudlians, Rory Storm and the Hurricanes, and for the

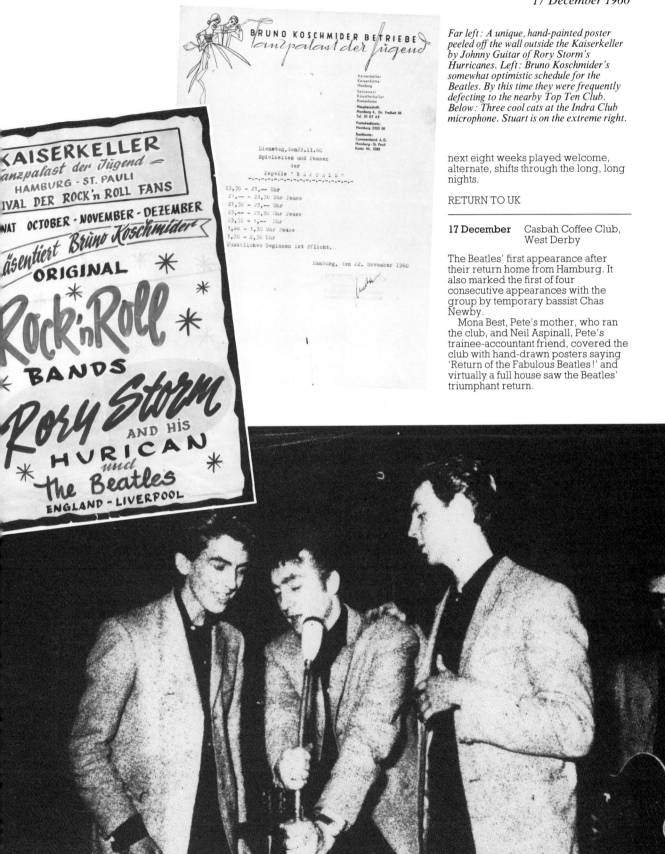

BRUNO KOSCHMIDER BETRIEBE
*Tanzpalast der Jugend*

Kaiserkeller
Kaiserhütte
Hamburg
Sansssouci
Künstlerkeller
Bremerhaven
Hauptanschrift:
Hamburg 4, Gr. Freiheit 36
Tel. 31 07 63
Postscheckkonto:
Hamburg 2353 06
Bankkonto:
Commerzbank A.G.
Hamburg - St. Pauli
Konto Nr. 3382

Dienstag, den 22.11.60
Spielzeiten und Pausen
der
Kapelle "B E A T L E S"

19,30 - 21,-- Uhr
21,-- - 21,30 Uhr Pause
21,30 - 23,-- Uhr
23,-- - 23,30 Uhr Pause
23,30 - 1,-- Uhr
1,00 - 1,30 Uhr Pause
1,30 - 2,30 Uhr

Pünktliches Beginnen ist Pflicht.

Hamburg, den 22. November 1960

*Far left: A unique, hand-painted poster peeled off the wall outside the Kaiserkeller by Johnny Guitar of Rory Storm's Hurricanes. Left: Bruno Koschmider's somewhat optimistic schedule for the Beatles. By this time they were frequently defecting to the nearby Top Ten Club. Below: Three cool cats at the Indra Club microphone. Stuart is on the extreme right.*

KAISERKELLER
*Tanzpalast der Jugend* —
HAMBURG - ST. PAULI —
...IVAL DER ROCK'n ROLL FANS
...NAT OCTOBER - NOVEMBER - DEZEMBER
...äsentiert Bruno Koschmider
ORIGINAL
Rock'n Roll
BANDS
Rory Storm
AND HIS
HURICAN
und
the Beatles
ENGLAND - LIVERPOOL

next eight weeks played welcome, alternate, shifts through the long, long nights.

RETURN TO UK

**17 December**    Casbah Coffee Club, West Derby

The Beatles' first appearance after their return home from Hamburg. It also marked the first of four consecutive appearances with the group by temporary bassist Chas Newby.

Mona Best, Pete's mother, who ran the club, and Neil Aspinall, Pete's trainee-accountant friend, covered the club with hand-drawn posters saying 'Return of the Fabulous Beatles!' and virtually a full house saw the Beatles' triumphant return.

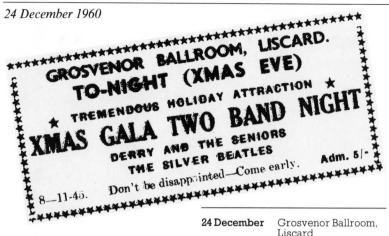

**GROSVENOR BALLROOM, LISCARD.**
**TO-NIGHT (XMAS EVE)**
★ TREMENDOUS HOLIDAY ATTRACTION ★
**XMAS GALA TWO BAND NIGHT**
DERRY AND THE SENIORS
THE SILVER BEATLES
Adm. 5/-
8—11-45. Don't be disappointed—Come early.

*The management of the Grosvenor clearly couldn't adjust to the Beatles' name change.*

**24 December**  Grosvenor Ballroom, Liscard

With the threat of violence slightly decreased, rock sessions had returned to the Grosvenor with the Wallasey Corporation in charge. The Beatles, playing their first true public performance after Hamburg (the Casbah being a strictly members-only club), shared the bill with Derry and the Seniors. The two groups received ten guineas each.

**27 December**  Town Hall Ballroom, Hatton Hill Road, Litherland, Liverpool

If any one live performance in the Beatles' career could be described as the turning point it was this, their penultimate gig in 1960. Their career was not without hiccups in the future but, in reality, the group never looked back after this night.

**31 December**  Casbah Coffee Club, West Derby

The last occasion that Chas Newby played guitar in the Beatles.

## Other engagements played

The only semi-regular performances of the Quarry Men/Beatals in early 1960 were at the Friday afternoon Students' Union dances in the school hall of the Liverpool College of Art, Hope Street, during John Lennon and Stuart Sutcliffe's final year of education there. All record of the dates has long since vanished. As the group was without enough amplifiers (there was, remember, a new guitarist in the group) the union was prevailed upon to provide them with one, on the proviso that it never left the building. It did: the Beatles were to use this amplifier (albeit irregularly) until 1962.

The Beatals played during an interval break on one Sunday afternoon in early 1960 at the original Cassanova Club, situated above the Temple Restaurant in Temple Street, Liverpool city centre. The venue was opened on 10 January 1960 by Cass and the Cassanovas, who were frustrated at the lack of opportunities to play in the city, and it operated on Thursday, Friday and Saturday nights, and Sunday afternoons.

In addition to their unspecifiable occasional Monday-night appearances at the Jacaranda Coffee Bar between the end of May and mid-August, the Silver Beatles may well have fulfilled other unannounced and unadvertised dates there during this period as they or Allan Williams saw fit, especially with the permanent absence from late June of the resident group, the Royal Caribbean Steel Band. On one occasion, probably in late June, they backed Royston Ellis, the teenage 'beat poet', while he recited some of his work.

For one week in early July the Silver Beatles fulfilled their infamous strip club booking at the New Cabaret Artistes. See pages 34 and 35 for details.

On very rare occasions (probably just once or twice in mid-1960) the Silver Beatles played for an afternoon in the cellar of a shebeen run by Allan Williams' business partner, Lord Woodbine: the New Colony Club, situated in a semi-derelict house at 80 Berkley Street, Liverpool 8, in the heart of the city's vice area.

The precise dates of the Beatles' few, sporadic and, for obvious reasons, unannounced appearances at the Top Ten Club, 136 Reeperbahn, in Hamburg are now lost for ever, if they were ever noted down at all. In addition to impromptu jamming with Tony Sheridan and his group, the Jets, they also performed there alone on one or two occasions towards the end of their stay in Hamburg, at the end of November.

## Engagements not played

The author could find no evidence, or likely indication, that the group played at the Casbah Coffee Club in 1960 other than on the two dates listed for 17 and 31 December.

The tour of Scotland with Johnny Gentle in May was over nine days, not a fortnight, as has always been reported. And it did *not* visit Glasgow, Edinburgh or Galashiels, as suggested by past authors of Beatles books.

Aside from the engagements detailed in the chronological listing, the Beatles did not undertake any other bookings in and around Liverpool in 1960. They did not, for example, perform at halls like the Aintree Institute or Hambleton Hall until January 1961, nor did they ever appear at the Litherland Town Hall before 27 December 1960. One must conclude from this that Stuart Sutcliffe received the kick to his head which it is believed either directly caused, or at least hastened, his early death two years later, outside the Lathom Hall in Seaforth on 14 May 1960, not outside the Litherland Town Hall, as has been reported in a great many Beatles books.

The Beatles' almost-legendary foray down to Aldershot took place in December 1961, not in December 1960, as reported in Philip Norman's *Shout!*

# THE MUSIC

This is an attempt to detail the live performance repertoire of the Beatles (and their other incarnations) in 1960, showing – where possible – the group's vocalist, the composer(s) of the song and the name of the artist/group who recorded the version which influenced them. It is, in all likelihood, an incomplete guide.

| Song title | Main vocalist(s) | Composer(s) | Influential version (year) |
| --- | --- | --- | --- |
| Ain't She Sweet[1] | John | Yellen/Ager | — |
| All Shook Up | Paul | Blackwell/Presley | Elvis Presley (1957) |
| Apache | (Instrumental) | Lordan | The Shadows (1960) |
| Bad Boy | John | Williams | Larry Williams (1959) |
| Be-Bop-A-Lula | John | Vincent/Davis | Gene Vincent and his Blue Caps (1956) |
| Begin the Beguine | ? | Porter | Pat Boone (1957) ? |
| Blue Moon of Kentucky | Paul | Monroe | Elvis Presley (1954) |
| Blue Suede Shoes[2] | John | Perkins | Carl Perkins (1956) and Elvis Presley (1956) |
| Bony Moronie | John | Williams | Larry Williams (1957) |
| Carol | John | Berry | Chuck Berry (1958) |
| Cathy's Clown | ? | Everly/Everly | The Everly Brothers (1960) |
| Catswalk[3] | (Instrumental) | McCartney | — |
| Clarabella | Paul | Pingatore | The Jodimars (1956) |
| C'mon Everybody | ? | Cochran/Capehart | Eddie Cochran (1959) |
| Corrine, Corrina | ? | Trad. arr. McCoy/Chatman/Williams/Parish | Joe Turner (1956) or Ray Peterson (1960) |
| Crying, Waiting, Hoping | George | Holly | Buddy Holly (1959) |
| Dance in the Street | ? | Davis/Welch | Gene Vincent and his Blue Caps (1958) |
| Darktown Strutters Ball | ? | Brooks | Joe Brown and the Bruvvers (1960) |
| Dizzy Miss Lizzy | John | Williams | Larry Williams (1958) |
| Don't Forbid Me | ? | Singleton | Pat Boone (1957) ? |

1 The version most likely to have prompted the Beatles to perform this song would be Gene Vincent's 1956 rock recording. But since John Lennon's vocal rendition sounds quite different to Vincent's it seems apparent that John arranged his own, unique, version.

2 The Beatles mostly performed the composer Carl Perkins' version.

3 When this tune was released on record by the Chris Barber Band in 1967 it was re-titled 'Catcall'.

| Song title | Main vocalist(s) | Composer(s) | Influential version (year) |
|---|---|---|---|
| Don't Let the Sun Catch You Cryin'[4] | Paul | Greene | Ray Charles (1960) |
| Fools Like Me | John | Clement/Maddux | Jerry Lee Lewis (1959) |
| Glad all Over[5] | George | Schroeder/Tepper/Bennett | Carl Perkins (1957) |
| Gone, Gone, Gone | ? | Perkins | Carl Perkins (1959) |
| Good Golly Miss Molly | Paul | Blackwell/Marascalco | Little Richard (1958) |
| Gypsy Fire Dance | ? | ? | ? |
| Hallelujah, I Love Her So | Paul | Charles | Ray Charles (1956) and Eddie Cochran (1960) |
| Harry Lime (*Third Man* Theme)[6] | (Instrumental) | Karas | Anton Karas (1949) |
| Heavenly | ? | Twitty/Nance | Conway Twitty (1959) or Emile Ford and the Checkmates (1960) |
| Hello Little Girl | John | LENNON/McCartney | — |
| Hey, Good Lookin'[7] | ? | Williams | — |
| High School Confidential | Paul | Lewis/Hargrave | Jerry Lee Lewis (1958) |
| Home[8] | ? | Van Steeden/Clarkson/Clarkson | ? |
| Honey Hush | ? | Turner | Joe Turner (1953) or Johnny Burnette and the Rock 'n' Roll Trio (1957) |
| Hound Dog | John | Leiber/Stoller | Elvis Presley (1956) |
| Hully Gully | ? | Smith/Goldsmith | The Olympics (1959) |
| I Forgot to Remember to Forget | George | Kesler/Feathers | Elvis Presley (1955) |
| I Got a Woman | John | Charles/Richards | Ray Charles (1954) and Elvis Presley (1956) |
| I Remember | ? | Cochran/Capehart | Eddie Cochran (1959) |
| I'm Gonna Sit Right Down and Cry (Over You) | John | Thomas/Biggs | Elvis Presley (1956) |
| It's a Long Way to Tipperary | ? | Judge/Williams | Traditional |
| It's Now or Never | ? | DiCapua/Schroeder/Gold/Capurro | Elvis Presley (1960) |
| It's so Easy | ? | Holly/Petty | Buddy Holly and the Crickets (1958) |
| Jailhouse Rock | John | Leiber/Stoller | Elvis Presley (1958) |

4 Different to the same-titled song taken to number six in the charts by Gerry and the Pacemakers in May 1964.

5 Different to the same-titled song taken to number one in the charts by the Dave Clark Five in January 1964.

6 Chet Atkins, a favourite of the Beatles and George Harrison in particular, released a version of this tune in July 1960 which *may* have led to the group's version.

7 The Beatles performed their own arrangement of this 1951 Hank Williams hit which borrowed from both Williams' original and a cover version by Carl Perkins.

8 The Mills Brothers recorded a version of this song in June 1960 which may have influenced the Beatles thereafter. It is not known who influenced them to perform it before then.

| Song title | Main vocalist(s) | Composer(s) | Influential version (year) |
|---|---|---|---|
| Johnny B. Goode | John | Berry | Chuck Berry (1958) |
| Lawdy Miss Clawdy | ? | Price | Lloyd Price (1952) |
| Lend Me your Comb | John/Paul | Twomey/Wise/Weisman | Carl Perkins (1957) |
| Like Dreamers Do | Paul | Lennon/McCARTNEY | — |
| Little Queenie | Paul | Berry | Chuck Berry (1959) |
| Long Tall Sally | Paul | Johnson/Penniman/Blackwell | Little Richard (1956) |
| Love Me Tender[9] | Stuart Sutcliffe | Presley/Matson | Elvis Presley (1956) |
| Love of the Loved | Paul | Lennon/McCARTNEY | — |
| Lucille | Paul | Penniman/Collins | Little Richard (1957) |
| Maybe Baby | ? | Holly/Petty | Buddy Holly and the Crickets (1958) |
| Mean Woman Blues | ? | Demetrius | Jerry Lee Lewis (1957) or Elvis Presley (1957) |
| Midnight Special (Prisoner's Song)[10] | ? | Traditional | Lonnie Donegan and his Skiffle Group (1956) |
| Money (That's What I Want) | John | Gordy/Bradford | Barret Strong (1959) |
| Moonglow and the theme from *Picnic* | ? | Hudson/De Lange/Mills/Duning/Allen | The McGuire Sisters (1956) |
| Nothin' Shakin' (but the Leaves on the Trees) | George | Colacrai/Fontaine/Lampert/Cleveland | Eddie Fontaine (1958) |
| The One after 909 | John | Lennon/McCartney | — |
| Ooh! My Soul | Paul | Penniman | Little Richard (1958) |
| Over the Rainbow | Paul | Harburg/Arlen | Gene Vincent and his Blue Caps (1959) |
| Peggy Sue | John | Holly/Allison/Petty | Buddy Holly (1957) |
| Ramrod | (Instrumental) | Casey | Duane Eddy with the Rebels (1958) |
| Raunchy | (Instrumental) | Justis/Manker | Bill Justis and his Orchestra (1957) |
| Red Sails in the Sunset | Paul | Kennedy/Williams | Joe Turner (1959) or Emile Ford and the Checkmates (1960) |
| Reelin' and Rockin' | ? | Berry | Chuck Berry (1958) |
| Rock and Roll Music | John | Berry | Chuck Berry (1957) |
| Roll over Beethoven[11] | John | Berry | Chuck Berry (1956) |
| Searchin' | Paul | Leiber/Stoller | The Coasters (1957) |
| September Song | ? | Anderson/Weill | Johnny Ray (1959) |

**9** Although the composers are credited as Presley/Matson this song was actually written by Ken Darby, musical director of the *Love Me Tender* film. Vera Matson is Darby's wife.

**10** Duane Eddy recorded a version of this song in November 1960 which may have influenced the Beatles thereafter.

**11** In later years George Harrison assumed the lead vocal.

| Song title | Main vocalist(s) | Composer(s) | Influential version (year) |
|---|---|---|---|
| Shakin' all Over | ? | Heath | Johnny Kidd and the Pirates (1960) |
| Shimmy Shimmy | John/Paul | Massey/Schubert | Bobby Freeman (1960) |
| Short Fat Fanny | John | Williams | Larry Williams (1957) |
| Shout | John/Paul/George | Isley/Isley/Isley | The Isley Brothers (1959) |
| Slow Down | John | Williams | Larry Williams (1958) |
| Summertime | ? | Gershwin | Sam Cooke (1957) or Ray Charles (1958) |
| Sure to Fall (in Love with You) | Paul | Perkins/Claunch/Cantrell | Carl Perkins (1956) |
| Sweet Little Sixteen | John | Berry | Chuck Berry (1958) |
| Teenage Heaven | ? | Cochran/Capehart | Eddie Cochran (1959) |
| Tennessee | John | Perkins | Carl Perkins (1956) |
| That'll Be the Day | John | Holly/Allison/Petty | Buddy Holly and the Crickets (1957) |
| That's all Right (Mama) | Paul | Crudup | Elvis Presley (1954) |
| Think It Over | ? | Holly/Allison/Petty | Buddy Holly and the Crickets (1958) |
| Three Cool Cats | George | Leiber/Stoller | The Coasters (1959) |
| Three Steps to Heaven | ? | Cochran | Eddie Cochran (1960) |
| Too Much Monkey Business | John | Berry | Chuck Berry (1956) |
| True Love | ? | Porter | Bing Crosby and Grace Kelly (1956) or Elvis Presley (1957) |
| Tutti Frutti | Paul | Penniman/LaBostrie | Little Richard (1957) |
| Twenty Flight Rock | Paul | Cochran/Fairchild | Eddie Cochran (1957) |
| Well . . . (Baby Please Don't Go) | John | Ward | The Olympics (1958) |
| What'd I Say | Paul | Charles | Ray Charles (1959) |
| Whole Lotta Shakin' Goin' On | ? | Williams/David | Jerry Lee Lewis (1957) |
| Words of Love | John/George | Holly | Buddy Holly (1957) |
| The World Is Waiting for the Sunrise[12] | John/Paul | Lockhart/Seitz | Les Paul with Mary Ford (1953) |
| Yakety Yak | ? | Leiber/Stoller | The Coasters (1958) |
| You Are my Sunshine | ? | Davis/Mitchell | Duane Eddy (1960) |
| You Don't Understand Me | John | Massey | Bobby Freeman (1960) |
| You Were Meant for Me | ? | Freed/Brown | ? |
| You Win Again | John | Williams | Hank Williams (1952) or Jerry Lee Lewis (1958) |
| Youngblood | George | Leiber/Stoller/Pomus | The Coasters (1957) |
| Your True Love | George | Perkins | Carl Perkins (1957) |

**12** Performed only by the Nerk Twins, not the Beatles.

# 1961

The sight of Beatles-inspired hysteria among the patrons at the Town Hall ballroom, Litherland, on 27 December 1960, sent promoter Brian Kelly scurrying for his engagements diary before anyone else could beat him to the group.[1] He booked them for thirty-five dances, for around £6–£8 each, between January and March 1961 alone, and it was these bookings, above all others, which quickly and firmly established the Beatles as the premier rock combo and number one attraction on Merseyside.

With Chas Newby back at college, the bass position within the group once again fell vacant. This time though, a permanent move was made and after George had refused an invitation from John to take up the instrument Paul assumed the role, switching from his position on rhythm guitar and/or piano. Initially he played a cheaply-constructed Solid 7 model, strung with three strings surreptitiously snipped from a convenient piano, and held upside down because he was left-handed. But when the Beatles next returned to Hamburg he saved enough money to purchase an unusual Hofner model, shaped like a violin.[2]

The hectic life for the Beatles in the 12 months of 1961 was a dramatic contrast to the uncertainties and tribulations of the previous year, a fact perfectly traceable by the course of their live bookings. On their return from Hamburg in December 1960, aside from the last handful of dates procured for the group by Allan Williams, responsibility for finding and negotiating bookings fell to Pete Best and his mother,

Mona. (Both were adept at the art because Pete's father, Johnny Best, was a locally-famous boxing promoter, with a regular column on the sport in the *Liverpool Echo*.) On a great many occasions the Bests had no alternative but to double- or even triple-book the Beatles in a single day, such was the demand. And these weren't just 20-minute sessions. Often the group would play two three-hour gigs in one night, sometimes just hours after a two-hour lunchtime session.

Of course none of the groups in those heady days had very much equipment to handle. In early 1961 the Beatles had just three guitars, three amplifiers (sometimes) and one drum kit. More often than not they would use microphones supplied by a promoter which he, in turn, would hire if he couldn't afford to own them himself. None of the apparently essential sophisticated equipment of the eighties had been invented back then, nor did anyone appear to require

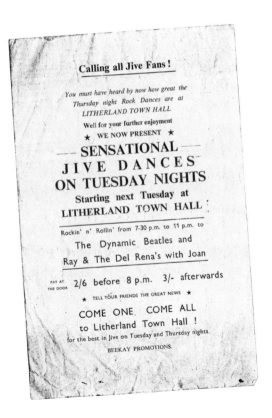

Calling all Jive Fans !

*You must have heard by now how great the Thursday night Rock Dances are at*
LITHERLAND TOWN HALL

Well for your further enjoyment

★ WE NOW PRESENT ★

— SENSATIONAL —
JIVE DANCES
ON TUESDAY NIGHTS
Starting next Tuesday at
LITHERLAND TOWN HALL

Rockin' n' Rollin' from 7-30 p.m. to 11 p.m. to

The Dynamic Beatles and
Ray & The Del Rena's with Joan

PAY AT THE DOOR 2/6 before 8 p.m. 3/- afterwards

★ TELL YOUR FRIENDS THE GREAT NEWS ★

COME ONE. COME ALL
to Litherland Town Hall !
for the best in jive on Tuesday and Thursday nights.

BEEKAY PROMOTIONS.

---

**1** Kelly's long-time claim that he posted bouncers outside the Beatles' dressing-room door on 27 December 1960, not to prevent fans from getting in but to stop other, rival, promoters from engaging them, can be largely dismissed from the fact that David Forshaw, promoter at the St John's Hall in Bootle, had remarkably easy access to the group after the dance had finished, and duly engaged them for three gigs.

**2** During the course of researching this book, the author spoke with numerous, independent witnesses on Merseyside who insist that on many occasions during Paul's initial few months on bass, he had the lead tucked, not into an amplifier, but into his pocket.

such things. These days even the smallest pub band will utilize a sound-mixing desk; in Liverpool in 1961 the volume knob on the (often home-made) amplifier was simply turned to maximum.

Nonetheless, the frequency of the bookings, the distance between the halls, and the late finishing times, made the need for a van and, if possible, a regular driver, nothing short of essential if the group was to progress. It was here that Neil Aspinall, friend of Pete Best, proved invaluable to the Beatles. Rapidly tiring of his correspondence course in accountancy, Aspinall found the life, comparative excitement, and cash-in-hand existence of 'road managing' far more attractive than preparing a trial balance. For £80 he bought an old Commer van and soon became their permanent go-fer.[3]

One thing that hadn't changed since 1960 or, for that matter, in decades, was the rumbustious and, sometimes literally, razor-sharp atmosphere at some Merseyside dance halls. Although the Teddy Boy era was on the wane, the violent thuggery at these gatherings was still little short of terrifying, and most of the venues the Beatles played in 1961 were no place for the meek or faint-hearted. Merseyside machismo, seemingly, has often to be publicly aired in order to

be credible. Both Neil Aspinall and Paul McCartney remember, with some trepidation, those days of old, particularly at one beat venue, the Hambleton Hall in Huyton. Aspinall had the odious duty of loading and unloading the Beatles' van there, under the watchful eyes, and heavy breath, of the local toughs, who would have been only too pleased to wade gleefully into action at the drop of a wrong word. Every time Aspinall humped gear into the hall he had to lock the van carefully, lest he came back outside to find the remaining equipment, indeed even the van, gone. McCartney recalls that whenever they played 'Hully Gully' there it would end in fighting. One night rival gangs even turned fire extinguishers against each other, in addition to their usual array of weapons.

One place remarkably free of such entertainment was the dingy cellar underneath number 10 Mathew Street, Liverpool city centre, known as the Cavern Club, a venue played by the Quarry Men in 1957 and 1958. Since that time it had changed hands, and was owned by one Ray McFall, formerly the accountant to Alan Sytner, the club's previous owner. McFall had taken over the reins on 3 October 1959, at the birth of the massive trad jazz boom in Britain, and he, not unnaturally, maintained Sytner's pro-jazz, anti-beat policy for the club. But by mid-1960 the craze was virtually over (though its major stars largely remained) and McFall began to look further afield for his entertainment – even to rock and roll.

---

**3** Today, in 1986, Aspinall is *still* employed by the Beatles, as a director and caretaker of their ill-fated, lumbering Apple empire.

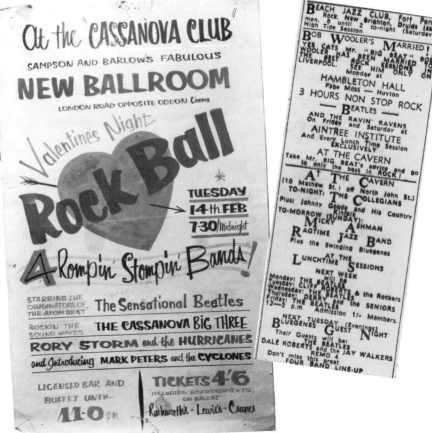

*Right: Paul McCartney amended this early poster, changing Beetles to Beatles with a black pen. Far right: Adverts from the Liverpool Echo, including one for the Beatles' night-time debut in the Cavern Club on 21 March. Note they were playing lunchtime sessions there before this time, including one the previous day.*

For a short while a few top Liverpool beat groups played the club as interval attractions – though not always to the liking of the jazz audience – until eventually, on Wednesday 25 May 1960, while the Silver Beetles were up in Scotland backing Johnny Gentle, the Cavern Club held its first all-beat night, headlined by Cass and the Cassanovas and Rory Storm and the Hurricanes.

It took quite some time, nine months in fact, for the Beatles to gain entry into the establishment, and it was largely due to the efforts of Mona Best and Bob Wooler, the local dance MC/compere now resident at the Cavern Club, who championed the Beatles' cause in the ear of McFall. Mrs Best in particular was very persistent, and had first telephoned McFall about 'her son's group' on 4 December 1960, just three days after Pete had returned home, deported, from Hamburg.

The Beatles made their debut at the Cavern Club at the lunchtime session on Tuesday 21 February 1961, three and a half years after John Lennon and his Quarry Men cronies had skiffled their way through an August 1957 evening there, and one month prior to the Beatles' first night-time appearance at the venue, as guests of that curious jazz/rock hybrid, the Swinging Bluegenes, on 21 March – the date previously accepted as the Beatles' Cavern Club debut, but which can now be seen to be incorrect. One thing is for sure: over the next two and a half years the Cavern Club was the Beatles' home and, in Liverpool at least, the two names were synonymous. At a time when it was unfashionable for a group to monopolize a venue, the Beatles took up residency at the Cavern Club, and made an exclusive arrangement with it which precluded them from playing at certain other leading Merseyside venues like the Iron Door Club (after it returned to that name under new management from the Liverpool Jazz Society and the Storyville Jazz Club) and Orrell Park Ballroom. These places, in turn, booked their own resident groups like the Searchers and the Undertakers.

When the Beatles made their very last appearance at the Cavern Club in August 1963, with Britain effectively on the verge of becoming Beatle-mad, Bob Wooler checked back through the club diaries – now tragically destroyed – and counted their appearances at the venue. He concluded that it was their 292nd, and with that announcement the figure was committed to history. But much as I have searched, delved and cajoled I could not discover any more than 274 of these. Intriguingly though, the magic figure of precisely 292 can be arrived at by some mathematical manipulation, and I suspect that this is what happened:

| | |
|---|---:|
| The number of Beatles gigs at the Cavern Club | 274 |
| Four of those 274 were all-night sessions in which the Beatles performed two stage-spots. These were counted, then, as entirely separate appearances. Add, therefore, an extra | 4 |
| Beatles appearances on the MV *Royal Iris*, organized exclusively by the Cavern Club | 4 |
| Cancelled or postponed bookings | 10 |
| | 292 |

Away from the statistics, there is no denying the importance of the Cavern Club in the shaping and history of the Beatles. It was here, in a former fruit and vegetable warehouse 18 stone steps below street level, that they honed their precocious talent. And it was here that they formed their incredible rapport with the Cavern Club audience – their audience. For an initial fee of £15 a night, or £5 a lunchtime session, the Beatles rocked the city from their grimy underground lair, and went from nobodies to the biggest show-business phenomenon Britain has ever produced.

The Cavern Club was the stuff that all good rock and roll poetry is made of, and a health inspector's nightmare. It had no ventilation, no dramatic lighting other than a set of 60-watt white bulbs starkly pointing down at the stage, dreadfully inadequate lavatory arrangements, no tables, no curtains, no carpets, no booze, no fights – and most certainly no room. For Beatles performances hundreds would squeeze into the claustrophobic, subterranean hothouse, where the sweat would, literally, stream down the bare-brick walls and arches, and where the stench and steam would hang in the air like a barrage balloon, endangering the lives of the electric guitar heroes perched on the creaky wooden stage. That, in itself, was just two feet off the ground, and the same distance from the outstretched arms of the kneeling, clamorous girls who made up the front row.

The Cavern Club girls idolized, and romanticized about, the Beatles. At each and every performance they would desperately strive to attract the attention of one or other of the group in the hope of an acknowledgement or perhaps even a date. Two minutes before the Beatles took to the stage there would be

*This page: Cavern Club memorabilia.*
*Opposite: Four leather-clad Beatles sweat it out in the Cavern, circa November 1961.*

a mass, ritualistic, final preening session among the girls. The dust of compact powder would clog the air, hair curlers and rollers would be removed and frantic back-combing would take place. Many of these fans even formed themselves into little groups or gangs, like the Cement Mixers or The Woodentops and it was not unusual for a nominated leader to telephone either Paul on GAR 6922, George on GAR 4596, John on GAT 1696 or Pete on STA 1556 to request a certain song for a certain gig. Far from being annoyed, the Beatles actively encouraged this kind of rapport and genuinely yearned for such contact in later years when they were playing venues so vast and cold that they were 200 yards or more away from the nearest fan.

Another important effect of the Cavern Club on the Beatles in 1961 was the way it helped to shape and define the widely differing personalities within the group. It was here that John's sharp, cutting edge, his imperious personality, his defiant stage stance – legs astride, head back, guitar thrust high on chest – all took shape. While girls were never quite sure how to handle John, his apparent arrogance was much modelled by the Cavern Club's male clientele. Paul, meanwhile, attracted the girls' eyes, with his good looks, charming stage patter and earnest politeness. George remained mostly in the background, studiously awaiting his guitar solos. But his youthful features, lop-sided smile and droll humour did not go without their female admirers. Mostly though, the girls went for Pete Best, the self-effacing, reticent drummer who would quietly, and without expression, provide the Beatles' solid backbeat. His natural air of detachment, and his monotone voice, would send the hearts of the female Cavernites a-fluttering.

With hindsight, people have said that the Cavern Club made the Beatles and, to a certain extent, that is true. But the Beatles also made the Cavern, and through them it became the world's unlikeliest but most celebrated show-business venue in the mid-sixties. And when the Beatles grew too big for it, and moved away, the Cavern began to wither, and not all the Billy J. Kramers in the world could have stopped it. It died twice, firstly in 1966 when Ray McFall went bankrupt, and then, after it had been re-opened, in 1973, when it was demolished to make way for an underground air vent, with shocking disregard for its significance. Liverpool was to rue that thoughtless act for ten years as hundreds of thousands of tourists from all over the world flocked to the city to stare at a piece of wasteland. In 1984, at tremendous expense – though not the council's money – the cellar club was identically re-created just a few inches from where it had once stood, and re-opened to the public.

But for true afficionados who experienced the club's heyday, the city can never be excused.

Back in 1961 though, shortly after their Cavern Club debut, the Beatles were off for their second trip to Hamburg. Coming just three months after George Harrison, Paul McCartney and Pete Best's enforced departure from the country it was no easy matter to arrange, and a great many promises of good behaviour were made in a series of letters from Pete and Mona Best to the German authorities. Fortunately the Beatles now had allies in Hamburg working on their behalf too. Bass player Stuart Sutcliffe, who had returned to Liverpool long after the others, in late February 1961, had gone back in advance of the others to pursue his blossoming romance with Astrid Kirchherr and an artistic career at the city's fine State College of Art. Another ally was Peter Eckhorn, owner of the Top Ten Club, who had made the hurried agreement with the Beatles on 30 November 1960 for a month's engagement in April. With this collective help the big breakthrough finally came in a letter to Pete Best from the West German Immigration Office which gave him and Paul a one-year lifting of the ban by 'special concession of the Foreign Department'. As an advance against their forthcoming weekly wages, Eckhorn paid 158 DM to the authorities on behalf of Best and McCartney – the cost of sending them home the previous winter – and with George Harrison now turned eighteen years of age the way was finally clear for the group to return.

A few days before leaving Liverpool they got together at the Best household and telephoned Eckhorn to negotiate the final contract. It was a standard gruelling Hamburg engagement – they were required on stage from 7 p.m. until 2 a.m. on Mondays to Fridays, and from 7 p.m. until 3 a.m. on weekends, always with a 15-minute break in every hour. The salary was a modest 35 DM per man per day. Eckhorn's all-in accommodation, though dingy – old army bunk-beds in the attic four flights above the club – was certainly superior to the behind-the-cinema-screen lodgings proffered the previous year by Bruno Koschmider. On Friday 24 March, after playing that same lunchtime in the Cavern Club, the Beatles set off from Lime Street station on the long train journey to Hamburg. They took to the stage on 27 March, though their contract wasn't due to commence until 1 April, and happily began the 14-week haul through a twice-extended contract until 2 July.

Now domiciled permanently in Hamburg, Stuart's playing days with the Beatles were all but over, though he did perform the occasional evening with them for old times' sake and also played on one or

*Bottom: Three dancing girls, dubbed The Shimmy-Shimmy Queens by compere Bob Wooler, pose for Dick Matthews' camera at the Aintree Institute on 19 August 1961 while the Beatles warm up for their night's work in the background. Below: By the autumn the Beatles' local fame had brought them their first fan club.*

BEATLES FAN CLUB

Membership Card
• • • • • • • • • •

1961 — 62 SEASON
ENDING 31st AUGUST, 1962

Thursday

Dear Peter, Don't be surprised at his *among green* etter, everything has worked out fine Paul will ring you, or ring Paul as soon as you have this. Best of luck

Stuart.

One thing I forgot to tell Paul, and that is that you both must pay Peter Eckhorn 79 D.M each his this the cost of sending you home.

The lifting of the deportation ban is only valid for 1 year then you can have it renewed. One thing they made clear, if you have any trouble with the Police, no matter how small then you've had it forever. (Drunkeness, fighting, women etc).

bye bye.

Stuart.

**jacaranda enterprises**

23 SLATER STREET LIVERPOOL 1 / ROYAL 6544

A. R. Williams

20th April, 1961.

Dear All,

I am very distressed to hear you are contemplating not paying my commission out of your pay as was agreed in our contract for your engagement at the Top Ten Club.

May I remind you, seeing you are all appearing to get more than a little swollen-headed, that you would not even have smelled Hamburg if I had not made the contacts, and by Law it is illegal for any person under contract to make a contract through the first contract.

I would also point out that the only reason you are there is through the work that I did and if you had tried yourselves to play at the Top Ten without a bonafide contract and working through a British Government approved Agency you would not be in Germany now.

Remember in your last contract under Koschmider you agreed not to play 30 weeks from terminating that contract, the only reason you managed get out of that was again through myself. So far as you are concerned he kept that contract.

So you see Lads, I'm very annoyed you should welsh out of your agreed contract. If you decide not to pay I promise you that I shall have you out of Germany inside two weeks through several legal ways and don't you think I'm bluffing.

I will also submit a full report of your behaviour to the Agency Members Association of which I am a full member, and every Agent in England is a member, to protect Agents from artistes who misbehave and welsh out of agreements.

So if you want to play in Liverpool for all the local boys you go straight ahead and welsh on your contract. Don't underestimate my ability to carry out what I have written.

-continued-

two occasions with other visiting Merseyside groups. Perhaps because of this ex-Beatle status it was Stuart who was assigned the unpleasant task of writing, on the group's behalf, back to Allan Williams in Liverpool, announcing that as they themselves had negotiated the booking with Eckhorn, they were refusing to pay Williams his weekly commission. Williams was livid, claiming – as he does to this day – that *he* had first taken the Beatles to Hamburg, *he* arranged the Eckhorn contract, and *he* helped quash Paul and Pete's deportation ban. On 20 April he wrote a tersely worded letter to the group threatening to exact damaging retribution if they went ahead and reneged on their, regrettably verbal, agreement. This he could probably have done should he have felt so disposed but, as time passed, the situation cooled down. In retrospect one can see that perhaps Williams was wronged, but the group probably felt he had outgrown his usefulness and were seeking a way of cutting their ties with him which, by this time, were very thin anyway. In 1961 Williams had found the Beatles just two engagements – both at the Grosvenor Ballroom in Liscard – and since they were now established with promoter Brian Kelly, Bob Wooler, the compere for various promotions, and Cavern Club owner Ray McFall, they could afford to sever the last vestiges of any link with the hapless Williams for ever.

Hamburg was Hamburg, the same as before.

*Correspondence relating to the Beatles' second visit to Hamburg, March–July 1961. Top: A letter from Hamburg—domiciles Stuart Sutcliffe to Pete Best. Above: Part of Allan Williams' angry 20 April letter.*

```
HGR      /   5.12.1961                    TRANSLATION


                                    BERT KAEMPFERT PRODUKTION


              A G R E E M E N T

    Between

              1) John W. Lennon          )
              2) James Paul McCartney     )        as Group called
              3) George Harrison          )         The Beatles
              4) Peter Best               )
    domiciled as follows :-

              1) 251, Manlove Ave., Woolton 25, Liverpool
              2) 20 Forthlin Road, Liverpool 18
              3) 25 Upton Green, Speke, Liverpool 24.
              4) 8, Haymans Green, Liverpool 12
    hereinafter referred to as the "Group",
                        and
    BERT KAEMPFERT PRODUKTION
              Inselstr. 4, Hamburg
    hereinafter referred to as "Produktion",
    IT IS AGREED AS FOLLOWS :-


                                      Cont'd. ./...
```

Uproarious, immoral, clamorous, a veritable hotbed of vices *verboten* yet, somehow, charming too. The Beatles were glad to be back, and this time they even had a small but élite following, mostly friends of Astrid Kirchherr. Although Stuart had effectively left the Beatles he and Astrid attended the Top Ten Club on most evenings, and Astrid continued to photograph them whenever she could. It was during this Hamburg visit that she cut Stuart's hair into the style which would eventually become known as the Beatle-cut – long, clean, brushed forward, and with a fringe. At first the mere sight of Stuart was enough to send the four Beatles into paroxysms of laughter, but after a while they grew to like it and, within a few months – with the exception of Pete Best – they were to restyle their rock-and-roll quiffs in the same way.

Without a doubt the highlight of this second Hamburg jaunt was their first-ever professional recording session, which led to the release of their debut disc. At the Top Ten Club, in addition to their own performances, the Beatles were regularly backing Tony Sheridan, the 20-year-old English singer, already a veteran of British TV pop shows, whose presence in Hamburg the previous November had tempted the starry-eyed Beatles to break their contract with Bruno Koschmider by playing at a rival venue. In Germany Sheridan was contracted to make

*Top: The Beatles in the Cavern Club.*
*Above: Part of the translation of the brief contract, dated 12 May 1961, which led to the Beatles' first-ever recordings, with Tony Sheridan.*

61

records with Deutsche Grammophon, under the auspices of its popular music label Polydor, and one night in April 1961 Alfred Schacht, the European director of co-ordination for the Aberbach publishing organization, walked into the Top Ten to speak with Sheridan, and saw the Beatles. Schacht was impressed by the Sheridan/Beatles union and later discussed with his friend Berthold (Bert) Kaempfert – the 37-year-old German orchestra leader/composer/arranger/conductor who had recently scored an American number one hit with 'Wonderland by Night' – the possibility of recording them together for Polydor. On 12 May the Beatles were invited to Kaempfert's office to discuss a recording and publishing contract and willingly agreed to sign up.

One morning a few days later, at eight o'clock sharp, not long after the group had wearily climbed the four flights of stairs from the Top Ten Club to their welcome beds in the attic, two taxis arrived to take them and their equipment to the recording studio. This, despite Kaempfert's prestige, was no more than an infants' school, and the recording took place on the stage, with the curtain closed. Five numbers were taped that day, for which the four Beatles (Stuart Sutcliffe most certainly did not play on the recordings, as has been claimed elsewhere, although he did attend the session as an observer) received a flat session fee of 300 DM each, in lieu of all future rights and royalties. On three numbers – rocked-up versions of 'My Bonnie Lies over the Ocean', 'When the Saints Go Marching In' and the Sheridan ballad 'Why (Can't You Love Me Again)' – the Beatles actually backed Sheridan. Of the remaining two, one was 'Ain't She Sweet', the old Eddie Cantor vaudeville hit newly arranged and sung by John Lennon, and the other was a guitar instrumental composed by the unique team of Lennon and George Harrison. Initially the track did not have a title and 'Beatle Bop' was among the names considered until they finally plumped for 'Cry for a Shadow', a play on the name of the Cliff Richard instrumental backing group they so despised for their set stage movements, the Shadows.

In August, after the Beatles had returned home to Liverpool, Polydor released two of the songs, 'My Bonnie' and 'The Saints' (as they titled them) on a single, credited to Tony Sheridan and the Beat Brothers, and it eventually reached number five on the West German hit parade, selling a reputed 100,000 copies in the process. The label had been afraid to use the word Beatles lest it was confused with the similar-sounding word 'peedles', north German slang for the male organ.[4]

*Below: Bob Wooler introduces the Beatles as they complete setting-up, Aintree Institute, 19 August 1961. Bottom and right: Action shots of John and Paul later in the year, at the Tower Ballroom, New Brighton, and Cavern Club respectively.*

and the Beatles felt that there was a real danger that fame and fortune might elude them. The group were uncrowned kings of Merseyside, in great demand at all the dance halls, and they had made a record. Yet they were also quickly growing tired and restless with the monotony of Cavern appearance after Cavern appearance, much as they all loved the venue. It was a dead end, Liverpool was a dead end, and they had no idea how to escape. For the next four months the youthful Beatles marked time and watched life pass them by.

As far as the Beatles were concerned, the only real excitement to hit the local rock and roll set-up at this time was the launching of its very own bi-weekly newspaper by Bill Harry, former Art College friend of John Lennon and Stuart Sutcliffe. He called it *Mersey Beat*, a phrase which was to be picked up by the mass media two years later when Liverpool groups overran the British pop music charts in the wake of the Beatles' success.[5]

For several months Bill Harry, and his fiancée Virginia Sowry, had been visiting local jive halls, talking to groups, and making notes about the burgeoning beat scene. They had quickly realized how parochial it was: groups in one area of town had little or no knowledge of other groups or opportunities in other areas. With this in mind they hit upon the idea of a special newspaper – in essence the very first music 'fanzine'. Harry was the editor, publisher, writer, chief sub and layout man. And he even hand-distributed initial issues around the city's newsagents, record stores, dance halls and music shops. He was

Their second Hamburg stint completed, the Beatles arrived back in England around 11 July and immediately rejoined the fast and furious merry-go-round of Merseyside engagements. There was no doubt now that they were something really quite special, yet nothing seemed to be happening for them. Liverpool may just as well have been the North Pole as far as London pop impresarios were concerned,

---

**4** The background information about the sessions comes from the memories of Pete Best and Tony Sheridan, Philip Norman's Beatles biography *Shout!* and research by the author. The song details come from an article in *Mersey Beat* printed just one month after the session, so one can presume that they are accurate. Yet it all differs quite considerably from the recording information supplied with a compact disc pressing of Sheridan/Beatles material in December 1984. This states that six songs were recorded over two days – 22/23 June 1961 – at Harburg Friedrich Ebert Halle, Hamburg: 'Ain't She Sweet', 'Cry for a Shadow', 'The Saints', 'Why', 'My Bonnie' and 'Nobody's Child', and that one further song 'If You Love Me Baby' was taped the following day, 24 June, at Studio Rahlstedt, Hamburg.

The period becomes even murkier when one compares a second article in *Mersey Beat*, in May 1962, with the session details. The article states that during the Beatles' stint at the Star-Club in April 1962 they recorded two more numbers with Sheridan under the direction of Bert Kaempfert, before the enforced cessation of their contract by Brian Epstein. (This is confirmed by correspondence between Epstein and Kaempfert – see page 92 – and by Pete Best's book *Beatle!*, yet the official recording details do not mention it.) The songs were 'Sweet Georgia Brown' and 'Swanee River'. Contrary to this, yet again, the session details indicate that 'Sweet Georgia Brown' was recorded on 21 December 1961 (the Beatles were not even in Hamburg then) and there is no mention at all of 'Swanee River'. 'Swanee River' does indeed sound like it features the Beatles' backing except for a saxophone break which may well have been added later, perhaps at the same time that Sheridan completely re-recorded the vocals to 'Sweet Georgia Brown', in early 1964.

Precisely what was recorded, and when, may never be clearly determined.

**5** Actually, although Harry can rightly be credited with great insight, partly instigating, and furthering, the Liverpool beat music success story, he did not originate the title 'Mersey Beat' as he claims. The nightly *Liverpool Echo* newspaper had a weekly Saturday column spotlighting the local jazz scene under the title *Mersey Beat* which started on 30 November 1957 and ran for a year.

also, of course, quick to promote his friends, and page two of the very first issue, 6–20 July 1961, carried a brilliantly witty article, written by John Lennon before the Beatles had gone to Hamburg in March, entitled 'Being a Short Diversion on the Dubious Origins of Beatles'. It was Lennon's first printed prose, and the same style was to be fêted three years later when *In his own Write*, his book of similarly inspired lunacy, topped the best sellers.

Two weeks before John Lennon's 21st birthday on 9 October he received a generous coming-of-age gift of £40 from his Aunt Elizabeth in Sutherland, Scotland, and he and Paul McCartney immediately decided to take off to Paris for a fortnight's break.[6] In a letter from Hamburg, Stuart Sutcliffe had mentioned to John that Jurgen Vollmer would be in Paris. Jurgen was a friend of Astrid and one of the small band of Beatles followers in Hamburg, who had also photographed them on numerous occasions at the Top Ten Club. John and Paul were keen to meet him again and wasted little time in getting there. Although they spent most of the trip lounging around left-bank cafés until their money ran out (thus precluding a planned foray into Spain), and enjoying the bohemian lifestyle, John and Paul also observed the typically French music scene, attending a Johnny Hallyday show at the Paris Olympia, and a rock music club in Montmartre. One other retrospectively important event happened during the trip – Jurgen finally persuaded John and Paul to restyle their hair permanently like his own, and Stuart Sutcliffe's, indeed, like most French teenagers'. The Beatle haircut was there to stay.

On 9 November 1961 the lunchtime session at the Cavern Club had a rather curious visitor, the handsome, eligible, well-spoken and dapper, 27-year-old gentleman manager of NEMS (an acronym for North End Music Stores), a prosperous record store situated in nearby Whitechapel, one of the main thoroughfares in Liverpool city centre. His name was Brian Samuel Epstein, and quite what he was doing there even he was really at a loss to explain. Nor, for that matter, has it ever become crystal clear how he came to discover the place, or seek out the Beatles.

---

**6** During the course of his research I have been able to prove that this two-week holiday was not taken without the knowledge of George Harrison and Pete Best, or indeed Merseyside rock promoters, as has long been suggested by authors of Beatles books, indeed even by the Beatles themselves. The clear 15-day break in engagements unquestionably proves otherwise, as does the sudden, hectic, prebooked resumption from 15 October.

**7** *A Cellarful of Noise*, Souvenir Press, 1964.

## Dances at the Grosvenor

Derry and the Seniors have been playing to packed halls since their return from Germany and Wallasey Corporation Entertainments have been fortunate in re-engaging the Seniors for tonight's dance at the Grosvenor.

On Tuesday afternoon Mrs. Shaw presents another in her ladies' olde tyme and modern sequence dances, and in the evening Paramount take over for their strict tempo dance '21-Plus' night.

Friday night brings another top professional group "The Beatles" to the ballroom. This band also has recently returned from a highly successful Continental tour.

*Opposite: 1961 memorabilia, including, bottom left, the Operation Big Beat ticket sold by NEMS. Centre: a Beatles' repertoire list prepared one night by John Cochrane, drummer with Wump and his Werbles (!) to prevent duplication of song material. Far right: a typical page from the* Liverpool Echo *classifieds.*

One school of thought – supported by Epstein's own autobiography[7] – follows this theory: Stuart Sutcliffe sent a few copies of 'My Bonnie', the Sheridan/Beatles record, across from Hamburg to Liverpool, and George Harrison had given a copy to Bob Wooler one Saturday night in August, on a bus *en route* for the Aintree Institute. Bob, of course, plugged the disc relentlessly at his almost-nightly circuit of disc-jockey/compere engagements on Merseyside, constantly urging people to demand the disc at record shops in the hope of persuading someone to import officially a few copies from West Germany. One youth who heard Wooler's promotion of the disc, at the Hambleton Hall, was 18-year-old Raymond Jones from Huyton, and – so the legend goes – at three o'clock in the afternoon on Saturday 28 October, sporting a leather jacket and jeans, Jones walked into NEMS in Whitechapel and asked manager Brian Epstein for the disc. Epstein was nonplussed, having – so he said – heard of neither the record nor the group. But Epstein promised to do some research and, if possible, order Jones a copy. On the following Monday morning two girls made a similar enquiry, and Epstein determined to find out why a disc about which he knew nothing, and which had not even been listed in the infallible weekly record-industry publication *Record Retailer*, was in demand.

He placed telephone calls to specialist record importers but no one seemed to have heard of the

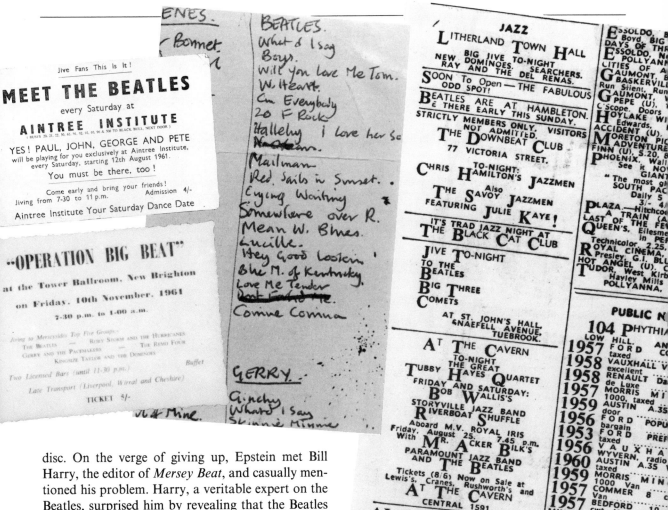

disc. On the verge of giving up, Epstein met Bill Harry, the editor of *Mersey Beat*, and casually mentioned his problem. Harry, a veritable expert on the Beatles, surprised him by revealing that the Beatles were a Liverpudlian group and not, as Epstein had quite reasonably assumed, German. He further pointed out that they were regularly to be found less than two hundred yards away from NEMS, in a place called the Cavern Club.

Harry himself remembers the situation quite differently. He claims that Epstein had been one of the chief vendors of *Mersey Beat* since its inception four months previously and, furthermore, had taken great interest in its contents, including the Beatles. This claim is supported by two facts. Firstly, Epstein ordered, and sold, twelve dozen copies of the paper's second issue, in which the bold headline 'Beatles Sign Recording Contract!', an article, and a photograph of the group completely dominated the front page.

Secondly, Epstein volunteered to write a regular record review column in the paper, commencing with issue three. Although he may well have been uninterested in rock and roll, it is, nonetheless, still very hard to believe – as some authors have implied – that he would then have failed to read, or at least casually glance through, the rest of each issue.[8] The real truth is probably a blend of the two stories. One further piece of evidence against Epstein's account of the events was uncovered by the author in the process of researching this book: that by 27 October, or even earlier, NEMS was selling tickets, which carried the Beatles' name at the head of a list of groups, for Sam Leach's first Operation Big Beat dance at the New Brighton Tower Ballroom.

---

**8** It should be pointed out, though, that Epstein's review column in the 31 August–14 September issue, did *not* actually appear on the same page as 'Well Now – Dig This!' by Bob Wooler, the much-celebrated, sagacious article proudly extolling the virtues of the Beatles virtually two years before anyone else caught on. The two items were only put together in the compilation of the retrospective book *Mersey Beat: The Beginnings of the Beatles* (Omnibus Press, 1977), which reproduced facsimile articles and/or pages from the newspaper.

One thing is for certain. On 9 November, wearing a neatly pressed pin-striped suit, and tie, with his attaché-case tucked under his arm, and flanked by his similarly attired shop assistant, Alistair Taylor, Brian Epstein descended the eighteen stone steps into the Cavern Club and another world opened up for him. In a BBC-North-East radio interview two and a half years later he recalled the events of that day. 'It was pretty much of an eye-opener, to go down into this darkened, dank, smoky cellar in the middle of the day, and to see crowds and crowds of kids watching these four young men on stage. They were rather scruffily dressed – in the nicest possible way or, I should say, in the most attractive way – black leather jackets and jeans, long hair of course. And they had a rather untidy stage presentation, not terribly aware, and not caring very much, what they looked like.[9] I think they cared more even then for what they sounded like . . . I immediately liked what I heard. They were fresh and they were honest, and they had what I thought was a sort of presence and – this is a terribly vague term – star quality. Whatever that is, they had it, or I sensed that they had it.'

In short, Epstein was transfixed. History has since revealed, of course, that he was a homosexual, and various authors and 'experts' have explored this fact in an effort to explain Epstein's fascination with the Beatles. Whether or not this *was* the reason will always be open to conjecture, but for the purposes of this book it is entirely irrelevant. The fact remains that after the lunchtime session was over Epstein struggled through the sweaty teenage hordes to the Cavern Club's minuscule bandroom to meet the Beatles. He had, after all, theoretically gone there on business – to find out more about their record backing Tony Sheridan in order that he could import 200 copies. He first encountered George Harrison, and a slightly sarcastic jibe: 'What brings Mr Epstein here?' Brian explained about the enquiries for their record, found the answers he required, heard the disc, courtesy of Cavern Club DJ Bob Wooler, and left.

Throughout the remainder of November Brian found himself returning to the Cavern Club whenever the Beatles were on, always managing to grab a few hurried words with them. No immediate friendship seems to have been struck but the Beatles were slightly flattered by his attentions. As the days passed though, and Epstein discovered more and more

*Below and opposite: The Beatles, warming up, and in performance, at the Aintree Institute on 19 August 1961. Classic shots of the Beatles in the pre-Brian Epstein period: leather-clad rock and rollers playing scruffy suburban jive halls.*

about them, a vague idea of somehow 'fathering' the group germinated. It was of course preposterous – as everyone to whom he mentioned it quickly reminded him. Nevertheless he began to quiz record company sales reps and record store owners in London about the intricacies of pop music management, and he even went to the Blue Angel Club and

**9** This, although Epstein didn't say it, included smoking, eating and swearing on stage, telling private jokes and laughing among themselves, turning their backs on the audience, and suddenly stopping a song half way through. All in all, a typical 1961 Beatles' Cavern Club performance.

sought out Allan Williams to ask his advice. 'What should I do?' enquired Brian, to which Williams – still bitter over the recent Hamburg episode – characteristically replied, 'Brian, don't touch 'em with a fucking bargepole!' – a tip he was to regret somewhat in the ensuing years . . . .

Although still unsure and unsettled about precisely what he was going to propose to the Beatles, Epstein invited them to a meeting in the offices behind his shop on 3 December at 4:30 p.m. John, George and Pete, together with Bob Wooler (he never did discover quite why he was there) all arrived at the appointed time. But no Paul. Half an hour elapsed and Brian, a stickler for punctuality, was getting pretty hot under the collar. Eventually George was asked to telephone Paul and find out why he was so late; he returned with the message that Paul had just got up and was in the bath. Epstein was furious and ranted about how late McCartney was going to be for this, an important meeting. But George, with his wonderfully dry wit and lop-sided smile, retorted, 'Yes, he may be late but he'll be very clean!' Eventually Paul did arrive and the six-strong party retired to a local milk bar tentatively to discuss business to

their mutual advantage. The Beatles' reaction was not unfavourable, and another meeting was set for the following Wednesday afternoon, 6 December.

In the intervening three days Epstein consulted his family solicitor, E. Rex Makin, and sought his advice. It wasn't exactly positive, and Makin, who had known Brian all his life, was sceptical about what he saw as another scheme in which the young Epstein would surely lose interest before too long. But Epstein was not to be deterred, and when Wednesday afternoon arrived he put his proposals and terms to the Beatles. He would require 25 per cent of their gross fees on a weekly basis. In return for this he would assume responsibility for arranging their bookings which, he stressed, would be better organized, more prestigious, and in uncharted areas further afield than Liverpool. He further vowed that the group would never again play a date for less than £15 – a bold and rather brash promise to make in 1961 – except for Cavern Club lunchtime sessions, where he would ensure their £5 fee was doubled to £10. But more than all of this he dangled before the Beatles the biggest carrot of all – he would extricate them from their West German recording contract

and would then use his influence as one of the north-west's biggest record retailers to get the Beatles a decent deal with a major British recording company.

Coming from a man who had no previous pop management experience, to a provincial group which up until then had taken their musical career comparatively lightly, this was pretty strong talk. There was an awkward silence while the four Beatles pondered the proposals. Then John, on behalf of the group, blurted, 'Right then, Brian. Manage us. Now where's the contract, I'll sign it.' But there was no contract – yet. The one Brian had been given by a friend in the business – a typical management/artist document – had so disgusted him with its meanness and exploitation, and enslavement of the artist, that he steadfastly refused to utilize it. Instead, using it as a guide, he modified and adapted the terms to draw up a much fairer agreement.

Four days later, on Sunday 10 December, another meeting was held, this time at the Casbah Coffee Club, where the Beatles ritually congregated before going out for their night's work. John, Paul, George and Pete all agreed in principle to the contract and vowed that, subject to Brian attempting to carry through his promises, they would eventually sign. This duly happened in the NEMS office after the Beatles' Cavern Club lunchtime session on 24 January 1962. Interestingly though, while Alistair Taylor dutifully and lawfully witnessed the contract by countersigning it in five places, only four other signatures graced the paper; Brian Epstein did not add his own. Perhaps, in his own mind at least, ever the gentleman, he still wanted truly to prove himself to the group before he was seen to be 'capturing' them. In fact, he wasn't to sign for a further nine months. The group though was totally oblivious to this triviality – nor did it really matter to either party or affect their relationship. To all intents and purposes, from that moment, on the afternoon of Wednesday 24 January 1962, Brian Epstein was the Beatles' first, and only, real manager.

An example of the Gargantuan task that Epstein was voluntarily taking on can be seen from the reaction – or lack of it – to Operation Big Beat, Sam Leach's mighty dance presentation at the New Brighton Tower Ballroom on 10 November 1961. Over 3,000 paying customers turned up to see the top beat groups on Merseyside in a marathon five-and-a-half-hour session. Yet not only was the event predictably ignored by all of the blinkered London-based musical papers, but the two daily Liverpool newspapers, the *Post* and *Echo*, and even the two locally based weekly papers, the *Wallasey News* and *Birkenhead News*, ignored it too. Not one single men-

tion anywhere, neither before the gig nor after. But Epstein did it – singlehandedly he transformed this pulsating but insular scene into the biggest popular music boom the whole of Britain has ever seen. Within just two short years, all *five* of the groups participating in Operation Big Beat would have London recording contracts.

The one concession the *Liverpool Echo* did make to popular music at that time was a disc review column entitled 'Off the Record' which ran every Saturday, written, mysteriously, under the pen name of Disker. Early in December 1961 Epstein wrote to Disker in the hope of soliciting a favourable mention for the Beatles in his column. But when the reply arrived it came not from the *Echo* but from London and, strangely, from someone at Decca Records. Disker, it transpired, was the *nom de plume* of Tony

*Above: The Beatles at Sam Leach's Operation Big Beat on 10 November. Left: Setting up at Aldershot on 9 December with members of Ivor Jay and the Jaywalkers.*

Barrow, a London-based Liverpudlian who, in addition to being a freelance journalist, was a full-time sleeve-note writer for Decca. Barrow's reply was not discouraging and Epstein travelled down to London to meet him. But when they met, and Epstein played Barrow a crudely recorded, scratchy acetate of the Beatles playing in the Cavern Club, Barrow was visibly unimpressed, and he further disappointed Epstein by emphasizing that 'Off the Record' was precisely that – a column in which new records were reviewed. He could not deviate from that ruling and mention a group which didn't have a release.

But there was something about Epstein and his group that nagged away at Barrow. To this day he can't really explain what it was – just a gut feeling perhaps – but after Epstein had left his office Barrow made a couple of internal telephone calls around Decca. One of these was to the sales department which, as Barrow expected, in turn contacted the A&R (artists and repertoire) men, and gently explained that an important company client was touting a group. It would be tactful, they suggested, if Decca gave them a try-out. The head of A&R was Dick Rowe, and he had been in the game long enough to know that it would be unwise, and bad for company business, if he refused. So it was that in mid-December 1961, probably on the 13th or 20th, Rowe's young assistant, Mike Smith, was despatched to Liverpool to witness a full Beatles performance in the group's best possible surroundings, the Cavern Club. There was great excitement in the Cavern that night – for the first time ever an A&R man would be in attendance. A major breakthrough indeed.

Smith liked what he saw, not enough to warrant an immediate contract admittedly, but sufficiently enough to arrange a second audition quickly, this time to take place in a real recording studio, Decca's own, in north London. The inexperienced Smith simply wanted Rowe to see the group before he boldly went ahead and signed them up.

The date was set for 1 January 1962.

**5 January**     Town Hall, Litherland

The first of 35 dates between January and March 1961 for promoter Brian Kelly, who ran 'Beekay' dances at various halls in North Liverpool. Many of these dates were booked immediately after the group's sensational appearance for Kelly at this hall on 27 December 1960.

In the audience on this particular evening were Johnny Guitar and Ringo Starr from Rory Storm and the Hurricanes. They had returned from Hamburg on 4 January.

**6 January**     St John's Hall,
Oriel Road,
Bootle, Lancashire

The organizer of this dance, 17-year-old Dave Forshaw, was the only promoter other than Brian Kelly to enter the Beatles' dressing room after the Litherland date on 27 December. He swiftly booked them for three monthly dates. On this first occasion he paid them £6 10s, a fee easily recouped since the hall was filled almost to capacity on this night. Clearly, word of the Beatles' prowess was spreading fast.

**7 January**     Aintree Institute,
Longmoor Lane,
Aintree, Liverpool

The first of 31 Beatles appearances at this venue, situated – as Brian Kelly almost always pointed out in his advertisements – 'Behind the Black Bull' pub, not far from the famous Aintree racecourse, home of the annual Grand National Steeplechase.

The favourite pastime among one faction at the Institute was to lob chairs at all and sundry, including the group on stage.

**8 January**     Casbah Coffee Club,
West Derby

**13 January**     Aintree Institute,
Aintree

**14 January**     Aintree Institute,
Aintree

**15 January**     Casbah Coffee Club,
West Derby

**18 January**     Aintree Institute,
Aintree

The Beatles were paid £8 10s for this appearance.

**19 January**     Alexandra Hall,
College Road,
Crosby, Liverpool

Another Beekay (Brian Kelly) venue.

**20 January**     Lathom Hall, Seaforth

A celebrated return to the site of the Silver Beats' (Silver Beetles) first-ever date, eight months previously.

**21 January**     Lathom Hall, Seaforth
and   Aintree Institute,
Aintree

Two gigs for Brian Kelly in one night. The Aintree appearance was unadvertised.

**22 January**     Casbah Coffee Club,
West Derby

**25 January**     Hambleton Hall,
St David's Road,
Page Moss,
Huyton, Liverpool

The first of sixteen engagements for promoters Wally Hill and Vic Anton at this desperate-looking municipal building on the eastern edge of Liverpool.

**26 January**     Town Hall, Litherland

**27 January**     Aintree Institute,
Aintree

**28 January**     Lathom Hall, Seaforth
and   Aintree Institute,
Aintree

Come and Jive at Merseyside's Best Jive Dance
**AINTREE INSTITUTE**
**THIS SATURDAY and every Saturday**
— CARNIVAL —
Hats, Balloons etc.
FARON AND THE TEMPEST TORNADOES
THE BEATLES FROM HAMBURG
Your Compere — DYNAMIC BOB WOOLER
7-30 to 11 p.m.     Admission 4/-
THIS FRIDAY. DOMINOES, RAVERNS ............... 2/6
NEXT WED. CLIFF ROBERTS, Senior Service Gift Night 2/6

**LOOK !**
**THREE TOP GROUPS AGAIN**
NEXT WEDNESDAY NIGHT AT HAMBLETON HALL
Page Moss, Huyton
— What a terrific line up for —
WEDNESDAY, 25th JANUARY 1961
● The Sensational Beatles
● Derry & The Seniors
● Faron & The Tempest Tornadoes
YES! You must come along early and bring your friends!
PAY AT THE DOOR   2/6 before 8 p.m.   3/- afterwards
NOTE! No admission after 9-30 p.m.

| | |
|---|---|
| **29 January** | Casbah Coffee Club, West Derby |
| **30 January** | Lathom Hall, Seaforth |

Again, the Beatles were paid £8 10s for their night's work.

| | |
|---|---|
| **1 February** | Hambleton Hall, Huyton |
| **2 February** | Town Hall, Litherland |
| **3 February** | St John's Hall, Bootle |

The second of Dave Forshaw's bookings, for which the Beatles were paid an increased fee of £7 10s.

*Above: Extract from Dave Forshaw's diary, showing his booking of the Beatles on 3 February and their fee.*

| | |
|---|---|
| **4 February** | Lathom Hall, Seaforth |
| **5 February** | Blair Hall, Walton Road, Walton, Liverpool |

The Beatles' first engagement with Peak Promotions which ran jive dances at four venues, the Holyoake Hall in Smithdown Road, the David Lewis Club in Great George Place, the Columba Hall in Widnes, and this one. The only one of these the Beatles didn't ever play was the Columba Hall.

| | |
|---|---|
| **6 February** | Lathom Hall, Seaforth |
| **8 February** and | Aintree Institute, Aintree Hambleton Hall, Huyton |

Two dances for two different promotions in one evening. The venues are several miles apart, so newly acquired road manager Neil Aspinall had some hurried driving to do.

| | |
|---|---|
| **10 February** and | Aintree Institute, Aintree Lathom Hall, Seaforth |
| **11 February** and | Lathom Hall, Seaforth The Cassanova Club, Sampson and Barlow's New Ballroom, London Road, Liverpool |

Two dates in one evening, the second of which was the first of a great many they were to undertake for local promoter Sam R. Leach.

Notes: The Cassanova Club had moved to these premises from the site in Temple Street two days earlier, on 9 February.

THE CASSANOVA "ROCK 'N' SWING" CLUB
OPENING THIS THURSDAY, FEB. 9, 7.30-12 P.M. SAMPSON & BARLOW'S NEW BALLROOM, LONDON ROAD. FIVE STOMPING BANDS!!!
THE CASSANOVA'S BIG THREE
THE FABULOUS REMO 4
RORY STORM & the HURRICANES
TOMMY & THE METRONOMES
BENNY & THE BLACK CATS
LIVERPOOL'S LATEST SWINGING SENSATIONS!
MARK PETER & VINCE WADE
ALSO INTRODUCING "THE ATOM BEAT!!"
TICKETS 5/- (INCLUDES REFRESHMENTS). RUSHWORTH'S, LEWIS'S, &c. LIMITED TICKETS AT DOOR.
ALSO
NEXT TUESDAY, FEBRUARY 14.
A "VALENTINE'S NIGHT ROCK BALL"!!!
SAMPSON & BARLOW'S NEW BALLROOM, LONDON ROAD.
ANOTHER GREAT ROCKING LINE UP!!
STARRING
THE SENSATIONAL BEATLES!!
THE CASSANOVAS BIG THREE!!
RORY STORM'S "ATOM BEAT" HURRICANES!!
ALSO PRESENTING
MARK PETERS AND CYCLONES! THE
TICKETS 4/6 (INCLUDES REFRESHMENTS) ALSO AVAILABLE AT RUSHWORTH'S, LEWIS'S & CRANE'S.
"ALL THIS FABULOUS ENTERTAINMENT" AT
THE CASSANOVA CLUB!!!
TO-MORROW NIGHT! WEDNESDAY!!
AT THE "HIVE OF JIVE"
HAMBLETON HALL
PAGEMOSS-HUYTON
THE SENIOR WEATHERMAN (DERRY) FORECASTS A HOT TIME WITH A COOL STORM (RORY TYPE), HURRICANES, TEMPESTS AND TORNADOES, AND THE TEMPERATURE WILL BE FARON-HEIT. TAKE NOTE!!! THERE WILL ALSO BE AN INVASION OF BOPPIN' BEATLES!
GO GO GO MAN GO
IT'S THE WEDNESDAY NIGHT SHOW
AINTREE INSTITUTE
BEATLES BEATLES
DERRY AND THE SENIORS
JEAN DAY AND THE JANGO BEATS.

On 7 March 1963 this ballroom re-opened as the Peppermint Lounge, so named after the famous New York twist club. Contrary to other reports, the Beatles did *not* play here when it was under that name.

| | |
|---|---|
| **12 February** | Casbah Coffee Club, West Derby |
| **14 February** and | Cassanova Club Town Hall, Litherland |

Handbills for the Cassanova Club date detailed the Beatles as originators of The Atom Beat, a dance involving much foot stomping.

| | |
|---|---|
| **15 February** and | Aintree Institute, Aintree Hambleton Hall, Huyton |
| **16 February** and | Cassanova Club Town Hall, Litherland |
| **17 February** | St John's Hall, Snaefell Avenue, Tuebrook, Liverpool |

Mona Best, mother of the Beatles' drummer Pete, and owner of the Casbah Coffee Club, also ran some dances at this venue, not far from her home in West Derby. This was the first of eleven such Beatles engagements, and they were paid the handsome sum of £20.

Casbah Promotions PRESENT A

Big Beat Dance

ST. JOHNS HALL · SNAEFELL AVENUE
TUEBROOK LIVERPOOL
On FRIDAY, 17th FEBRUARY 1961
The BEATLES Rock Combo
GENE DAY & JANGO Beats
MISSION 3/6 (Doors Open 7-15 p.m.)
The Management Reserve the Right to Refuse Admission

| | |
|---|---|
| **18 February** [CANCELLED] and | Cassanova Club Aintree Institute, Aintree |

The Beatles were withdrawn from their date at the Cassanova Club, and it was re-scheduled for 28 February. Their place was taken by Rory Storm and the Hurricanes.

| | |
|---|---|
| **24 February** | Grosvenor Ballroom, Liscard |

The Beatles' first appearance across the Mersey in 1961.

| | |
|---|---|
| **25 February** and | Aintree Institute, Aintree Lathom Hall, Seaforth |

A far from easeful evening for George Harrison on the occasion of his eighteenth birthday.

| | |
|---|---|
| **26 February** | Casbah Coffee Club, West Derby |

*Above: Advert for the Beatles' Cavern Club debut, at lunchtime on 21 February. Their evening performance as 'The Boppin' Beatles' at the Cassanova Club is also mentioned. Inset: The Beatles' first appearance across the Mersey. Right: Promoter Dave Forshaw's amateur photo of the Beatles at St John's Hall, Bootle.*

| | |
|---|---|
| **19 February** | Casbah Coffee Club, West Derby |

| | |
|---|---|
| **21 February** Lunchtime | Cavern Club |
| Night and | Cassanova Club Town Hall, Litherland |

With this lunchtime date a long-established 'fact' can be totally dispelled. The Beatles did not make their debut at the Cavern Club on 21 March 1961; they made their *night-time* debut on that date, certainly, but their true first-time-at-the-venue performance (after the Quarry Men dates in 1957 and 1958) was on this day, a month previously.

This day also marked the first of many occasions when the Beatles would perform *three* engagements in one day.

| | |
|---|---|
| **22 February** and | Aintree Institute, Aintree Hambleton Hall, Huyton |

For the Aintree date the group received £7 2s.

| | |
|---|---|
| 28 February and | Cassanova Club Town Hall, Litherland |
| 1 March | Aintree Institute, Aintree |
| 2 March | Town Hall, Litherland |
| 3 March | St John's Hall, Bootle |
| 4 March | Aintree Institute, Aintree |
| 5 March | Casbah Coffee Club, West Derby |
| 6 March Lunchtime | Cavern Club |
| Night | Liverpool Jazz Society, 13 Temple Street, Liverpool |

Their second appearance at the Cavern Club, and their first at what had previously been, and was eventually to re-emerge as, the Iron Door Club.

| | |
|---|---|
| 7 March | Cassanova Club |
| 8 March Lunchtime | Cavern Club |
| Night | Aintree Institute, Aintree |
| and | Hambleton Hall, Huyton |
| 10 March Lunchtime | Cavern Club |
| Night | Grosvenor Ballroom, Liscard |
| and | St John's Hall, Tuebrook |

The Liscard engagement marked the last date ever arranged for the Beatles by Allan Williams. He hadn't booked them anywhere other than at this hall since their return from Hamburg three months previously.

| | |
|---|---|
| 11 March and | Aintree Institute, Aintree Liverpool Jazz Society |

The LJS date was a true innovation on the part of Sam Leach, by far the most adventurous and ambitious rock promoter to be found on Merseyside. He put on a 12-group, 12-hour, all-night session, commencing at 8 p.m. Saturday and finishing at 8 a.m. Sunday. The admission price was just 6s 6d (now 32½p) for LJS members and 7s 6d (37½p) for non-members. Although the attendance capacity of the cellar was 1000 people, around 2000 saw at least some part of the show. Leach was to hold many similar marathon Big Beat Sessions over the next two years at several venues, most – though not all – of which the Beatles attended.

| | |
|---|---|
| 12 March | Cassanova Club |

| | |
|---|---|
| 13 March | Liverpool Jazz Society |
| 14 March Lunchtime | Cavern Club |
| 15 March Lunchtime | Cavern Club |
| Afternoon | Liverpool Jazz Society |

After the Beatles' lunchtime spot at the Cavern Club (12:00–1:00 p.m. on this occasion), they shifted their equipment over Victoria Street and into the Liverpool Jazz Society for a five-hour afternoon session alternating with Rory Storm and the Wild Ones (Rory plus assorted guest musicians) and Gerry and the Pacemakers. The Beatles' first appearance was at 2:00 p.m.

| | |
|---|---|
| 16 March Lunchtime | Cavern Club |
| 17 March and | Mossway Hall, Moss Way, Croxteth, Liverpool Liverpool Jazz Society |

Contrary to information in other books, this was the Beatles' one and only ever engagement for Messrs McIver and Martin who, under the name of Ivamar, promoted at three venues in North Liverpool at this time: St Luke's Hall in Crosby (aka The Jive Hive), the Ivamar Club (Masonic Hall) in Skelmersdale, and the Mossway Hall in Croxteth.

| | |
|---|---|
| 19 March | Casbah Coffee Club, West Derby |

**20 March**
Lunchtime      Cavern Club

Night      Hambleton Hall,
                Huyton

**21 March**
Night      Cavern Club

The night-time debut of the Beatles in
Mathew Street.

**22 March**
Lunchtime      Cavern Club

**24 March**
Lunchtime      Cavern Club

Now eager to book the Beatles at every
conceivable opportunity, Ray McFall,
the Cavern Club owner, actually
engaged the Beatles to play this
lunchtime session just hours – literally

– before the group journeyed to
Hamburg for their second visit.

**VISIT TO HAMBURG**

**27 March–2 July** Top Ten Club,
(98 nights)      136 Reeperbahn

A twice-extended contract led to the
Beatles staying 14 weeks at the Top
Ten Club, playing a staggering total of
535 hours on stage.

*John, Paul and George performing vocal harmonies from the stage of the Top Ten Club, Hamburg.*

It was little wonder then that, just as on their first German trip in 1960, the Beatles' stamina and musical versatility improved dramatically as the visit wore on. When they returned to Liverpool they were simply untouchable.

RETURN TO UK

| 13 July | St John's Hall, Tuebrook |
|---|---|

Back to Merseyside with an opening date for Mrs Best at St John's Hall.

| 14 July | |
|---|---|
| Lunchtime | Cavern Club |
| Night | Cavern Club |

| 15 July | Holyoake Hall, Smithdown Road, Liverpool |
|---|---|

Aside from the Quarry Men engagements here and at St Barnabas Church Hall in 1957, this was – geographically – the closest the Beatles came to playing in Penny Lane, the road made famous in their 1967 song.

| 16 July | Blair Hall, Walton |
|---|---|

The first of three consecutive Sunday-night dates at this venue for Peak Promotions.

| 17 July | |
|---|---|
| Lunchtime | Cavern Club |
| Night | Town Hall, Litherland |

| 19 July | |
|---|---|
| Lunchtime | Cavern Club |
| Night | Cavern Club |

| 20 July | St John's Hall, Tuebrook |
|---|---|

| 21 July | |
|---|---|
| Lunchtime | Cavern Club |
| Night | Aintree Institute, Aintree |

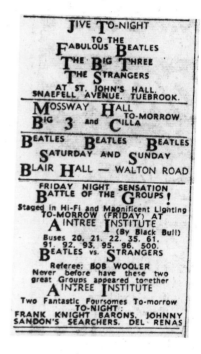

| 22 July | Holyoake Hall, Smithdown Road |
|---|---|

| 23 July | Blair Hall, Walton |
|---|---|

| 24 July | Town Hall, Litherland |
|---|---|

| 25 July | |
|---|---|
| Lunchtime | Cavern Club |
| Night | Cavern Club |

| 26 July | |
|---|---|
| Night | Cavern Club |

| 27 July | |
|---|---|
| Lunchtime | Cavern Club |
| Night | St John's Hall, Tuebrook |

Also on the bill with the Beatles at the St John's Hall were the Big Three, the remains of Cass and the Cassanovas after Brian Cassar had left the group and gone to London. On this night they also featured a young girl who occasionally sang with them, Cilla White – later, of course, to become world famous as songstress Cilla Black.

| 28 July | Aintree Institute, Aintree |
|---|---|

| 29 July | Blair Hall, Walton |
|---|---|

| 30 July | Blair Hall, Walton |
|---|---|

| 31 July | |
|---|---|
| Lunchtime | Cavern Club |
| Night | Town Hall, Litherland |

| 2 August | |
|---|---|
| Lunchtime | Cavern Club |
| Night | Cavern Club |

| 3 August | St John's Hall, Tuebrook |
|---|---|

| 4 August | |
|---|---|
| Lunchtime | Cavern Club |
| Night | Aintree Institute, Aintree |

| 5 August | |
|---|---|
| Night | Cavern Club |

An all-night session in which the Beatles shared the bill with noted jazz trumpeter Kenny Ball.

| 6 August | Casbah Coffee Club, West Derby |
|---|---|

| 7 August | Town Hall, Litherland |
|---|---|

LITHERLAND TOWN HALL
TO-NIGHT: BANK HOLIDAY SPECIAL
BEATLES — BEATLES
HEAR PETE BEST SING TO-NIGHT. 2/6
THE BLACK CAT CLUB
TO-NIGHT          TO-NIGHT

| 8 August | |
|---|---|
| Lunchtime | Cavern Club |

| 9 August | |
|---|---|
| Night | Cavern Club |

| 10 August | |
|---|---|
| Lunchtime | Cavern Club |
| Night | St John's Hall, Tuebrook |

| 11 August | |
|---|---|
| Night | Cavern Club |

| 12 August | Aintree Institute, Aintree |
|---|---|

| 13 August | Casbah Coffee Club, West Derby |
|---|---|

| 14 August | |
|---|---|
| Lunchtime | Cavern Club |

| 16 August | |
|---|---|
| Night | Cavern Club |

| 17 August | St John's Hall, Tuebrook |
|---|---|

For this evening the Beatles played as a five-man outfit, augmented by Johnny Gustafson, good-looking bassist with the Big Three, who were also on the night's bill of fare. Paul McCartney – in frivolous mood – moved around the stage and among the audience singing into a microphone *sans* guitar, in the style of the solo singers of the day.

| 18 August | |
|---|---|
| Lunchtime | Cavern Club |
| Night | Aintree Institute, Aintree |

| 19 August | Aintree Institute, Aintree |
|---|---|

| 20 August | Hambleton Hall, Huyton |
|---|---|

| 21 August | |
|---|---|
| Lunchtime | Cavern Club |

| 23 August | |
|---|---|
| Lunchtime | Cavern Club |
| Night | Cavern Club |

| 24 August | St John's Hall, Tuebrook |
|---|---|

| 25 August | |
|---|---|
| Lunchtime | Cavern Club |
| Night | Riverboat Shuffle aboard the MV *Royal Iris*, River Mersey |

The first of four floating Beatles performances, aboard the infamous Mersey vessel, the *Royal Iris*, colloquially known as the Fish and Chip Boat!

During the summer months Ray McFall, owner of the Cavern Club, booked the ferry for occasional 'shuffles', always providing a cross-section of entertainment in order to attract as many patrons as possible. Heading the bill on this occasion, and drawing in a large following, was Acker Bilk, clarinetist and spearhead of the trad jazz boom. Providing the beat music, and attracting a more youthful audience, were the Beatles. The three-and-a-quarter-hour jaunt began and ended at the Pier Head.

| | |
|---|---|
| **26 August** | Aintree Institute, Aintree |
| **27 August** | Casbah Coffee Club, West Derby |
| **28 August** Lunchtime | Cavern Club |
| **29 August** Lunchtime | Cavern Club |
| **30 August** Night | Cavern Club |
| **31 August** | St John's Hall, Tuebrook |
| **1 September** Lunchtime | Cavern Club |
| Night | Cavern Club |
| **2 September** | Aintree Institute, Aintree |
| **3 September** | Hambleton Hall, Huyton |
| **5 September** Lunchtime | Cavern Club |
| Night CANCELLED | Cavern Club |
| **6 September** Night | Cavern Club |
| **7 September** Lunchtime | Cavern Club |
| Night | Town Hall, Litherland |
| **8 September** | St John's Hall, Tuebrook |
| **9 September** | Aintree Institute, Aintree |

| | |
|---|---|
| **10 September** | Casbah Coffee Club, West Derby |
| **11 September** Lunchtime | Cavern Club |
| **13 September** Lunchtime | Cavern Club |
| Night | Cavern Club |
| **14 September** | Town Hall, Litherland |
| **15 September** Lunchtime | Cavern Club |
| Night and | Grosvenor Ballroom, Liscard |
| | Village Hall, East Prescot Road, Knotty Ash, Liverpool |

Two evening engagements for the Beatles on different sides of the Mersey which, combined with the lunchtime session at the Cavern Club, meant that the group gave three separate performances, each at different venues, in less than twelve hours.

The Liscard date marked the Beatles' first appearance 'across the water' in six months, while the Knotty Ash dance, promoted by Mona Best, marked their debut at this fine, mock-Tudor style village hall in the area made famous as the home of comedian Ken Dodd, and his 'jam butty mines'.

| | |
|---|---|
| **16 September** | Aintree Institute, Aintree |
| **17 September** | Hambleton Hall, Huyton |
| **19 September** Lunchtime | Cavern Club |
| **20 September** Night | Cavern Club |
| **21 September** Lunchtime | Cavern Club |
| Night | Town Hall, Litherland |

A star-studded evening before a capacity crowd in Litherland as Brian Kelly books Liverpool's top three outfits. 'No bands like pro bands', as he proudly bills the Beatles, Gerry and the Pacemakers and Rory Storm and the Hurricanes. Three-and-a-half 'rocking hours' for just 3s (15p)!

## THE BEATLES TO VISIT WALLASEY

For Paramount's final night in their Friday series at the Grosvenor Ballroom, they have managed to secure the Beatles, recently returned from a highly successful tour of Germany. This will be their first appearance in Wallasey following their return and together with the house band, Cliff Roberts and the Rockers, a terrific programme is assured. For this final night dancing will commence at 7-45 p.m. (doors open 7-30 p.m.) and run non-stop until 11 p.m. Patrons are advised to attend at the commencement of dancing because the Beatles will be playing early due to a late engagement in Liverpool.

PARAMOUNT PRESENT **GROSVENOR BALLROOM** PRESENT

NEXT FRIDAY — 15th SEPTEMBER
★ FINAL NIGHT IN THE PRESENT ROCK SERIES ★
TERRIFIC ALL STAR BILL  THE FABULOUS

# BEATLES

(Making their first Wallasey appearance since their German tour)
Supported by Cliff Roberts & The Rockers
ADMISSION 4/-
NON-STOP 7.45 — 11 p.m.
(THE BEATLES PLAY EARLY, SO COME EARLY).

AND FOR STRICT TEMPO DANCERS
**DANCING every TUESDAY**
WITH THE HIGNETT QUARTET.
Admission 2/6

BEEKAY PRESENTS
THE BEST JIVE DANCES AT
**Litherland Town Hall**
EVERY MONDAY and THURSDAY
This Monday:—
7-30 — 11 p.m.
RAY & The DEL RENAS—CY & The CIMARRONS
Admission 2/6

Next Thursday:—
**NO** BANDS LIKE PRO BANDS
WELL DIG THIS!!!
★ **BEATLES** ★
PLUS
**Jerry & the Pacemakers**
PLUS
**Golden boy RORY STORM**
MR. SHOWMANSHIP and THE HURRICANES.

★ WHAT A FABULOUS NIGHT
★ ONLY PRO. BANDS
★ COME EARLY TO BE SURE OF ADMISSION
7-30—11 p.m. 3½ Rocking Hours. Members 3/-
ANOTHER BEEKAY DANCE

# ST. JOHN BRIGADE DISAPPOINTED

## Poor Attendance At Star Matinee

THERE was a disappointing response by the general public to Sunday's star matinee at the Albany Cinema, Maghull, said Mr. G. Timpson, secretary of the Waterloo Ambulance and Nursing Division of the St. John Ambulance Brigade and organiser of the show.

The matinee, to raise funds for a new ambulance for the division, attracted only two-thirds of the people expected, in spite of the fact that top comedian Ken Dodd was the star of the show.

The division had hoped to raise £500 from the charity concert, but the final figure looks like being only about a quarter of this.

" So it seems that the ambulance is as far away as ever," Mr. Timpson told the Herald.

This was disappointing considering all the work the Division had done in this area throughout the summer.

The three-hour concert was presented by Liverpool agent Jim Gretty, who organised a host of Merseyside club artists for the show. Compered by Arthur Scott, of the Everton Supporters' Club, the concert was a variety of musical acts spiced with the comedy of Ken Dodd.

### OPERA AND " ROCK "

A Sunday afternoon show has to rely mainly on musical acts, and this caused the performance to have an air of " sameness " about it. But the organisers tried hard to vary the acts, presenting everything from operatic arias to the pounding rock'n'roll beat of Liverpool's Beatles Rock Group.

Country and Western fans were catered for by Hank Walters and the Dusty Road Ramblers, who got the show off to a fine start, followed by tenor Les Arnold, an ex-miner from St. Helens. Pop Singer Joe Cordova followed with a selection of popular songs, and this led on to the music and comedy of Dave Dunn and Jim Markey, who have appeared on radio and television.

The deep baritone of coloured artist Lennie Rens was heard in a selection of popular Negro songs, and Canadian Shirley Gordon sang a number of light operatic numbers. The first half was closed by pop singer Bert King and instrumentalists The Eltones.

After the interval, the undoubted star was Ken Dodd, with his zany comedy, large teeth and fly-away hair. He had the crowd eating out of his hand in ten seconds flat, and could have gone on with his act all night. He was ably supported by local singer Denis Smerdon, who sang the soliloquy from " Carousel," and glamorous vocalist Edna Bell, from Maghull.

A Trad jazz item was given by Jackie Owen and the Joe Royal Trio.

The Beatles closed the show with their own brand of feet-tapping Rock.

### CIVIC PATRONS

The performance was attended by the Mayor and Mayoress of Crosby (Alderman F. T. Sutton and Mrs. E. F. Darwin), the Chairman of West Lancs. R.D.C., Councillor R. Phillips, with Mrs. Phillips; and the Chairman of Maghull Parish Council, Councillor H. Prescott, with Mrs. Prescott, who were invited to a reception after the show at the Alt Hotel.

Ken Dodd and numerous officers and ladies of the St. John Ambulance Brigade also attended the reception. Mr. Dodd was introduced in turn to all the guests.

| | |
|---|---|
| **22 September** | Village Hall, Knotty Ash |
| **23 September** | Aintree Institute, Aintree |
| **24 September** | Casbah Coffee Club, West Derby |
| **25 September** Lunchtime | Cavern Club |
| **27 September** Lunchtime | Cavern Club |
| Night | Cavern Club |
| **28 September** | Town Hall, Litherland |
| **29 September** Lunchtime | Cavern Club |
| Night | Village Hall, Knotty Ash |

The Beatles' last performance before John and Paul took off for a two-week vacation in Paris.

A report from the Crosby Herald on the Beatles' unusual Maghull gig.

| | | |
|---|---|---|
| **15 October** Afternoon | | Albany Cinema, Northway, Maghull, Liverpool |
| Night | | Hambleton Hall, Huyton |

The Albany Cinema date marked the Beatles' first booking after John and Paul's return – and a most unusual one at that.

Liverpool variety agent Jim Gretty, a country and western guitarist since the thirties, specializing in charity work, and also part-time guitar salesman at Hessy's music store in Liverpool (it was Gretty who sold John Lennon his first guitar in 1957), put on this Sunday afternoon variety – in the true sense of the word – concert, typical of the old-tyme music hall days, in Maghull, a sleepy village north of Aintree. All proceeds went to the local branch of the St John Ambulance Brigade.

Topping the 16-act three-hour bill was comedian Ken Dodd, ably supported by tenors, a Lowry organist, trad jazz and country and western outfits, and a singer of operatic arias. The Paris trip and other live bookings meant that this gig punctuated a rare eight-week absence from the Casbah. The Beatles, hopelessly out of place on such a bill, and performing before an audience of the local mayor, councillors and civic dignitaries, closed the show with a ten-minute thrash, having been switched to that position from the ignominy of the first post-interval spot in an attempt by Ken Dodd to revive the flagging, and sadly disappointing, audience.

| | |
|---|---|
| **16 October** Lunchtime | Cavern Club |
| **17 October** | David Lewis Club, Great George Place (Nile Street Entrance), Liverpool |

The Beatles' first, and only, appearance at this venue also marked the first-ever venture by the one-month-old Beatles Fan Club.

| | |
|---|---|
| **18 October** Lunchtime | Cavern Club |
| Night | Cavern Club |
| **19 October** | Town Hall, Litherland |

A legendary date in the annals of Merseybeat, but also one which, over the years, has become exaggerated out of all proportion.

Booked alongside the Beatles on this typical Thursday-night Beekay bill were Gerry and the Pacemakers. Midway through the evening someone suggested that, as a break from routine, the two groups should join forces for one night to become, as it were, the Beatmakers. They duly took to the stage – George on lead guitar, Paul on rhythm, Pete Best sharing his drum kit with Freddy Marsden, Les Maguire on saxophone, Les Chadwick on bass, John Lennon at the piano and Gerry Marsden on lead guitar and vocals. Karl Terry, leader of the group Karl Terry and the Cruisers, who were also on the bill, also joined in the fun, joining in on the vocals.

The union was not intended to be permanent, indeed it was never again attempted, despite frequent opportunities for the two groups to do so.

**20 October**
Lunchtime    Cavern Club

Night    Village Hall,
Knotty Ash

**21 October**
Night    Cavern Club

This booking could really be counted as two engagements, with the Beatles playing both before and after midnight during this Saturday Cavern Club all-nighter.

**22 October**    Casbah Coffee Club,
West Derby

**24 October**
Lunchtime    Cavern Club

**25 October**
Night    Cavern Club

**26 October**
Lunchtime    Cavern Club

**27 October**    Village Hall,
Knotty Ash

**28 October**    Aintree Institute,
Aintree

**29 October**    Hambleton Hall,
Huyton

**30 October**
Lunchtime    Cavern Club

**31 October**    Town Hall, Litherland

**1 November**
Lunchtime    Cavern Club

Night    Cavern Club

**3 November**
Lunchtime    Cavern Club

**4 November**
Night    Cavern Club

*Underneath the arches . . . George Harrison socialising with Rory Storm in the Cavern Club, November 1961.*

**7 November**
Lunchtime    Cavern Club

Night    Merseyside Civil
Service Club,
Lower Castle Street,
Liverpool
and    Cavern Club

The first of four consecutive, block-booked, appearances at the Merseyside Civil Service Club, a venue new to the Beatles but one which had featured groups like Rory Storm and the Hurricanes weekly for almost a year.

The Beatles were not a great success here, and weren't re-booked after these four appearances.

**8 November**
Night    Cavern Club

**9 November**
Lunchtime    Cavern Club

Night    Town Hall, Litherland

One of the most important (if not THE most important) dates in the Beatles' history. For in attendance amid the predominantly young, female, lunchtime Cavern Club throng, far from inconspicuous in his pin-striped suit, was local record store owner and manager, 27-year-old Brian Epstein.

By a complete coincidence to this meeting of Epstein and the Beatles, though most certainly symbolic of its future outcome, this date also marked the last-ever appearance by the Beatles at the shabby ballroom of the Litherland Town Hall.

**10 November**    Tower Ballroom,
Promenade,
New Brighton,
Wallasey, Cheshire
and    Village Hall,
Knotty Ash

A spectacularly busy evening for the Beatles. Main attraction was undoubtedly the Tower Ballroom engagement, the first of many occasions they were to play this huge hall, capable of holding a 5000-strong audience.

Over 3000 were packed in to witness this, the first Operation Big Beat in Liverpool, run on a grand American-style scale by ambitious promoter Sam Leach. (Leach had previously 'tested the water' with a run of Big Beat Sessions at the Civic Hall in Ellesmere Port, Cheshire, in July 1961, in which the Beatles did not participate.)

Between 7:30 p.m. and 1:00 a.m. five top groups played alternate shifts on stage. The Beatles' first spot was at 8:00 p.m., after which they dashed back, via the Mersey tunnel, to appear on stage at the Knotty Ash Village Hall. The evening was rounded off in fine style back at the Tower with a second spot at 11:30 p.m., and a frantic, hair-raising car race back under the River Mersey to Liverpool city centre with Rory Storm and the Hurricanes which very nearly resulted in a bloody and premature end to the lives of the latter group's members.

Note: The first advertisement for the Tower Ballroom gig in the *Liverpool Echo*, carried in the 27 October edition, included the name of NEMS among the various ticket outlets. This pre-dates, by 24 hours, Brian Epstein's first knowledge of the group's name as he describes their discovery.

| | |
|---|---|
| **11 November** | Aintree Institute, Aintree |

After the performance, the Beatles headed for the Liverpool Jazz Society to attend a party thrown by Sam Leach to celebrate the success of the previous evening at the Tower Ballroom.

| | |
|---|---|
| **12 November** | Hambleton Hall, Huyton |

| | |
|---|---|
| **13 November** | |
| Lunchtime | Cavern Club |

| | |
|---|---|
| **14 November** | |
| Night | Merseyside Civil Service Club |
| and | Cavern Club |

| | |
|---|---|
| **15 November** | |
| Lunchtime | Cavern Club |
| Night | Cavern Club |

| | |
|---|---|
| **17 November** | |
| Lunchtime | Cavern Club |
| Night | Village Hall, Knotty Ash |

| | |
|---|---|
| **18 November** | |
| Night | Cavern Club |

| | |
|---|---|
| **19 November** | Casbah Coffee Club, West Derby |

| | |
|---|---|
| **21 November** | |
| Lunchtime | Cavern Club |
| Night | Merseyside Civil Service Club |

| | |
|---|---|
| **22 November** | |
| Night | Cavern Club |

| | |
|---|---|
| **23 November** | |
| Lunchtime | Cavern Club |

| | |
|---|---|
| **24 November** | Casbah Coffee Club, West Derby |
| and | Tower Ballroom, New Brighton |

After fulfilling their Casbah engagement, the Beatles moved on to

*Above: Pete and Paul clowning with Emile Ford at the Tower Ballroom, New Brighton on 24 November. Below: The Beatles, with Paul gulping air, backing Davy Jones in the Cavern Club on 8 December.*

New Brighton for another Sam Leach presentation, Operation Big Beat II.

The Beatles' 11:00 p.m. spot was considerably enlivened by the surprise unannounced appearance in the ballroom of two top black singers of the day, Britain's Emile Ford and America's UK-domiciled Davy Jones. Jones leapt on stage to join the Beatles for two numbers, while Ford performed similarly with backing by a delighted Rory Storm and the Hurricanes.

| | |
|---|---|
| **26 November** | Hambleton Hall, Huyton |

| | |
|---|---|
| **27 November** | |
| Lunchtime | Cavern Club |

| | |
|---|---|
| **28 November** | Merseyside Civil Service Club |

| | |
|---|---|
| **29 November** | |
| Lunchtime | Cavern Club |
| Night | Cavern Club |

| | |
|---|---|
| **1 December** | |
| Lunchtime | Cavern Club |
| Night | Tower Ballroom, New Brighton |

The Beatles headed this five-and-a-half-hour, six-group, Big Beat Session at the Tower, attended by 2000 people.

| | |
|---|---|
| **2 December** | |
| Night | Cavern Club |

| | |
|---|---|
| **3 December** | Casbah Coffee Club, West Derby |

| | |
|---|---|
| **5 December** | |
| Lunchtime | Cavern Club |

| | |
|---|---|
| **6 December** | |
| Night | Cavern Club |

**8 December**

Lunchtime      Cavern Club

Night           Tower Ballroom,
                New Brighton

A big day for the Beatles, with Sam Leach booking Davy Jones to headline his seven-act bill at the Tower, and Ray McFall booking him for a lunchtime Cavern Club gig. The Beatles actually backed Jones at both venues, as well as performing their customary spot themselves.

South African-born singing star Danny Williams, then sitting at number four on the hit parade with 'Moon River', and destined for the top position three weeks later, was in Liverpool for a week's engagement at the Cabaret Club so he too was added to the New Brighton bill just days before the event.

**9 December**    The Palais Ballroom,
                Queens Road,
                Aldershot, Hampshire
        and     The Blue
                Gardenia Club,
                Greek Street,
                Soho, London

An historic date in Beatles folklore : their first-ever live performance 'down south', and their first-ever London gig. Not that southerners knew much about it : the Aldershot date, owing to a major blunder, was unadvertised and attracted a measly eighteen people, while the London performance was a spur-of-the-moment whim to jump on stage in a night club/café run by an old friend.

If the minute attendance at the Aldershot gig suggests an air of impetuous planning, certainly the idea was a good one. Liverpool promoter Sam Leach had shrewdly come to realize that as no London agents or record company executives would ever come to Liverpool, he would, instead, take the Liverpool groups to see them. Fine in principle, but in reality, Leach's geographical familiarity with the south of England was somewhat wayward, and instead of choosing a venue in Greater London he ended up booking five consecutive Saturdays at the Palais Ballroom in Aldershot, an uninspiring military outpost thirty-seven miles south-west of London. Not surprisingly, his optimistic invitations to London's top pop impresarios went unheeded.

This, the first of the bookings, was billed on posters and handbills as a Battle of the Bands between the Beatles and the totally unknown London combo, Ivor Jay and the Jaywalkers (not related in any way to the hit group Peter Jay and the Jaywalkers). Leach claims that he also placed a substantial advertisement in the local newspaper, the *Aldershot News*, proudly heralding the Big Beat Session. But unfortunately, and totally unbeknownst to him, he says, the paper refused to accept his cheque since he was not a regular advertiser. Nor could they

*Above : One-ninth of the total audience dance while the Beatles valiantly play on during the eventful Aldershot fiasco on 9 December.*

contact him as he hadn't thought to give them his home address. The advert did not appear.

Come the day of the gig, tired and aching from the nine-hour van journey down from Liverpool, the group discovered – much to their horror – that they faced the prospect of playing to an empty hall. Their only solution was to rush around the town's two coffee bars, and pubs, shouting, 'Hey ! There's a dance on at the Palais tonight,' and offer everybody free admission. Eighteen people turned up. To their credit, the Beatles valiantly played on, while Sam Leach went out among the dancers imploring them to spread out so as to look more numerous.

At the end of the evening the Liverpudlian entourage drowned their sorrows in southern Watney's brown

ale and played a soccer match with bingo balls on the dance floor. In 1983, Paul McCartney remembered the evening as 'the time we couldn't get arrested', despite, it seems, every effort to deliberately cause a scene. Indeed, although they weren't actually taken into custody, the police were waiting for them outside the hall and ordered them out of town, never to return.

In their youthful exuberance, at one o'clock in the morning and with nowhere to stay overnight, they headed for the bright lights of London, and a club run by their old friend Brian Cassar, former leader of Cass and the Cassanovas. The Soho club was small and very obscure, and the few late-night patrons hardly raised a collective eye when the Beatles (minus George who was busy chatting up a London fan) jumped on stage to perform an impromptu set.

As Sunday dawn was breaking the Beatles set off back to Liverpool, their southern adventure over.

Note : The following Saturday, 16 December, Leach brought Rory Storm and the Hurricanes down for Battle of the Bands II with Ivor Jay. This time the advertisement did appear in the *Aldershot News*, and 210 paying customers turned up. Despite the encouraging attendance Leach, by this time, was disgruntled and dissatisfied with Aldershot, and he cancelled his booking for the three remaining dances.

| | | | | | | |
|---|---|---|---|---|---|---|
| **10 December** | Hambleton Hall, Huyton | | Added to the bill at the last moment were Cass and the Cassanovas, a one-night reunion of Brian Cassar and the Big Three. | | **23 December** Night | Cavern Club |

Another all-night session.

| | |
|---|---|
| **11 December** Lunchtime | Cavern Club |

| | |
|---|---|
| **16 December** Night | Cavern Club |

| | |
|---|---|
| **26 December** | Tower Ballroom, New Brighton |

| | |
|---|---|
| **13 December** Lunchtime | Cavern Club |
| Night | Cavern Club |

| | |
|---|---|
| **17 December** | Casbah Coffee Club, West Derby |

| | |
|---|---|
| **27 December** Night | Cavern Club |

This evening was billed as The Beatles' Xmas Party.

| | |
|---|---|
| **19 December** Lunchtime | Cavern Club |

| | |
|---|---|
| **15 December** Lunchtime | Cavern Club |
| Night | Tower Ballroom, New Brighton |

| | |
|---|---|
| **20 December** Night | Cavern Club |

| | |
|---|---|
| **29 December** Night | Cavern Club |

Another typical Sam Leach presentation – five groups playing five-and-a-half hours' entertainment.

| | |
|---|---|
| **21 December** Lunchtime | Cavern Club |

| | |
|---|---|
| **30 December** Night | Cavern Club |

## Other engagements played

In the three months prior to April 1961 – between the group's first and second trips to Hamburg – the Beatles found time in their increasingly busy schedule to play two small venues twenty miles up the coast from Liverpool, in Southport, Lancashire. One was the ATC Club, Birkdale, where they reportedly received the grand sum of £1 10s between them, and the second was the Labour Club, Devonshire Road, High Park. Neither of these bookings was advertised, and the author has been unable to pinpoint any precise dates.

The Beatles are understood to have played in at least two Liverpool labour clubs in 1961, although no records of such engagements have survived, nor were the bookings ever advertised.

After a lunchtime session in the Cavern Club the Beatles occasionally moved on to an afternoon drinking establishment, the Starline Club in Windsor Street, Liverpool, for extra rehearsals. Apparently they also fulfilled one or two evening performances here too, but these were unadvertised and untraceable by the author.

The author has been unable to confirm a 1961 appearance by the Beatles at a Sunday afternoon dance in the hall at Allerton Synagogue in Booker Avenue, West Allerton, Liverpool.

One Sunday evening towards the end of the year, possibly 5 November, the Beatles played at the Glenpark Club in Lord Street, Southport.

British disc jockey and TV personality Jimmy Savile recalls the Beatles playing on two occasions at the Three Coins Club in Fountain Street, Manchester, Lancashire. Only one of these, the second date, was advertised, but as the first was for a fee of just £5 that would seem to date it in the pre-Epstein period. Since the Three Coins did not open for business until 14 October 1961, and they only engaged live groups on a Sunday, this perhaps further narrows the date down to either 5 November or 19 November.

## Engagements not played

One night early in 1961 the Beatles, complete with equipment, set out for an engagement, procured by telephone, at the Yew Tree Hotel in Wythenshawe, south of Manchester, a venue which nightly advertised The Biggest Show in the North. But when they arrived they discovered not a beat-music club but one of the typical northern variety clubs, of the *Wheeltappers and Shunters* tradition, breeding ground for British comedians over several decades. The manager of the Yew Tree, accustomed to seeing artistes clad in at least suits, if not full evening dress, was suitably horrified at the Beatles' scruffy, leather-clad appearance, and the discovery that they played filthy rock and roll music, and refused them admission.

The Beatles' 29 July appearance at Blair Hall, Walton, was originally scheduled for Holyoake Hall, Smithdown Road, Liverpool.

Although noted rock promoter Lewis Buckley is known to have written to the Beatles in late 1961 and offered them engagements in Crewe and/or Northwich, Cheshire, it is certain that the group were unable to accommodate him. Buckley also approached other Liverpool groups like Rory Storm and the Hurricanes and had more success. The Beatles did eventually play for Buckley, but not until Brian Epstein had been established as manager.

# THE MUSIC

This is an attempt to detail the live-performance repertoire of the Beatles in 1961, showing – where possible – the group's vocalist, the composer(s) of the song and the name of the artist/group who recorded the version which influenced the group. It is, in all likelihood, an incomplete guide.

| Song title | Main vocalist(s) | Composer(s) | Influential version (year) |
|---|---|---|---|
| Ain't She Sweet[1] | John | Yellen/Ager | — |
| Bad Boy | John | Williams | Larry Williams (1959) |
| Be-Bop-A-Lula | John | Vincent/Davis | Gene Vincent and his Blue Caps (1956) |
| Besame Mucho | Paul | Velazquez/Skylar | The Coasters (1960) |
| Blue Moon of Kentucky | Paul | Monroe | Elvis Presley (1954) |
| Blue Suede Shoes[2] | John | Perkins | Carl Perkins (1956) and Elvis Presley (1956) |
| Bony Moronie | John | Williams | Larry Williams (1957) |
| Boys | Pete Best | Dixon/Farrell | The Shirelles (1960) |
| Carol | John | Berry | Chuck Berry (1958) |
| Catswalk[3] | (Instrumental) | McCartney | — |
| Clarabella | Paul | Pingatore | The Jodimars (1956) |
| C'mon Everybody | ? | Cochran/Capehart | Eddie Cochran (1959) |
| Corrine, Corrina | ? | Trad. arr. McCoy/ Chatman/Williams/ Parish | Joe Turner (1956) or Ray Peterson (1960) |
| Cry for a Shadow | (Instrumental) | Lennon/Harrison | — |
| Crying, Waiting, Hoping | George | Holly | Buddy Holly (1959) |
| Dance in the Street | ? | Davis/Welch | Gene Vincent and his Blue Caps (1958) |
| Darktown Strutters Ball | ? | Brooks | Joe Brown and the Bruvvers (1960) |
| Dizzy Miss Lizzy | John | Williams | Larry Williams (1958) |
| Don't Forbid Me | ? | Singleton | Pat Boone (1957) ? |
| Everybody's Trying to Be my Baby | George | Perkins | Carl Perkins (1958) |

1 The version most likely to have prompted the Beatles to perform this song would be Gene Vincent's 1956 rock recording. But since John Lennon's vocal rendition sounds quite different to Vincent's it seems apparent that John arranged his own, unique, version.

2 The Beatles mostly performed the composer Carl Perkins' version.

3 When this tune was released on record by the Chris Barber Band in 1967 it was re-titled 'Catcall'.

| Song title | Main vocalist(s) | Composer(s) | Influential version (year) |
|---|---|---|---|
| Falling in Love Again (Can't Help It) | Paul | Hollander | Marlene Dietrich (1930) |
| Fools Like Me | John | Clement/Maddux | Jerry Lee Lewis (1959) |
| Glad all Over[4] | George | Schroeder/Tepper/Bennett | Carl Perkins (1957) |
| Good Golly Miss Molly | Paul | Blackwell/Marascalco | Little Richard (1958) |
| Hallelujah, I Love Her So | Paul | Charles | Ray Charles (1956) and Eddie Cochran (1960) |
| Heavenly | ? | Twitty/Nance | Conway Twitty (1959) or Emile Ford (1960) |
| Hello Little Girl | John | LENNON/McCartney | — |
| Hey, Good Lookin'[5] | ? | Williams | — |
| High School Confidential | Paul | Lewis/Hargrave | Jerry Lee Lewis (1958) |
| The Hippy Hippy Shake | Paul | Romero | Chan Romero (1959) |
| Hold Me Tight | Paul | Lennon/McCARTNEY | — |
| The Honeymoon Song[6] | Paul | Theodorakis/Sansom | Manuel [and the Music of the Mountains] (1959) |
| Hound Dog | John | Leiber/Stoller | Elvis Presley (1961) |
| Hully Gully | ? | Smith/Goldsmith | The Olympics (1959) |
| I Forgot to Remember to Forget | George | Kesler/Feathers | Elvis Presley (1955) |
| I Got a Woman | John | Charles/Richards | Ray Charles (1954) and Elvis Presley (1956) |
| I Got to Find my Baby | John | Berry | Chuck Berry (1960) |
| I Just Don't Understand | John | Wilkin/Westberry | Ann-Margret (1961) |
| I Remember | ? | Cochran/Capehart | Eddie Cochran (1959) |
| I Wish I Could Shimmy Like my Sister Kate | John | Piron | The Olympics (1961) |
| I'm Gonna Sit Right Down and Cry (over You) | John | Thomas/Biggs | Elvis Presley (1956) |
| It's Now or Never | ? | DiCapua/Schroeder/Gold/Capurro | Elvis Presley (1960) |
| Johnny B. Goode | John | Berry | Chuck Berry (1958) |
| Kansas City/Hey-Hey-Hey-Hey![7] | Paul | Leiber/Stoller/Penniman | Little Richard (1959) |
| Lawdy Miss Clawdy | ? | Price | Lloyd Price (1952) |
| Leave my Kitten Alone | John | John/Turner/McDougal | Little Willie John (1959) |
| Lend Me your Comb | John/Paul | Twomey/Wise/Weisman | Carl Perkins (1957) |

**4** Different to the same-titled song taken to number one in the charts by the Dave Clark Five in January 1964.

**5** The Beatles performed their own arrangement of this 1951 Hank Williams hit which borrowed from both Williams' original and a cover version by Carl Perkins.

**6** Since Manuel's original version of 'The Honeymoon Song' was purely instrumental, and the only pre-1961 vocal version of the song was recorded in French by Petula Clark, one must presume that Paul McCartney studied the song's sheet music in order to learn the lyrics.

**7** This medley of two songs recorded separately by Little Richard in 1959 was not the Beatles' idea. Richard himself recorded the same medley in 1959 and it is this version which the Beatles cover.

| Song title | Main vocalist(s) | Composer(s) | Influential version (year) |
|---|---|---|---|
| Like Dreamers Do | Paul | Lennon/McCartney | |
| Little Queenie | Paul | Berry | Chuck Berry (1959) |
| Lonesome Tears in my Eyes | John | Burnette/Burnette/Burlison/Mortimer | The Johnny Burnette Trio (1956) |
| Long Tall Sally | Paul | Johnson/Penniman/Blackwell | Little Richard (1956) |
| Love Me Tender[8] | Stuart Sutcliffe | Presley/Matson | Elvis Presley (1956) |
| Love of the Loved | Paul | Lennon/McCartney | |
| Lucille | Paul | Penniman/Collins | Little Richard (1957) |
| Mailman, Bring Me no More Blues | ? | Roberts/Katz/Clayton | Buddy Holly and the Crickets (1957) |
| Matchbox | Pete Best | Perkins | Carl Perkins (1957) |
| Maybe Baby | ? | Holly/Petty | Buddy Holly and the Crickets (1958) |
| Mean Woman Blues | ? | Demetrius | Jerry Lee Lewis (1957) or Elvis Presley (1957) |
| Memphis, Tennessee | John | Berry | Chuck Berry (1959) |
| Money (That's What I Want) | John | Gordy/Bradford | Barret Strong (1959) |
| New Orleans | ? | Guida/Royster | Gary 'US' Bonds (1961) |
| Nothin' Shakin' (but the Leaves on the Trees) | George | Colacrai/Fontaine/Lampert/Cleveland | Eddie Fontaine (1958) |
| The One after 909 | John | Lennon/McCartney | |
| Ooh! My Soul | Paul | Penniman | Little Richard (1958) |
| Over the Rainbow | Paul | Harburg/Arlen | Gene Vincent and his Blue Caps (1959) |
| Peggy Sue | John | Holly/Allison/Petty | Buddy Holly (1957) |
| Please Mister Postman | John | Holland/Bateman/Gordy | The Marvelettes (1961) |
| Red Hot | John | Emerson | Ronnie Hawkins (1959) |
| Red Sails in the Sunset | Paul | Kennedy/Williams | Joe Turner (1959) or Emile Ford and the Checkmates (1960) |
| Reelin' and Rockin' | ? | Berry | Chuck Berry (1958) |
| Road Runner | ? | McDaniel | Bo Diddley (1960) |
| Rock and Roll Music | John | Berry | Chuck Berry (1957) |
| Roll over Beethoven[9] | John or George | Berry | Chuck Berry (1956) |
| Save the Last Dance for Me | John | Pomus/Shuman | The Drifters (1960) |
| Searchin' | Paul | Leiber/Stoller | The Coasters (1957) |
| September in the Rain | Paul | Dubin/Warren | Dinah Washington (1961) |

**8** Although the composers are credited as Presley/Matson this song was actually written by Ken Darby, musical director of the *Love Me Tender* film. Vera Matson is Darby's wife.

**9** It was probably during this year that the lead vocal for this song was assumed by George Harrison from John Lennon.

| Song title | Main vocalist(s) | Composer(s) | Influential version (year) |
|---|---|---|---|
| Shakin' all Over | ? | Heath | Johnny Kidd and the Pirates (1960) |
| The Sheik of Araby | George | Smith/Snyder/Wheeler | Fats Domino (1961) |
| Shimmy Shimmy | John/Paul | Massey/Schubert | Bobby Freeman (1960) |
| Short Fat Fanny | John | Williams | Larry Williams (1957) |
| Shout | John/Paul/George | Isley/Isley/Isley | The Isley Brothers (1959) |
| Slow Down | John | Williams | Larry Williams (1958) |
| So How Come (No One Loves Me) | George | Bryant | The Everly Brothers (1960) |
| Sure to Fall (in Love with You) | Paul | Perkins/Claunch/Cantrell | Carl Perkins (1956) |
| Sweet Little Sixteen | John | Berry | Chuck Berry (1958) |
| Take Good Care of my Baby | George | Goffin/King | Bobby Vee (1961) |
| Teenage Heaven | ? | Cochran/Capehart | Eddie Cochran (1959) |
| Tennessee | John | Perkins | Carl Perkins (1956) |
| That's all Right (Mama) | Paul | Crudup | Elvis Presley (1954) |
| Thirty Days | John | Berry | Chuck Berry (1955) |
| Three Cool Cats | George | Leiber/Stoller | The Coasters (1959) |
| Three Steps to Heaven | ? | Cochran | Eddie Cochran (1960) |
| Till there Was You | Paul | Willson | Peggy Lee (1961) |
| To Know Her Is to Love Her[10] | John | Spector | The Teddy Bears (1958) |
| Too Much Monkey Business | John | Berry | Chuck Berry (1956) |
| Tutti Frutti | Paul | Penniman/LaBostrie | Little Richard (1957) |
| Twenty Flight Rock | Paul | Cochran/Fairchild | Eddie Cochran (1957) |
| Well . . . (Baby Please Don't Go) | John | Ward | The Olympics (1958) |
| What'd I Say | Paul | Charles | Ray Charles (1959) |
| Whole Lotta Shakin' Goin' On | ? | Williams/David | Jerry Lee Lewis (1957) |
| Wild in the Country | Pete Best | Peretti/Creatore/Weiss | Elvis Presley (1961) |
| Will You Love Me Tomorrow? | John | Goffin/King | The Shirelles (1961) |
| Wooden Heart[11] | Paul | Twomey/Wise/Weisman/Kaempfert | Elvis Presley (1960) |
| Words of Love | John/George | Holly | Buddy Holly (1957) |
| You Don't Understand Me | John | Massey | Bobby Freeman (1960) |
| You Win Again | John | Williams | Hank Williams (1952) or Jerry Lee Lewis (1958) |
| Youngblood | George | Leiber/Stoller/Pomus | The Coasters (1957) |
| Your Feet's too Big | Paul | Benson/Fisher | Fats Waller (1939) or Chubby Checker (1961) |
| Your True Love | George | Perkins | Carl Perkins (1957) |

10 Originally written and recorded as 'To Know Him Is to Love Him'.

11 Like Presley's version, Paul McCartney sang the lyrics in part-German and part-English. This was a particular favourite, for obvious reasons, with Hamburg audiences.

1962

**THE**

# BEATLES

Come and meet

**" PETE, PAUL, JOHN and GEORGE "**

The Group Everyone has been asking for — Now they're here, at the

# KINGSWAY

## NEXT MONDAY — ONLY 2/6

Come and hear them play their latest record, It's Sensational

# COMMENTARY

At eleven o'clock on the morning of Monday 1 January 1962, a cold and icy New Year's Day, John Lennon, Paul McCartney, George Harrison and Pete Best sat in the reception area at Decca studios, 165 Broadhurst Gardens, West Hampstead, London, and waited for the summons that would take them into the big time. And waited. And waited. While Brian Epstein had travelled down by train, for the four Beatles it had been a nightmare ten-hour journey, hunched in an old van overcrowded with all their equipment, battling against heavy New Year's Eve snowstorms which caused driver/road manager Neil Aspinall to lose his way near Wolverhampton.

Mike Smith, the A&R man who had seen the Beatles at the Cavern Club, and who would be supervising the audition, was late, following an all-night New Year's party. The Beatles were fidgety and Epstein was angry, sensing that Smith's delay was a slight on their importance. But eventually Smith did arrive and shepherded the motley Liverpudlians into the studio. There was an immediate problem: Smith was aghast at the state of the Beatles' amplifiers, battered and ragged veterans of more than 300 tough Merseyside dance dates and long Hamburg nights, and insisted the group use unfamiliar studio equipment instead.

Eventually everyone readied themselves, the daunting red light went on, and the session commenced. With so much at stake the Beatles were ill at ease and restrained, lacking their customary vocal and instrumental cohesion. But they soldiered on, eventually laying down fifteen songs, rather unrepresentative of their typical stage repertoire but each one chosen with great care by Brian Epstein to highlight the Beatles' versatility. There were three Lennon–McCartney compositions, two eccentric arrangements of old standards, seven cover versions of fifties songs – encompassing rock and roll, rhythm and blues, and country and western styles – two soft ballads and a contemporary chart hit. At the end of the two-hour session Smith hurried the group out of the studio because he was running late for a second audition he was supervising, with an Essex-based group, Brian Poole and the Tremeloes from Barking. But he still seemed pleased with the Beatles, and their chance of landing a prized recording contract

appeared distinctly favourable. The group returned to Liverpool to await the good news.

In that first week of January 1962 the Beatles' horizon looked decidedly bright. Three days after the Decca audition, on 4 January, *Mersey Beat* published the results of its first-ever group popularity poll. The Beatles were convincingly clear winners over their nearest rivals, Gerry and the Pacemakers, the Remo Four, Rory Storm and the Hurricanes, and Johnny Sandon and the Searchers.[1] The following day saw the official British release by Polydor (under pressure from Brian Epstein) of 'My Bonnie' by Tony Sheridan and the Beatles. The likelihood of it scoring a chart hit was extremely remote, as Epstein knew, but the notoriety and prestige to be gained from having a UK record release was quite considerable. The Beatles added it to their stage repertoire, with John Lennon assuming Sheridan's lead vocal; Epstein added such phrases as 'Polydor Recording Artistes!' or 'Hear the Beatles play their new record' to dance advertisements, posters and handbills.

By the end of January – after, unofficially, just one month and, officially, just one week, under Brian Epstein – the Beatles had a decent management contract, a record in the shops, a possible contract with the mighty Decca organization in the offing, an audition with BBC radio lined up for 12 February, a much superior Hamburg engagement to fulfil, money in their pockets, and a rota of new, vastly improved venues to play. Out went the great majority of the Beatles' 1961 venues, deemed by Epstein to be unsuitable for the 1962 model. Out went the Beatles' uncaring attitude, their childish stage antics, and their renowned reputation for tardiness. Out too went the group's hit-and-miss music presentation, to be replaced by one or two precise, pre-arranged, tight sets of never more than sixty minutes a time.

But perhaps the most significant transformation of all was contained in the large brown paper bags

---

1 In the respective bedrooms of all four Beatles lay dozens of *Mersey Beat*s, all with the voting coupons neatly clipped out, but since every other group on Merseyside had cheated in just the same way the possibility of any unfair advantage was ruled out.

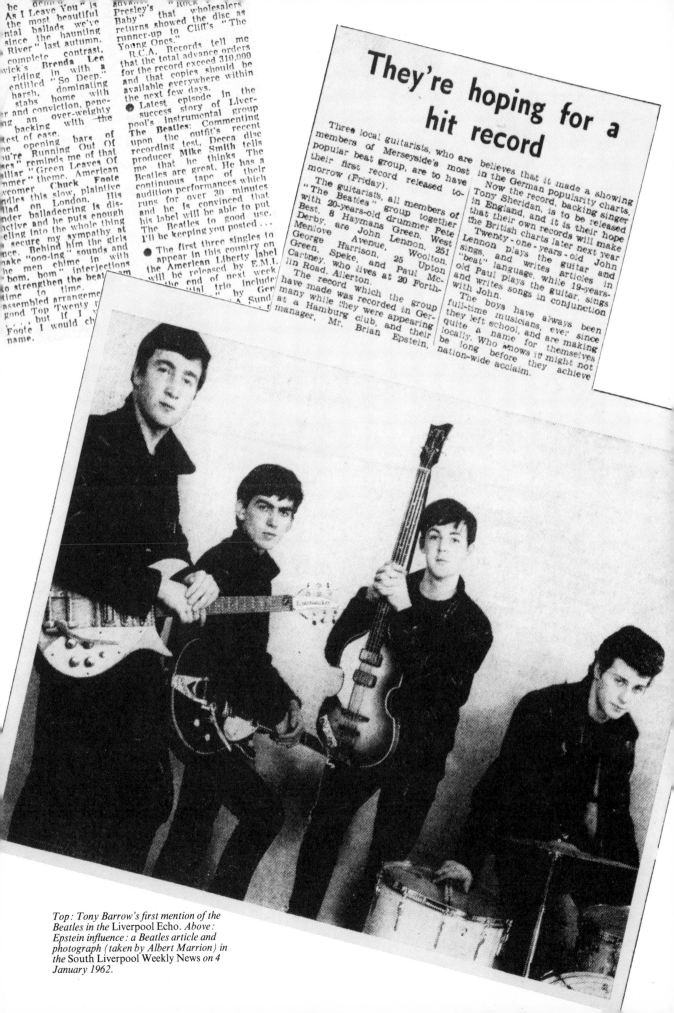

As I Leave You" is
the most beautiful
ntal ballads we've
since the haunting
River" last autumn,
complete contrast,
wick's **Brenda Lee**
riding in with a
entitled "So Deep,"
harsh, dominating
stabs home with
r and conviction, pene-
an over-weighty
backing with the
st of ease.
he opening bars of
ou're Running Out Of
es" reminds me of that
ullar "Green Leaves Of
mmer" theme. American
wcomer **Chuck Foote**
ndles this slow, plaintive
llad on London. His
nder balladeering is dis-
nctive and he puts enough
eling into the whole thing
secure my sympathy at
nce. Behind him the girls
 make "ooo-ing" sounds and
he men chime in with
bom, bom" interjections
o strengthen the beat from
ime to time.
assembled arrangeme
good Top Twenty
but if I
Foote I would ch
name.

advance "ROCK
Presley's
Baby" that wholesalers
returns showed the disc as
runner-up to Cliff's "The
Young Ones."

R.C.A. Records tell me
that the total advance orders
for the record exceed 310,000
and that copies should be
available everywhere within
the next few days.

● Latest episode in the
success story of Liver-
pool's instrumental group
**The Beatles:** Commenting
upon the outfit's recent
recording test, Decca disc
producer **Mike Smith** tells
me that he thinks The
Beatles are great. He has a
continuous tape of their
audition performances which
runs for over 30 minutes
and he is convinced that
his label will be able to put
The Beatles to good use.
I'll be keeping you posted . . .

● The first three singles to
appear in this country on
the American Liberty label
will be released by E.M.I.
the end of next week
vital trio include
by Ger
A Sund

# They're hoping for a hit record

Three local guitarists, who are
members of Merseyside's most
popular beat group, are to have
their first record released to-
morrow (Friday).

The guitarists, all members of
"The Beatles" group together
with 20-years-old drummer Pete
Best, 8 Haymans Green, West
Derby, are John Lennon, 251
Menlove Avenue, Woolton.
George Harrison, 25 Upton
Green, Speke, and Paul Mc-
Cartney, who lives at 20 Forth-
lin Road, Allerton.

The record which the group
have made was recorded in Germany while they were appearing
at a Hamburg club, and their
manager, Mr. Brian Epstein,

believes that it made a showing
in the German popularity charts.

Now the record, backing singer
Tony Sheridan, is to be released
in England, and it is their hope
that their own records will make
the British charts later next year

Twenty - one - years - old John
Lennon plays the guitar and
sings, and writes articles in
"beat" language, while 19-years-
old Paul plays the guitar, and
writes songs in conjunction
with John.

The boys have always been
full-time musicians, ever since
they left school, and are making
quite a name for themselves
locally. Who knows it might not
be long before they achieve
nation-wide acclaim.

*Top: Tony Barrow's first mention of the
Beatles in the* Liverpool Echo. *Above:
Epstein influence: a Beatles article and
photograph (taken by Albert Marrion) in
the* South Liverpool Weekly News *on 4
January 1962.*

carried by each of the Beatles on 24 March into the dressing room of that night's engagement, the Barnston Women's Institute, on the Wirral. For inside each bag was a brand new £40 grey, brushed tweed lounge suit, with pencil-thin lapels and a matching tie, all bought from bespoke tailor Beno Dorn in Birkenhead. From that very moment out, for ever, went the Beatles' desperately dishevelled stage appearance: the black leather outfits, or jeans, and plimsolls. If the group really wanted to make it to the top, Epstein continually reminded them, they had to have a professional attitude and approach, and presentable, respectable appearance. Various Beatles in turn – but principally John Lennon – put up a struggle before bowing to the common sense of Epstein's statement. They had had their own, unique, way for two years and got precisely nowhere in the world of pop music. Anything was worth a try.

On 7 March 1962 at 8:00 p.m. the Beatles congregated around three microphones in the Playhouse Theatre, St John's Road, Manchester, and recorded their debut broadcast session for BBC radio. Even without a finalized record contract, the Beatles had managed to pass their BBC audition on 12 February, and had been booked by producer Peter Pilbeam to appear on his show *Teenager's Turn (Here We Go)*,

*June 1962. Another photo session with Albert Marrion, the four Beatles this time each dressed in a natty Beno Dorn suit, shirt and tie.*

alongside the resident Brad Newman, the Trad Lads, and the Northern Dance Orchestra. When the recording started and the Beatles performed three numbers, Roy Orbison's 'Dream Baby (How Long Must I Dream?)', Chuck Berry's 'Memphis, Tennessee' and the Marvelettes' 'Please Mister Postman', the specially invited Playhouse audience broke into spontaneous, ecstatic applause. At that moment Epstein and the Beatles saw, for the first time, that their infectious brand of music really could catch on outside the confines of Merseyside or Hamburg. Their dream was not an impossibility.[2]

But within days of the four Beatles eagerly tuning their respective radios into the BBC Light Programme wavelength, and hearing their own sound coming from the speakers, they and Brian Epstein received a bombshell of immense proportions. Decca turned them down.

If the Beatles themselves were incensed and disillusioned at their failure, Brian Epstein was positively smarting in the face of his first hitch. The capture of a recording contract was *the* essential ingredient in his master plan to establish the Beatles in the entertainment world. And it had seemed such a formality too. Decca's Mike Smith had seen the group on two occasions and been enthusiastic both times. And why had the company taken two months to decide that the Beatles were unsuitable for their requirements? The reason put forward: that they sounded too much like the Shadows, and that – besides – 'guitar groups are on the way out' was pure folly.

Epstein vowed to pursue the matter and travelled to London to meet Dick Rowe, the head of Decca's singles A&R department, and S. A. Beecher-Stevens, the company's sales manager. But the Decca men could not be budged. Kindly, but somewhat conciliatorily, they cooed, 'The Beatles won't go, Mr Epstein. We know these things. You have a good record business in Liverpool, why not stick to that?' The red-faced, hot-headed Epstein quickly lost his remaining cool. 'You must be out of your minds,' he ranted, 'these boys are going to explode. I am com-

pletely confident that one day they will be bigger than Elvis Presley!' The important Decca men afforded themselves a wry smile; they heard that one every day from every manager of every struggling pop group in the land.

Although convinced in his beliefs, Epstein had a foot in the door at Decca and was reluctant to sever the tenuous link altogether. He toyed with the idea of offering to buy up 3000 copies of any Beatles single released by the company, but then decided against it. He also, the next day, had a meeting with Tony Meehan, former Shadows drummer and then an independent producer, with a view to buying some studio time at a cost of £100 and having Meehan professionally produce a single. But Meehan kept the ever-punctual Epstein waiting and when the meeting finally started he was disparaging towards the Beatles, viewing them as just another no-hope group taking up his valuable time. Epstein, in indignation, dropped the idea.[3]

With the benefit of hindsight, the real reason behind Decca's now infamous rejection of the Beatles is simple to comprehend. Mike Smith, only two years in the A&R department, auditioned two beat groups on 1 January 1962 – the Beatles and Brian Poole and the Tremeloes – but because of his relative inex-

---

**2** This session was the start of a long and enormously productive relationship between the Beatles and BBC radio, and the group recorded three more programmes in 1962, on 11 June, 25 October and 27 November.

**3** This account of Brian Epstein's meeting with Tony Meehan, based on Epstein's autobiography *A Cellarful of Noise*, differs from Meehan's own version, recounted to the author in November 1984. Meehan says that his five-minute chat with Epstein was 'friendly and constructive' and places the blame for Decca's mis-handling of the Beatles squarely on Dick Rowe. 'It was simply a dreadful corporate blunder,' rues Meehan.

*Below: Brian's hard-earned and much-improved contract for the Beatles' next Hamburg trip. Below: Bert Kaempfert's gracious waiving of his Beatles contract, enabling Brian Epstein to seek a UK deal without complication.*

perience Dick Rowe permitted him to sign just one of them. He chose the latter group, not because they were more promising but purely and simply because they were based in Barking, just eight miles from his office. They would be far easier, and cheaper, to work with than a group based 200 miles away. So Decca Records let the Beatles go and, more than coincidentally, began its disastrous slide into oblivion.

While the Beatles, and in particular John Lennon, had convinced themselves that Epstein had lost them their chance of a recording contract by his interfering with what they knew best – their music – by insisting that they perform *his* selection of material rather than their more familiar repertoire, their next trip to Hamburg came along. The seeds of the visit – their third – had been sown in late December 1961 when Peter Eckhorn, owner of the Top Ten Club, accompanied by singer Tony Sheridan, came over to Liverpool to sign up some groups for 1962. But when Eckhorn approached the Beatles he came up against a new obstacle. Brian Epstein. And Epstein – in keeping with his stated management policy, and keen to assert his proprietary role in his first-ever dealings with a Hamburg club owner – wanted more money for the Beatles' services than the group had previously required: 500 DM per man per week. Eckhorn was flabbergasted at the thought of paying 2000 DM a week for a pop group and offered an already generous maximum of 450 DM per man. Epstein magnanimously agreed to consider the deal and let Eckhorn know his decision in due course. Eckhorn left Liverpool without the Beatles contract on 30 December 1961. Three weeks later Horst Fascher, former bouncer at both Bruno Koschmider's Kaiserkeller and Eckhorn's Top Ten clubs, arrived in Liverpool. He had been lured away from Eckhorn by Manfred Weissleder, a prominent Hamburg club owner who was planning to open an enormous rock venue, as yet unnamed but tentatively titled The Twist Club, eclipsing even the sizable Top Ten. Fascher was appointed as manager and sent to England with musician Roy Young to get – no expense spared – the biggest opening night attraction possible for the club, the Beatles. Fascher, too, came up against Epstein but was better prepared than his adversary Eckhorn had been. The desired 500 DM per man was duly offered and a contract was drawn up then and there, engaging the Beatles for seven weeks, from 13 April until 31 May 1962.

The Beatles' train-travelling days were over, with Epstein extravagantly arranging for the group to fly to Hamburg. On Wednesday 11 April John, Paul and Pete flew out of Ringway Airport, Manchester, bound for Hamburg. George, who was unwell, flew

# Mother flies home with son's body

An Aigburth mother returned home from Hamburg last Monday with the body of her son, who had died suddenly. Mrs. Millie Sutcliffe, aged 54, of 37 Aigburth Drive flew to Germany last Friday night after she had received a telegram telling her that her 21-years-old son Stuart had died last Tuesday in the arms of his German fiancee while being sped in an ambulance to a Hamburg Hospital.

Stuart's father, Mr. Charles Sutcliffe, was sailing for South America, but he cannot be told of the tradegy for at least another three weeks as he has a bad heart and the news could prove fatal. The family have arranged for a padre to meet the ship in Buenos Aires and break the news to Mr. Sutcliffe.

Stuart—whose whole life was devoted to painting—went to Germany 18-months-ago with a city skiffle group. He intended staying in Germany for only three months, but while there he met 23-years-old Astrid Kirchner, and he decided to stay on and enter Hamburg College of Art. They planned to marry when he had finished his course in June.

A former pupil of Prescot Grammar School and the Liverpool College of Art, Stuart was described by a master as a brilliant student.

In a recent art exhibition in Liverpool, millionaire John Moores bought one of Stuart's paintings. Said his 20-years-old sister Joyce: "Stuart lived for painting. His whole life was devoted to the subject, and his greatest wish was to have an exhibition of his own in Liverpool."

A few weeks ago, he paid a surprise visit to his family, but his sister said that he appeared very quiet and not at all his usual self.

Joyce added: "We had a letter last Monday saying that Stuart had been taken ill and doctors could not diagnose the trouble."

A post-mortem was made before Mrs. Sutcliffe flew home on Sunday with her son's body. A blood clot on the brain was given as the cause of his death.

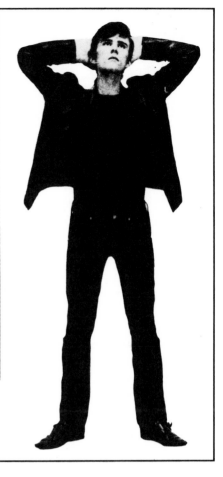

*The death of Stuart Sutcliffe: Sutcliffe was possibly the first, but certainly not the last of the Beatles' close associates to die tragically.*

out the following day with Brian Epstein. But when the first entourage arrived in Hamburg they were met at the airport by a distraught Astrid Kirchherr. Stuart Sutcliffe, her fiancé, a truly gifted artist, the former Beatles bass player, and John Lennon's closest friend, was dead, aged just 21. He had died of a brain haemorrhage the previous day, 10 April, in Astrid's arms, in an ambulance *en route* for the hospital.

Although they reacted in widely differing ways, John, Paul and Pete were utterly devastated by the loss of their friend. As was George Harrison, and even Brian Epstein who, in his short time with the Beatles, had heard much about Sutcliffe's talents. On Friday 13 April, the same day the Beatles opened at the by now re-named and christened Star-Club, Stuart's grieving mother, Millie Sutcliffe, arrived in Hamburg to undergo the dreadful ritual of formally identifying her dead son, and to take him back home to rest in Liverpool.

Over the following two decades, into the eighties, a school of thought developed believing that Stuart's death was a direct result of a fight outside a Liverpool dance hall after a Silver Beetles gig in 1960, during which he received a hefty kick to the head.

Brian Epstein, having overseen the Beatles' safe arrival in Hamburg, met Manfred Weissleder, owner of the Star-Club, and observed the first two nights of the Beatles' seven-week stint there, flew back to England and prepared himself for one last all-or-nothing onslaught on the record companies. Armed with the only tangible result of the failed audition for Decca – two reel-to-reel tapes containing the fifteen allegedly ill-chosen songs – Epstein travelled by train from Liverpool to London.

He went first to Pye, then to Oriole and Philips, and then to EMI's two giant labels, Columbia (which housed, among others, Cliff Richard), and HMV. At each and every one the reply was the same: a polite, or impolite, but always emphatic 'No'. In desperation, on the morning of 8 May 1962, Brian Epstein walked into the huge HMV record store on London's Oxford Street. He had heard that it contained a small department which, for a £1 10s fee, could transfer tape recordings on to black acetate discs. Epstein rightly believed that this would be a more impressive way to present the Beatles' music than with unwieldy tapes. As the engineer, Ted Huntly, was cutting the discs, he could not help but listen to them, and was sufficiently impressed to ask Epstein whether the publishing rights to the three Lennon–McCartney songs 'Love of the Loved', 'Hello Little Girl' and 'Like Dreamers Do' were still available. When he ascertained that they were, he excused himself to an adjoining office, picked up the internal telephone, and dialled a number. Situated on the top floor of the building, above the shop, was the headquarters of Ardmore and Beechwood, long-standing British music publishers and a subsidiary of EMI Publishing.

Within minutes, tightly clutching his newly-pressed, sweet-smelling acetates, Epstein was in the office of 55-year-old Sidney Coleman, the director and general manager of the company, and talking business. Coleman, too, liked the sound of the Beatles, and offered to publish at least two of the three Lennon–McCartney compositions. But while Epstein was cheered with this offer, the first piece of good news he had received during his long and fruitless search, what he *really* wanted for the Beatles was a recording – not a publishing – contract. Coleman could see the point and offered to refer Epstein to a friend of his, George Martin, head of A&R at Parlophone Records, another subsidiary of EMI, though much less prestigious and successful than the illustrious Columbia and HMV. Coleman phoned Martin's secretary Judy Lockhart-Smith (later to be Martin's second wife), and arranged for Epstein to go across Oxford Street to EMI's principal building on Manchester Square, and make an appointment. This done, a meeting with George Martin was set for the following day, Wednesday 9 May, at the Abbey Road recording studios in St John's Wood, north London.

Brian Epstein spent a sleepless night at the Green Park Hotel in Half Moon Street, situated off Piccadilly, and in the morning took a taxi to Abbey Road where he met Martin for the first time. Martin was unlike any A&R man Epstein had come across. He was clearly well educated, and well spoken, but without being snobbish or superior. And at 36 years old he was certainly the youngest head of A&R of any major label in Britain. Martin was only too aware that he was in charge of EMI's 'joke label' – christened thus not just because it released many comedy records, but because it was the poor relation of EMI, with the smallest budget and releases-to-hits ratio – despite having Adam Faith and Shane Fenton on its roster. He liked the look of Epstein, the earnest, extremely polite manager of an unknown Liverpool pop group. Epstein began on his sanguine sales pitch,

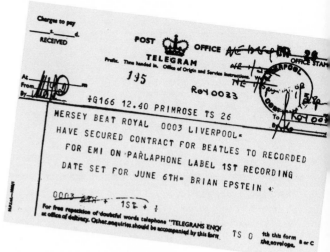

*Brian Epstein's telegram to* Mersey Beat. *The date, 9 May, and the place of despatch, Primrose (Hill, near Abbey Road studios), prove every account of the Beatles story to date wrong (see footnote).*

saying how huge the Beatles were on Merseyside, and then expressing great, and by now well-practised, mock-surprise when Martin said that he hadn't heard of them. Then Epstein played Martin the discs cut the previous day, and held his breath.

There was something in the music, a certain indefinable quality, which appealed to George Martin as to no other A&R man. The unusual, quirky harmonies perhaps, the rough-hewn yet somehow pleasant-sounding instrumentation. Martin, it must be said, wasn't *over*impressed, just sufficiently curious to offer Epstein a provisional recording contract for the Beatles. Shortly after midday, Epstein left Abbey Road studios cock-a-hoop, and veritably sprinted to the post office on nearby Wellington Road to convey the good news to the interested parties. He telephoned first his parents, and then sent two telegrams. The first, to the Beatles in Hamburg, read, 'Congratulations boys. EMI request recording session. Please rehearse new material.' The second, to Bill Harry at *Mersey Beat*, read, 'Have secured contract for Beatles to recorded [sic] for EMI on Parlaphone [sic] label. First recording date set for June 6th.' Two days *before* that first session/commercial test, on Monday 4 June, the Beatles and EMI Records signed and sealed their first contract.[4]

The Beatles' seven-week engagement at the Star-Club came to an end on 31 May, and on 2 June the

---

4 All the dates and venues in this, and the preceding three paragraphs, are correct, and have been taken from infallible, documentary evidence, including surviving telegrams and letters, and the actual EMI contract. Yet this very, unshakeable evidence completely differs from and contradicts every previously published report of the sequence of events, including even Brian Epstein's and George Martin's autobiographies, published in 1964 and 1979

group flew back to Ringway Airport, Manchester. After a well-deserved two days of rest, punctuated only by a private Cavern Club rehearsal behind-closed-doors, the group travelled to EMI House in Manchester Square, in London's West End, on 4 June to sign their prestigious contract. Two days later, on Wednesday 6 June, the group arrived at Abbey Road studios for their debut recording session. All but the ever-reticent drummer Pete Best got on famously with George Martin. He himself impressed the Beatles by revealing that it was he who had produced the solo comedy records by Goons members Peter Sellers and Spike Milligan. John Lennon and George Harrison, particularly, counted these records among their personal favourites. The Beatles, meanwhile, impressed Martin with their irrepressible, irreverent humour, and their apparent ease in what were usually nerve-wracking conditions. One quote, which has since gone down in Beatles folklore, sums up both the group's humour and that first meeting with Martin, and merits a repeat mention here. Martin, his assistant Ron Richards, and recording engineer Norman Smith (a decade later to score three surprise Top Ten hits of his own, under the name of Hurricane Smith) had come to the end of a long, stern lecture about the rights, wrongs, whys and wherefores of recording, and what they would expect from the Beatles in the future. During this time the four Beatles had sat very quietly and attentively. Then George Martin said, 'Right. Is there anything you don't like?' A long hush followed, with each Beatle glancing from one to another, before George Harrison took a long, serious look at Martin and spoke above the silence. 'Yeah. I don't like your tie!'

Four songs were taped on that first visit to Abbey Road, under the principal direction not of George Martin but his assistant, Ron Richards. The first, 'Besame Mucho', was a rock arrangement of an old standard, while the other three were all Lennon–McCartney compositions: 'P.S. I Love You', 'Ask Me Why' and 'Love Me Do'.

The Beatles rejoined the Merseyside nightly engagements scene on 9 June, their enormous popularity undiminished despite their two-month absence. At a Welcome Home night at the Cavern the club's record attendance figure was shattered.

Long queues, stretching the length of Mathew Street, would form hours before Beatles appearances there, even the lunchtime gigs. On 11 June a coachload of Cavernites, with their four Beatle heroes on board, made its way to the Playhouse Theatre in Manchester for the group's second BBC radio recording. After the programme had been taped Beatles hysteria spread to the nearby Manchester streets and, in the mêlée, the coach returned to Liverpool without Pete Best, left stranded and alone. It was to prove a symbolic moment for the luckless Beatles drummer.

That summer of 1962 Brian Epstein was booking the Beatles into ever-improving local venues, and slowly but surely – and certainly with more than a little naïvety – securing them invaluable out-of-town dates too, in such places as Stroud, Northwich, Rhyl, Doncaster, Swindon, Morecambe and Lydney. On 7 June Brian and his brother, Clive John Epstein, put down an initial share capital of £100 on a new venture designed to control Brian's show-business aspirations. Sixteen days later NEMS Enterprises was officially registered. And on 28 June the Beatles made their debut at the Majestic Ballroom in Birkenhead, not in itself a particularly auspicious event but, put into its proper perspective, a prominent landmark, and one which can be seen to illustrate perfectly the way Brian Epstein was handling the Beatles in the crucial middle months of 1962.

The Majestic was a Top Rank venue, one of 28 such ballrooms dotted around the UK which belonged to the massive entertainments giant. From Bill Marsden, manager of the Majestic at Birkenhead, Epstein ascertained the name of the company's theatre division manager, L. B. (Len) Fancourt, and wrote to him praising the Beatles and announcing their availability to Top Rank. Fancourt filed this with the dozens of similar letters received every week from hopeful pop-group managers. He sent Epstein the standard reply – a list of all the names and addresses of every ballroom they operated, with a short note to the effect of 'try them yourself'. Epstein did just that. From Aberdeen to Plymouth and Crewe to Kilburn each and every ballroom manager received an immaculately typed letter, on newly-designed NEMS Enterprises notepaper, beginning with the grandiloquent opening gambit 'L. B. Fancourt has personally suggested I write to you concerning the possible engagement of my group, the Beatles . . . .' These letters invariably also carried a line like 'I must tell you that the group is very heavily booked as far ahead as October [or whatever month was three months after the post date] but I might just be able to squeeze you in . . . .' Amazingly, it worked, and the Beatles were to play eleven of the twenty-eight

*Two typical mid-1962 Beatles engagements,
one at a Wirral jazz club, the other
supporting a major star of the day.*

Top Rank ballrooms within twelve months of the Birkenhead debut.

During the Beatles' first eight weeks back in England after Hamburg, from 6 June to 31 July, they fulfilled a staggering total of 61 live engagements, plus two recording sessions – one for EMI and the other for the BBC. Each week Brian Epstein would prepare neatly typed 'accounts statements' for the four Beatles and Neil Aspinall, showing precise details of the past seven days' bookings with fees, expenses and commission all calculated to the last penny, and also giving details and relevant instructions for the coming week's engagements. Here Brian would stress the need for punctuality and smart appearance, and underline – often literally – why each and every gig was of particular importance to the group. The week's bookings would invariably include a Wednesday-night session and a quota of two or three lunchtime gigs at the Cavern Club (usually in the form of Monday, Wednesday, Friday one week, Tuesday and Thursday the next), plus at least one 'major' appearance, either in Southport, on the Wirral, or out of town. At these engagements Epstein would incongruously break the Beatles' one-hour stage spot into two separate half-hour sets, to tantalize the audience and also prepare the Beatles for the day when they would hit the big time. This, after all, was how the *stars* appeared live.

In Skegness, Lincolnshire, 161 miles away across the breadth of Britain, one of the most incredible strokes of good fortune in show-business history was about to touch a small-built, sad-eyed, 22-year-old Liverpudlian, earning a meagre summer wage playing drums with a group called Rory Storm and the Hurricanes at the town's Butlin's holiday camp. His name was Richard Starkey, known as Ritchie to his friends, or Ringo Starr on stage, and on 14 August 1962 he was plucked from almost certain obscurity to the bosom of the Beatles in one fell swoop.

The Beatles had been contemplating the dismissal of Pete Best for some considerable time and, in their own deliberate way, were gradually divorcing him from their activities. Best, for example, did not learn of the group's failure at the Decca audition for some time after the others because they 'forgot' to tell him. A plan was hatching in the minds of John, Paul and George to oust him once and for all. It was based largely on jealousy. Jealousy of Pete's good looks, and the way he attracted the better girls. But it also had deeper, more fundamental roots. Best's drumming ability, though adequate, was quite limited, and was almost certainly unsuitable for recording purposes, a theory echoed by George Martin after the

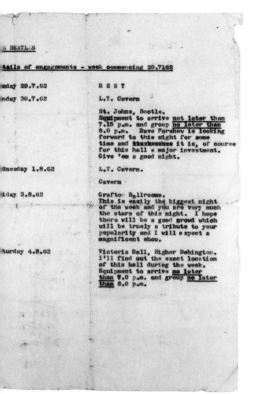

*One of Brian's accounts sheets for Paul McCartney, showing dates played, fees received, expenses and net total, and the week's engagements to come. Precious few of these important documents exist today.*

6 June session. Best's personality was also markedly different from those of the other three Beatles. They were witty, brash and exuberant, he was painfully shy and reserved. He had also steadfastly refused to restyle his hair into the Beatle cut like the other three and, as a consequence, he *looked* out of place too. These were the principal reasons behind Best's dismissal, and while so-called 'insiders' privy to the group may still claim, as always, that they know other, more salacious reasons, the remaining Beatles had decided that enough was enough. Best had to go.

Despite the aforementioned alleged shortcomings, it was still shabby treatment for the lad who had served the group unstintingly from their hapless, drummer-less, Silver Beatles days, through three lengthy Hamburg seasons, and over two hundred Cavern Club performances. He had shared in the heartaches and the headaches, the glory and the gloom, controlled the Beatles' bookings before Epstein, and made his home – the Casbah – their home. The Beatles had had two years in which to remove him, but didn't, and now with the group beginning to reap the benefits of the long, hard slog, with money rolling in and an EMI recording contract secured, he was out. Cut and dried. It was the most underhand, unfortunate and unforgivable chapter in the Beatles' monumental rise to power.

Brian Epstein, as manager, was given the thankless, unsavoury task of breaking the news to Pete Best, and summoned him to a meeting in his office at the NEMS Whitechapel shop at eleven o'clock on the morning of Thursday 16 August. Half an hour later a dumbstruck Best, along with his buddy Neil Aspinall, was drowning his sorrows in Liverpool ale. Within hours the news leaked out and there was a minor uproar among Beatles fans, for many of whom Pete Best was the favourite. Brian Epstein needed protection to walk down Mathew Street for a few days, and his shining new Ford motor car was badly scratched. And on 19 August, after the Beatles performed at the Cavern Club with Ringo Starr for the first time, there were scuffles outside the club, and George Harrison received a shining black left eye.

For Pete Best the agony of then sitting on the sidelines and watching the Beatles scale unparalleled heights in show business throughout the rest of the decade was compounded by his abysmal failure to become a success himself. In September 1962, out of an act of kindness and largesse, Brian Epstein set Best up as drummer in another Liverpool combo, Lee Curtis and the All-Stars,[5] managed by Epstein's friend Joe Flannery whose brother Peter actually was 'Lee Curtis' (so named because his favourite singer was the American, Curtis Lee). But although the group was second only to the Beatles in travelling

---

5 Epstein initially offered Best the opportunity of joining the Merseybeats but he turned this down.

# RICHARD REALISES A BOYHOOD AMBITION

**R**ICHARD STARKEY always wanted to be a drum. From when he was a small boy he was alv tapping his fingers.

He has been in hospital twice, and has had 12 operations, several of them major ones.

When he came out last time after two years spent mostly in bed, he looked around for something to do—and started his fingers tapping again.

So he saved up and spent £10 on a second-hand drum kit and set about teaching himself to play.

After two months' hard practice he joined a group. And now, with a new drum kit costing £125, he is entertaining hundreds of teenagers at a Pwllheli (North Wales) holiday camp as a member of Rory Storm's Hurricanes.

All five of them Liverpool lads, are packing the camp's rock and calypso ballroom each evening for three-hour jive sessions.

Working a 16-hour week they spend their spare time joining in all the fun of the camp, swimming, sport and sunbathing.

"It's as good as a holiday—and we get paid for it," said 20-years-old Richard—he lives in Admiral Grove, Dingle—during a break in the rock session.

His suntanned face broke into a smile as he added: fabulous."

## PROFESSIONAL CAREEF

Richard—he plays under name of Ringo Starr—is second ex-pupil of St. C. of E. School, Dingle, to n a professional career in and roll.

The first—Ronnie Wychei now carving a niche for hin as Billy Fury.

It is the group's biggest tract so far; before they fi dates at Liverpool jazz clubs had a spot in a rock show Liverpool Stadium in May, wh starred Gene Vincent and was have featured Eddie Cochr But he was killed a few d before.

Led by ex-cotton samplen Rory Storm (his real name Alan Caldwell) whose home at 54 Broadgreen Road, Stone croft, the group has been pla ing together for just 10 month

The other members — L Walters, 22 (bass guitar an vocal), Ty Brian, 19 (lea guitarist), Johnny Guitar, (rhythm guitar and vocal) and Richard, all belonged to othe groups before that.

When they finish their 1 week engagement

*Mementos from Ringo Starr's pre-Beatles career. Above: Performing stand-up drumming with the Eddie Clayton Skiffle Group at the Wilson Hall, Garston, 23 May 1957. Right: A local newspaper article dated 25 August 1960. Bottom: Looning on stage with the Hurricanes at St Luke's Hall, Crosby, October 1961. Opposite: Standing, left, with Rory and the Hurricanes, Butlins Pwllheli summer 1960. Also left to right: Ty Brian, Rory, Lou Walters (Wally), Johnny Guitar.*

down to London to record, they became bogged down in the quagmire of Liverpool combos trying to make the charts in 1963, and eventually Curtis left to pursue a solo career. The group, re-named Pete Best and the All-Stars, plodded on, and in July 1964, under the revised name of the Pete Best Four, they released a flop single for Decca, 'I'm Gonna Knock on your Door'. Although the record came about as a result of his ex-Beatle status, Best was finding the tag a considerable, inescapable millstone around his neck. Eventually he succumbed to the avaricious demands of a few American record-industry sharks, and released a succession of dire, low-budget records, culminating in one dreadful 1966 album, deceptively and quite deliberately titled *Best of the Beatles. They* ensured he styled his hair into a Beatle Cut. But there was worse to come, and by 1968 Pete Best had abandoned his show-business career for ever in favour of a steady job in a Liverpool bakery. From there he moved into a clerical position in local government, which is where he is to this day. For many years Best remained a recluse, shying away from all journalists, radio and TV men attempting to interview him, but in 1978 he re-surfaced in the role of technical adviser to an American television production, *Birth of the*

*Beatles*, and in 1985 his autobiography, *Beatle!*, was published.

It is a little-known but most certainly true and verifiable fact that Brian Epstein initially approached sturdy Johnny Hutchinson of the Big Three to fill the vacancy in the Beatles, but Hutch, who disliked the Beatles intensely, turned the job down. So on the morning of Tuesday 14 August Brian Epstein, and then John Lennon, called Butlin's in Skegness and put out a message over the camp's public address system for Richard Starkey to come to the telephone. As it transpired, Ringo had been unsettled with Rory Storm and the Hurricanes for some time. After graduating through the Eddie Clayton Skiffle Group in 1957 and 1958, he first drummed with the Raving Texans on 25 March 1959 at the Mardi-Gras club in Mount Pleasant, Liverpool, though he didn't join the group on a permanent basis until that November, by which time, via a succession of three name changes, they had become Rory Storm and the Hur-

ricanes.[6] In May 1960 the band secured a valuable summer season engagement at Butlin's in Pwllheli, North Wales, commencing 4 June, but Ringo announced that he wasn't going; he was getting married that same month. But the wedding was cancelled, and Ringo went to Butlin's instead and then, in October, on to Hamburg with the group to play at the Kaiserkeller. It was here that Ringo first came into regular contact with the Beatles. The two parties took an almost immediate liking to one another, and it was Starr, not Pete Best, who accompanied Walter Eymond and the Beatles to the tiny recording studio in Hamburg to record 'Summertime' that October.

One year later, in October 1961, after a second summer engagement at Butlin's in Pwllheli, Ringo became restless again. He had always been

---

6 The other two names were, in September 1959, Al Storm and the Hurricanes, and in October 1959, Jett Storm and the Hurricanes.

*Rocking at the Cavern Club with a new drummer.*

enamoured with Wild West movies so he wrote to the Houston Chamber of Commerce in Texas, USA, expressing interest in emigration. But while the reply was not unfavourable, Ringo became disheartened by the sight of so many application forms and abandoned the idea. Nevertheless, three months later, he did quit the Hurricanes to work overseas, though not in Houston but in Hamburg. On 30 December 1961 he left Lime Street station with Peter Eckhorn and Tony Sheridan, to be the drummer behind Sheridan in the house band at the Top Ten Club. But by March 1962[7] Ringo had grown tired of the argumentative Sheridan, and he left Hamburg for a re-claimed place with Rory Storm on a working holiday in France and then, back in England, for a third season with Butlin's, this time at Skegness.

When John Lennon's telephone call came through offering Ringo the chance to join the Beatles for an initial 'wage' of £25 per week, Rory Storm and his group were just fifteen days away from completing the three-month Butlin's stint. But the Beatles' need was urgent, and as Ringo had been keen to join them for quite some time – he had even sat in with them

on two occasions when Pete Best was ill[8] – he gave Rory three days' notice, and on Saturday 18 August 1962 took his place at the drum kit behind the Beatles at the Hulme Hall in Port Sunlight, near Birkenhead. On that night the Fab Four was born.

Pete Best wasn't the only casualty in the saga surrounding the appointment of Ringo Starr in the Beatles. The popularity of Rory Storm and the Hurricanes, at one time arguably the top rock group on Merseyside, had already suffered a considerable slump as a result of the group's long and regular absences away from the bustling Liverpool scene. Placed fourth in the 1961 *Mersey Beat* group popularity poll, they dropped to seventeenth in the 1962 ballot. After Starr's departure they tried a succession of drummers without any joy and when, in the wake of the Beatles' success, every major record company in Britain rushed to Liverpool to sign up anybody or everybody, the likeable and talented Rory somehow missed the boat. He released just a handful of obscure records over the years without success, including one, a rock version of the *West Side Story* song, 'America', on Parlophone in November 1964 which was actually produced by Brian Epstein. But the fickle hand of fate had chosen to leave Rory behind. On 15 August 1965, on the same night that the Beatles played to a world-record-breaking crowd of 55,600 people at their celebrated Shea Stadium gig in New York, Rory Storm and the

---

**7** Ringo was not, as has been suggested in many Beatles books, in Hamburg in April 1962 when the Beatles arrived in town to play at the Star-Club.

**8** Both were Cavern Club lunchtime sessions, the dates untraceable by the author.

Hurricanes were still to be found playing at the Orrell Park Ballroom in Liverpool. And on 27 September 1972, at the age of 32, Rory, depressed over the death of his father eight months previously, died in a double suicide pact with his mother, Violet.

The Best/Starr controversy had one further complication – Neil Aspinall. Neil was a close friend of Pete and for a while had actually lived in the Best household in Hayman's Green, West Derby. But he was also the Beatles' loyal, hard-working road manager, and a good one at that. When Pete Best was sacked from the group Aspinall was left sitting on the fence, with the unenviable problem of whom to side with. To Brian Epstein's and the remaining Beatles' everlasting relief, he chose them.

On 22 August, four days after Ringo Starr had joined the Beatles, a camera crew from Granada Television came down to the Cavern Club lunchtime session and captured on celluloid not just the only film of the Beatles playing in the Cavern but also the first of hundreds of television appearances the group would make in the ensuing years.[9] It is remarkable for one other reason too. Right at the very end of the soundtrack one can clearly hear a lone voice in the audience cry 'We want Pete!' Amazingly, the hectic activities of this one week in August were still not over, for less than 24 hours after the visit from the Granada film crew, on Thursday 23 August, John Lennon married Cynthia Powell at the Mount Pleasant Register Office in Liverpool. And that night, the centuries-old customary wedding-night ritual was forsaken in favour of an important Beatles gig at the Riverpark Ballroom in Chester.

Although the Beatles' initial EMI recording session on 6 June had been a success, the numbers taped were not deemed to be of sufficiently good quality, so on 4 September John, Paul, George and Ringo flew down to London from Liverpool Airport to attend a second session with George Martin at Abbey Road studios. It was, of course, Ringo Starr's first recording, and Martin knew nothing of the sacking of Pete Best or of his replacement. Two numbers were taped at this session, 'Love Me Do', and 'How Do You Do It', the latter a song composed by Mitch Murray, a typical-of-the-era pop tunesmith from Tin Pan Alley. The Beatles thoroughly resented having to perform a song they didn't like, or choose themselves, although this was established procedure in the late fifties and early sixties. (Indeed it was the Beatles who singlehandedly revolutionized the role of the artist in the recording studio, and their in-house success sounded the death knell for Tin Pan Alley.) The group made no attempt to disguise their patent dislike for the Mitch Murray song throughout the recording session.

Yet again Martin was dissatisfied, and he summoned the Beatles down to London for a third attempt one week later, on 11 September. This time

*Making a mockery of the long-held view that EMI didn't promote 'Love Me Do', here is a full-page advert they put in* Record Retailer *a week before release. It was the only time EMI did this, for any artist/group, in the entire year.*

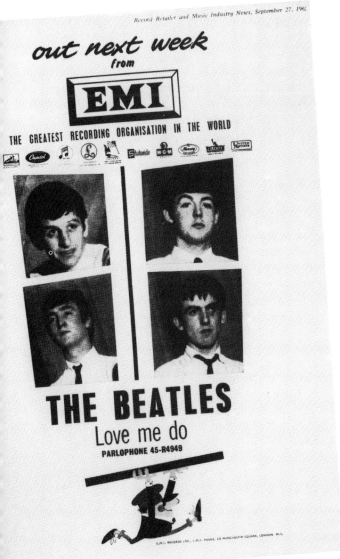

*Record Retailer and Music Industry News, September 27, 1962*

---

**9** The Beatles appeared on television on four occasions in 1962: on Granada's *People and Places* on 17 October (live) and 17 December (live); on TWW's *Discs-A-GoGo* on 3 December (live) and on Associated-Rediffusion's *Tuesday Rendezvous* (live) on 4 December. A further appearance planned for Granada's *People and Places*, on 2 November, was scrapped. It was to have been pre-recorded on 29 October. The film shot in the Cavern Club was of poor quality and was not shown on television until after the Beatles were famous.

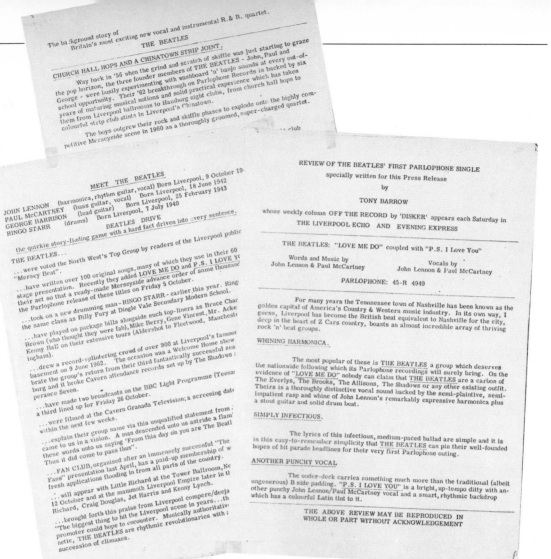

The background story of
Britain's most exciting new vocal and instrumental R.& B. quartet.

THE BEATLES

## CHURCH HALL HOPS AND A CHINATOWN STRIP JOINT.

Way back in '56 when the grind and scratch of skiffle was just starting to graze the pop horizon, the three founder members of THE BEATLES - John, Paul and George - were busily experimenting with washboard 'n' banjo sounds at every out-of-school opportunity. Their '62 breakthrough on Parlophone Records is backed by six years of maturing musical notions and solid practical experience which has taken them from Liverpool ballrooms to Hamburg night clubs, from church hall hops to colourful strip club stints in Liverpool's Chinatown.

The boys outgrew their rock and skiffle phases to explode onto the highly competitive Merseyside scene in 1960 as a thoroughly groomed, super-charged quartet.

... club

## MEET THE BEATLES

JOHN LENNON (harmonica, rhythm guitar, vocal) Born Liverpool, 9 October 19.
PAUL McCARTNEY (bass guitar, vocal) Born Liverpool, 18 June 1942
GEORGE HARRISON (lead guitar) Born Liverpool, 25 February 1943
RINGO STARR (drums) Born Liverpool, 7 July 1940

## BEATLES DRIVE

the quickie story-finding game with a hard fact driven into every sentence.

THE BEATLES...

...were voted the North West's Top Group by readers of the Liverpool public "Mersey Beat".

...have written over 100 original songs, many of which they use in their 60 stage presentation. Recently they added LOVE ME DO and P.S. I LOVE YO their act so that a ready-made Merseyside advance order of some thousand the Parlophone release of these titles on Friday 5 October.

...took on a new drumming man - RINGO STARR - earlier this year. Ring the same class as Billy Fury at Dingle Vale Secondary Modern School.

...have played on package bills alongside such top-liners as Bruce Chan Brown (who thought they were fab), Mike Berry, Gene Vincent, Mr. Acke Kenny Ball on their extensive tours (Aldershot to Fleetwood, Manchester ingham).

...drew a record-splintering crowd of over 900 at Liverpool's famous basement on 9 June 1962. The occasion was a Welcome Home show brate the group's return from their third fantastically successful sea burg and it broke Cavern attendance records set up by The Shadows a perance Seven.

...have made two broadcasts on the BBC Light Programme (Teena a third lined up for Friday 26 October.

...were filmed at the Cavern Granada Television; a screening dat within the next few weeks.

...explain their group name via this unqualified statement from : came to us in a vision. A man descended unto us astride a flam these words unto us saying 'From this day on you are The Beatl Thus it did come to pass thus".

...FAN CLUB, organised after an immensely successful "The Fans" presentation last April, has a paid-up membership of w fresh applications flooding in from all parts of the country.

...will appear with Little Richard at the Tower Ballroom, N 12 October and at the mammoth Liverpool Empire later in th Richard, Craig Douglas, Jet Harris and Kenny Lynch.

...brought forth this praise from Liverpool compere/deeja "The biggest thing to hit the Liverpool scene in years...th promoter could hope to encounter. Musically authoritativ netic, THE BEATLES are rhythmic revolutionaries with a succession of climaxes.

## REVIEW OF THE BEATLES' FIRST PARLOPHONE SINGLE

specially written for this Press Release

by

### TONY BARROW

whose weekly column OFF THE RECORD by 'DISKER' appears each Saturday in
THE LIVERPOOL ECHO AND EVENING EXPRESS

THE BEATLES: "LOVE ME DO" coupled with "P.S. I Love You"

| Words and Music by | Vocals by |
|---|---|
| John Lennon & Paul McCartney | John Lennon & Paul McCartney |

PARLOPHONE: 45-R 4949

For many years the Tennessee town of Nashville has been known as the golden capital of America's Country & Western music industry. In its own way, I guess, Liverpool has become the British beat equivalent to Nashville for the city, deep in the heart of Z Cars country, boasts an almost incredible array of thriving rock 'n' beat groups.

### WHINING HARMONICA.

The most popular of these is THE BEATLES a group which deserves the nationwide following which its Parlophone recordings will surely bring. On the evidence of "LOVE ME DO" nobody can claim that THE BEATLES are a carbon of The Everlys, The Brooks, The Allisons, The Shadows or any other existing outfit. Theirs is a thoroughly distinctive vocal sound backed by the semi-plaintive, semi-impatient rasp and whine of John Lennon's remarkably expressive harmonica plus a stout guitar and solid drum beat.

### SIMPLY INFECTIOUS.

The lyrics of this infectious, medium-paced ballad are simple and it is in this easy-to-remember simplicity that THE BEATLES can pin their well-founded hopes of hit parade headlines for their very first Parlophone outing.

### ANOTHER PUNCHY VOCAL

The under-deck carries something much more than the traditional (albeit ungenerous) B side padding. "P.S. I LOVE YOU" is a bright, up-tempo ditty with another punchy John Lennon/Paul McCartney vocal and a smart, rhythmic backdrop which has a colourful Latin tint to it.

THE ABOVE REVIEW MAY BE REPRODUCED IN
WHOLE OR PART WITHOUT ACKNOWLEDGEMENT

## NEMS ENTERPRISES LTD
DIRECTORS: B. AND C. J. EPSTEIN

12-14 WHITECHAPEL, LIVERPOOL, 1 TELEPHONE ROYAL 7895

BE/BA:

4th October 1962

Dear Jack,

Have you been able to find anymore engagements for THE BEATLES? I'm enclosing a copy of the new 'Press Release' which we have just issued.

Kindest regards,

Yours sincerely,
Brian Epstein.

Jack Fallon Esq.,
Messrs. Cana Variety Agency,
5, Wardour Street,
LONDON W.1

*Extracts from Tony Barrow's press release for 'Love Me Do', independent of EMI's own. It contained a carefully worded biography, individual pen portraits and even a small selection of suggested jokes about the group's name.*

he took no chances and booked in a session drummer, Andy White, to take the place of a dismayed-looking Ringo Starr who had to be content with shaking a tambourine or maracas. Three more numbers were recorded, all Lennon–McCartney compositions: an early, slow, version of 'Please Please Me', 'Love Me Do' and 'P.S. I Love You'. At last George Martin was happy, and for the Beatles' first single he chose the 4 September version of 'Love Me Do' as the A-side (later re-pressings substituted the second version of the song, with Ringo just on tambourine), and the 11 September recording of 'P.S. I Love You' as the flip-side.[10]

On Friday 5 October 1962 the great event happened – the Beatles' debut single was released. One week later it crept into the *Record Retailer* chart at position 49. There was a very strong suspicion in

10 All of the recording details are taken from original, indubitable, EMI session sheets. Once again the information contained therein, reprinted here, contradicts all previously reported accounts of the events, based on memory or journalistic assumptions.

LITTLE RICHARD at the Empire

amptonshire. He had, quite by chance, discovered the home telephone number of Arthur Howes, Britain's leading concert promoter at that time, who ran 'package shows' (a now outmoded idea, in which six or seven acts would perform for around ten minutes each, twice nightly, in a different town each day) at virtually every major theatre or cinema with a stage in Britain. When Howes answered the phone Brian launched into his usual sales pitch, now backed by the added weight of a chart record, and opportunistically asked for some dates. There and then, amazingly, Howes provisionally booked the Beatles on to a Helen Shapiro package set for February 1963 and, to see what the Beatles were like, a one-night bill headed by the suave, yodelling Australian, Frank Ifield, at the Embassy Cinema in Howes' home town of Peterborough on 2 December.[11] Although he offered the group £80 a week (to be shared between all four members) for the Shapiro tour, for the Ifield date he couldn't guarantee any fee, just travelling expenses. Brian accepted the offer and, to show his gratitude, gave Howes the option on all future Beatle tours. But on the night of the Ifield gig, during both houses, the Beatles' ten-minute spots were greeted with stony silence. It hadn't struck anyone that an Ifield audience might not be suited to the Beatles' brand of rock and roll, played at maximum volume. The night was an unmitigated disaster. Howes, though, could see that the boys had talent and kept his option on the Beatles' nationwide touring rights. Not only did he immediately confirm their place on the Shapiro tour, but within two days he had also booked them into a second package, with American stars Tommy Roe and Chris Montez, set for March 1963.

Before all that could happen, two separate fortnight engagements at the Star-Club, Hamburg, arranged many months previously, still had to be fulfilled. And between the first one, from 1 to 14 November, and the second, from 17 to 31 December, the Beatles made their fourth visit of the year to George Martin in the Abbey Road studios. On Monday 26 November they recorded their second single, scheduled for release early in January 1963. Both sides were again Lennon–McCartney originals, the A-side being a revised version of 'Please Please Me', the song first attempted on 11 September, while the reverse was 'Ask Me Why', publicly aired on BBC radio's *Teenager's Turn* programme as far back as 11 June.

Liverpool, and in the record industry as a whole, that Brian Epstein hyped the disc by buying up 10,000 copies over the three months from October to December 1962. Certainly the record led an extremely erratic, up and down, chart career. Epstein always denied this claim vehemently although, since his death, close business friends and associates have admitted that it was almost certainly true. Whatever the circumstances, eleven weeks later, on 27 December, 'Love Me Do' peaked at number 17 on the charts, a most encouraging debut.

Three days prior to the celebrated release of the Beatles' first single, on 2 October, Brian Epstein and the group drew up a solid, legally binding, five-year management contract. This time Epstein even signed his name.

As 'Love Me Do' began its slow climb up the record charts, so the Beatles began to spread their wings and fulfil bookings further afield. On Sunday 28 October, just hours before the group were to take the stage at the prestigious Liverpool Empire theatre for the first time, Brian Epstein made a trunk telephone call down to Peterborough in North-

---

**11** Research has revealed, conclusively, that the Beatles' spot on the Shapiro tour *was* arranged *before* the Peterborough date, contrary to Howes' own recollection.

*A serious mid-afternoon rehearsal in the Cavern Club, behind closed doors, crafting the sound that would rock 1963.*

For the Beatles, after the long, long wait, suddenly it was all happening. In addition to their ever-increasing schedule of non-Liverpool gigs, there was a sudden rush of radio and television appearances to fulfil, promoting 'Love Me Do'. They topped the second *Mersey Beat* popularity poll with consummate ease and were even voted fifth in an end-of-year *New Musical Express* national poll for the Best British Vocal Group, and seventh in the Best British Small Group category, a remarkable achievement on the strength of one single by an 'unknown' northern combo. It was with the greatest reluctance then that the group returned to Hamburg for the fifth and final time on 17 December, to support Johnny and the

Hurricanes at the Star-Club. They were leaving behind them open-ended opportunities to keep their flag flying. Put simply, they really didn't want to go, and when they arrived in Hamburg they could think of little else but getting back home and working hard to consolidate their small foothold on the charts.

Early on New Year's Eve the Beatles' very last Hamburg club performance was captured on tape[12] on a portable Grundig recorder owned by portly Ted Taylor, leader of the Liverpool group King Size Taylor and the Dominoes, who were also playing a residency at the Star-Club. The recording, released on record 15 years later, in 1977, is rough – both in audio quality and performance quality. The Beatles sound tired and irritable and apply little care in their presentation. They had outgrown the Star-Club, they had outgrown Hamburg, and having made excellent use of their unique experiences there, the time had come for them to move on to greater things.

---

**12** During the course of researching this book, the author has been able to prove, conclusively, that the recording took place on this very night.

**3 January**
| | |
|---|---|
| Lunchtime | Cavern Club |
| Night | Cavern Club |

**5 January**
| | |
|---|---|
| Lunchtime | Cavern Club |

**6 January**
| | |
|---|---|
| Night | Cavern Club |

**7 January**     Casbah Coffee Club, West Derby

**9 January**
| | |
|---|---|
| Lunchtime | Cavern Club |

**10 January**
| | |
|---|---|
| Night | Cavern Club |

**11 January**
| | |
|---|---|
| Lunchtime | Cavern Club |

**12 January**
| | |
|---|---|
| Night and | Cavern Club |
| | Tower Ballroom, New Brighton |

Another two-gig night for the Beatles. Their spot at the Tower Ballroom took place at 11:30 p.m., as makeshift headliners of the show, Screaming Lord Sutch, billed as the top act of the night, having failed to arrive.

**13 January**     Hambleton Hall, Huyton

The Beatles' last-ever appearance at this hall, much, one would imagine, to their everlasting relief. This was certainly not the type of venue Brian Epstein wanted his group to be seen in.

**14 January**     Casbah Coffee Club, West Derby

**15 January**
| | |
|---|---|
| Lunchtime | Cavern Club |

**17 January**
| | |
|---|---|
| Lunchtime | Cavern Club |
| Night | Cavern Club |

**19 January**
| | |
|---|---|
| Lunchtime | Cavern Club |
| Night | Tower Ballroom, New Brighton |

**20 January**
| | |
|---|---|
| Night | Cavern Club |

**21 January**     Casbah Coffee Club, West Derby

**22 January**
| | |
|---|---|
| Lunchtime | Cavern Club |
| Night | Kingsway Club, Promenade, Southport, Lancashire |

The lunchtime spot at the Cavern Club was the first of five experimental one-hour lunch sessions, half the usual duration. The admission price was one shilling.

The evening gig is a good illustration of the initial Epstein influence on the Beatles – the venues they would play under his aegis. No longer the scruffy, violent, suburban jive halls, but respectable, civilized clubs. Places with a real stage, real curtains and real dressing rooms – even real carpets – as befitting the Beatles' new-found status.

There was also considerable emphasis on promotion, with cleverly structured advertisements exaggerating the Beatles' achievements, and a news release/article and photograph of the group sent to the local newspaper in advance of the engagement.

**24 January**
| | |
|---|---|
| Lunchtime | Cavern Club |
| Night | Cavern Club |

**26 January**
| | |
|---|---|
| Lunchtime | Cavern Club |
| Night and | Cavern Club |
| | Tower Ballroom, New Brighton |

**27 January**     Aintree Institute, Aintree

The Beatles' last engagement at this venue, and for Beekay, promoter Brian Kelly. For Brian Epstein, who ferried the group to and from the gig in his car, the evening ended in fury when Kelly paid the Beatles' £15 fee in handfuls of loose change. Epstein was angered at what he saw as a slight to the group's importance and not only did he ensure that they never played for Kelly again but he also saw fit to mention the incident in his autobiography two years later.

**28 January**     Casbah Coffee Club, West Derby

TWIST AROUND THE TOWER
TOWER BALLROOM, NEW BRIGHTON
To-night, Friday, January 12, 7.30 p.m. to 1 a.m. – The Greatest Show on Merseyside. starring that horrible. hairy Monster
SCREAMING LORD SUTCH
(X Certificate)
AND HIS HORDE OF SAVAGES
WITH PHILIPS RECORDING ARTISTS
MEL (King of Twist) TURNER
AND THE BANDITS
Also Mersey Beat Poll Winners.
THE BEATLES (After 11.30 p.m.)
RORY STORM AND THE HURRICANES
THE STRANGERS
We introduced The Twist to Merseyside. New we present another lead – A Sensational Twist Exhibition Team
MR. TWIST & THE TWISTETTES

**29 January**    Kingsway Club,
Southport

The second of three consecutive,
block-booked, appearances at this
venue. As the club was licensed to sell
alcohol the beat groups had to play in
an upstairs ballroom without a bar in
order that under-18s could be
admitted.

**30 January**
Lunchtime    Cavern Club

**31 January**
Night    Cavern Club

**1 February**
Lunchtime    Cavern Club

Night    The Beatle Club,
Thistle Café,
Banks Road,
West Kirby,
Wirral, Cheshire

The West Kirby date marked an
important step in the Beatles' career:
the first booking fully organized by
Brian Epstein after the signing of the
management contract seven days
previously, and the first on which he
took a commission.

GRAND OPENING OF
THE BEATLE CLUB
THISTLE CAFE, Banks Road, West Kirby
To-morrow, Thursday Feb. 1, 7.30-11.30.
Starring Merseyside's Premier Beat Group
THE BEATLES
and STEVE DAY & THE DRIFTERS.
Tickets 4/6, Strothers. Membership
forms available.

The engagement perfectly
personifies Epstein at that time. The
venue was a dance instruction hall
behind, and above, a café in a sleepy
dormitory village on the River Dee, ten
miles from Liverpool. It was not a
regular haunt for beat groups so
Epstein was able to persuade the
lessor of the hall, somewhat
magnanimously, into calling it The
Beatle Club, a true misnomer since,
after this engagement, the group
never returned there! This, anyway,
was billed as the Grand Opening Night
and the Beatles' fee was quite
substantial for the time – £18. Brian's
commission, to cover petrol, oil, and
other miscellaneous expenses, was
just 10 per cent – specially reduced for
this celebratory occasion.
According to Sam Leach, who
occasionally promoted at the Thistle
Café, a suspected case of laryngitis
prevented John Lennon from playing
this important date. He claims that he
saved the day for Brian Epstein by
persuading Rory Storm (who didn't
play guitar) to line up alongside Paul,
George and Pete as a temporary
replacement Beatle. It should be said
however that this claim is seriously
doubted by no lesser people than
George Harrison and Neil Aspinall,
who remember no such occurrence.

**2 February**    Oasis Club,
45/47 Lloyd Street,
Manchester,
Lancashire

TONY SMITH'S JAZZMEN
OASIS    OASIS
LLOYD STREET, off ALBERT SQUARE.
7 30    TO-NIGHT    7 30
FOR THE FIRST TIME IN MANCHESTER
POLYDOR'S GREAT RECORDING STARS
THE BEATLES
THE BEATLES
PLUS!    PLUS!    PLUS!
THE ALLAN DENT
JAZZ BAND
TWIST OR BUST AT THE BEST
FRIDAY NIGHT IN TOWN.
3/6    MEMBERS    3/6

Another important career landmark:
aside from the Aldershot gig two
months previously, this was the
Beatles' first professionally organized
out-of-town date. Epstein's influence is
beginning to show.
Tony Stuart, manager of the Oasis on
behalf of the owners, Kennedy Street
Enterprises, booked the Beatles for the
club on three further occasions over
the next year.

**3 February**
Night    Cavern Club

**4 February**    Casbah Coffee Club,
West Derby

Pa's gone down the dog
track; Mother's playin'
Bingo, but everyone else is
going to see the

BEATLES

Last Appearance at the

KINGSWAY

NEXT MONDAY

PLUS

QUIET ONES

**5 February**
Lunchtime    Cavern Club

Night    Kingsway Club,
Southport

With this lunchtime date the Cavern
Club reverted back to the customary
two-hour session.

**7 February**
Lunchtime    Cavern Club

Night    Cavern Club

**9 February**
Lunchtime    Cavern Club

Night    Cavern Club
and    Technical
College Hall,
Borough Road,
Birkenhead, Cheshire

The first of three consecutive,
successful, Friday-night bookings for
the Technical College.

**10 February**    Youth Club, St Paul's
Presbyterian
Church Hall,
North Road,
Tranmere,
Birkenhead, Cheshire

Another unusual Beatles venue,
booked by Epstein, and not half a mile
from the technical college where the
group had played the previous
evening.

**11 February**    Casbah Coffee Club,
West Derby

Note: on 12 February the Beatles went
to audition for BBC radio in Manchester.

**13 February**
Lunchtime    Cavern Club

**14 February**
Night    Cavern Club

**15 February**
Lunchtime    Cavern Club

Night    Tower Ballroom,
New Brighton

With a Panto Ball set for the following
evening it was only natural there
should be a Pre-Panto Ball. This was it.
Terry Lightfoot and his New Orleans
Jazz Band shared the bill with the
Beatles, watched by 3500 customers.

**16 February**    Technical
College Hall,
Birkenhead
and    Tower Ballroom,
New Brighton

The college date was part of its annual
Panto celebrations. The Tower date
was a regular Sam Leach promotion.

**17 February**
Night    Cavern Club

**18 February**    Casbah Coffee Club,
West Derby

**19 February**
Lunchtime    Cavern Club

**20 February**    Floral Hall,
Promenade,
Southport, Lancashire

Probably the Beatles' biggest date under Epstein thus far : the Floral Hall being a real theatre, with gold lamé curtains and tiered seats.
  The evening was billed, to attract the largest possible audience, as a Rock 'n' Trad Spectacular. In addition to the Beatles four other rock groups were on the bill, including Gerry and the Pacemakers and Rory Storm and the Hurricanes, while the trad element was supplied by the Chris Hamilton Jazzmen.

**21 February**
Lunchtime    Cavern Club

Night    Cavern Club

**23 February**
Lunchtime    Cavern Club

Night    Tower Ballroom,
New Brighton
  and    Technical
College Hall,
Birkenhead

Two separate Beatles appearances at the Tower, at 9:00 and 10:45 p.m. In between, the group had time to sneak away for a half-hour set at the college.

**24 February**
Night    YMCA,
Birkenhead Road,
Hoylake,
Wirral, Cheshire
  and    Cavern Club

The YMCA date was not, surprisingly, an Epstein booking but the result of much perseverance by club organizer Charles Tranter who, eager to book the Beatles for some time (he first approached them for a dance on 8 September 1961 but the Beatles were otherwise engaged), finally presented himself at the door of Mrs Mona Best and offered a generous £30 fee for this one appearance. Unfortunately for Tranter the crowd at the YMCA did not share his enthusiasm for the Beatles, quickly grew dissatisfied with the group's over-long introductions and pauses between songs, and booed them off stage! Tranter also recalls that as the group wore black leather outfits he presumed that they were meant to signify real insects, and duly advertised them as such: The Beetles.
  The Cavern appearance took place after midnight, during another of the club's all-night sessions.

**25 February**    Casbah Coffee Club,
West Derby

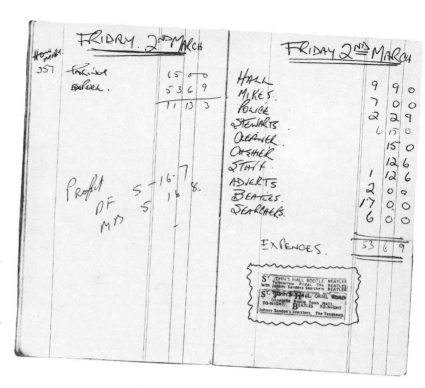

*Promoter Dave Forshaw's diary entry for 2 March, showing the Beatles' fee of £17, an attendance of 357 and profit of over £11.*

**26 February**    Kingsway Club,
Southport

**27 February**
Lunchtime    Cavern Club

**28 February**
Night    Cavern Club

**1 March**
Lunchtime    Cavern Club

Night    Storyville Jazz Club,
13 Temple Street,
Liverpool

The Beatles had already played this venue, when it was known as the Liverpool Jazz Society. In September 1962 it would become the Iron Door Club.

**2 March**    St John's Hall,
Bootle
  and    Tower Ballroom,
New Brighton

The Bootle date was a slight reversion to habitats of old : inglorious suburban jive halls. But it was played because young promoter Dave Forshaw always saved and worked hard to occasionally present a top-line act for his clientele.
  Later in the evening the Beatles went across the Mersey for another Tower date, billed on this occasion as a Mad March Rock Ball.

**3 March**
Night    Cavern Club

**4 March**    Casbah Coffee Club,
West Derby

**5 March**
Lunchtime    Cavern Club

Night    Kingsway Club,
Southport

**6 March**
Night    Cavern Club

**8 March**    Storyville Jazz Club

Note : On 7 March the Beatles recorded their first-ever BBC radio appearance, transmitted a day later on *Teenager's Turn (Here We Go).*

**9 March**
Lunchtime    Cavern Club

Night    Cavern Club

**10 March**    Youth Club, St Paul's
Presbyterian
Church Hall,
Tranmere

A return date, precisely one month after the first appearance.

| | |
|---|---|
| **11 March** | Casbah Coffee Club, West Derby |
| **13 March** Lunchtime | Cavern Club |
| **14 March** Night | Cavern Club |
| **15 March** Lunchtime | Cavern Club |
| Night | Storyville Jazz Club |

The Storyville date was titled the Beatles' Farewell Party. Farewell to the Storyville that is – they were never to play there again.

| | |
|---|---|
| **16 March** Night | Cavern Club |
| **17 March** | Village Hall, Knotty Ash |

A special event for promoter Sam Leach: his engagement night. Leach had assumed the responsibility to promote beat nights at this venue after Mona Best relinquished her rights following six months' activity.

Billing the evening as a St Patrick's Night Rock Gala, Leach booked the Beatles and Rory Storm and the Hurricanes in order to attract a bumper crowd and pay for his engagement party in Huyton, which began after the evening's rock and roll proceedings had ended. Both groups then attended the party which, in true Liverpool style, did not end until the following afternoon.

| | |
|---|---|
| **18 March** | Casbah Coffee Club, West Derby |
| **20 March** Night | Cavern Club |
| **21 March** Lunchtime | Cavern Club |
| **22 March** Night | Cavern Club |
| **23 March** Lunchtime | Cavern Club |
| Night | Cavern Club |

| | |
|---|---|
| **24 March** | Heswall Jazz Club, Barnston Women's Institute, Barnston Road, Heswall, Wirral, Cheshire |

The first of three Beatles appearances at this glorious venue also marked the Beatles' stage debut in suits.

| | |
|---|---|
| **25 March** | Casbah Coffee Club, West Derby |
| **26 March** Lunchtime | Cavern Club |
| **28 March** Lunchtime | Cavern Club |
| Night | Cavern Club |
| **29 March** | Odd Spot Club, 89 Bold Street, Liverpool |

The Beatles' first appearance at this night club in Liverpool city centre, which had opened on 9 December 1961.

*Above: An Epstein-designed handbill, grandly touting the Beatles' claims to fame. The 'European Tour' was simply their next trip to Hamburg.*

**30 March**

Lunchtime    Cavern Club

Night    Cavern Club

**31 March**    Subscription Rooms, Stroud, Gloucestershire

Another important date: the Beatles' first southern engagement under Brian Epstein, and only their second ever – preceded of course by Sam Leach's unfortunate Aldershot débâcle in December 1961.

Actually, Epstein's choice of southern venue was equally, if not more, wayward than Leach's had been, although at least this dance was booked through a reputable London agent, the Cana Variety Agency. John (Jack) Fallon who runs Cana also promoted dances, predominantly in the western counties, under another company, Jaybee Clubs, hence the booking. The Beatles were to play four different Jaybee venues in all.

Note: The Canadian-born Fallon was also a reputable double-bass and violin player, having performed with many of the music greats down the years, including Guy Lombardo and Duke Ellington. Long established as a studio session man, Fallon received a telephone call on 12 July 1968 summoning him for a night's work at Abbey Road studios. It was only when he arrived there that he was informed he was needed to play the country fiddle on a Beatles session – Ringo Starr's first recorded composition 'Don't Pass Me By'. The Beatles had no idea that Fallon was also a musician, and despite the hectic activities of the previous six years, they actually remembered him and spent some considerable time together reminiscing about the Subscription Rooms in Stroud!

**1 April**    Casbah Coffee Club, West Derby

**2 April**

Lunchtime    Cavern Club

Night    Pavilion Theatre, Lodge Lane, Liverpool

The Pavilion date was a most unusual booking, for the Beatles shared the bill with the Royal Waterford Showband, specially flown in from Ireland for the occasion. The evening was promoted by local variety agent Jim Gretty and it marked the one and only Beatles appearance at the 'Pivvy', long established as Liverpool's first and foremost striptease theatre.

Note: The Quarry Men did perform here once or twice in late fifties skiffle contests.

| DATE | BAND | BAND FEE | STAFF | | BOUNCERS STEWARDS | | CLOAKROOMS | | SUNDRIES |
|---|---|---|---|---|---|---|---|---|---|
| 1962 FEB 3rd | Clinton Ford - Charlie Galbraith Sounds Incorporated | 646 | 80 32 | - - 10 - | 9 | 10 - | 12 | - - | 4 10 - |
| 10th | Checkmates Midnights | 450 | 50 5 | - - - - | 7 | 10 - | 15 | 10 - | Train fare Transport Phone Colin Segeler Till |
| 17th | Russ Sainty R. Rousers | 534 | 35 6 | - - - - | 4 | 19 9 | 16 | 5 - | |
| 24th | Shane Fenton Dukes | 522 | 55 5 | - - - - | 7 | 10 - | 7 | 10 - | Hall adv. left. |
| MARCH 3rd | Cliff Bennett + Rebel Rousers Cir. R. Rousers | 498 | 45 6 | - - - - | 4 | 14 - | 14 | 15 - | |
| 10th | Duke D'Monde R. Rousers | 279 | 30 6 | - - - - | 4 | 14 - | 16 | 5 - | |
| 17th | Mike Berry R. Rousers | 566 | 35 6 | - - - - | 5 | 11 - | 14 | 10 - | |
| 24th | Stranges Midnights | 470 | 30 5 | - - - - | 8 | 11 - | 14 | 10 - | 5 5 |
| 31st | The Beatles R. Rousers | 466 | 30 6 | - - - - | 5 | 11 - | 14 | 10 - | |

**4 April**

Lunchtime    Cavern Club

Night    Cavern Club

**5 April**

Night    Cavern Club

A special Cavern Club Beatles appearance, presented by their fan club.

*Above: Jaybee Clubs' accounts sheet for early 1962. The attendance figure, to the right of the names, shows the Beatles attracted one of the lowest gates. Top: The Beatles' first appearance at the Odd Spot Club in Liverpool. Below: A special treat for the fan club.*

THE BEATLES FAN CLUB
PRESENTS

"THE BEATLES FOR THEIR FANS"

OR AN EVENING WITH GEORGE, JOHN, PAUL & PETE

GUEST ARTISTES WILL INCLUDE

THE FOUR JAYS

AND THE BEATLES' FAVOURITE COMPERE

BOB WOOLER

7-30 p.m., THURSDAY, APRIL 5th, 1962

AT THE CAVERN

TICKETS 6/6d.

Ticket holders will receive a FREE PHOTOGRAPH and may apply for FREE Membership of the Fan Club. (See over).

**6 April**

Lunchtime      Cavern Club

Night           Tower Ballroom,
New Brighton

The Tower date was a two-and-a-half-hour Beatles Farewell Ball, prior to their imminent Hamburg trip. They shared the bill with Emile Ford and the Checkmates.

**7 April**

Night           Casbah Coffee Club,
West Derby
and   Cavern Club

The Beatles' last two Liverpool performances for two months had to take place without George Harrison who had been taken ill. Brian Epstein, mindful of the impending and important Hamburg engagement, refused George permission to take to the stage.

**VISIT TO HAMBURG**

**13 April–31 May**    Star-Club,
(except 20          39 Grosse Freiheit,
April, Good       St Pauli
Friday)
(48 nights)

Seven weeks at the Star-Club, Hamburg's big new plush rock venue. The Beatles were required to play four hours one night, and three the next, always with a one-hour-on, one-hour-off system. By 31 May, at the end of the

*A selection of memorabilia relating to Beatles engagements, spring/summer 1962. Left to right : A poster for the gig with Emile Ford, star of 1959 and 1960, at the Tower Ballroom, New Brighton. A handbill announcing the opening of the biggest rock club in Hamburg yet, the Star-Club. A handbill for the beneficial gig with Bruce Channel, and one for a Big Beat Bargain Night, the Beatles' first appearance in St Helens.*

group's third lengthy Hamburg stint within two years, another 172 gruelling hours' stage time had been toiled.

For two of the seven weeks the Beatles shared the bill with Little Richard, and later with Gene Vincent.

RETURN TO UK

**6 June** CANCELLED

Night/         Cavern Club

A Welcome Home celebration planned for this evening was postponed in mid-May until 9 June because the Beatles were down at EMI's Abbey Road studios in London for their first recording session.

**9 June**

Night           Cavern Club

This Beatles Welcome Home Show appearance smashed the existing attendance record at the Cavern Club, as 900 vociferous youngsters crammed themselves into the underground

sweatbox to see their idols.

For the next twelve days the Cavern Club had the Beatles under exclusive contract.

**12 June**

Lunchtime      Cavern Club

Night           Cavern Club

Note : On 11 June the Beatles recorded their second BBC radio appearance, on *Here We Go*. It was transmitted on 15 June.

**13 June**

Lunchtime      Cavern Club

Night           Cavern Club

**15 June**

Lunchtime      Cavern Club

Night           Cavern Club

**16 June**

Night           Cavern

**19 June**

Lunchtime      Cavern Club

Night           Cavern Club

**20 June**

Lunchtime      Cavern Club

Night           Cavern Club

**21 June**        Tower Ballroom,
                   New Brighton

Although unadvertised as such, this
was the first of many occasions in the
second half of 1962 when Brian Epstein
would shrewdly book top-line acts of
the day to appear on Merseyside in
order that the Beatles could be seen to
support them on the bill, or maybe
even upstage them. On this occasion it
was Bruce Channel who headlined, just
five weeks after scoring a Top Ten hit
with 'Hey! Baby'.

The evening was of further,
unexpected benefit. Channel's
harmonica player, Delbert McLinton,
so inspired John Lennon that his
influence would be clearly heard on
nearly all of the Beatles' recorded
output until 1964.

**22 June**
Lunchtime          Cavern Club

Night              Cavern Club

**23 June**        (Victory)
                   Memorial Hall,
                   Chester Way,
                   Northwich, Cheshire

The first of six Beatles appearances at
this up-market venue in Northwich, a
famous Cheshire salt-mining town, 25
miles south-east of Liverpool. The
promoter, Lewis Buckley, ran beat
music dances all over Britain, so a
good, impressive performance was
all-important.

**24 June**        Casbah Coffee Club,
                   West Derby

This was the Beatles' last-ever
appearance at the Casbah, which,
approaching three years' activity,
finally closed down at the end of June
after a death in the Best family.

**25 June**
Lunchtime          Cavern Club

Night              Plaza Ballroom,
                   Duke Street,
                   St Helens, Lancashire

The St Helens date was another
important booking: the Beatles' first for
Whetstone Entertainments, a company
which ran two other ballrooms in the
Merseyside area, the Orrell Park in
Liverpool and the Riverpark in
Chester. The Beatles' fee was £25.

Before the gig Epstein wrote a note
to the Beatles stating that Whetstone
'control 16 venues in the Northwest'
but this was a careful fabrication to
chivvy his group. He well knew that 13
of the 16 were exclusively bingo halls.

**27 June**
Lunchtime          Cavern Club

Night              Cavern Club

**28 June**        Majestic Ballroom,
                   Conway Street,
                   Birkenhead, Cheshire

Not just the first of 17 Beatles

appearances at this venue but also,
very importantly, the group's first
booking with Top Rank, Britain's
premier entertainment organization at
that time, encompassing theatres,
cinemas, dance halls and bingo clubs.
They also operated 28 venues for beat
music throughout the country, mostly,
though not all, named Majestic. The
Beatles were to play 11 of these in the
ensuing year.

**29 June**
Lunchtime          Cavern Club

Night              Tower Ballroom,
                   New Brighton

Following his two successful ventures
the previous winter, and an
unnumbered occasion on 9 March
without the Beatles, Sam Leach
presented Operation Big Beat III at the
Tower. Ten Merseyside groups,
headed by the Beatles, performed in a
'cavalcade of rock 'n' twist' during the
five-and-a-half-hour show.

**30 June**        Heswall Jazz Club,
                   Barnston Women's
                   Institute,
                   Heswall

**1 July**
Night              Cavern Club

Also appearing on the Cavern Club
bill on this occasion was Gene Vincent.
The night was something of a reunion
as the Beatles and Vincent had met and
become friendly in Hamburg.

2 July — Plaza Ballroom, St Helens

The second of the Beatles' four consecutive Monday-night bookings at this venue.

3 July
Lunchtime — Cavern Club

4 July
Night — Cavern Club

5 July — Majestic Ballroom, Birkenhead

6 July — Riverboat Shuffle aboard the MV *Royal Iris*, River Mersey

Another floating Beatles performance on board the Fish and Chip Boat, presented by the Cavern Club. Once again the Beatles shared the bill with Acker Bilk, who was still in the Top Ten with 'Stranger on the Shore' (an apt title to perform on a Riverboat Shuffle!) more than six months after its release.

7 July — Golf Club Dance, Hulme Hall, Bolton Road, Port Sunlight, Birkenhead, Cheshire

8 July
Night — Cavern Club

9 July — Plaza Ballroom, St Helens

10 July
Lunchtime — Cavern Club

11 July
Night — Cavern Club

12 July
Lunchtime — Cavern Club

Night — Majestic Ballroom, Birkenhead

13 July — Tower Ballroom, New Brighton

14 July — Regent Dansette, High Street, Rhyl, Flintshire, Wales

This, the Beatles' first-ever performance in Wales, took place in a ballroom situated, like so many snooker and billiards clubs of the day, above a branch of Burtons.

15 July
Night — Cavern Club

16 July
Lunchtime — Cavern Club

Night — Plaza Ballroom, St Helens

17 July — McIlroy's Ballroom, Havelock Square, Swindon, Wiltshire

The Beatles' third southern date.

18 July
Lunchtime — Cavern Club

Night — Cavern Club

19 July — Majestic Ballroom, Birkenhead

The Beatles' Thursday-night season at this venue, which had run over three weeks from 28 June to 12 July, was extended for one more week due to popular demand.

20 July
Lunchtime — Cavern Club

21 July — Tower Ballroom, New Brighton

22 July
Night — Cavern Club

23 July — Kingsway Club, Southport

24 July
Lunchtime — Cavern Club

25 July
Lunchtime — Cavern Club

Night and — Cavern Club Cabaret Club, 28 Duke Street, Liverpool

The Cabaret Club booking was a curious one – an attempt by Brian Epstein to break the Beatles into the cabaret circuit. Although the group received a £15 fee, this unadvertised performance was akin to an audition – which they failed miserably. The co-manager of the club at the time, Bob Woodward, remembers the audience response as nil, and the Beatles playing so loud that they set the windows rattling. He didn't book them again.

26 July — Cambridge Hall, Lord Street, Southport, Lancashire

The first of two consecutive evenings presented by NEMS Enterprises (Brian Epstein) showcasing Joe Brown and his Bruvvers, and the Beatles. At the time, Brown stood at number three in the charts with 'A Picture of You', one of Epstein's favourite pop records and also a new feature of the Beatles' own stage act, sung by George Harrison. On this and the following evening Allan Williams lent administrative assistance to Epstein.

27 July — Tower Ballroom, New Brighton

The second Joe Brown presentation by Epstein

**28 July**
Night and Cavern Club
Majestic Ballroom,
Birkenhead

**30 July**
Lunchtime Cavern Club

Night (Blue Penguin Club),
St John's Hall,
Bootle

Another return to the 1961 stamping ground in Bootle, thanks to the efforts of Dave Forshaw, the likeable young promoter who always saved so hard to afford the Beatles whenever possible.

**1 August**
Lunchtime Cavern Club

Night Cavern Club

**3 August** Grafton Rooms,
West Derby Road,
Liverpool

The first-ever rock show at this pre-war *palais de danse*, promoted by local man Albert Kinder. The Beatles headed the bill which included Gerry and the Pacemakers and the Big Three.
Note: The Quarry Men did perform here in late-fifties skiffle contests.

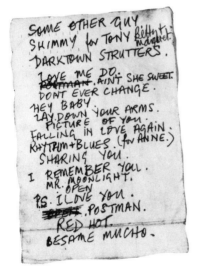

*Paul's draft of the Beatles' repertoire for the Grafton gig.*

**4 August** Victoria Hall,
Village Road,
Higher Bebington,
Wirral, Cheshire

Another unusual Beatles venue. So few groups ever played there, that initially even Brian Epstein didn't know how to find the hall.

**5 August**
Night Cavern Club

**7 August**
Lunchtime Cavern Club

Night Cavern Club

**8 August** CANCELLED
Night Cavern Club
Co-op Ballroom,
Doncaster, Yorkshire

The Beatles were excused their regular Cavern Club Wednesday-night appearance, this time on a bill with Shane Fenton (later Alvin Stardust) and the Fentones, in order that they could fulfil the more prestigious (!) booking in Doncaster, 86 miles across the Pennines.

**9 August**
Lunchtime Cavern Club

**10 August** Riverboat Shuffle
aboard the
MV *Royal Iris*,
River Mersey

Just over one month after boating down river with Acker Bilk, this time the Cavern Club presented the Beatles with Johnny Kidd and the Pirates, two years after they had hit the top of the charts with the immortal 'Shakin' all Over'. Also sailing down the muddy Mersey on this occasion were the Dakotas, the instrumental group later teamed up by Brian Epstein with Billy J. Kramer.

**11 August** Odd Spot Club,
Liverpool

**12 August**
Night Cavern Club

**13 August**
Lunchtime Cavern Club

Night Majestic Ballroom,
High Street,
Crewe, Cheshire

Another Top Rank venue – this one used to bill its beat nights as 'The biggest rock since Blackpool rock'! This was the first of two consecutive Monday-night Beatles appearances here.

**15 August**
Lunchtime Cavern Club

Night Cavern Club

The night-time Cavern Club gig marked the last-ever appearance of Pete Best with the Beatles, two years and three days after he had joined them.

**16 August** Riverpark Ballroom,
off Love Street,
Chester, Cheshire

What should have been one of the Beatles' more successful evenings, with the first of four (unconsecutive) Thursday-night bookings in this beautiful Cheshire town, was marred by the non-appearance of Pete Best, dismissed from the group by Brian Epstein a few hours before the gig. At the time Best had said that he would fulfil the Chester engagement but, hardly surprisingly, during the course of the day, he decided against it. Johnny Hutchinson of the Big Three was drafted in as replacement at the eleventh hour.

**17 August** Majestic Ballroom,
Birkenhead
and Tower Ballroom,
New Brighton

Once again Johnny Hutchinson stood in for the Beatles on drums, playing at both engagements. Oddly, the Big Three also had a booking on this date, at the Orrell Park Ballroom, so *they* had to find a replacement.

**18 August** Horticultural
Society Dance,
Hulme Hall,
Bolton Road,
Port Sunlight,
Birkenhead, Cheshire

The first day, and first-ever appearance, of Ringo Starr in the Beatles. The four had just two hours' rehearsal before they took to the stage.
The Beatles were to eventually appear four times at this venue, situated in the beautiful self-contained village of Port Sunlight, created by Viscount Leverhulme in 1888 for the

▲ Fifty-one-year-service veteran, Mr Charles Henry Taylor, receives good wishes for a happy retirement from Mr J. Lee, manager of Hard Soaps Department

◄ Playing music with a beat for the Horticultural Society's dance at Hulme Hall after the Summer Show on Saturday, 18th August, will be The Beatles, one of the North's leading rhythm groups

employees of his soap business, now the thriving multi-national giant, Unilever. The official attendance capacity of Hulme Hall was 450 but, unofficially, 500 paying customers would be squeezed in on Beatles nights.

**19 August**
Night                  Cavern Club

**20 August**          Majestic Ballroom,
                       Crewe

**21 August**  ~~CANCELLED~~
Lunchtime              Cavern Club

This Cavern Club booking was switched to the following day, 22 August, at the request of Granada Television.

**22 August**
Lunchtime              Cavern Club

Night                  Cavern Club

The lunchtime session was a momentous occasion, for it brought television cameras into the Cavern Club cellar for the first time in several years. As a direct result of viewers' letters, TV producers from the Manchester-based company Granada had watched the Beatles in action at the Cambridge Hall, Southport, on 26 July and at the Cavern Club on 1 August and, impressed by what they saw, sent a crew down on this lunchtime and filmed the Beatles performing two songs, 'Some other Guy' and 'Kansas City/Hey-Hey-Hey-Hey!', for a programme entitled *Know the North*. Unfortunately the conditions in the Cavern Club were not conducive to good filming and the results were largely unsatisfactory. The footage was shelved and not transmitted until much later on, when the Beatles were famous. Now it stands as the only movie film in existence of the Beatles

playing in the Cavern Club, although, tragically, just the clip of 'Some other Guy' has survived the years.

**23 August**          Riverpark Ballroom,
                       Chester

This, amazingly, was how John Lennon spent his wedding night: playing with the Beatles in Chester.

**24 August**
Lunchtime              Cavern Club

Night                  Majestic Ballroom,
                       Birkenhead

**25 August**          Marine Hall Ballroom,
                       Esplanade,
                       Fleetwood, Lancashire

The Beatles' first, and only, appearance in this northern coastal town, famous for its fishing industry.

**26 August**
Night                  Cavern Club

Also appearing on this night's bill of fare was Mike Berry, who had enjoyed a Top Thirty hit in October 1961 with 'Tribute to Buddy Holly'.

**28 August**
Night                  Cavern Club

An irregular Tuesday-night Cavern Club gig by the Beatles, switched in mid-August to allow the group to fulfil a booking in Morecambe on 29 August.

**29 August**  ~~CANCELLED~~
Night                  Cavern Club

                       Floral Hall Ballroom,
                       Promenade,
                       Morecambe, Lancashire

The first of two Beatles gigs at this seaside resort.

*From Port Sunlight's own works magazine. This was the only advertisement for the date but it was enough to pack the hall.*

**30 August**
Lunchtime              Cavern Club

Night                  Riverpark Ballroom,
                       Chester

**31 August**          Town Hall,
                       Town Hall Chambers,
                       Lydney,
                       Gloucestershire

The first of a Friday/Saturday double-engagement with Jaybee Clubs.

114

**1 September**   Subscription Rooms,
Stroud

A return to the venue played on 31
March 1962.

**2 September**
Night           Cavern Club

**3 September**
Lunchtime       Cavern Club

Night           Queen's Hall,
Widnes, Lancashire

The first of three consecutive Monday-
night NEMS presentations in Widnes, the
industrial town on the Mersey twelve
miles south of Liverpool. The Beatles,
naturally, headlined each one, and
though the support groups varied from
week to week, Rory Storm and the
Hurricanes – back from their Butlin's
stint on 1 September – appeared on
the first two occasions. They initially
bore malice over the fact that their
drummer, Ringo Starr, had just been
snatched from them, but this passed.
   On 4 September the Beatles flew
down to London for a recording
session at the EMI studios.

**5 September**
Lunchtime       Cavern Club

Night           Cavern Club

The Beatles were unable to make their
usual Wednesday-night Cavern Club
session because they had stayed on in
London longer than expected after the
recording session the previous day.
The lunchtime spot had been switched
in advance to the following day.

**6 September**
Lunchtime       Cavern Club

Night           Rialto Ballroom,
Upper Parliament
Street/
Stanhope Street,
Liverpool

The Rialto date was a Sam Leach
presentation, though it was at a Top
Rank venue. Surprisingly, this was the
Beatles' debut at the Rialto, although
the Quarry Men did perform here once
or twice in late-fifties skiffle contests.

**7 September**   Newton Dancing
School,
Village Hall,
Thingwall Road,
Irby, Heswall,
Wirral, Cheshire

Another auspicious Beatles booking!

**8 September**   YMCA,
Whetstone Lane,
Birkenhead, Cheshire
and   Majestic Ballroom,
Birkenhead

**9 September**
Night           Cavern Club

Also on the bill was Clinton Ford, the
British singer with two Top Thirty hit
singles to his credit. He was originally
booked to appear on 2 September.

**10 September**
Lunchtime       Cavern Club

Night           Queen's Hall, Widnes

**12 September**
Night           Cavern Club

As well as performing their customary
set, the Beatles also backed a 16-year-
old female discovery, Simone Jackson.
On the bill, too, were Freddie and the
Dreamers.
   Note: A camera crew from Granada
television was not in the Cavern Club
on this night, as suggested at the time
in *Mersey Beat*.
   On 11 September the Beatles had
spent the day back at the Abbey Road
recording studios.

**13 September**
Lunchtime       Cavern Club

Night           Riverpark Ballroom,
Chester

The fourth and final Thursday-night
Beatles appearance at this venue.

**14 September**   Tower Ballroom,
New Brighton

Sam Leach's Operation Big Beat V. Six
groups, headed by the Beatles, played
a five-and-a-half-hour session.
   Note: Operation Big Beat IV had
taken place while the Beatles were
otherwise engaged, on 3 August.

**15 September**   (Victory)
Memorial Hall,
Northwich

**16 September**
Night           Cavern Club

**17 September**
Lunchtime       Cavern Club

Night           Queen's Hall, Widnes

**19 September**
Night           Cavern Club

**20 September**
Lunchtime       Cavern Club

**21 September**   Tower Ballroom,
New Brighton

A special five-group evening to
celebrate Rory Storm's birthday.

| | |
|---|---|
| **22 September** | Majestic Ballroom, Birkenhead |

| | |
|---|---|
| **23 September**<br>Night | Cavern Club |

| | |
|---|---|
| **25 September** | Heswall Jazz Club, Barnston Women's Institute, Heswall |

An unusual mid-week (Tuesday) engagement at the WI.

| | |
|---|---|
| **26 September**<br>Lunchtime | Cavern Club |
| Night | Cavern Club |

| | |
|---|---|
| **28 September**<br>Lunchtime | Cavern Club |
| Night | Riverboat Shuffle aboard the MV *Royal Iris*, River Mersey |

The Beatles' third and last nautical experience of the summer season, headlining with Lee Castle and the Barons.

| | |
|---|---|
| **29 September** | Oasis Club, Manchester |

A return visit to the scene of the Beatles' first major engagement under Brian Epstein.

| | |
|---|---|
| **30 September**<br>Night | Cavern Club |

| | |
|---|---|
| **2 October**<br>Lunchtime | Cavern Club |

| | |
|---|---|
| **3 October**<br>Night | Cavern Club |

| | |
|---|---|
| **4 October**<br>Lunchtime | Cavern Club |

| | |
|---|---|
| **6 October** | Horticultural Society Dance, Hulme Hall, Port Sunlight |

Prior to this third engagement in Port Sunlight, the Beatles put in a personal appearance at Dawson's Music Shop in Widnes, where they signed copies of their first record, 'Love Me Do', released the previous day.

| | |
|---|---|
| **7 October**<br>Night | Cavern Club |

| | |
|---|---|
| **8 October**<br>Lunchtime | Cavern Club |

This lunchtime Cavern Club appearance was cancelled because the Beatles had to travel down to London for an evening recording for the Radio Luxembourg programme *The Friday Spectacular* at EMI House in Manchester Square. The programme was broadcast on 12 October. On 9 October the group stayed in London and visited music journalists and the weekly pop newspapers, to give interviews promoting the release of 'Love Me Do'.

| | |
|---|---|
| **10 October**<br>Lunchtime | Cavern Club |
| Night | Cavern Club |

| | |
|---|---|
| **11 October** | Rialto Ballroom, Liverpool |

Billed as a Rock 'n' Twist Carnival, this evening was organized by Liverpool University.

| | |
|---|---|
| **12 October**<br>Lunchtime | Cavern Club |
| Night | Tower Ballroom, New Brighton |

The Tower Ballroom date marked Brian Epstein's most ambitious venture yet: a five-and-a-half-hour, 12-act presentation, spearheaded by the legendary American rocker, Little Richard. The evening was an enormous success, and Epstein re-

booked Richard to assume top billing at another NEMS presentation he had scheduled for the Empire Theatre, Liverpool, on 28 October.

For the Beatles the experience of playing second on a 12-act bill to Little Richard was enormous. Enormous is also the only way to describe the degree of embarrassment the group suffered when they bumped into Pete Best backstage at the Tower. He was there in his new role as drummer with Lee Curtis and the All-Stars.

| | |
|---|---|
| **13 October**<br>Night | Cavern Club |

| | |
|---|---|
| **15 October** | Majestic Ballroom, Birkenhead |

| | |
|---|---|
| **16 October** | La Scala Ballroom, Runcorn, Cheshire |

The Beatles' first-ever appearance in Runcorn, a town 14 miles south of Liverpool

| | |
|---|---|
| **17 October**<br>Lunchtime | Cavern Club |
| Night | Cavern Club |

Note: Between these two gigs, in the early evening, the Beatles made their television debut, appearing live singing 'Love Me Do' on the Granada show *People and Places* from the company's Manchester studios.

| | |
|---|---|
| **19 October**<br>Lunchtime | Cavern Club |

| | |
|---|---|
| **20 October** | Majestic Ballroom, Witham, Hull, Yorkshire |

Another Top Rank venue, and at 128 miles from Liverpool the furthest one from home the Beatles had played to date.

| | |
|---|---|
| **21 October**<br>Night | Cavern Club |

| | |
|---|---|
| **22 October** | Queen's Hall, Widnes |

Another NEMS showcase for the Beatles. Also on the bill were Lee Curtis and the All-Stars, and another face-to-face encounter with Pete Best.

| | |
|---|---|
| **26 October**<br>Lunchtime | Cavern Club |
| Night | Public Hall, Preston, Lancashire |

Surprisingly, the Beatles' debut in this major Lancashire town just thirty miles north-west of Liverpool.

On 25 October the Beatles had recorded a third appearance on the BBC radio programme *Here We Go*. It was broadcast on 26 October.

NEMS ENTERPRISES present     B 63     **BAND PASS**

# LITTLE RICHARD
## AT
# THE TOWER
BALLROOM, NEW BRIGHTON

**FRIDAY 12 OCTOBER 1962**

7-30 p.m. to 1-0 a.m.

Late transport to all areas

A Bob Wooler Production

**ADVANCE TICKET 10/6**

with THE BEATLES
The Big Three
Billy Kramer with The Coasters
The Dakotas with Pete MacLaine
The Four Jays
Lee Curtis and The All Stars
The Mersey Beats
Rory Storm and The Hurricanes
The Undertakers

THE BEATLES     spielen im    ★ Star-Club
Hamburg-St. Pauli

**27 October**     Recreations
Association Dance,
Hulme Hall,
Port Sunlight

The Beatles' fourth and final
appearance at this venue. Prior to
going on stage the group recorded a
radio interview for the patients of
Cleaver and Clatterbridge Hospitals,
both situated on the Wirral.

**28 October**     Empire Theatre,
Liverpool

A most important engagement for the
Beatles, for not only were they part of
an eight-act, star-studded, non-
Liverpool groups NEMS presentation
bill, but this was also their first-ever
appearance (barring the Quarry Men's
auditions) at the Empire and the
group's first real 'pop package show',
with two separate houses, at 5:40 and
8:00 p.m.
    Heading the bill, once again, was
Little Richard, while the other acts
included pop luminaries of the time,
Craig Douglas (whom the Beatles
actually backed, in addition to
performing their own set), Jet Harris
(former Shadows bassist), Kenny
Lynch, and Sounds Incorporated.
Epstein had hoped to book Sam Cooke
too, but he was unavailable.
    To the hard core of Liverpool fans
the group had really made the big time.

**VISIT TO HAMBURG**

**1–14 November**     Star-Club,
(14 nights)     Grosse Freiheit

A brief return to the Star-Club, the first
time the Beatles had officially played in
the same club on successive trips.
Their fee was an increased 600 DM per
man per week.
    Another 49 stage hours to add to the
enormous Hamburg experience,
though by this time the group didn't
need it as much.

**RETURN TO UK**

**17 November**      Jubilee Hall,
Chapel Street,
Dukinfield, Cheshire

Matrix Hall,
Fletchamstead
Highway, Coventry,
Warwickshire

The Beatles' first-ever Midlands
engagement. In London the night
before the group had recorded a
second appearance on the Radio
Luxembourg show *The Friday
Spectacular*. It was transmitted on
23 November. The Dukinfield
engagement was cancelled after Brian
Epstein and the management had
failed to agree terms, so Brian quickly
lined up the Coventry gig.

*The Star-Club's promotional handout
picture of the Beatles, showing the group en
route for another Hamburg slog.*

**18 November**
Night     Cavern Club

Another highly successful Welcome
Home night.

**19 November**
Lunchtime     Cavern Club

Night     Adelphi Ballroom,
New Street,
West Bromwich,
Staffordshire

This return visit to the Midlands
necessitated an 85-mile afternoon dash
down from the north.

**20 November**     Floral Hall, Southport

Another two-performance theatre
appearance.

**21 November**
Lunchtime     Cavern Club

Night     Cavern Club

The lunchtime session, originally
slated for the Remo Four, was played
by the Beatles in a swap for the 23
November gig.

*In this article from the* Peterborough Standard *the reviewer left the reader in little doubt as to what he thought of the Beatles' performance. Does he still only remember Frank Ifield?*

| 22 November | Majestic Ballroom, Birkenhead |

**23 November** ~~CANCELLED~~
Lunchtime    Cavern Club

Night    Tower Ballroom, New Brighton

The lunchtime gig at the Cavern Club was fulfilled by the Remo Four because the Beatles had gone down to London for an audition with BBC television, arranged so that producers could see whether the group had any TV potential. It took place at 12:20 p.m. in St James Hall, Gloucester Terrace, London W2. Four days later, Brian Epstein learned that they had failed!

Afterwards the group sped back to Merseyside for an unusual engagement at the Tower Ballroom, the 12th annual Lancashire and Cheshire Arts Ball. Sharing the bill with the Beatles were Billy Kramer and the Coasters (prior to Epstein signing Kramer to a management contract, adding a spurious initial, J, and severing the Coasters link in favour of the Dakotas), the Llew Hird Jazz Band and the one-and-only Clan McCleod Pipe Band!

**24 November**    Royal Lido Ballroom, Central Beach, Prestatyn, Flintshire, Wales

Only the Beatles' second-ever Welsh engagement, following the gig in nearby Rhyl four months previously.

**25 November**
Night    Cavern Club

**28 November**
Night    Cavern Club
   and    Young Idea Dance, 527 Club, Lewis's Department Store, Ranelagh Street, Liverpool

Two engagements in one night, the second of which was a staff dance held on the top floor of Lewis's, arguably the premier department store in Liverpool.

On 26 November the Beatles had returned to Abbey Road studios in London to record their second single, while on the following day they stayed in the capital and recorded an appearance on the BBC radio programme *The Talent Spot*. It was broadcast on 4 December.

**29 November**    Majestic Ballroom, Birkenhead

**30 November**
Lunchtime    Cavern Club

Night    Town Hall, Market Street, Earlestown, Newton-le-Willows, Cheshire

Brian Epstein always referred to this Earlestown date when he stated that the Beatles played in Warrington in 1962.

The night was billed as The Big Beat Show No. 2 and was presented by T&T Vicars Sports and Social Club (Football Section)!

**1 December**    (Victory) Memorial Hall, Northwich
   and    Tower Ballroom, New Brighton

The Beatles were added to the New Brighton bill just one day before the gig, in order to boost flagging ticket sales. It meant a hurried journey up from Northwich and a very late-night spot on stage.

**2 December** ~~CANCELLED~~
Night    Cavern Club

Embassy Cinema, Broadway, Peterborough, Northamptonshire

This fine piece of opportunism by Brian Epstein backfired disastrously when the Beatles simply bombed on this

---

# I'll remember Frank Ifield
## — says *Lyndon Whittaker*

IT IS EASY TO SEE why Frank Ifield has been so popular in this country. No pseudo American accent; no sulky Presley look. Frank Ifield is himself and he flashed many a happy smile as he breezed through a confident performance at the Embassy on Sunday.

As expected his well-known hit songs "I remember you," "Lovesick blues" and "She taught me how to yodel" were sung in addition to "Lonesome Me" and "Lucky devil".

Ifield came well up to expectations, but the supporting artists failed to please. Just a year ago, Billy Fury, Eden Kane, Karl Denver, The Allisons and Chas. McDevitt all appeared on the same show. Since then there has been a gradual decline in the standard of supporting artists.

"The exciting Beatles" rock group quite frankly failed to excite me. The drummer apparently thought that his job was to lead, not to provide rhythm. He made far too much noise and in their final number "Twist and Shout" it sounded as though everyone was trying to make more noise than the others. In a more mellow mood, their "A taste of honey" was much better and "Love me do" was tolerable.

Young vocalist Susan Cope seemed more confident than when she last appeared at the Embassy on the Bobby Vee Show, and she introduced a little piano playing into her

---

Frank Ifield bill. The experience may have been good, but the damage to the group's collective ego was extensive. Ray McFall at the Cavern Club graciously waived the contracted Beatles gig for this day.

**5 December**
Lunchtime    Cavern Club

Night    Cavern Club

Note: On 3 and 4 December the Beatles appeared live on television, on *Discs-A-GoGo* and *Tuesday Rendezvous* respectively. On both programmes they sang 'Love Me Do'.

**6 December**    Club Django, Ground Floor, Queen's Hotel, Promenade, Southport, Lancashire

Club Django – as the name implies – was essentially a jazz preserve, but the management were too aware of the Beatles' escalating success to let an opportunity of booking the group pass them by.

**7 December**
Lunchtime    Cavern Club

Night    Tower Ballroom, New Brighton

The Beatles headed a seven-group line-up.

**8 December**    Oasis Club, Manchester

118

**9 December**
Night          Cavern Club

The Beatles' record producer George Martin and his assistant Judy Lockhart-Smith attended this performance.

**10 December**
Lunchtime      Cavern Club

**11 December**   La Scala Ballroom, Runcorn

The Beatles' second Runcorn date though, unlike the first occasion, this was a NEMS presentation.

**12 December**
Lunchtime      Cavern Club

Night          Cavern Club

**13 December**   Corn Exchange, St Paul's Square, Bedford, Bedfordshire

Another southern engagement, arranged by the promoters following the withdrawal of the artiste originally booked to appear, Joe Brown.

**14 December**   Music Hall, The Square, Shrewsbury, Shropshire

In Jaybee country but, in fact, a major booking with promoter Lewis Buckley. Most top acts of the day played here.

**15 December**   Majestic Ballroom, Birkenhead

Two entirely separate gigs in one night. During the evening the Beatles performed a standard Majestic booking. Then, at midnight, the first-ever *Mersey Beat* poll awards show (for 1962) began. As winners of the poll (for the second year in succession) the Beatles closed the show at four o'clock in the morning, and were also presented with a handsome plaque by editor Bill Harry.

The poll runners-up, on stage immediately prior to the Beatles, were Lee Curtis and the All-Stars, so there was another encounter with Pete Best.

**16 December**
Night          Cavern Club

The Beatles' last Cavern Club appearance of 1962.

On 17 December the group appeared live on Granada television's programme *People and Places*.

### VISIT TO HAMBURG

| 18–31 December (except 25 December) (13 nights) | Star-Club, Grosse Freiheit |
| --- | --- |

The Beatles grudgingly left England, and their chart record, radio, TV and increasingly prestigious live bookings, for the probably unnecessary, and most certainly unwanted, fifth and final club trip to Hamburg. Despite the increased fee of 750 DM per man per week, all the four Beatles could think about was getting back home to England to capitalize on their success.

The final 42 hours on the Star-Club stage brought their gruelling Hamburg experience to a total of approximately 800 hours. Quite how valuable the work tied up in this staggering statistic was to prove in the ensuing four years, 1963 to 1966, was, at this point, beyond comprehension.

The Beatles had served their apprenticeship, and served it the hard way. They were now ready to take on whatever the world could throw at them.

RETURN TO UK

---

**Other engagements played**
None

**Engagements not played**
A series of planned Beatles engagements in Chester in March 1962 was cancelled and it was another five months before the group made their debut in the Cheshire town.

There is no evidence whatsoever to support a claim that the Beatles played at the Kraal Club in New Brighton, Cheshire, in 1962. Most Liverpool rock groups played there but not, it seems, the Beatles.

The Beatles did not play live at the Silver Blades Ice Rink in Prescot Road, Liverpool, during this or any other year, contrary to popular belief. In fact, the Beatles did not perform live in any ice rink at any time, unlike virtually every other group on Merseyside and elsewhere.

The Beatles first played in Sheffield, Yorkshire, in February 1963, not in November 1962 as claimed in one book on the group.

The Beatles did not perform live in Nuneaton, Warwickshire, despite claims to that effect in the Beatles' first-ever press release, issued at the time of the release of 'Love Me Do' and illustrated on page 102. The only beat venue in that town was the Co-operative Ballroom, and the promoter from the early sixties there has assured the author that, sadly, he never booked the group.

Brian Epstein's grand whole-page advertisement in *Mersey Beat* in December 1962 mentioned that the Beatles had played in Blackpool. This was not strictly true. The Beatles were in fact *provisionally* booked for a short season in late 1962 at the Picador Club in Bloomfield Road, Blackpool, but this was cancelled by the manager of the club after what he saw as a poor television appearance by the group on the Granada show *People and Places*. Epstein may, however, have been referring to the Beatles' 25 August gig in nearby Fleetwood.

The Beatles did not play at the Klic Klic Klub in Stanley Street, Southport, Lancashire, in 1962, despite lingering local rumours to the contrary. The Klub did not actually open for business until 12 January 1963, and even then the Beatles never played there.

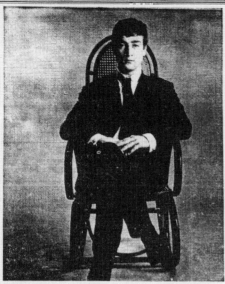

LEFT
**JOHN LENNON**

RIGHT
**PAUL McCARTNEY**

BOTTOM LEFT
**GEORGE HARRISON**

BOTTOM RIGHT
**RINGO STARR**

# 1962 the BEATLES

## YEAR OF ACHIEVEMENT

★ WON "MERSEY BEAT" POPULARITY POLL (2nd YEAR)

★ VOTED FIFTH IN NEW MUSICAL EXPRESS POLL FOR BEST BRITISH VOCAL GROUP

★ E.M.I. RECORDING CONTRACT

★ FOUR B.B.C. BROADCASTS

★ FOUR T.V. APPEARANCES

★ TWO LUXEMBOURG BROADCASTS

★ TWO HAMBURG ENAGEMENTS

★ ENTERED THE TOP FIFTY WITHIN TWO DAYS OF "LOVE ME DO" RELEASE

★ HIT NO 21 IN THE CHARTS WITH "LOVE ME DO" THEIR FIRST DISC

★ APPEARED WITH LITTLE RICHARD, FRANK IFIELD, JOE BROWN, JET HARRIS, GENE VINCENT, JOHNNY AND THE HURRICANES, CRAIG DOUGLAS and many others.

★ APPEARED AT LIVERPOOL (EMPIRE), BIRMINGAM, MANCHESTER, HULL, DONCASTER, CREWE, STROUD, COVENTRY, SHREWSBURY, BEDFORD, PETERBOROUGH, PRESTON, BLACKPOOL, etc., etc.

---

AND IN 1963

★ **'Please, Please Me'**
Released by Parlophone
JANUARY 11th

★ Appearances in 'Thank Your Lucky Stars,' 'Saturday Club,' and B.B.C. T.V. (January).

★ **Scottish Tour**
(JANUARY)

★ **Helen Shapiro Tour**
(FEBRUARY)

★ **'Love Me Do'**
RELEASE AMERICA, CANADA AND GERMANY
TOMMY ROE/CHRIS MONTEZ TOUR (MARCH)
AND WHO KNOWS !

---

Sole Direction:
**Brian Epstein,**
Nems Enterprises Ltd.,
12/14 Whitechapel,
Liverpool, 1
ROYal 7895

Recording Manager:
**George Martin,**
EMI Records Limited,
20, Manchester Square,
London W.1

Press Representative:
**Tony Calder**
    **Enterprises**
15, Poland Street,
London W. 1

Road Manager:
**Neil Aspinall**

Fan Club Secretary:
**Miss R. Brown**
90, Buchanan Road,
Wallasey, Cheshire

# THE MUSIC

This is an attempt to detail the live performance repertoire of the Beatles in 1962, showing – where possible – the group's vocalist, the composer(s) of the song and the name of the artist/group who recorded the version which influenced the group. It is, in all likelihood, an incomplete guide.

| Song title | Main vocalist(s) | Composer(s) | Influential version (year) |
| --- | --- | --- | --- |
| Ain't She Sweet[1] | John | Yellen/Ager | — |
| Anna (Go to Him) | John | Alexander | Arthur Alexander (1962) |
| Ask Me Why | John | LENNON/McCartney | — |
| Baby it's You | John | M. David/Bacharach/Williams | The Shirelles (1961) |
| Bad Boy | John | Williams | Larry Williams (1959) |
| Beautiful Dreamer | Paul | Foster | Slim Whitman (1954) |
| Be-Bop-A-Lula | John | Vincent/Davis | Gene Vincent and his Blue Caps (1956) |
| Besame Mucho | Paul | Velazquez/Skylar | The Coasters (1960) |
| Boys[2] | Pete Best or Ringo | Dixon/Farrell | The Shirelles (1960) |
| Carol | John | Berry | Chuck Berry (1958) |
| Catswalk[3] | (Instrumental) | McCartney | — |
| Clarabella | Paul | Pingatore | The Jodimars (1956) |
| C'mon Everybody | ? | Cochran/Capehart | Eddie Cochran (1959) |
| Crying, Waiting, Hoping | George | Holly | Buddy Holly (1959) |
| Dance in the Street | ? | David/Welch | Gene Vincent and his Blue Caps (1958) |
| Darktown Strutters Ball | ? | Brooks | Joe Brown and the Bruvvers (1960) |
| (There's a) Devil in her Heart[4] | George | Drapkin | The Donays (1962) |
| Dizzy Miss Lizzy | John | Williams | Larry Williams (1958) |
| Don't Ever Change | George | Goffin/King | The Crickets (1962) |
| Dream | George | Miller | Cliff Richard and the Shadows (1961) |
| Dream Baby (How Long Must I Dream?) | Paul | Walker | Roy Orbison (1962) |
| Everybody's Trying to Be my Baby | George | Perkins | Carl Perkins (1958) |

1 The version most likely to have prompted the Beatles to perform this song would be Gene Vincent's 1956 rock recording. But since John Lennon's vocal rendition sounds quite different to Vincent's it seems apparent that John arranged his own, unique, version.

2 Pete Best sang the lead vocal until August 1962. There-after Ringo Starr assumed the role.

3 When this tune was released on record by the Chris Barber Band in 1967 it was re-titled 'Catcall'.

4 The Donays were an all-girl group so this was originally titled '(There's a) Devil in his Heart'.

| Song title | Main vocalist(s) | Composer(s) | Influential version (year) |
|---|---|---|---|
| Falling in Love Again (Can't Help It) | Paul | Hollander | Marlene Dietrich (1930) |
| Glad all Over[5] | George | Schroeder/Tepper/Bennett | Carl Perkins (1957) |
| Hallelujah, I Love Her So | Paul | Charles | Ray Charles (1956) and Eddie Cochran (1960) |
| Hello Little Girl | John | LENNON/McCartney | — |
| Hey! Baby | Paul | Channel/Cobb | Bruce Channel (1962) |
| The Hippy Hippy Shake | Paul | Romero | Chan Romero (1959) |
| Hold Me Tight | Paul | Lennon/McCARTNEY | — |
| Honey Don't[6] | John | Perkins | Carl Perkins (1956) |
| The Honeymoon Song[7] | Paul | Theodorakis/Sansom | Manuel [and the Music of the Mountains] (1959) |
| I Fancy me Chances | ? | Lennon/McCartney | — |
| I Forgot to Remember to Forget | George | Kesler/Feathers | Elvis Presley (1955) |
| I Got a Woman | John | Charles/Richards | Ray Charles (1954) and Elvis Presley (1956) |
| I Got to Find my Baby | John | Berry | Chuck Berry (1960) |
| I Just Don't Understand | John | Wilkin/Westberry | Ann-Margret (1961) |
| I Remember You | Paul | Mercer/Schertzinger | Frank Ifield (1962) |
| I Saw Her Standing There | Paul | Lennon/McCARTNEY | — |
| I Wish I Could Shimmy Like My Sister Kate | John | Piron | The Olympics (1961) |
| If You Gotta Make a Fool of Somebody | Paul | Clark | James Ray (1961) |
| I'm Gonna Sit Right Down and Cry (Over You) | John | Thomas/Biggs | Elvis Presley (1956) |
| I'm Talking about You | John | Berry | Chuck Berry (1961) |
| Johnny B. Goode | John | Berry | Chuck Berry (1958) |
| Kansas City/Hey-Hey-Hey-Hey![8] | Paul | Leiber/Stoller/Penniman | Little Richard (1959) |
| Leave my Kitten Alone | John | John/Turner/McDougal | Little Willie John (1959) |
| Lend Me your Comb | John/Paul | Twomey/Wise/Weisman | Carl Perkins (1957) |
| Like Dreamers Do | Paul | Lennon/McCARTNEY | — |
| Little Queenie | Paul | Berry | Chuck Berry (1959) |
| Lonesome Tears in my Eyes | John | Burnette/Burnette/Burlison/Mortimer | The Johnny Burnette Trio (1956) |
| Long Tall Sally | Paul | Johnson/Penniman/Blackwell | Little Richard (1956) |

5 Different to the same-titled song taken to number one in the charts by the Dave Clark Five in January 1964.

6 John Lennon sang lead vocals on this song until approximately August 1963, after which Ringo Starr took over.

7 Since Manuel's original version of 'The Honeymoon Song' was purely instrumental, and the only pre-1961 vocal version of the song was recorded in French by Petula Clark, one must presume that Paul McCartney studied the song's sheet music in order to learn the lyrics.

8 This medley of two songs recorded separately by Little Richard in 1959 was not the Beatles' idea. Richard himself recorded the same medley in 1959 and it is this version which the Beatles cover.

| Song title | Main vocalist(s) | Composer(s) | Influential version (year) |
|---|---|---|---|
| Love Me Do | Paul | Lennon/McCartney | — |
| Love of the Loved | Paul | Lennon/McCartney | — |
| Lucille | Paul | Penniman/Collins | Little Richard (1957) |
| Mama Said | ? | Dixon/Donson | The Shirelles (1961) |
| Matchbox[9] | Pete Best or John | Perkins | Carl Perkins (1957) |
| Memphis, Tennessee | John | Berry | Chuck Berry (1959) |
| Money (That's What I Want) | John | Gordy/Bradford | Barret Strong (1959) |
| Mr Moonlight | John | Johnson | Dr Feelgood (1962) |
| My Bonnie Lies over the Ocean[10] | John | Trad. arr. Sheridan | Tony Sheridan and the Beatles (1961) |
| Nothin' Shakin' (but the Leaves on the Trees) | George | Colacrai/Fontaine/ Lampert/Cleveland | Eddie Fontaine (1958) |
| The One after 909 | John | Lennon/McCartney | — |
| Ooh! My Soul | Paul | Penniman | Little Richard (1958) |
| Open (Your Lovin' Arms | George | Knox | Buddy Knox (1962) |
| Over The Rainbow | Paul | Harburg/Arlen | Gene Vincent (1959) |
| Peppermint Twist | Pete Best | Dee/Glover | Joey Dee and the Starliters (1962) |
| A Picture of You | George | Beveridge/Oakman | Joe Brown and the Bruvvers (1962) |
| Pinwheel Twist | Paul | Lennon/McCartney | — |
| Please Mister Postman | John | Holland/Bateman/ Gordy | The Marvelettes (1961) |
| Please Please Me | John/Paul | Lennon/McCartney | — |
| P.S. I Love You | Paul | Lennon/McCartney | — |
| Red Hot | John | Emerson | Ronnie Hawkins (1959) |
| Red Sails in the Sunset | Paul | Kennedy/Williams | Joe Turner (1959) or Emile Ford and the Checkmates (1960) |
| Reminiscing | George | Curtis | Buddy Holly (1962) |
| Road Runner | ? | McDaniel | Bo Diddley (1960) |
| Rock and Roll Music | John | Berry | Chuck Berry (1957) |
| Roll over Beethoven | George | Berry | Chuck Berry (1956) |
| Save the Last Dance for Me | John | Pomus/Shuman | The Drifters (1960) |
| Searchin' | Paul | Leiber/Stoller | The Coasters (1957) |
| September in the Rain | Paul | Dubin/Warren | Dinah Washington (1961) |
| Sharing You | George | Goffin/King | Bobby Vee (1962) |
| The Sheik of Araby | George | Smith/Snyder/Wheeler | Fats Domino (1961) |

**9** Pete Best sang the lead vocal until August 1962. Thereafter John Lennon assumed the role. The Beatles did not perform this song live after 1962 but when, in 1964, they released a studio version on record, Ringo Starr sang lead vocal.

**10** The Sheridan/Beatles single of this song – titled simply 'My Bonnie' – credited the composer as Trad. arr. Sheridan although it was first written by Charles T. Pratt (under the pseudonyms J. T. Wood and H. T. Fulmer) in 1881. A rock version of the song was first realized on disc by Ray Charles in 1958.

| Song title | Main vocalist(s) | Composer(s) | Influential version (year) |
|---|---|---|---|
| Sheila | George | Roe | Tommy Roe (1962) |
| Shimmy Shimmy | John/Paul | Massey/Schubert | Bobby Freeman (1960) |
| A Shot of Rhythm and Blues | John | Thompson | Arthur Alexander (1961) |
| Slow Down | John | Williams | Larry Williams (1958) |
| So How Come (No One Loves Me) | George | Bryant | The Everly Brothers (1960) |
| Soldier of Love (Lay Down your Arms) | John | Cason/Moon | Arthur Alexander (1962) |
| Some other Guy | John/Paul | Leiber/Stoller/Barrett | Ritchie Barrett (1962) |
| Sure to Fall (in Love with You) | Paul | Perkins/Claunch/Cantrell | Carl Perkins (1956) |
| Sweet Little Sixteen | John | Berry | Chuck Berry (1958) |
| Take Good Care of my Baby | George | Goffin/King | Bobby Vee (1961) |
| A Taste of Honey | Paul | Marlow/Scott | Lenny Welch (1962) |
| That's All Right (Mama) | Paul | Crudup | Elvis Presley (1962) |
| Three Cool Cats | George | Leiber/Stoller | The Coasters (1962) |
| Till there Was You | Paul | Willson | Peggy Lee (1961) |
| Tip of my Tongue | Paul | Lennon/McCARTNEY | — |
| To Know Her Is to Love Her[11] | John | Spector | The Teddy Bears (1958) |
| Too Much Monkey Business | John | Berry | Chuck Berry (1956) |
| Twenty Flight Rock | Paul | Cochran/Fairchild | Eddie Cochran (1957) |
| Twist and Shout | John | Russell/Medley | The Isley Brothers (1962) |
| Well . . . (Baby Please Don't Go) | John | Ward | The Olympics (1958) |
| What a Crazy World We're Living in | George | Klein | Joe Brown (1962) |
| When I'm Sixty-Four | Paul | Lennon/McCARTNEY | — |
| Where Have You Been all my Life? | John | Mann/Weil | Arthur Alexander (1962) |
| Wild in the Country | Pete Best | Peretti/Creatore/Weiss | Elvis Presley (1961) |
| Will You Love Me Tomorrow? | John | Goffin/King | The Shirelles (1961) |
| Wooden Heart[12] | Paul | Twomey/Wise/Weisman/Kaempfert | Elvis Presley (1960) |
| Words of Love | John/George | Holly | Buddy Holly (1957) |
| You Don't Understand Me | John | Massey | Bobby Freeman (1960 |
| You Really Got a Hold on Me | John | Robinson | [Smokey Robinson and] The Miracles (1962) |
| Youngblood | George | Leiber/Stoller/Pomus | The Coasters (1957) |
| Your Feet's too Big | Paul | Benson/Fisher | Fats Waller (1939) or Chubby Checker (1961) |
| Your True Love | George | Perkins | Carl Perkins (1957) |

**11** Originally written and recorded as 'To Know Him Is to Love Him'.

**12** Like Presley's version, Paul McCartney sang the lyrics in part German and part English. This was a particular favourite, for obvious reasons, with Hamburg club audiences.

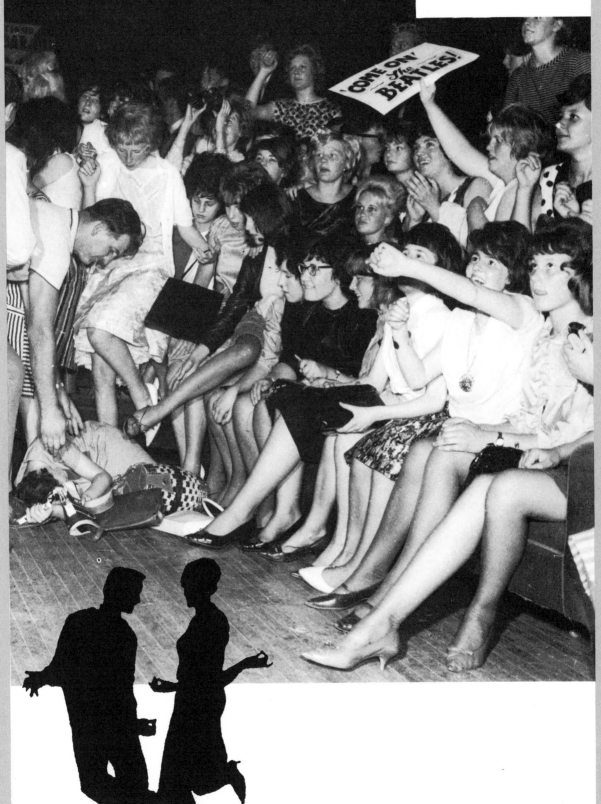

**1963**

The year it all went berserk, 1963, started in fairly quiet fashion, with the Beatles on a five-engagement tour of Scotland during the worst British winter weather for decades. The tour had been booked the previous November through Jack Fallon at the Cana Variety Agency with Albert Bonici, a Scottish promoter, at a cost to Bonici of just £42 per night. Although the bad weather actually caused the cancellation of the first of the five dates, and Bonici lost money on the tour, Brian Epstein had written into the contract a clause offering Bonici an exclusive option on all future Beatles appearances in Scotland. This, together with Epstein's verbal agreement with Arthur Howes, effectively tied up any future Beatles tours in the United Kingdom.

The Beatles' second single, the punchy, effervescent 'Please Please Me', was released by EMI on the following Friday, 11 January, and it wasn't long before it was following 'Love Me Do' into the charts, entering on 17 January. But whereas 'Love Me Do' had staged an oddly varied, up and down, run on the hit parade, 'Please Please Me' ran a more traditional course: a key television appearance and favourable press reviews leading to valuable radio airplay and healthy sales, importantly this time not just centred around Liverpool and the north-west of England, but on a national scale. Indeed a great many of the Beatles' home-town fans, naturally possessive of the group after two years' exclusive ownership, resisted buying the disc lest it became a big success and took the Beatles out of their Merseyside grasp and into the national view.

It was not long before this fear became a reality. As 'Please Please Me' took a fast and firm grip on the charts so the Beatles' circle of live bookings grew ever larger and their Liverpool appearances fewer and further apart. Six Cavern Club gigs in January, three in February, none in March, tells its own tale. But the Beatles had worked hard for this situation, driven relentlessly with style and panache by Brian Epstein. In the 12 months of 1963 the Beatles slogged their way through the most uncompromising, punishing and utterly ruthless schedule of concert tours, one-night appearances, recording sessions, radio recordings, television appearances, photo-graphic sessions and press interviews. They dodged no one and no assignment. Everyone could have access to the group, no reasonable demand was refused. Never before had a pop group, or any musical act/artiste, exerted themselves quite so much.

After a rapid climb 'Please Please Me' hit the prized and once so unattainable number one spot on the *New Musical Express* singles chart for the week ending 22 February, initially sharing the position with Frank Ifield's 'The Wayward Wind' before, one week later, occupying the summit alone. The seemingly impossible mountain had been scaled and, not unnaturally, the Beatles and Brian Epstein, their friends, families, associates and employees, were absolutely ecstatic. The group was about to start on the second phase of their comparatively low-key tour of Britain with Helen Shapiro when word of the number-one chart placing came through in a telegram from the *NME*. In the Cavern Club on 19 February, just as the Beatles were due on stage, Bob Wooler proudly announced the news. It was met with stony, sombre, silence. But throughout the rest of Britain, in the audiences on the Shapiro tour, the Beatles became *the* attraction. Suddenly it became their tour.

Increasingly rapturous receptions and steadily growing tumult greeted the Beatles everywhere on the tour immediately following the one with Shapiro, this time with two American artistes, Tommy Roe and Chris Montez. Admittedly neither star was exceptionally big in the UK, both having scored just a couple of chart hits here. But they *were* American, and no British act had ever superseded an American act. The Beatles did – and they were clearly both pleased and embarrassed by it at the same time – having, by audience demand, to assume top-of-the-bill status over the Americans. The Beatles were, if anything, powerless to stop it and as bemused as everyone else over what was happening.

The tour with Roe and Montez concluded at the end of March but there was no respite in the Beatles' barrage of Britain. Throughout April, as the deeply packed snow finally began to thaw, the group covered England north, south, east and west on a nightly rota of ballroom appearances. Their third single, 'From

Below: The Beatles down south, in Chatham, Kent, on 12 January. Bottom: Back in the Cavern Club but yearning for pastures new, January 1963.

*Right: By audience demand, the Beatles were promoted from third to top act on the Roe/Montez tour, playing the all-important closing spot. This programme shows how one member of the audience recorded the alteration. Below: From the days when the NME took front-page advertisements, this is Arthur Howes' spread for his spring promotions.*

your programme for tonight

1  The Terry Young Six
2
3  Debbie Lee
4  Tony Marsh
5  Chris Montez  TOMMY ROE
   THE BEATLES

Interval

6  The Terry Young Six
7  The Viscounts
8  Tony Marsh
9  TOMMY ROE  CHRIS MONTEZ
   The Beatles

God Save the Queen

New Musical Express—February 22, 1963

# CLIFF

Registered at the G.P.O. as a Newspaper

## LOVE
(MAKES THE WORLD GO ROUND)
PAUL ANKA on RCA 1326

## ESO BESO
PAUL ANKA on RCA 1318

SPANKA MUSIC LTD. ALL ENQUIRIES TO
K.P.M. 21 DENMARK STREET, W.C.2  TEM 3856

# MUSICAL EXPRESS

WORLD'S LARGEST CIRCULATION OF ANY MUSIC PAPER
—WEEKLY SALES EXCEED 200,000 (MEMBERS OF ABC)

# SEDAKA
ALICE IN WONDERLAND
RCA 1331
RCA VICTOR

---

★ ARTHUR HOWES *Presents:* STARS FROM THE HIT PARADE ★

## FRANK IFIELD AND BIG ROAD SHOW

| | | | | |
|---|---|---|---|---|
| Sun., Mar. 10th | Coventry | Coventry Theatre | 6.00 & 8.30 | |
| Sun., Mar. 17th | Kingston | A.B.C. | 5.15 & 7.45 | |
| Sat., Mar. 23rd | Brighton | Hippodrome | 6.00 & 8.40 | |
| Sun., Mar. 24th | Bournemouth | Winter Gardens | | |

| | | | | |
|---|---|---|---|---|
| Sat., Mar. 30th | Cardiff | Sophia Gdns. Pav. | 6.00 & 8.40 | |
| Sun., Mar. 31st | Bristol | Colston Hall | 5.30 & 7.45 | |
| Tues., Apr. 2nd | Manchester | Ardwick Apollo | 6.30 & 8.45 | |
| Wed., Apr. 3rd | Huddersfield | A.B.C. | 6.15 & 8.30 | |
| Thur., Apr. 4th | Stockton | Globe | 6.15 & 8.30 | |
| Fri., Apr. 5th | Sheffield | City Hall | | |
| Sat., Apr. 6th | Bradford | Gaumont | 6.00 & 8.30 | |

★ ★ ★
## HELEN SHAPIRO
### THE BEATLES
DANNY WILLIAMS ★ KENNY LYNCH
THE HONEYS ★ THE KESTRELS
RED PRICE BAND ★ DAVE ALLEN

| | | | |
|---|---|---|---|
| Sat., Feb. 23rd | Mansfield | Granada | 6.15 & 8.30 |
| Sun., Feb. 24th | Coventry | Coventry Theatre | 6.00 & 8.30 |
| Tues., Feb. 26th | Taunton | Gaumont | 6.25 & 8.40 |
| Wed., Feb. 27th | York | Rialto | 6.40 & 8.45 |
| Thur., Feb. 28th | Shrewsbury | Granada | 6.15 & 8.30 |
| Fri., Mar. 1st | Southport | Odeon | 6.25 & 8.40 |

| | | | |
|---|---|---|---|
| Sat., Mar. 2nd | Sheffield | City Hall | 6.15 & 8.40 |
| Sun., Mar. 3rd | Hanley | Gaumont | 6.15 & 8.40 |

## HELEN SHAPIRO
THE KESTRELS ★ THE HONEYS ★ DAVE ALLEN

| | | | |
|---|---|---|---|
| Sat., Mar. 16th | Birmingham | Town Hall | |
| Sun., Mar. 17th | Derby | Gaumont | 6.00 & 8.30 |

## JET HARRIS & TONY MEEHAN
DANNY WILLIAMS ★ RED PRICE BAND

| | | | |
|---|---|---|---|
| Mon., Mar. 18th | Maidstone | Granada | 6.20 & 8.30 |
| Wed., Mar. 20th | Aylesbury | Granada | 7.00 & 9.10 |

| | | | |
|---|---|---|---|
| Thur., Mar. 21st | Cheltenham | Odeon | 6.30 & 8.45 |
| Fri., Mar. 22nd | Plymouth | A.B.C. | 6.15 & 8.30 |
| Sat., Mar. 23rd | Cardiff | Sophia Gdns. Pav. | 6.00 & 8.40 |

★ ★
## TOMMY ROE ★ CHRIS MONTEZ
(In association with Evelyn Taylor)
THE BEATLES ★ THE VISCOUNTS ★ DEBBIE LEE
TONY MARSH ★ TERRY YOUNG SIX

| | | | |
|---|---|---|---|
| Sat., Mar. 9th | East Ham | Granada | 6.45 & 9.00 |
| Sun., Mar. 10th | Birmingham | Hippodrome | 5.30 & 8.00 |
| Tues., Mar. 12th | Bedford | Granada | 7.00 & 9.10 |
| Wed., Mar. 13th | York | Rialto | 6.40 & 8.45 |
| Thur., Mar. 14th | Wolverhampton | Gaumont | |

| | | | |
|---|---|---|---|
| Fri., Mar. 15th | Bristol | Colston Hall | 6.30 & 8.45 |
| Sat., Mar. 16th | Sheffield | City Hall | 6.10 & 8.40 |
| Sun., Mar. 17th | Peterborough | Embassy | 5.30 & 8.00 |
| Mon., Mar. 18th | Gloucester | A.B.C. | 6.15 & 8.30 |
| Tues., Mar. 19th | Cambridge | A.B.C. | 6.15 & 8.30 |
| Wed., Mar. 20th | Romford | Ritz | 6.45 & 9.00 |
| Thur., Mar. 21st | Croydon | A.B.C. | 6.45 & 9.00 |
| Fri., Mar. 22nd | Doncaster | Gaumont | 6.15 & 8.50 |

| | | | |
|---|---|---|---|
| Sat., Mar. 23rd | Newcastle | City Hall | 6.30 & 8.40 |
| Sun., Mar. 24th | Liverpool | Empire | 5.40 & 8.00 |
| Tues., Mar. 26th | Mansfield | Granada | 6.20 & 8.30 |
| Wed., Mar. 27th | Northampton | A.B.C. | 6.30 & 8.45 |
| Thur., Mar. 28th | Exeter | A.B.C. | 6.15 & 8.30 |
| Fri., Mar. 29th | Lewisham | Odeon | 7.00 & 9.15 |
| Sat., Mar. 30th | Portsmouth | Guildhall | 6.30 & 8.50 |
| Sun., Mar. 31st | Leicester | De Montfort Hall | |

*Above: Americans Chris Montez and Tommy Roe flanked by the four pretenders from England. Right: the Beatles start their third UK tour of the year, and it's only May.*

Me to You', was released on 12 April so there were a few radio and television appearances to be slotted in too, promoting the disc. As can be seen in the illustrated newspaper articles, localized Beatles-inspired mayhem and hysteria had definitely started by this time, some six months before it picked up on a national scale in the wake of Fleet Street's sudden awareness of the happening. *Why* the mayhem started, and why it was necessary, was, is, and always will be, a mystery, defying social psychologists and historians then as now. It just *happened.* Certainly the Beatles were not the first to be subjected to such vocal adulation. Frank Sinatra, in his prime, had sent the bobby-soxers swooning and screaming. Johnny Ray too, in the mid-fifties. And in the yet-young rock and roll era Elvis Presley in the USA and Cliff Richard in Britain had already inspired similar scenes without ever knowing how or why. Talent, which the Beatles had in profusion, was not the only answer, witness the meteoric rise to fame a decade later of the Bay City Rollers. The Beatles too were baffled by it and – initially at least – more than a little flattered. But this was to turn into anger and resentment before very long as they became stifled by the very madness of it all.

When 'From Me to You' took an almighty leap into the *New Musical Express* chart, landing, feet first, at number six and ready for a lengthy spell at number one within one further week, it was clear to all that here really was something bright, fresh and new on the music scene. Strangely, for a while, the Beatles had been attempting to gauge what the next pop music fad might be. Might it be Latin-beat, calypso-rock, a resurgence of twist music? But what they hadn't considered was what actually happened: they, the Beatles, *created* the next scene. It was them, or Mersey beat, or the Mersey sound or even 'The Invasion of the Liverpoplians' as one pop paper hack ludicrously dubbed it.

The Beatles' 'overnight success' had some quite remarkable side effects. Firstly, unfashionable Liverpool suddenly became El Dorado. *The* place to be. Phenomenal numbers of record company A&R

men, agents, managers and tour promoters rushed up to Merseyside *en masse* waving pens and dotted lines. It wasn't long before Liverpool had broken the long-established London stranglehold and taken over the pop charts, with Gerry and the Pacemakers, Billy J. Kramer and the Dakotas, Cilla Black, the Searchers, the Fourmost, the Swinging Blue Jeans (renamed from the Swinging Bluegenes), and the Merseybeats all following in the wake of the Beatles. To say that they all owed their success to the Beatles would actually be a great understatement, for without Epstein and the Beatles opening the metaphorical floodgates it is highly unlikely that any of them would have achieved national success. Few of them lasted the distance anyway, and those that did were largely – though not all – the ones managed by Brian Epstein. For after the Beatles had established a foothold on the charts with 'Love Me Do', Epstein had begun to expand his NEMS Enterprises umbrella to cover first the Big Three, the Merseybeats (though only for a short time and a contract was never signed) and Gerry and the Pacemakers, and then, soon afterwards, Billy J. Kramer and the Dakotas, the Four-most, Cilla Black and Tommy Quickly. Not all were successes – Quickly just couldn't find the 'hit formula' and the Big Three quit NEMS before very long because they preferred to remain true to their rhythm and blues roots, and not become what they saw as 'family entertainers'. Two groups, the Swinging Blue Jeans and King Size Taylor and the Dominoes, actually turned down management offers from Epstein. But those that did stay – often fuelled by freely donated, exclusive, Lennon—McCartney tunes – swamped the charts in 1963.[1] In the 52 hit parades published in

---

1 This was not the only benefit these artists gleaned by being in the same management organization as the Beatles. They also secured an enormous number of the live bookings offered to the Beatles which were impossible or inappropriate for the Beatles to fulfil. Rarely did Brian Epstein ever allow a promoter to go away empty-handed without another NEMS act instead. The careers of Gerry and the Pacemakers and Billy J. Kramer, to name but two, both got away to an immediately healthy start partly because they had played engagements in major halls and ballrooms north and south even before they had any chart success – gigs clearly slated by promoters for the Beatles.

*April . . . and the mayhem commences. This article describes the scenes in Kilburn, during the Beatles' second London gig.*

# Screaming teenagers flock to hear the Beatles

"**F**ANTASTIC. I've never known anything like it." That was the verdict of Ron Stoten, harassed manager of the State ballroom, Kilburn, on Tuesday evening.

He had spent an exhausting evening trying to hold back hundreds of hysterical, screaming teen-agers who had flocked to the State to see (and hear) the fabulous Beatles.

A capacity audience of over 1,000 (many more had to be turned away) swarmed round the stage, straining to get near the four boys from Liverpool (average age 20).

Amid piercing screams from the female element in the audience The Beatles put everything they'd got into some really sensational, throbbing numbers.

## FAMOUS SONGS

They ripped out their famous hit-parade songs, "Love Me Do" and "Please Please Me," then brought in one or two tracks from their new LP.

With Ringo Starr bashing out a tremendous, hypnotic beat at the back on the drums, the other three, John Lennon, George Harrison and

riotous than the first one, then it was.

Attacking the numbers with the same gusto (and that throbbing beat) The Beatles pounded out "Twist and Shout," "Taste Of Honey" and "Baby It's You."

But the highlight of their dynamic performance — to me at any rate — was their new record, released last week.

It's called, "From Me To You," and once again it is their own composition.

This number has a gorgeous

sound and was vigorously put over.

I shall be very surprised if it doesn't shoot up the hit-parade.

## BEST OF ALL

There are probably nearly 1,000 people already ordering their copies from their record shops.

This number went down best of all and there were several cries of "Encore" at the end.

Footnote: Negotiations are at present going on between the State ballroom and Brian Epstein (manager of The Beatles and Gerry and the Pacemakers) for Gerry and the Pacemakers (No 1 this week with "How Do You Do It") to do a similar spot at the State within the next few weeks.

The queues are probably already forming!

**PICTURES NEXT WEEK**

Michael Shepherd photos

n maybe, but if you "dig" beat ballads "Beatles"
en you'll know why these girls screamed as the
n through "With love from me to you."

pool lads, all in their
nties, brought a touch
Alley stardust to
Thursday night, For
hour in the Co-op.
treet, 300 screaming
d and twisted to the
thm of beat ballads
les."

to one another as though almost
two years of one night stands was
all in a day's work—which for them,
of course, is exactly what it is.

They ran the inevitable gauntlet
of female autograph hunters as they
tried to wind down and get changed
in time to get back to Liverpool for
a well-earned rest.

**BOUNCERS"**

as deafening and the
ere keyed up to a

Inside the hall, the teenagers were
still going strong to the music of
"Shaun and Sum People." Out of

---

1963 by *Record Retailer* three of these acts scored a total of 45 weeks in the Top Ten. Combined with the Beatles' tally of 40 weeks, Brian Epstein's groups accounted for 85 Top Ten placings. In December 1961 Epstein had been a record-store owner. By December 1963 he had helped to revitalize and revolutionize the British record industry as never before.

A second side effect of the Beatles' staggering success was the way it dramatically – and quickly – altered the grass-roots level of the British music scene. From as remarkably early as March or April 1963, throughout the length and breadth of Britain, the concept of beat/rock and roll music radically, noticeably, changed. An astonishing number of new clubs and venues opened to cater for this sudden upsurge in interest. Almost every town of medium-to-large population had one. And to fill these clubs thousands of Beatles-style, self-contained (i.e. writing and singing), leaderless groups were quickly formed, many of them later to swamp the once all-American British charts, indeed even the all-American American charts. Even the once-blasé media became interested, firstly of course, from about May 1963, on a localized scale with local and provincial newspapers affording the subject unprecedented column inches, and eventually, by the

autumn, on a national basis too, when Fleet Street finally picked up on the boom. Even the BBC began to realize what was happening and gave pop music its largest chunk of radio and television air time to date.

By the early summer of 1963 the Beatles were permeating all the echelons of the suddenly burgeoning pop business. After a stream of appearances on multitudinous radio shows, the BBC offered the group their own series. *Pop Go the Beatles* initially ran over four weekly programmes, from 24 May to 17 June, before it was extended for a further eleven weeks from 2 July. The four weekly music papers – *Melody Maker, New Musical Express, New Record Mirror* and *Disc* – were giving the Beatles' hectic activities blanket coverage, while the myriad weekly teenage girls' magazines, from *Valentine* to *Boyfriend*, had not been slow in picking up on the new fad either, with regular features, colour pin-up posters and 'interviews' with the Beatles. A publisher named Sean O'Mahony had already launched, with great success, *Beat Monthly*, a magazine predominantly featuring the Beatles and other Liverpool groups, and his preparations for the Beatles' own official magazine, *The Beatles Monthly Book*, were almost complete, with the initial issue going to press in early July for 1 August publication. Television too, particularly the

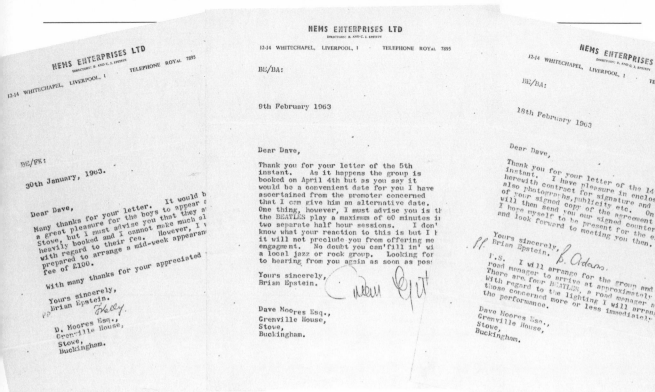

NEMS ENTERPRISES LTD
DIRECTORS: B. AND C. J. EPSTEIN
12-14 WHITECHAPEL, LIVERPOOL, 1    TELEPHONE ROYAL 7895

BE/FK:

30th January, 1963.

Dear Dave,

Many thanks for your letter.  It would b
a great pleasure for the boys to appear a
Stowe, but I must advise you that they a'
heavily booked and I cannot make much al
with regard to their fee.  However, I '
prepared to arrange a mid-week appearan'
fee of £100.

With many thanks for your appreciated

Yours sincerely,
pp Brian Epstein.

D. Moores Esq.,
Grenville House,
Stowe,
Buckingham.

---

NEMS ENTERPRISES LTD
DIRECTORS: B. AND C. J. EPSTEIN
12-14 WHITECHAPEL, LIVERPOOL, 1    TELEPHONE ROYAL 7895

BE/BA:

9th February 1963

Dear Dave,

Thank you for your letter of the 5th
instant.   As it happens the group is
booked on April 4th but as you say it
would be a convenient date for you I have
ascertained from the promoter concerned
that I can give him an alternative date.
One thing, however, I must advise you is th
the BEATLES play a maximum of 60 minutes ir
two separate half hour sessions.   I don'
know what your reaction to this is but I h
it will not preclude you from offering me
engagment.   No doubt you can'fill in' wi
a local jazz or rock group.   Looking for
to hearing from you again as soon as pos'

Yours sincerely,
Brian Epstein.

Dave Moores Esq.,
Grenville House,
Stowe,
Buckingham.

---

NEMS ENTERPRISES LTD
DIRECTORS: B. AND C. J. EPSTEIN
12-14 WHITECHAPEL, LIVERPOOL, 1    TELEPH

BE/BA:

18th February 1963

Dear Dave,

Thank you for your letter of the 14th
instant.   I have pleasure in enclosing
herewith contract for signature and ret
also photographs, publicity etc.   On rec
of your signed copy of the agreement we
will then send you our signed counterpar
I hope myself to be present for the engag
and look forward to meeting you then.

Yours sincerely,
pp Brian Epstein.
B. Adams.

P.S.   I will arrange for the group and the
road manager to arrive at approximately 4.3
There are four BEATLES, a road manager and
With regard to the lighting I will arrange
those concerned more or less immediately bef
the performance.

Dave Moores Esq.,
Grenville House,
Stowe,
Buckingham.

---

commercial network, had felt the groundswell of opinion from British youth quite early. ABC screened an all-Liverpool edition of *Lucky Stars (Summer Spin)* (the summer version of *Thank your Lucky Stars*), headed by the Beatles, on 29 June. And on the charts the Beatles reigned supreme. Their magnificent debut LP *Please Please Me*, a refreshing, zestful change from the dire, penny-pinching albums normally released by artists after a hit single, hit the top of the *Record Retailer* chart on 11 May and remained unmovable for 30 straight weeks ... until it was dislodged by the Beatles' own follow-up.

From 18 May until 9 June the Beatles toured Britain again – their third such jaunt in as many months. The tour had been conceived back in March by a Manchester-based promoting company, Kennedy Street Enterprises, as a vehicle for top American guitarist Duane Eddy to visit the country. The Beatles were also included in the package, for the first and only time in Britain on a non-Arthur Howes tour. Problems quickly beset Eddy's planned visit and at one stage Ben E. King and the Four Seasons were lined up to replace him. That too fell through, and in late March Kennedy announced that they had secured Roy Orbison to be the top attraction. They were wrong. The Beatles, who admired and were influenced by Orbison in their formative years (Orbison was a real star, with nine hits to his credit in less than three years, four of them of Top Ten rank,

including a number one), completely dominated the tour and relegated Orbison to second fiddle. Within a week of the tour's commencement the cover of the souvenir programme was back at the printer's, changing the priority of star billing:

### ROY ORBISON
### THE BEATLES

### THE BEATLES
### ROY ORBISON

Brian Epstein was besieged with offers for the Beatles. A garden fête appearance here, a merchandising endorsement there. And as for live bookings, there wasn't a promoter in the land who wasn't eager to engage them for a show. What a difference a year can make! As in all such cases of sudden national fame, it actually took quite a while for Epstein and the Beatles to reap any financial gain from the new situation. In June and July the group were still fulfilling live dates contracted back in March and April, at fees ridiculously small by comparison to what they could really command. In similar, past circumstances, it was not uncommon for whingeing pop singer/group managers to claim that their artiste 'had suddenly been taken ill' and would be unable to fulfil a certain booking. Brian Epstein would have none of this, and was strictly honourable in all of his dealings. Certainly he attempted to *buy* the Beatles out

**NEMS ENTERPRISES LTD**
DIRECTORS: B. AND C. J. EPSTEIN

12-14 WHITECHAPEL, LIVERPOOL, 1    TELEPHONE ROYAL 7895

BE/BA:

20th February 1963

Dear Dave,

Thank you for your letter and also for
returning the contract signed by yourself.
I regret, however, that it is necessary
for me to request that the contract be
endorsed by a representative of Stowe School
itself over twentyone years of age. As
otherwise the contract is not strictly speaking
legal. As I am assuming you will have no
difficulty in obtaining such signature I enclose
herewith our signed counterpart.

We will use our own microphones and amplification
and will naturally be grateful for any assistance
which your electricians can give to our road
manager in setting up. When the group arrives I
suggest that it will be best for them to proceed
to the hall and see the layout etc. but I have
no doubt that they will be delighted to look around
the school and to meet some of the boys. I am
pleased that you are arranging for a meal for us
after the performance. I'm not at present sure
whether we will return to London (from where we will
have come) or stay nearby the same night. Is there
a good hotel in the district?

Many thanks again for your co-operation.

Yours sincerely
Brian Epstein

---

**NEMS ENTERPRISES LTD**
DIRECTORS: B. AND C. J. EPSTEIN

12-14 WHITECHAPEL, LIVERPOOL, 1    TELEPHONE ROYAL 7895

BE/J/BA:

11th March 1963

Dear David,

Thank you for your recent letter, enclosing £1. 10. 6
for the BEATLES L.P. Record; I am enclosing your receipt
and, as soon as the record is available, a copy will be
sent to you.

… have today written to the Green Man Hotel at Syresham
… see if they can accommodate the group and, if this
possible, it would be appreciated if you could show
… the way; after which they will take you back to
…ol.

…egard to autographs, the boys will be very pleased
… these for you during the time they are at the

… forward to seeing you.

…ely,

…an Epstein

*An unusual gig to say the least – dignified
Stowe School receives a visit from the
Beatles, after a request from one of the
pupils. Above: Some of the correspondence
relating to the booking. Left: Rocking the
Roxburgh Hall underneath the hallowed
Latin.*

Police hold back the mob—there had been nothing like it since Johnnie Ray.

*From the* Daily Herald, *14 October 1963.*

of a booking on one or two occasions – perhaps because he felt that the date would be a retrogressive step, or if he considered the hall to be unsafe or unable to contain the group's fan following – but he never, ever reneged on a signed contract. Almost every agent or dance/concert promoter consulted during the course of researching this book told me of his scrupulously fair business dealings without any prompting.

In July the Beatles' lengthy series of summer bookings in seaside towns commenced. This included weekly 'residencies' in Margate, Weston-super-Mare, the Channel Islands, Llandudno, Bournemouth and Southport, as well as various one-nighters in four other towns. In between these dates were packed miscellaneous club and ballroom appearances, BBC radio sessions and more recordings for EMI at Abbey Road studios. On 1 July the Beatles taped what would become their fourth single release, the epoch-making 'She Loves You', while throughout the rest of the month the group somehow found time to squeeze in most of the recording sessions for

# Beatles

## WHAT A SUNDAY NIGHT AT THE PALLADIUM!

HERALD REPORTER

EARLY 2,000 teenage girls, screaming "We Want The Beatles," battled through a pant-police cordon outside the London Palladium t night.

'he battle reached its climax minutes after the curtain ne down at the close of I T V's Sunday Night at the ladium.

### SMUGGLED

ince mid-morning, Liverpool's Beatles group — John inon, Paul McCartney, George Harrison and Ringo .rr — had been prisoners in the Palladium while the nagers surged outside.

Extra police stood at the gangways while more sealed the stage door.

But when the Beatles, with their bobbed haircuts, ished their 12-minute act, the trouble really started.

Screaming girls launched themselves against the police ending helmets flying and constables reeling.

Police vans sealed off the front of the theatre so that e Beatles could be smuggled out.

### CHASED

The pop group dived down the theatre steps into a . The teenagers charged forward and the Beatles' car nt off into Oxford Street chased by the crowd.

Stage-doorman George Cooper said: "There's been thing like it since American singer Johnnie Ray came re in 1955."

their second album, to be titled *With the Beatles*. EMI wisely chose to delay the release of this LP until sales of the first one, *Please Please Me*, had started to subside.

On 3 August 1963 the Beatles gave their last-ever live performance at the Cavern Club, and an historic era was brought to an end. The Cavern could no longer contain the vast and fast-growing legions of Beatles fans, nor for that matter could Liverpool contain the Beatles themselves. They were destined for far greater horizons, and not just in Britain. In the remaining three years that the Beatles were giving concerts they performed in Liverpool on just four more occasions.

By now the obstreperous scenes before, during and after every single Beatles gig had become little short of maniacal, and dangerous to all concerned – fans and Beatles alike. The worst part was nearly always the problem of how the group could escape, unscathed, from the stage door to their van – shielded as best he could by the none-too-large frame of the ever-reliable road manager Neil Aspinall – and thence from the car park out on to the open road. Two important decisions were made: Neil Aspinall, and the Beatles, would have a second assistant, genial Mal Evans, a Liverpudlian from 28 Hillside Road, Mossley Hill, former bouncer at the Cavern Club and latterly a post office engineer. 'Big Mal', as he became known, was liked by everyone and an essential part of the Beatles' working lives from the moment he met them with the van at Ringway Airport, Manchester, on the group's return from a five-night visit to Jersey and Guernsey on 11 August. The second decision had the typical Brian Epstein touch. The Beatles, Epstein vowed, would not accept any more bookings for venues of stature less than a theatre. No more small clubs, no more ballrooms. The remaining ballroom engagements, long-booked, from August onwards, were of course fulfilled, but no more contracts were negotiated. While undoubtedly a matter of high prestige, the decision had, anyway, been virtually forced on Epstein by the awesome scenes at the Beatles' summer gigs, and the horrifying thought that one of 'the boys' might be physically hurt if they continued to play such venues where the stage did not have the height required to hold off the seething crowds of fans.

As far as Fleet Street – and therefore the Great British General Public – was concerned, real Beatlemania (in itself a Fleet Street term coined at this time) first occurred in London on Sunday 13 October. After the Beatles had returned from justly deserved vacations and made a swift three-day return to Scotland, they appeared on the ATV programme *Val Parnell's Sunday Night at the London Palladium*, a long-running British variety show of music-hall tradition, broadcast live every week from the famous theatre in the heart of London. The next day Fleet Street gleefully reported the scenes of mayhem in Argyll Street which greeted the arrival of the Beatles in their professionally chauffeured Austin Princess – an Epstein-orchestrated display of grandeur which beat van-travelling any day. Even during the show people recall that the clamorous noise from the kids outside in the street was sufficient to permeate the

Police hold back the fans—and the Beatles keep on singing

# POLICE BATTLE ON STAGE AT BEATLES SHOW

SCREAMING girls, struggling policemen, a constable's helmet rolling on the floor. It's those Beatles again.

This was the scene at a ballroom in Buxton, Derbyshire, when police had to go on stage to keep frenzied teenagers from the Merseyside pop group.

More riots over the Beatles followed yesterday.

AT LEICESTER 3,000 teenagers queued for 16 hours to buy tickets to see the group.

## SCREAMING

When the ticket office opened, 70 police, some with dogs, struggled with the screaming mob as they charged the door.

Hundreds of fans were showered with glass splinters after the crowd had swayed into a shop window and broken it.

Fifty fans fainted and were treated by ambulance men. Five were taken to hospital, suffering from exhaustion.

Two roads were closed to traffic while the battle went on. The fans bought all 4,900 tickets for two shows at the city's De Montfort Hall.

## WAITING

AT BIRMINGHAM, 30 miles away, fans waited six hours to see the Beatles arrive at television studios to record a programme.

When they arrived 3,500 teenagers stormed the studios. They were held back by 50 police.

More police had to be brought up to help the Beatles make their getaway from a side door after the recording.

*Beatlemania grips the English towns of Luton and Buxton, and the Swedish capital city Stockholm, providing ample copy and countless column-inches for the Beatles-hungry media but provoking little imagination from copy-writers.*

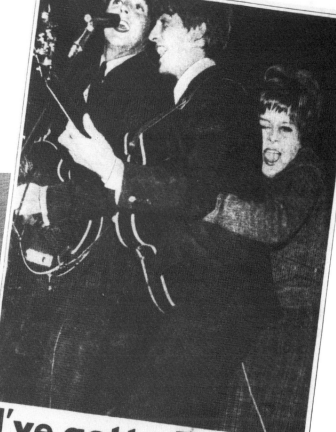

# I've gotta Beatle!

SHE'S the envy of thousands of British teenagers — this Swedish girl who has actually grabbed herself a Beatle.

The Merseyside riot-rousers were belting out their hit tunes in Stockholm at the week-end when this local lass went berserk. She rushed on to the stage and jumped ecstatically on to the back of lead guitarist George Harrison. Afterwards George said: " It wasn't very funny at the time. But so long as you can keep on playing it's not too bad."

When the Beatles gave their second performance police reinforcements were c a l l e d in. They managed to prevent screaming fans from climbing on to the stage.

The Beatles end their tour of Sweden next Thursday. Look out, England!

# I've gotta ticket!

THIS girl's got herself the next best thing to a Beatle—a ticket for one of their shows. And she weeps with joy in a friend's arms.

She queued all Saturday night in the cold at New-castle - upon - Tyne. She was pushed and jostled and trodden on. But fin-ally she was rewarded at the ticket office.

Yesterday morning there was panic when someone shouted: " The office is open." More than 200 youngsters were hurt as a section of the 4,200-strong crowd surged forward and trampled on them.

### SCUFFLE

Ambulance crews were kept busy treating casual-ties. Three people were taken to hospital with minor injuries.

One of those who had to have treatment was a senior woman police offi-cer. Chief Inspector Olive McVay.

She was hurt when she helped a policeman to break up a scuffle between youths.

Police sent in bottles of

sal volatile to revive hun-dreds of young people affected by nervous strain and exposure.

While the injured were being treated. Superin-tendent John Martin drove along beside the two-mile queue and warned:

" Unless you calm down

I will stop the sale of all tickets and cancel the concerts."

All the panic was really unnecessary. For after the queue had been served 500 tickets were still left.

These were sold to an-other queue which formed in the afternoon.

theatre walls and actually appear on the telecast. The theory put forward by Philip Norman in his 1981 Beatles biography *Shout!*, that all of the editors and journalists of Fleet Street, seemingly in mass agreement, actually invented the high drama – and, in essence, Beatlemania – to suit their own ends, is really beyond credence. True, at one stage in the day there were, as Norman claims, only a handful of girls milling about outside the staid theatre, but that was during the afternoon rehearsals. By the evening, according to several independent eye-witnesses, the street was positively buzzing with activity and fans.

Philip Norman's other theory – that the press were eagerly seeking something bright, happy, fun and above all clean, to report, in the aftermath of the lingering enormous public scandal surrounding Cabinet Minister John Profumo – is, on the other hand, quite believable and probably an accurate summation of the events and thinking prevalent at that time.

On 15 October, two days after the Palladium show, and one day after the Beatles-inspired street scenes had received blanket coverage in the press, there was yet more fodder for the suddenly Beatles-hungry media. It was officially announced that, back in late August, the group had received, and secretly accepted, an invitation from top entertainment impresario Bernard Delfont to appear before Queen Elizabeth the Queen Mother and Princess Margaret at the annual Royal Command (Variety) Performance. That night, 15 October, the Beatles were giving a one-night stand at the Floral Hall in Southport – the last of a great many performances they gave in the pretty town on the Lancashire coast – and they were besieged in their dressing room by journalists seeking views on the group's confirmed royal approval. Were they 'selling out'? it was asked. The Beatles said no . . . but felt that, deep down, perhaps they were. Every year after 1963 Brian Epstein had to endure merciless pleas from Delfont *et al* for the group to appear on the show a second time, but the Beatles steadfastly held their ground and refused.

After another live date, in Buxton, Derbyshire, the taping of both radio and television appearances, for *Easy Beat* and *Thank your Lucky Stars* respectively, and two long recording sessions at Abbey Road studios, during which they cut both sides of their next single, 'I Want to Hold your Hand' and 'This Boy', the Beatles took off to Sweden for their first-ever foreign tour. Worth £2000 to the group, the trip ran from 23 to 31 October and was no less gruelling than their British itinerary had been: the Beatles gave five concerts (nine shows), and recorded appearances on Swedish radio and television pop shows during their

**NOVEMBER 10** ON CHANNEL 8

*\* 7.28 The Royal Variety Performance*

IN THE PRESENCE OF
HER MAJESTY
QUEEN ELIZABETH
THE QUEEN MOTHER

AT THE
**Prince of Wales Theatre,
London**
on November 4

PRESENTED BY BERNARD DELFONT IN ASSOCIATION WITH LESLIE A. MACDONNELL, O.B.E.
IN AID OF THE VARIETY ARTISTES BENEVOLENT FUND: ORGANISING SECRETARY ARTHUR SCOTT

**THE BEATLES**
WILFRID BRAMBELL and HARRY H. CORBETT
Steptoe and Son
MARLENE DIETRICH
CHARLIE DRAKE
MICHAEL FLANDERS and DONALD SWANN
BUDDY GRECO
DICKIE HENDERSON
JOE LOSS AND HIS ORCHESTRA
SUSAN MAUGHAN
NADIA NERINA
WITH Desmond Doyle, Christopher Newton, Keith Rosson AND Ronald Plaisted
LUIS ALBERTO DEL PARANA and LOS PARAGUAYOS
HARRY SECOMBE and the 'Pickwick' Company
TOMMY STEELE and members of 'Half a Sixpence' Company

*Queen Elizabeth, The Queen Mother*

ERIC SYKES and HATTIE JACQUES
SPECIALITIES BY
CLARK BROTHERS
FRANCIS BRUNN
BILLY PETCH DANCERS
PINKY and PERKY
The Prince of Wales Theatre Orchestra
UNDER THE DIRECTION OF
HAROLD COLLINS
THE SHOW DIRECTED BY
ROBERT NESBITT
UNDER THE PERSONAL SUPERVISION OF
BERNARD DELFONT
ORGANISER FOR THE FUND
ARTHUR SCOTT
TELEVISION DIRECTION BY
BILL WARD

ATV Network Presentation
(Wilfrid Brambell and Harry H. Corbett, Pinky and Perky, and Eric Sykes televised by arrangement with B.B.C.)
See pages 3, 4, 5 and 7

short stay. Sweden too, judging by press and public reaction, succumbed to the Beatles just as thoroughly as Britain had done. Beatlemania, it seemed, had travelled over the North Sea with the Beatles, engulfing even the non-English-speaking among the Swedish teenagers. At the Stockholm show George Harrison was all but dragged from the stage by adoring fans.

Strangely, the jaunt to Sweden is best remembered for the *aftermath*, the Beatles' homecoming into London Airport on 31 October from Arlanda, Stockholm. Despite a heavy downpour of rain, several hundreds of screaming fans, many sporting the now-famous Beatle haircut – fashioned seemingly so many years ago by Astrid Kirchherr in Hamburg – thronged the rooftop gardens of the Queen's Building and created a din so piercing that it actually drowned the noise of the SAS Caravelle's engines. Representatives of Fleet Street and the BBC were out in force too, with 50 photographers, and as many journalists, bustling around the four surprised Beatles as they descended the steps of the plane and witnessed the first of a hundred so-called 'airport receptions'.

The celebrated Royal Command Performance took place on Monday 4 November at the Prince of Wales Theatre in Coventry Street, London. There were the by-now-expected scenes of Beatlemania outside the theatre: thousands of screaming teenagers

The minutiae of Beatlemania, as reported
faithfully by the weekly pop paper Disc.
Reporters reached for their thesaurus in
their quest for new superlatives to
describe identical manic scenes in
different ways.

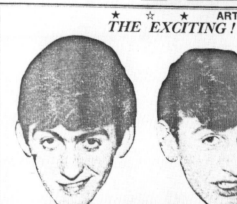

*Side-stage snapshots of the Beatles in full cry,
with the audience, though unshown, doubtless
in the same state. Britain, autumn 1963.*

being valiantly held in check by rows of strong, arm-linked London policemen. For once the arrival of the Royals was overshadowed, and by four young men from Liverpool who played rock and roll music. Had the country gone mad? Inside the theatre the Beatles wooed and won over their bejewelled audience as quickly and effectively as they once, long ago, captured a Cavern Club assembly. Performing on the same bill as Pinky and Perky may not have been the Beatles' idea of fame, nor, for that matter, was playing for socialites and debutantes. But, as usual in such situations, the Beatles' instinctive and lovably impudent wit took over and won the day. Before launching into 'Twist and Shout' – hardly, one would think, a suitable choice of song for so austere an occasion or so sedate an audience – John Lennon stepped up to the microphone. 'For this number we'd like to ask your help,' he said. 'Will the people in the cheaper seats clap your hands? All the rest of you, if you'll just rattle your jewellery.' Brian Epstein, sitting proudly in his tuxedo amid the royal gathering, was overcome with joy for 'his boys', and more than a little relieved that he had now stopped squirming in his seat over what John had *threatened* to say, backstage before the show. 'I'll just tell 'em to rattle their fuckin' jewellery,' had been Lennon's original, pithy version of the famous ad-lib.

Real, unstoppable, all-conquering Beatlemania was now well and truly under way. All of the 100,000 available tickets for the London run of *The Beatles' Christmas Show*, an enterprising Epstein-conceived seasonal extravaganza encompassing music and comedy acts largely supplied from his NEMS stable of artistes, sold out within 25 days of going on sale. And all over Britain teenagers in their thousands were queuing overnight in wintry conditions, and causing scenes of mayhem, just to get tickets for the Beatles' autumn tour when the box-offices opened. The tour had been first announced back in June, and it was their fourth package tour jaunt around Britain in ten months, visiting 34 towns, two shows per night. The Beatles' second album, *With the Beatles*, largely recorded back in the relative sanity of July, was released on 22 November to record advance orders of 270,000. One week later it had topped the half-million mark, this astonishing, record-breaking figure guaranteeing not only an instant number-one placing on the album chart but an appearance for the LP in the *singles* chart too (in those days calculated purely on the sales of discs, size immaterial). On 13 August the Beatles' EP release 'Twist and Shout' had become the first of its genre to sell 250,000 copies and qualify for silver status. 'She Loves You', the Beatles' fourth single, over a million copies sold and number one since August, was finally displaced in the first week of December by the group's fifth release, 'I Want to Hold your Hand'. Record-splintering advance orders of 1,000,000 copies in the UK did not, as was feared in the Beatles' camp, temper the disc's eventual sales, and it lodged itself at number one for six weeks, right through the Christmas period. The record had had orders of 500,000 on 5 November, just *one day* after it was first announced and 24 days before it was released.

In the newspaper columns boys were being sent home from school all over the country for sporting Beatle haircuts, a Beatle ballet was being planned,[2] a trendy vicar – Reverend Ronald Gibbons of the Trinity Methodist Church in Basildon, Essex – and several politicians, were invoking the Beatles' name to garner personal publicity, and questions were being raised in Parliament about the cost of the police protection afforded the group in London – protection, it was screamingly obvious, that was nothing short of essential if the limbs of John, Paul, George and Ringo were to remain intact.

For the Beatles themselves it was already beyond a joke and the cause of much resentment. Madness! Having to wear elaborate disguises to walk in public; being victims of an attempted joke kidnap by university students for a Rag Day stunt; their families and homes in a state of permanent siege; having guitars and clothes stolen from dressing rooms; and Brian Epstein having to appeal to fans not to hurl missiles on to the stage – mostly jelly-babies, or whole *packets* of jelly-babies because George Harrison had once jokingly remarked that they were his favourite brand of confection. Being smuggled in and out of each town on the tour was more akin to an army exercise than a rock group on the road. And once inside a theatre they could do nothing but remain cooped up in dingy dressing rooms, prisoners of their own fame.

---

**2** Titled *Mods and Rockers*, it was presented by the Western Theatre Ballet Company at the Prince Charles Theatre, London, from 18 December 1963 until 11 January 1964, giving a total of 30 performances.

On stage it was no better – performing before audiences so uncontrollable that the incessant, piercing, screaming not only ruled out the chance of any amplified sound being heard in the audience but prevented *the Beatles themselves*, in those days of comparatively primitive PA equipment, from hearing their own voices, harmonies or instrumentation. Even a batch of Vox AC60 amplifiers, double the strength of their AC30s, which were delivered to the Beatles on 30 November by Jennings Musical Industries, were unable to overcome the screams. After six years of musical progression on stage, the Beatles' advancement stopped dead there and then, and their playing became, instead, more stilted and ragged with every concert at which they couldn't even hear a count-in to enable the four to start playing a song at the same time.

The tumultuous year of 1963 ended with the name of the Beatles, as one newspaper reported in a special Beatle edition, 'engraved upon the heart of the nation'. They completely dominated all the media outlets over Christmas – newspapers, magazines, stage and cinema screen, radio and television. The music charts were positively swamped with Beatles records, not only by them but about them, *viz* comedienne Dora Bryan's 'All I Want for Christmas Is a Beatle'. In 1963 £6,250,000 had been paid for Beatles records.

Satisfied that the Beatles were now established, never again would Brian Epstein put them through such a punishing year. At least, not domestically. The horizons were broadening: at the end of July the Beatles had been booked into the Olympia Theatre

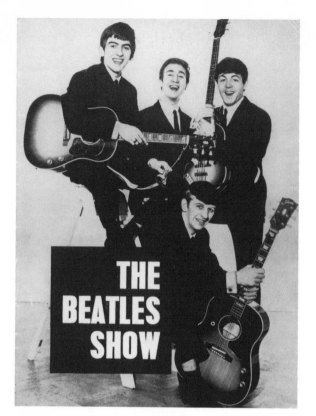

*Above right: The contract for the Beatles'
14 December concert, drawn up months in
advance, on 26 July. As usual, the fee was
good but modest compared to the group's
earning power by the time the concert came
around.*

in Paris for a three-week run in January 1964, a visit
mooted as early as April 1963. On the evening of 29
October, while the Beatles were on tour in Sweden,
Brian Epstein and the film company United Artists
concluded an agreement for the Beatles' first full-
length movie, shooting to commence in March 1964.
On 18 November Epstein received a £1000-per-day
offer from Cape Town impresario Peter Toerie for
the Beatles to make a short tour of South Africa early
in 1964. This was turned down. And in mid-
December 1963 Epstein signed a contract for the
Beatles to tour Australasia the following June.

On 5 November, the day after the Beatles' appearance in the Royal Command Performance, Brian
Epstein took Billy J. Kramer across to the United
States of America for a promotional visit. While there
Epstein met Ed Sullivan, the bluff, powerful and
somewhat difficult host of America's top-rated and
long-established CBS television programme *The Ed
Sullivan Show*. Sullivan, who had heard about the
Beatlemania rampant across the Atlantic, and who
thought it would be amusing for America to see this
latest, crazy-British fad, was flabbergasted by

Epstein's insistence that the Beatles, unknowns in the
USA, receive top billing on his show. He only grudgingly conceded when he learned that, in order to
achieve this accolade, Epstein was willing to accept
a huge cut in the group's appearance money. On the
evening of 11 November 1963 the two impresarios
reached agreement. For the paltry total of $10,000
the Beatles would make three appearances on the
show, two of them live – on 9 and 16 February 1964,
and also tape an insert for transmission on 23 February. Sullivan would also pay the Beatles' round-trip
air fares and their hotel bills in New York and Miami.
It was probably the best investment Sullivan ever
made, but Epstein was equally happy with the deal.

Finally, before flying home to England, Epstein
met with executives of Capitol Records, EMI's North
American arm, and persuaded them to handle the
single 'I Want to Hold your Hand'. Capitol had
earlier turned down their option on previous Beatles
singles, which had instead been picked up and
released by small independent labels in the USA
without any great success. 'I Want to Hold your
Hand' was scheduled for American release on 13
January 1964. Seventeen days earlier, on 26 December, owing to substantial consumer demands after
early, promotional radio airplay, Capitol rush-
released the record . . . .

## TOUR OF SCOTLAND

**2 January**  Longmore Hall,
Keith, Banffshire

The first night of the Beatles' first-ever
proper tour – a return visit to the town
played as support to Johnny Gentle on
25 May 1960 – was cancelled owing to
the diabolical weather conditions
which had the whole of Scotland in an
icy grip. Snowdrifts made virtually all
of the Highland roads impassable, and
the Beatles hadn't a chance of getting
through to Keith in time to fulfil the
engagement.

The tour had got away to a bad start
even before this setback. Due to the
inclement weather the Beatles' flight
from London to Edinburgh Airport on
2 January (the group had flown to
London from Hamburg on 1 January and
spent the night there) was
switched at the last moment to land at
Aberdeen – too late to notify Neil
Aspinall who turned up at Edinburgh
with a vanload of Beatles equipment
but no Beatles to meet.

**3 January**     Two Red Shoes
Ballroom,
Elgin, Morayshire

At last the tour got under way. This
ballroom was slightly L-shaped, which
meant that some of the dancers were
unable to see the Beatles on the stage.

**4 January**     Town Hall, Dingwall,
Ross and Cromarty

**5 January**     Museum Hall,
Henderson Street,
Bridge of Allan,
Stirlingshire

---

THE MUSEUM HALL,
BRIDGE OF ALLAN
SATURDAY, 5th JANUARY

THE "LOVE ME DO" BOYS

**THE BEATLES**

also ROY PURDON and the
TELSTARS

8.30 p.m. to 11.45 p.m. Late Transport

Admission, Five Shillings

Tickets from Preston Travel Service

Next week—Top Recording Star—
EDEN KANE

---

**6 January**     Beach Ballroom,
Sea Beach, Aberdeen,
Aberdeenshire

The last night of the five-date tour,
though the Beatles stayed on in
Scotland for another two days and
travelled down to Glasgow for a live
appearance on the Scottish Television
(STV) children's programme *Round-Up*
on Tuesday 8 January, where they
performed their upcoming single
release 'Please Please Me'.

END OF TOUR

**10 January**     Grafton Rooms,
Liverpool

The Beatles' first home-town
engagement for nearly a month,
heading a five-act bill. The evening
was a resounding success, with a
record-breaking attendance crowding
into the large Grafton Rooms. One
enterprising fan stole 100 tickets a few
days before the gig only to find that
they were numbered and declared
invalid.

---

AT THE CAVERN CLUB
10 MATHEW St. (Off North John St.)
TO-NIGHT:
THE FOUR MOSTS.
GERRY AND THE PACEMAKERS.
THE DELRENAS.
SONNY WEBB AND THE CASCADES.
TO-MORROW (Saturday)—
JOHNNY SANDON AND THE
REMO FOUR
THE ZENITH SIX
GROUP ONE.
SUNDAY—
JOHNNY AND MIKE WITH THE
SHADES
DALLAS JAZZ BAND
THE SWINGING BLUEGENES
THE BLUE MOUNTAIN BOYS
VIC AND THE SPIDERMEN
LUNCHTIME SESSIONS
NEXT WEEK.
MON.: GERRY LEVENE AND THE
AVENGERS.
TUES.: THE BIG THREE.
WED.: JOHNNY SANDON WITH THE
REMO FOUR.
THURS.: THE BEATLES.
We at the Cavern congratulate The
Beatles on the success of their first
record. It has been in the "charts"
now for 14 weeks and stands currently
at No. 17 (New Record Mirror). "Please
Please Me" should do even better than
"Love Me Do." and as "D.J." said
last night, should go right up the Hit
Parade. ALL THE BEST, BOYS!

---

**11 January**
Lunchtime     Cavern Club

Night     Plaza Ballroom,
Halesowen Road,
Old Hill, near Dudley,
Staffordshire
and     Ritz Ballroom,
York Road,
King's Heath,
Birmingham,
Warwickshire

Although the Beatles successfully
made the hazardous afternoon journey
south from Liverpool to Old Hill,
violent blizzards meant that they were
unable to traverse the 11 miles from
there to King's Heath to fulfil the
second part of a double booking in the
Midlands. It was the coldest night in the
area for seven years. The King's Heath
date was rearranged for 15 February.

**12 January**     Invicta Ballroom,
High Street,
Chatham, Kent

The Beatles' southernmost
engagement to date.

**14 January**     Wolverham Welfare
Association Dance,
Civic Hall,
Whitby Road,
Ellesmere Port,
Wirral, Cheshire

After a day's 'break' on 13 January, in
which the Beatles travelled to Aston
Road North, Aston, Birmingham, to
tele-record their debut appearance,
miming 'Please Please Me', on the
influential ABC programme *Thank your
Lucky Stars* (transmitted on Saturday
19 January), the group returned to the
dance circuit with this, their only-ever
date in Ellesmere Port, the industrial
town 19 miles south of Liverpool. A
capacity crowd of 700 packed the hall.

**17 January**
Lunchtime     Cavern Club

Night     Majestic Ballroom,
Birkenhead

While the evening of 16 January was
spent in the privacy of the Playhouse
studios in Manchester recording
another session for BBC radio, on the
17th the Beatles were back gigging at
a familiar stamping ground, the

Majestic Ballroom in Birkenhead. Every ticket for the dance was sold in advance, much to the patent disappointment of an extra 500 fans angrily locked outside the doors.

| 18 January | Floral Hall Ballroom, Morecambe |

| 19 January | Town Hall, High Street, Congleton, Cheshire |

El Rio Club, El Rio Dance Hall, Queen Victoria Street, Macclesfield, Cheshire

Town Hall Ballroom, Pauls Moss, Dodington, Whitchurch, Shropshire

The Macclesfield date was only a provisional booking and was rearranged for the following week after the Whitchurch gig came up. The Congleton gig was similar but never re-booked.

| 20 January Night | Cavern Club |

| 23 January | Emporium Ballroom, Doncaster, Yorkshire |

| Night | Cavern Club |

Having spent the evening of 21 January in London recording another appearance on the Radio Luxembourg programme *The Friday Spectacular* (transmitted on 25 January), 22 January recording three BBC radio programmes (*Pop Inn, Saturday Club* and *The Talent Spot*) at three different locations, and the morning of 23 January returning north to Liverpool (without, incidentally, the van's windscreen, and in freezing conditions), the Beatles could have been excused for feeling a little tired after taking to the stage in the Cavern Club! The Doncaster booking was cancelled a fortnight beforehand.

| 24 January | Assembly Hall, Mold, Flintshire, Wales |

| 25 January | Baptist Youth Club Dance, Co-operative Hall, Market Street, Darwen, Lancashire |

## Teenagers Entertained By TV Stars

" Fabulous ! " That was the comment everyone made who heard " The Beatles " at the Co-operative Hall, on Friday night.

Delayed by fog, the Group went on the stage five minutes after arriving to give a rip-roaring 60 minute performance such as Darwen youths have never heard in the town before !

Right from the first minute of their appearance the audience showed their delight in more ways than one. A packed hall; a star Group ably supported by local Groups namely : The Mustangs, The Electones, The Mike Taylor Combo; combined to make a very successful night.

" The Beatles " were the main attraction at the dance held by the Baptist Youth Club. Mr. T. Proudfoot, who organised the dance, said " This was the climax to three dances which we held before, and it was well worth the work involved."

Everyone who attended — and many more — are asking the question " When are they coming again ?" The answer ? As soon as possible ! ! ! !

| 26 January and | El Rio Club, Macclesfield King's Hall, Stoke-on-Trent, Staffordshire |

Twenty-one miles separated this double booking. At the El Rio gig, rearranged from 19 January, the Beatles were supported by local combo Wayne Fontana and the Jets, Fontana later finding fame with another group, the Mindbenders.

| 27 January | Three Coins Club, Fountain Street, Manchester, Lancashire |

A return visit to the club part-owned by disc jockey Jimmy Savile, first played by the Beatles soon after it opened in late 1961.

| 28 January | Majestic Ballroom, Westgate Road, Newcastle-upon-Tyne, Northumberland |

| 29 January | Astoria Ballroom, Wilson Street, Middlesbrough, Yorkshire |

This gig was only provisionally booked. It was Eden Kane, not the Beatles, who wowed the Middlesbrough clientele on this night.

| 30 January Lunchtime | Cavern Club |

| 31 January Lunchtime | Cavern Club |

| Night | Majestic Ballroom, Birkenhead |

There was such a demand for tickets for this Majestic date that the Beatles gave two entirely separate performances, at 8:00 p.m. and 11:00 p.m. Although standard practice in theatres, this was an unheard of arrangement for a ballroom.

**1 February** Assembly Rooms,
Corporation Street,
Tamworth,
Staffordshire
and Maney Hall,
Sutton Coldfield,
Warwickshire

Another double engagement in the
Midlands, this time eight miles apart.

### TOUR WITH HELEN SHAPIRO (PART ONE)

**2 February** Gaumont Cinema,
New Victoria Street,
Bradford, Yorkshire

The first night of the Beatles' first-ever
*nationwide* tour, bottom of a six-act bill
headed by sixteen-year-old Londoner
Helen Shapiro, voted as the Best British
Female Singer in 1961 and 1962.
    The Beatles' repertoire on this
opening night was 'Chains', 'Keep
your Hands off my Baby' (John Lennon
taking lead vocal on a contemporary
hit for Little Eva), 'A Taste of Honey'
and 'Please Please Me'. Two other
songs, 'Love Me Do' and 'Beautiful
Dreamer' (the latter a rock version of
the old Bing Crosby crooner, written
as a poem in 1864) were used during
the remaining dates as prepared
alternatives.

BREAK IN TOUR

**3 February**
Night Cavern Club

The Beatles headed an eight-hour,
eight-band, Rhythm and Blues
Marathon.

**4 February**
Lunchtime Cavern Club

The Beatles' 152nd, and last, Cavern
lunchtime session

### SHAPIRO TOUR CONTINUED

**5 February** Gaumont Cinema,
Hallgate, Doncaster,
Yorkshire

**6 February** Granada Cinema,
St Peters Street,
Bedford, Bedfordshire

**7 February** Regal Cinema,
Kirkgate, Wakefield,
Yorkshire

**8 February** ABC Cinema,
Warwick Road,
Carlisle, Cumberland

Probably the highlight of an otherwise
uneventful tour happened *after* this
gig, when the Beatles, Helen Shapiro
and Kenny Lynch were ejected from a
Carlisle Golf Club dance at the Crown
and Mitre Hotel in the town centre.
Offence was taken after the Beatles had
been admitted to the ballroom wearing
leather jackets.

**9 February** Empire Theatre,
High Street,
Sunderland, Durham

*Peter Stringfellow announcing (though it
looks like he's singing with) the Beatles at
the Azena Ballroom.*

**10 February** Embassy Cinema,
CANCELLED Peterborough

The Beatles were excused duty from
this last night of the first leg of the tour
as they had to be in London first thing
in the morning of 11 February, bright
and fresh and ready for the 13-hour
session at EMI's Abbey Road studios in
which they would record their first LP.
Their place on the Shapiro bill, for this
one night, was taken by Peter Jay and
the Jaywalkers.

BREAK IN TOUR

**12 February** Azena Ballroom,
White Lane,
Gleadless,
Sheffield, Yorkshire
and Astoria Ballroom,
Oldham, Lancashire

The Sheffield engagement had been
scheduled to take place at the St
Aidan's Church Hall youth club in City
Road, Sheffield, but the police advised
that it should be moved to a venue
which could safely contain the
expected turn-out.
    The young man who ran the youth-
club dances, and who booked the
Beatles for an £85 fee, was none other
than Peter Stringfellow, 20 years on the

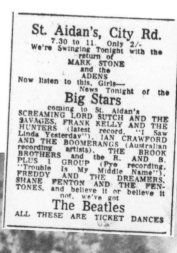

St. Aidan's, City Rd.
7.30 to 11. Only 2/-
We're Swinging Tonight with the
return of
MARK STONE
and the
ADENS
Now listen to this, Girls—
News Tonight of the
**Big Stars**
coming to St. Aidan's
SCREAMING LORD SUTCH AND THE
SAVAGES, FRANK KELLY AND THE
HUNTERS (latest record, "I Saw
Linda Yesterday"), IAN CRAWFORD
AND THE BOOMERANGS (Australian
recording artists), THE BROOK
BROTHERS and the R. AND B.
PLUS 1 GROUP (Pye recording,
"Trouble Is My Middle Name"),
FREDDY AND THE DREAMERS,
SHANE FENTON AND THE FEN-
TONES, and believe it or believe it
not, we've got
**The Beatles**
ALL THESE ARE TICKET DANCES

*13 February 1963*

*Two Beatles and three clearly happy fans pose for the camera, backstage at the Casino Ballroom, Leigh, on 25 February.*

millionaire owner of Stringfellow's, the Hippodrome and other large and highly successful night clubs in London and New York.

| **13 February** | Majestic Ballroom, Hull |
| --- | --- |

| **14 February** | Locarno Ballroom, West Derby Road, Liverpool |
| --- | --- |

A special dance to mark St Valentine's Night. It was the Beatles' first appearance at this venue although the Quarry Men did perform here once or twice in late-fifties skiffle contests.

| **15 February** | Ritz Ballroom, King's Heath, Birmingham |
| --- | --- |

The re-arranged engagement, postponed from 11 January. The situation was ideal for the Ritz promoters who now presented a group which featured in the Top Three of every singles chart that week, at the same cost as when they were a comparatively unknown act.

Sensational Farewell

# SHOWDANCE

NEMS ENTERPRISES PRESENT
at the
**QUEENS HALL, WIDNES**
**MONDAY, 18th FEBRUARY, 1963**
6-30    TWO SEPARATE SHOWS    8-45
Your own FAMOUS, FABULOUS, FANTASTIC
SENSATIONAL, MAGNIFICENT, SUPERB

# BEATLES

Stars of T.V., B.B.C., and PARLOPHONE RECORDS

PLUS

**BUDDY BRITTEN AND THE REGENTS**
(Decca Recording Artistes)

AND

**The Mersey Beats**

TICKETS (which MUST be purchased in advance)
FOR THE 6-30 p.m. SHOW **4/-**
Under 16's are welcome at this session.

FOR THE 8-45 p.m. SHOW **5/6**

*From* DAWSONS (Widnes and Runcorn)
THE MUSIC SHOP
and NEMS (Liverpool)

Note . . . **THE BEATLES**
WILL APPEAR ON STAGE
at 8-0 p.m. and 9-30 p.m.

THE DATE AGAIN—
**MONDAY, 18th FEBRUARY, 1963**

| **16 February** | Carfax Assembly Rooms, Oxford, Oxfordshire |
| --- | --- |

The Beatles' first booking with top London promoter John Smith. The group stayed overnight in the Midlands and on 17 February tele-recorded a second appearance for *Thank your Lucky Stars* (transmitted 23 February), again performing 'Please Please Me'.

| **18 February** | Queen's Hall, Widnes |
| --- | --- |

Another NEMS Enterprises' Showcase, with two separate houses. Both were sell-outs.

| **19 February** Night | Cavern Club |
| --- | --- |

The Beatles' first Cavern Club performance for more than a fortnight. The queue for admission formed *two days* beforehand. Also on the bill were Lee Curtis and the All-Stars. This was the last-ever occasion that any of the four Beatles set eyes on Pete Best.
    After the gig the Beatles travelled down through the night to London to appear live, performing two songs, on a BBC radio lunchtime show on 20 February. Then it was immediately back up north for the next engagement.

| **20 February** | Swimming Baths, St James Street, Doncaster, Yorkshire |
| --- | --- |

The pool, it should be stressed, was covered with boards . . . .

| **21 February** | Majestic Ballroom, Birkenhead |
| --- | --- |

Once again there were two separate houses, and the Beatles appeared at 7:30 p.m. and 11:30 p.m.

| **22 February** | Oasis Club, Manchester |
| --- | --- |

**TOUR WITH HELEN SHAPIRO (PART TWO)**

| **23 February** | Granada Cinema, Mansfield, Nottinghamshire |
| --- | --- |

| **24 February** | Coventry Theatre, Hales Street, Coventry, Warwickshire |
| --- | --- |

BREAK IN TOUR

| **25 February** | Casino Ballroom, Lord Street, Leigh, Lancashire |
| --- | --- |

**SHAPIRO TOUR CONTINUED**

| **26 February** | Gaumont Cinema, Corporation Street, Taunton, Somerset |
| --- | --- |

In the unceasingly terrible winter weather, Helen Shapiro was struck down with a heavy cold and was forced to miss this date. Danny Williams assumed top-of-the-bill status and Billie Davis, currently charting with 'Tell Him', was drafted in to pad out the bill.

| **27 February** | Rialto Theatre, Fishergate, York, Yorkshire |
| --- | --- |

Once again Helen Shapiro had to bow out of the proceedings due to illness.
    Travelling between York and Shrewsbury on the coach containing the entire entourage, John and Paul wrote the Beatles' next single, 'From Me to You'.

| **28 February** | Granada Cinema, Castle Gates, Shrewsbury, Shropshire |
| --- | --- |

With this date Helen Shapiro resumed her role as headliner, and Billie Davis left the tour.

**1 March** Odeon Cinema,
Lord Street,
Southport, Lancashire

**2 March** City Hall,
Barker's Pool,
Sheffield, Yorkshire

**3 March** Gaumont Cinema,
Piccadilly,
Hanley, Staffordshire

The final night of the tour. By this time the Beatles had been elevated on the bill from playing the ignominious first spot to the dizzy heights of the final act in the first half.

END OF TOUR

**4 March** Plaza Ballroom,
St Helens

The Beatles' first £100 booking.
The following day, 5 March, the group travelled to London to record three tracks at Abbey Road studios: their next single, 'From Me to You', the B-side 'Thank You Girl' and an early version of 'The One after 909'. On 6 March they returned north for another BBC radio recording session in Manchester.

**MERSEY BEAT SHOWCASE**

**7 March** Elizabethan Ballroom,
**(series of six** Co-operative House,
**one-night** Parliament Street,
**stands between** Nottingham,
**7 March and** Nottinghamshire
**16 June)**

An inspirational idea on the part of Brian Epstein: a one-night stand featuring fast growing stable of artistes, all beginning to enjoy great success. The Beatles, Gerry and the Pacemakers, the Big Three, and Billy J. Kramer and the Dakotas all appeared, as did the Cavern Club compere Bob Wooler. On this occasion the entire entourage actually travelled down from Liverpool with eighty fans on two coaches run by NEMS Enterprises for an all-in fare of 25 shillings!
This was the first of six such engagements interspersed over the following three months whenever opportunities arose. It became known as the Mersey Beat Showcase tour.

**RIALTO THEATRE** YORK
Manager: D. J. McCALLION Telephone 22119
**Wednesday, March 13th,** 6·40 & 8·45 p.m.
ARTHUR HOWES PRESENTS ON THE STAGE
AMERICA'S EXCITING
**CHRIS MONTEZ**
AMERICA'S FABULOUS
**TOMMY ROE**
**THE BEATLES**
THE TERRY YOUNG SIX :: Glamorous DEBBY LEE
THE VISCOUNTS :: YOUR 208 D.J. TONY MARSH
BOOKING NOW! Stalls and Circle 8/6, 6/6, 4/6.

**8 March** The Royal Hall,
Ripon Road,
Harrogate, Yorkshire

**TOUR WITH TOMMY ROE AND CHRIS MONTEZ**

**9 March** Granada Cinema,
Barking Road,
East Ham, London

Just six days after the conclusion of the Helen Shapiro tour – six days in which they fulfilled three live engagements, a recording session for EMI and a radio programme for the BBC – the Beatles were off again, gallivanting around a still-snowbound Britain on another package tour. Top billing this time was shared by two Americans, Tommy Roe and Chris Montez, though both were very quickly superseded – on the very first house of the first night in fact – by the seemingly all-conquering 'cheeky chappies' (as George Harrison remembers them), the Beatles.
The Beatles' repertoire on this tour comprised 'Love Me Do', 'Misery' (a song John and Paul had originally written for Helen Shapiro), 'A Taste of Honey', 'Do You Want to Know a Secret', 'Please Please Me' and 'I Saw Her Standing There'.

**10 March** Hippodrome Theatre,
Hurst Street,
Birmingham,
Warwickshire

**12 March** Granada Cinema,
Bedford

A three-man Beatles performance since a heavy cold kept John Lennon tucked up in bed. The songs, particularly 'Please Please Me', were re-arranged to allow George and Paul to take over John's vocal lines.
On 11 March, the Sunday respite from the tour, the Beatles recorded their third and final appearance on the Radio Luxembourg programme *The Friday Spectacular*. It was transmitted on 15 March.

**HIT BY INFLUENZA**
The influenza bug has hit the show, and The Beatles and the Terry Young Six both appeared with a man short.
In the case of The Beatles, John was missing. The rest of the group coped wonderfully in the absence of their lead singer.
George told me afterwards that the group's next "single" record was written by them in the coach as they travelled from York to Shrewsbury, following the Helen Shapiro show at the Rialto.
Despite having no lead singer, the boys struggled admirably with their hit number, Please Please Me. The rest of their programme was re-jigged for two-part singing. It included Misery (a new number they have written for Kenny Lynch), Till There Was You, and Do You Want To Know A Secret.

*Excerpt from the report on the Rialto, York engagement on 13 March.*

**13 March** Rialto Theatre, York

Still no John Lennon.

**14 March** Gaumont Cinema,
Snow Hill,
Wolverhampton,
Staffordshire

Another night without John Lennon, although he was fit enough to resume at Bristol on 15 March.

**15 March** Colston Hall,
Colston Street,
Bristol

**16 March** City Hall, Sheffield

Note: Prior to travelling to Sheffield the Beatles had gone from Bristol to London for a morning BBC radio session actually broadcast live on *Saturday Club*.

| | |
|---|---|
| **17 March** | Embassy Cinema, Peterborough |
| **18 March** | Regal Cinema, St Aldate Street, Gloucester, Gloucestershire |
| **19 March** | Regal Cinema, St Andrews Street, Cambridge, Cambridgeshire |
| **20 March** | ABC Cinema, South Street, Romford, Essex |
| **21 March** | ABC Cinema, London Road, (West) Croydon, Surrey |

Note: Before this gig the Beatles returned to the BBC studios in London to record a session for *On the Scene*.

| | |
|---|---|
| **22 March** | Gaumont Cinema, Doncaster |
| **23 March** | City Hall, Northumberland Road, Newcastle-upon-Tyne, Northumberland |
| **24 March** | Empire Theatre, Liverpool |

A celebrated return to the Beatles' home town, and their first Liverpool performance for more than a month.

| | |
|---|---|
| **26 March** | Granada Cinema, Mansfield |
| **27 March** | ABC Cinema, Abington Square, Northampton, Northamptonshire |
| **28 March** | ABC Cinema, London Inn Square, Exeter, Devon |
| **29 March** | Odeon Cinema, Loampit Vale, Lewisham, London |
| **30 March** | Guildhall, The Square, Portsmouth, Hants |
| **31 March** | De Montfort Hall, Granville Road, Leicester, Leicestershire |

END OF TOUR

| | |
|---|---|
| **4 April** | Roxburgh Hall, Stowe School, Stowe, Buckinghamshire |

This engagement, at a boys' public school – probably the Beatles' most unusual live gig – came about as a direct result of one Liverpudlian boy's interest in his home-town group.

The Beatles had not – as it may appear – enjoyed a break between 1 and 3 April. They recorded three radio programmes for the BBC.

| | |
|---|---|
| **5 April** | Swimming Baths, High Road Leyton, Leyton, London |

Note: Earlier in the evening, prior to the date at Leyton Baths, the Beatles also performed live 'behind closed doors' before EMI executives in Manchester Square, London, during a presentation ceremony to celebrate the award of the Beatles' first-ever silver disc, for the 'Please Please Me' single.

> **Pavilion Ballroom, Buxton**
> This **Saturday, 6th APRIL**
> 8 to 11.45 p.m.
> **THE BEATLES**
> plus
> **THE TRIXONS**
> Admission 6/-. Party Concessions
> Next Week: **Eric Delaney and his Band.**

| | |
|---|---|
| **6 April** | Pavilion Gardens Ballroom, St John's Road, Buxton, Derbyshire |
| **7 April** | Savoy Ballroom, South Parade, Southsea, Portsmouth, Hampshire |
| **9 April** | Ballroom, Gaumont State Cinema, Kilburn High Road, Kilburn, London |

Almost a home-from-home booking for the Beatles, this venue being just one mile from the Abbey Road recording studios. Prior to this gig the group were interviewed on the lunchtime BBC radio show *Pop Inn*, and then went to the studios of Associated-Rediffusion to appear live on the TV programme *Tuesday Rendezvous*.

| | |
|---|---|
| **10 April** | Majestic Ballroom, Birkenhead |

The Beatles' last appearance at this venue.

| | |
|---|---|
| **11 April** | Co-operative Hall, Long Street, Middleton, Lancashire |

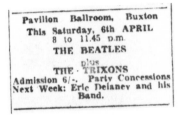

*A Cavern Club promotional handout.*

| | |
|---|---|
| **12 April** Night | Cavern Club |

A special Good Friday return to the Cavern Club, spearheading another eight-hour Rhythm and Blues Marathon.

| | |
|---|---|
| **15 April** | Riverside Dancing Club, Bridge Hotel, Teme Street, Tenbury Wells, Worcestershire |

Note: On 13 April the Beatles filmed their BBC-TV debut, in a programme featuring 'up and coming young talent' (and that included Jimmy Young!) called *The 625 Show*, broadcast on 16 April. This recording precluded the Beatles from putting in an advertised personal appearance – though they weren't scheduled to actually perform – at a football club dance at the Civic Hall in Uppermill, near Oldham. On 14 April the group then travelled to the ABC studios in Teddington, Middlesex to tele-record another appearance, singing 'From Me to You', on *Thank your Lucky Stars*, transmitted on 20 April. (After the recording the Beatles went across to the Crawdaddy Club in Richmond to see a new London group, the Rolling Stones.) On 16 April the Beatles appeared live from the Granada TV studios in Manchester on *Scene at 6.30*.

| 17 April | Majestic Ballroom,<br>Mill Street,<br>Luton, Bedfordshire |
|---|---|

| 18 April | Swinging Sound '63,<br>Royal Albert Hall,<br>Kensington Gore,<br>London |
|---|---|

During the first half of 1963 the BBC presented and broadcast live three concerts direct from this venue, each performed in front of an invited audience. The Beatles appeared in just this one, *Swinging Sound '63*, alongside 15 other artistes, and were the penultimate act, singing 'Twist and Shout' and 'From Me to You'.

It was after this show that Paul first met his fiancée-to-be, Jane Asher, who earlier in the evening had posed, screaming for the Beatles, for a *Radio Times* photographer.

## MERSEY BEAT SHOWCASE

| 19 April | King's Hall,<br>Stoke-on-Trent |
|---|---|

The second Mersey Beat Showcase date.

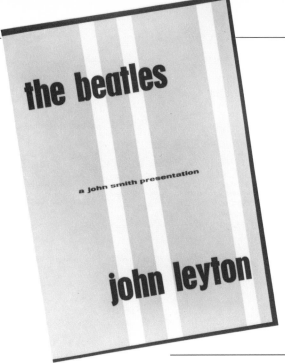

**DANCING AND WHIST**

**KING'S HALL, STOKE**

Chris Wainwright Promotions Ltd. present SATURDAY, APRIL 6th
Pye Recording Star
DANNY DAVIS
THE MARAUDERS    THE HOLLIES
THE D J.'s
Admission 6/-
pay at door
Licensed Bar : Buffet : Late Buses
No Admission after 9.30
SATURDAY, APRIL 13th
Hit Recorder of " Up on the Roof "
KENNY LYNCH
EASTER MONDAY. APRIL 15th
First Anniversary Gala Night
Free Holidays, Hairstyles, &c.
The Greatest Night of the Year
Admission 4/6 only
FRIDAY, APRIL 19th
Mersey Beat Show Case
Feating Hit Recorders of " Please
Please Me "
THE BEATLES :  THE BEATLES
Hit Recorders of " How do you do it ? "
JERRY AND THE PACEMAKERS
JERRY AND THE PACEMAKERS
Decca Recording Artists
THE BIG THREE and
BILLY CRAMER AND THE DAKOTAS
Compere: BOB WOOLLER
Advanced Tickets 10/- (or pay at door)
7.30 to 1 a.m
Don't Miss the All-Star Liverpool
Beat Show
SATURDAY APRIL 20th
SATURDAY, SPECTACULAR
Three Top Groups
SATURDAY, APRIL 27th
THE BROOKS BROTHERS

| 20 April | Ballroom, Mersey<br>View Pleasure<br>Grounds,<br>Overton Hills,<br>Frodsham,<br>Warrington, Cheshire |
|---|---|

The Beatles' first and only appearance at this venue, although other top Liverpool groups had played here fairly regularly since 1961.

| 21 April | *New Musical*<br>*Express* 1962–63<br>Annual Poll-winners'<br>All-star Concert,<br>Empire Pool,<br>Empire Way,<br>Wembley, Middlesex |
|---|---|
| and | Pigalle Club,<br>Piccadilly, London |

The Wembley performance marked probably the Beatles' biggest date yet – both in stature and in the size of venue. Eight thousand pop fans crowded into the arena to see a 14-act all-star bill, headed by Cliff Richard and the Shadows. Although the Beatles hadn't actually won a poll the *NME* slotted them in as penultimate act by virtue of their two recent chart-topping singles. They performed four songs, 'Please Please Me', 'From Me to You', 'Twist and Shout' and 'Long Tall Sally'.

The Pigalle Club booking was an odd one, and the Beatles only-ever gig at this fashionable restaurant/night club later to become the 'in' meeting place for the Mod movement.

| 23 April | Floral Hall, Southport |
|---|---|

## MERSEY BEAT SHOWCASE

| 24 April | Majestic Ballroom,<br>Seven Sisters Road,<br>Finsbury Park, London |
|---|---|

Another Mersey Beat Showcase in a Top Rank venue, this one situated close to the huge Finsbury Park Astoria cinema where the Beatles were to play on many future occasions. Two thousand people attended this evening.

## MERSEY BEAT SHOWCASE

| 25 April | Ballroom,<br>Fairfield Hall,<br>Park Lane,<br>Croydon, Surrey |
|---|---|

This Mersey Beat Showcase date was booked by promoter John Smith back in January, before the Beatles had a hit with 'Please Please Me' and before Gerry and the Pacemakers, Billy J. Kramer and the Big Three had emerged out of Liverpool. Smith, therefore, concerned that he might not fill the ballroom for one performance, let alone two, also booked in star singer/actor John Leyton to top the bill.

Three months later however, on the day of the gig, Leyton was taken ill and was unable to fulfil the booking. When Smith, abiding by the law, posted notices to that effect outside the ballroom's main entrance there was great cheering. No one had come to see him.

| 26 April | Music Hall,<br>Shrewsbury |
|---|---|

The first of two consecutive bookings for promoter Lewis Buckley.

| 27 April | (Victory)<br>Memorial Hall,<br>Northwich |
|---|---|

Note: The day after this gig, on 28 April, Paul, George and Ringo took off for a welcome 12-day holiday in Santa Cruz, Tenerife. John and Brian Epstein jetted to Spain.

| 11 May | Imperial Ballroom,<br>Carr Road,<br>Nelson, Lancashire |
|---|---|

Mayhem hit this northern industrial town in a big way as 2000 frantic teenagers crammed into the enormous Imperial Ballroom to see the Beatles.

# A great night for the fans at York 'pop' show

### By STACEY BREWER

NOT since Cliff Richard has York's Mecca-Casino rocked to such thunderous applause as it did last night for the Beatles, Gerry and the Pacemakers, and America's Roy Orbison.

The appreciation for the performers was spurred by the thought that it was the last show of the current series at the Mecca-Casino—so everybody let [go] just now.

The Beatles were a riot! They'd have sung a Liverpool bus time-table—and scored a hit. As it was, they concentrated on numbers like Some Other Guy, Do You Love You Go, and a tribute to Billy J. Kramer with Do You Want To Know A Secret.

### FROM HIT PARADE

There was also a little something called From Me To You, which happens to be top of the Hit Parade just now.

Gerry (a human fire-ball if ever there was one) and the Pacemakers closed the first half rather, they didn't just close it, they slammed it! The big number was How Do You Do It. Gerry's follow-up disc, I Like It, although released only last Friday, ran it a close second. In contrast, was a ballad styling of You'll Never Walk Alone.

Roy Orbison got the biggest "hand" I've ever heard at the Rialto. The show over-ran at both houses, and no wonder — when compere Tony March just couldn't make headway as 2,000 fans yelled for their pin-up Roy.

Don MacCallion, manager of the Mecca-Casino, must have felt glad he has Roy booked for a return date in York—on September 18 (with Billy J. Kramer plus Freddie and the Dreamers). Roy opened with Only The Lonely and followed with a selection including Cryin', Fallin', and, of course, his current chart entry, In Dreams.

He told me that when he finishes his British tour, he goes back to the US for a similar three-week tour in California. Then he has a couple of weeks off, when he plans "to relax and write more songs." He promises some new ones on his next visit to York.

The supporting bill last night included David Macbeth (Oh! Lonesome Me, A Very Good Year For Girls, My Golden Chance, etc.); Louise Cordet (I'm Just A Baby, Who's Sorry Now, and her latest record, Round And Around); and Ian Crawford (Some Kind-a Fun, Rythm Of The Rain, etc.). Erkey Grant provided a not-too-sharp contrast with a novelty version of Jezebel, and the Terry Young Combo played a couple of instrumentals on their own account, as well as backing the other solo artists.

## New Filey firm

New companies announced today by Jordan and Sons, Ltd., include:

Edwin Corrigan, Ltd. 11 Coble Landing, Filey, amusement caterers. Nominal capital £10,000 in £1 shares. Directors, Edwin Corrigan and Eliza J. Corrigan (also secretary), Coble Landing, Filey.

---

*The Beatles would have been amused to read that 'Do You Want to Know a Secret' was their tribute to Billy J. Kramer.*

| | |
|---|---|
| **14 May** | Rink Ballroom, Park Lane, Sunderland, Durham |

Note: On 12 May the Beatles had filmed another appearance at ABC studios for *Thank your Lucky Stars* (transmitted on 18 May), again performing 'From Me to You'.

| | |
|---|---|
| **15 May** | Royalty Theatre, City Road, Chester, Cheshire |

The Beatles' repertoire on this night comprised 'Some other Guy', 'Thank You Girl', 'Do You Want to Know a Secret', 'Please Please Me', 'You Really Got a Hold on Me', 'I Saw Her Standing There' and 'From Me to You'.

| | |
|---|---|
| **17 May** | Grosvenor Rooms, Prince of Wales Road, Norwich, Norfolk |

Note: On 16 May the Beatles appeared live on the BBC-TV programme *Pops and Lenny*, a children's puppet show, providing the musical interlude.

### TOUR WITH ROY ORBISON

| | |
|---|---|
| **18 May** | Adelphi Cinema, Bath Road, Slough, Buckinghamshire |

The opening night of the Beatles' third nationwide UK tour in as many months. Although Roy Orbison, whom the Beatles much admired, initially began as bill-topper, the Beatles very quickly – by audience demand – assumed the role. By the second week of the tour even the cover of the souvenir programme had been altered to reflect the change.

The Beatles' repertoire on this tour comprised 'Some other Guy', 'Do You Want to Know a Secret', 'Love Me Do', 'From Me to You', 'Please Please Me', 'I Saw Her Standing There' and 'Twist and Shout'.

| | |
|---|---|
| **19 May** | Gaumont Cinema, Hanley |

| | |
|---|---|
| **20 May** | Gaumont Cinema, Commercial Road, Southampton, Hampshire |

| | |
|---|---|
| **22 May** | Gaumont Cinema, St Helen's Street, Ipswich, Suffolk |

Note: On 21 May, the tour's 'rest day', the Beatles spent six hours in the BBC studios in London recording musical inserts for two programmes, *Saturday Club* and *Steppin' Out*.

| | |
|---|---|
| **23 May** | Odeon Cinema, Angel Row, Nottingham, Nottinghamshire |

| | |
|---|---|
| **24 May** | Granada Cinema, Hoe Street, Walthamstow, London |

Note: Before this gig the Beatles recorded the first in their own series of four special BBC radio programmes entitled *Pop Go the Beatles*.

| | |
|---|---|
| **25 May** | City Hall, Sheffield |

| | |
|---|---|
| **26 May** | Empire Theatre, Liverpool |

The Beatles' first home-town appearance in more than six weeks. They were fast outgrowing the city.

| | |
|---|---|
| **27 May** | Capitol Cinema, Dock Street, Cardiff, Glamorganshire, Wales |

| | |
|---|---|
| **28 May** | Gaumont Cinema, Foregate Street, Worcester, Worcestershire |

| | |
|---|---|
| **29 May** | Rialto Theatre, York |

| | |
|---|---|
| **30 May** | Odeon Cinema, Oxford Street, Manchester, Lancashire |

This concert was reviewed in the *Daily Express* by its northern show-business correspondent, Derek Taylor. Taylor subsequently became Brian Epstein's personal assistant, and then the Beatles' press officer, and went on to lead a highly colourful career with the Beatles and the music industry on both sides of the Atlantic.

| | |
|---|---|
| **31 May** | Odeon Cinema, High Street, Southend-on-Sea, Essex |

| | |
|---|---|
| **1 June** | Granada Cinema, Mitcham Road, Tooting, London |

Note: Before the two performances of this engagement, the Beatles spent *eight* hours in the studios of the BBC, recording the second and third programmes in their *Pop Go the Beatles* radio series.

| | |
|---|---|
| **2 June** | Hippodrome Theatre, Middle Street, Brighton, Sussex |

| | |
|---|---|
| **3 June** | Granada Cinema, Powis Street, Woolwich, London |

| | |
|---|---|
| **4 June** | Town Hall, Congreve Street, Birmingham, Warwickshire |

| | |
|---|---|
| **5 June** | Odeon Cinema, The Headrow, Leeds, Yorkshire |

NEMS ENTERPRISES PRESENT AT
**NEW BRIGHTON TOWER**
FOR ONE NIGHT ONLY 7·30 to 11·30
**FRIDAY. JUNE 14th.**
*Merseysides Greatest...*
**THE BEATLES** AND
**GERRY** *and the* **PACEMAKERS**
TICKETS
**6/.** *AT DOOR ON NIGHT* **7/.**
IN ADVANCE
A BOB WOOLER PRODUCTION
*PLUS 5 GREAT SUPPORTING GROUPS!!*
DON'T MISS
**FRIDAY. JUNE 28th.**
**JET HARRIS & TONY MEEHAN**

---

**7 June**  Odeon Cinema,
Renfield Street,
Glasgow, Lanarkshire,
Scotland

---

**8 June**  City Hall,
Newcastle-upon-Tyne

---

**9 June**  King George's Hall,
Northgate, Blackburn,
Lancashire

END OF TOUR

---

**10 June**  Pavilion,
North Parade,
Bridge Road,
Bath, Somerset

---

**12 June**  Grafton Rooms,
Liverpool

A special concert, arranged back in
February, in aid of the children's
charity, the NSPCC.

---

**13 June**  Palace Theatre Club,
Turncroft Lane,
Offerton, Stockport,
Cheshire
and  Southern Sporting
Club,
The Corona,
Birch Street,
Hyde Road,
Manchester,
Lancashire

A most unusual double booking – two
typical northern variety/cabaret night
clubs, ten miles apart.

---

## MERSEY BEAT SHOWCASE

**14 June**  Tower Ballroom,
New Brighton

A sensational return to an old stamping
ground – always one of the Beatles'
favourite venues – to play another
Mersey Beat Showcase presented by
NEMS Enterprises.

---

**15 June**  City Hall,
Fisherton Street,
Salisbury, Wiltshire

A surprise re-booking with Jaybee
Clubs, the promotion which booked
the Beatles into the historically
important Stroud engagement back in
March 1962. This dance was arranged
in April 1963 for the huge fee of £300
but, as the date approached, Brian
Epstein began to have serious
misgivings about playing such a
venue, and the safety of the Beatles. He
offered Jaybee £200 to cancel the
booking but was turned down. Over
1500 people crowded into the City
Hall.

### Big welcome for Beatles

AS the opening number struck
up, hundreds of youngsters
flocked on to the floor of Salisbury City Hall on Saturday, and
in a few moments it was packed
to capacity.
It was the first appearance in
Salisbury of a group who shot to
fame last year and have been
called the most exciting group
since the Shadows—the Beatles.
Queuing for tickets began as
early as 3 p.m. In all there were
about 1,500 teenagers—the largest
number ever to attend a personal
appearance locally.

---

## MERSEY BEAT SHOWCASE

**16 June**  Odeon Cinema,
South Street,
Romford, Essex

Another in the Mersey Beat Showcase
series, presented this time by John
Smith. Five more dates in the series,
planned for 17, 18, 19, 20 and 23 June,
were scrapped by Brian Epstein.
This was a truly remarkable booking
for – in what must surely be the only
time in popular music history – the
show's three main artistes, the Beatles,
Billy J. Kramer and the Dakotas, and
Gerry and the Pacemakers, actually
occupied numbers one, two and three
in that week's chart.

---

**21 June**  Odeon Cinema,
Epsom Road,
Guildford, Surrey

Note: Far from enjoying four days of
rest between 17 and 20 June, the
Beatles kept up their punishing
schedule. On 17 June they recorded
the fourth *Pop Go the Beatles*
programme for the BBC, on 18 June the
group returned north for Paul
McCartney's 21st birthday party in
Dinas Lane, Huyton, and on 19 June it
was back down to London for yet
another BBC session, for the show *Easy
Beat*.

---

**22 June**  Ballroom,
Town Hall,
Abergavenny,
Monmouthshire,
Wales

While George, Paul and Ringo
travelled on to Wales in the van with
road manager Neil Aspinall, John
Lennon stayed on in London to record
a controversially honest appearance
on the BBC-TV show *Juke Box Jury*,
transmitted a week later, on 29 June.
He reviewed songs by Cleo Laine, the
Tymes, Elvis Presley, Miriam Makeba,
Tom Glazer, Russ Conway, Paul and
Paula, and Julie Grant. After the
recording John flew down from
Battersea Heliport, London, to
Abergavenny in a helicopter specially
chartered by Brian Epstein at a cost of
£100. He touched down at the
Penypound football ground in
Abergavenny at 9:50 p.m., just in time
for the gig.

---

**25 June**  Astoria Ballroom,
Middlesbrough

Note: On 23 June the Beatles filmed an
appearance on ABC's *Lucky Stars
(Summer Spin)*, in a special all-
Liverpool edition transmitted on 29
June. They performed two songs,
'From Me to You' and 'I Saw Her
Standing There'. On 24 June the Beatles
recorded a session for the BBC radio
programme *Saturday Club*.

---

**26 June**  Majestic Ballroom,
Newcastle-upon-Tyne

The Beatles' last-ever performance in a
Top Rank ballroom, although they
were to continue utilizing the
company's extensive cinema and
theatre network.
After the show, in their Newcastle
hotel room, John Lennon and Paul
McCartney wrote the Beatles' next
single, 'She Loves You'.

---

**28 June**  Queen's Hall,
Sovereign Street,
Leeds, Yorkshire

Three thousand two hundred people
crammed into the vast Queen's Hall to
see the Beatles share the bill with Acker
Bilk and his Paramount Jazz Band.

**30 June**   ABC Cinema,
              Regent Road,
              Great Yarmouth,
              Norfolk

The first date in a ten week run of seaside performances. On this night the Beatles' repertoire comprised 'Some other Guy', 'Thank You Girl', 'Do You Want to Know a Secret', 'Misery', 'A Taste of Honey', 'I Saw Her Standing There', 'Love Me Do', 'From Me to You', 'Baby It's You', 'Please Please Me' and 'Twist and Shout'. The compere for this show was Ted Rogers.

**5 July**    Plaza Ballroom,
              Old Hill

The Beatles' second appearance at this venue, and a long-arranged date which Brian Epstein would have preferred to cancel but would not renege upon.
    Also on the bill was local combo Denny and the Diplomats, led by Denny Laine, future member of the Moody Blues and, eventually, Paul McCartney's post-Beatles group, Wings.
    On 1 July the Beatles recorded 'She Loves You' and 'I'll Get You' at EMI's Abbey Road studios, on 2 July they recorded, at the BBC studios in London, the first of 11 further programmes in the *Pop Go the Beatles* series, and on 3 July they recorded an insert for *The Beat Show* at the BBC studios in Manchester.

**6 July**    (Victory)
              Memorial Hall,
              Northwich

Note: Prior to this gig all four Beatles attended – and brought chaos to – the annual Northwich Carnival at Verdin Park, Northwich. Paul McCartney even crowned the new carnival queen. All good PR.

**7 July**    ABC Theatre,
              Church Street,
              Blackpool, Lancashire

Acting as compere on this and the following four Beatles gigs at this venue over the next two months was *Carry On* comedian Jack Douglas.

**8–13 July**   Winter Gardens,
(6 nights)      Fort Crescent,
                Margate, Kent

Six consecutive nights in Margate. The Beatles' twice-nightly repertoire comprised 'Roll over Beethoven', 'Thank You Girl', 'Chains', 'Please Please Me', 'A Taste of Honey', 'I Saw Her Standing There', 'Baby It's You', 'From Me to You' and 'Twist and Shout'.
    On the morning of 10 July the Beatles returned to London for a five-hour recording session at the BBC, in which they taped programmes six and seven

in the series *Pop Go the Beatles*. Then, in the late afternoon, they hurried back to Margate for their two performances at the Winter Gardens.

**14 July**   ABC Theatre,
              Blackpool

**19 and 20 July**   Ritz Ballroom,
(2 nights)           Promenade, Rhyl,
                     Flintshire, Wales

Two sell-out nights in north Wales, one year to the very week after the Beatles' inglorious Rhyl/Wales debut in the ballroom above Burton's tailor shop.
    On 16 and 17 July the group recorded four shows for BBC radio, and on 18 July recorded four tracks for their second LP at Abbey Road studios.

**21 July**   Queen's Theatre,
              Bank Hey Street,
              Blackpool, Lancashire

**22–27 July**   Odeon Cinema,
(6 nights)       The Centre,
                 Weston-super-Mare,
                 Somerset

**28 July**   ABC Cinema,
              Great Yarmouth

**31 July**   Imperial Ballroom,
              Nelson

Another riotous appearance in Nelson.
    On 30 July the Beatles resumed recording sessions for their second LP at EMI, laying down six tracks; they also managed to squeeze in a *Saturday Club* session for the BBC on the same evening, and record an interview for the programme *Non Stop Pop*.

**2 August**   Grafton Rooms,
               Liverpool

The Beatles returned to Merseyside after a seven-week absence to play for the last time at the Grafton.
    On 1 August the Beatles had recorded two more BBC radio shows.

**3 August**
Night          Cavern Club

All good things must come to an end – a suitable cliché, for after 274 Beatles appearances at the Cavern Club, spanning two and a half years, this was the very last.
    The Cavern Club had played a vital role, perhaps even *the* vital role, in shaping the Beatles' stature and grooming them for The Big Time. That time had come. Bob Wooler, the Cavern Club compere, remembers Brian Epstein promising that, one day, the Beatles would be back. It was not to be.
    Tickets for this gig went on sale on 21 July at 1:30 p.m. By 2:00 p.m. they were fully sold. The Beatles' fee was £300.

CALLING ALL BEATLE PEOPLE
THEY'RE BACK "HOME"
At the famous launching pad of Merseyside's great Beat Music ta
THE CAVERN
10 MATHEW STREET
(off North John Street)
TO-NIGHT — FOR ONE NIGHT ON
THE BEATLES
PLUS
Fontana Records "Big Find" Discov
THE MERSEY BEATS
Plus these four great groups:
THE ESCORTS
THE ROAD RUNNERS
THE SAPPHIRES
JOHNNY RINGO AND THE COLT
The show starts earlier than usual
6 P.M. TO 11.30 P.M.
PLEASE NOTE!
Admission to The Cavern Club will STRICTLY BY TICKET ONLY!
No Members or Visitors will be allow to pay at the door to-night!
ALL TICKETS NOW SOLD!
A COMPLETE SELL OUT!
Yet another mighty Cavern presentation

**4 August**   Queen's Theatre,
               Blackpool

There were so many Beatles fans outside the Queen's, blocking all entrances front and back, that the Beatles had to go through a builder's yard, up across some scaffolding and across to the roof of the theatre. They were then lowered down into the wings through a trap in the roof.

**5 August**   Urmston Show,
               Abbotsfield Park,
               Chassen Road,
               Urmston, Lancashire

An interesting engagement – the Beatles headed a four-act bill (including their old adversaries from the Decca audition, Brian Poole and the Tremeloes) playing inside a huge marquee at this annual south Manchester event. The compere was David Hamilton, later to become famous as a BBC disc jockey.

**6 and 7 August**   The Springfield
(2 nights)           Ballroom,
                     Janvrin Road,
                     St Saviour, Jersey,
                     Channel Islands

The first two of four nights in Jersey, promoted by John Smith. The Beatles' entire week in the Channel Islands cost Smith £1000.

**8 August**   Auditorium,
               Candie Gardens,
               St Peter Port,
               Guernsey, Channel
               Islands

The Beatles made the 30-mile journey

# BIG WELCOME FOR BEATLES

LIVERPOOL'S fabulous Beatles received a tumultuous welcome from packed houses at Candie Auditorium last night. This Northern beat group which has almost completely revolutionised the pop scene in a very short space of time, ripped through a nine number programme which included many tunes penned by group tunesmiths Paul McCartney and John Lennon.

This Baron Pontin presentation was a sell-out from the start. With the Beatles E.P. "Twist and Shout" currently at number three in the best selling disc charts these four lads who first took Britain by storm with the single release "Love Me Do" could do no wrong for the screaming, shouting Candie audience.

*The Beatles' one and only appearance in Guernsey, presented by Baron Pontin, great holiday-camp rival of Billy Butlin.*

across from Jersey to Guernsey in a 12-seater plane while their equipment travelled by ferry.

| | |
|---|---|
| **9 and 10 August** (2 nights) | The Springfield Ballroom, St Saviour, Jersey |

Back to Jersey for the last two nights of the week-long engagement.

| | |
|---|---|
| **11 August** | ABC Theatre, Blackpool |

| | |
|---|---|
| **12–17 August** (6 nights) | Odeon Cinema, Llandudno, Caernarvonshire, Wales |

Six days on the north Wales coast. On 14 August the Beatles sped across to Manchester to film an appearance on the Granada Television show *Scene at 6.30*. It was transmitted on 19 August.

| | |
|---|---|
| **18 August** | Princess Theatre, Torbay Road, Torquay, Devon |

Note: On their way south from Llandudno to Torquay the Beatles made a short diversion to Birmingham to film another appearance for *Lucky Stars (Summer Spin)*, transmitted on 24 August. They performed both sides of their forthcoming single, 'She Loves You' and 'I'll Get You'.

| | |
|---|---|
| **19–24 August** (6 nights) | Gaumont Cinema, Westover Road, Bournemouth, Hampshire |

Note: Midway through the week, on 21 August, the Beatles spent a morning and afternoon at EMI's Abbey Road recording studios re-mixing new material, before hurriedly returning to Bournemouth for the night's two performances.

| | |
|---|---|
| **25 August** | ABC Theatre, Blackpool |

| | |
|---|---|
| **26–31 August** (6 nights) | Odeon Cinema, Southport |

During this week the Beatles' repertoire comprised 'Roll over Beethoven', 'Thank You Girl', 'Chains', 'A Taste of Honey', 'She Loves You', 'Baby It's You', 'From Me to You', 'Boys', 'I Saw Her Standing There' and 'Twist and Shout'.

On the morning of 27 August the Beatles gave a private live performance, behind closed doors, at the Little Theatre in Hoghton Street, Southport, before BBC television cameras. It was shown in the programme *The Mersey Sound*, transmitted in London and the North on 9 October 1963, and nationally on 13 November.

| | |
|---|---|
| **4 September** | Gaumont Cinema, Worcester |

The first of a four-night run promoted by John Smith. Brian Epstein had granted Smith the booking because of the cancellation of several Mersey Beat Showcase dates allotted to Smith for late June.

On 3 September the Beatles spent eight and a half hours in the BBC studios in London recording the final three programmes in the series *Pop Go the Beatles*.

| | |
|---|---|
| **5 September** | Gaumont Cinema, Taunton |

| | |
|---|---|
| **6 September** | Odeon Cinema, Dunstable Road, Luton, Bedfordshire |

| | |
|---|---|
| **7 September** | Fairfield Hall, Croydon |

Note: Earlier in the afternoon – before the Croydon gig – the Beatles recorded another session for the BBC radio show *Saturday Club*.

| | |
|---|---|
| **8 September** | ABC Theatre, Blackpool |

Note: On 11 and 12 September the Beatles were back at Abbey Road studios recording more songs for their next LP.

| | |
|---|---|
| **13 September** | Public Hall, Preston |

Note: After the show Paul McCartney travelled 25 miles to the Imperial Ballroom in Nelson, arriving just after midnight, to appear on a panel judging the Imperial Miss 1963 contest, part of the annual Young Ones' Ball, sponsored by the local Nelson newspaper.

| | |
|---|---|
| **14 September** | (Victory) Memorial Hall, Northwich |

| | |
|---|---|
| **15 September** | Great Pop Prom, Royal Albert Hall, London |

The Beatles headed this afternoon show, the annual Great Pop Prom promoted by *Valentine, Marilyn* and *Roxy* magazines in aid of the Printers' Pension Corporation. Eleven other acts appeared, including the Rolling Stones. Disc jockey Alan Freeman was the compere.

On 16 September the Beatles took off for a holiday. John and his wife Cynthia travelled to Paris; George, with his brother Peter, visited his sister Louise, who had emigrated to St Louis, Missouri, in 1954; Paul and Ringo sunned themselves in Greece. All four Beatles returned to England on 2 October, and on 3 October got together at Abbey Road once more to add further finishing touches to their forthcoming album.

## MINI-TOUR OF SCOTLAND

| | |
|---|---|
| **5 October** | Concert Hall, Argyle Street, Glasgow, Lanarkshire |

The first of a three-night mini-tour of Scotland, promoted by Albert Bonici under his fortuitous exclusive agreement with Brian Epstein.

Before travelling north, on 4 October, the Beatles appeared live on the tenth edition of Associated-Rediffusion's new Friday night TV pop show *Ready Steady Go!* They performed 'Twist and Shout', 'I'll Get You' and 'She Loves You'.

**6 October**   Carlton Theatre, Arcade Halls, Sinclairtown, Kirkcaldy, Fifeshire

A concert presented by the management of Kirkcaldy's Raith Ballroom, unable to use their own premises because of Brian Epstein's new ruling that, where possible, the Beatles perform only in proper theatres. Fifteen hundred people attended each of the two houses.

**7 October**   Caird Hall, City Square, Dundee, Angus

END OF MINI-TOUR

**11 October**   Ballroom, Trentham Gardens, Trentham, Staffordshire

Note: On 9 October the Beatles had recorded another BBC session, this time the musical interlude to *The Ken Dodd Show*. It had been a long way since the Albany, Maghull show of 15 October 1961.

**13 October**   London Palladium Theatre, Argyll Street, London

The Beatles' biggest night to date, a celebrated top-of-the-bill performance on the top-rated variety show *Val Parnell's Sunday Night at the London Palladium*, transmitted live, nationwide, by ATV. Fifteen million people viewed the spectacle, and the next day all of the national daily newspapers reported scenes of uncontrollable mayhem outside the staid theatre, before, during and after the performance. The word Beatlemania was coined by one Fleet Street headline-writer and was quickly seized upon by the rest of the media.

The Beatles performed five songs on the show, 'I Want to Hold your Hand', 'This Boy', 'All my Loving', 'Money' and 'Twist and Shout'.

On 12 October the Beatles had spent the evening rehearsing for the Palladium show, behind locked doors at their fan club headquarters at 13 Monmouth Street, London.

**15 October**   Floral Hall, Southport

**19 October**   Pavilion Gardens Ballroom, Buxton

Note: On 16 October the Beatles recorded yet another BBC radio

*The Beatles, temporarily averting the demise of music hall on television.*

session, this time for *Easy Beat*. On 17 October they returned to EMI's Abbey Road studios to cut both sides of their next single, 'I Want to Hold your Hand' and 'This Boy', plus a retake of 'You Really Got a Hold on Me' for the next LP, and a special Christmas message for members of the Beatles fan club which was to be sent out free as a flexi disc in December. On 20 October the group filmed a further appearance on the ABC programme *Thank your Lucky Stars* (transmitted on 26 October) performing 'She Loves You'. On 23 October the Beatles finally completed sessions for their next album at Abbey Road studios, before flying to Sweden the same day.

**TOUR OF SWEDEN**

**25 October**   Nya aulan, Sundsta Läroverk, Karlstad

Not seven months after their concert at Stowe, it was very much 'back to school' for the Beatles as they kicked off their first true foreign tour in the unlikely setting of the new hall of a secondary school in tiny Karlstad. The Beatles' repertoire for their two shows here, at 7:00 p.m. and 9:00 p.m. and for the remainder of the short tour, comprised 'Long Tall Sally', 'Please Please Me', 'I Saw Her Standing There', 'From Me to You', 'A Taste of Honey', 'Chains', 'Boys', 'She Loves You' and 'Twist and Shout'.

Despite a wildly enthusiastic reception from screaming Swedish Beatlemaniacs, one man not so impressed was 'Johnny', the pop reviewer from local Karlstad newspaper *Nya Wermlands Tidning*. Johnny thought the Beatles terrible, their music corny and their playing out of rhythm, adding that the group should have been grateful that the fans' screams helped to drown out their awful performance. Johnny concluded the article with his opinion that the Beatles were of no musical importance whatsoever and that their support group, The Phantoms, decidedly outshone them.

On 24 October the Beatles recorded an appearance on the radio show *Pop '63* at the Karlaplansstudion in Stockholm.

**26 October**   Kungliga Hallen, Stockholm

Two shows.

**27 October**   Cirkus, Göteborg

Here they gave *three* performances in one day, at 3:00 p.m., 5:00 p.m. and 8:00 p.m.

**28 October**   Boråshallen, Borås

One performance, at 7:30 p.m., preceded by a half-hour spot during the mid-afternoon signing records at the Waldele record shop in Borås.

PRINCE OF WALES THEATRE
COVENTRY STREET, W.1.

*Licensed to and under the direction of BERNARD DELFONT*

*Manager* BRENT MAXFIELD

*Royal Performance*

*in the presence of*

Her Majesty Queen Elizabeth,
The Queen Mother

*In aid of the Variety Artistes' Benevolent Fund*

At 8.30 p.m. on the Evening of

Monday, November 4th, 1963

Her Majesty Queen Elizabeth, The Queen Mother

*will be received by*

Mr. BERNARD DELFONT          Mr. LESLIE A. MACDONNELL O.B.E.

Mr. ARTHUR SCOTT             Mr. BRENT MAXFIELD

Bouquets will be presented by
**Master David Delfont**
and
**Miss Dale Macdonnell**

**29 October**     Sporthallen, Eskilstuna

One show.

On 30 October, back in Stockholm, the Beatles tele-recorded an appearance on the Swedish TV pop show *Drop In*, transmitted on 3 November. On 31 October they took the morning SAS flight home to England.

END OF TOUR

## THE BEATLES' AUTUMN TOUR

**1 November**     Odeon Cinema, Winchcombe Street, Cheltenham, Gloucestershire

The Beatles' fourth nationwide tour of Britain inside nine months. Their repertoire for this one comprised 'I Saw Her Standing There', 'From Me to You', 'All my Loving', 'You Really Got a Hold on Me', 'Roll over Beethoven', 'Boys', 'Till there Was You', 'She Loves You', 'Money' and 'Twist and Shout'. The screaming was so loud that no one – not even the Beatles – could hear more than a few notes of it.

*Page three of the Royal Variety Show programme, annotated by all four Beatles and by Buddy Greco at the exclusive post-show party.*

**2 November**     City Hall, Sheffield

**3 November**     Odeon Cinema, Leeds

A few minutes of one of the two Beatles performances of this date was recorded for use in a court case involving the Performing Right Society. The tape no longer exists.

BREAK IN TOUR

**4 November**     Royal Variety Show, Prince of Wales Theatre, Coventry Street, London

The infamous Royal Command performance, in the presence of the Queen Mother and Princess Margaret, with Lord Snowdon. The Beatles, seventh on a nineteen-act bill, performed four songs, 'She Loves

You', 'Till there Was You', 'From Me to You' and 'Twist and Shout'. John's notorious jewellery-rattling witticism came before the last song. First Fleet Street and then – on 10 November when the show was televised over the entire ITV network – the whole of Britain capitulated.

## THE BEATLES' AUTUMN TOUR CONTINUED

**5 November**     Adelphi Cinema, Slough

**6 November**     ABC Cinema, Northampton

**7 November**     Adelphi Cinema, Middle Abbey Street, Dublin, Eire

The Beatles' first-ever appearance in Ireland. On 8 November they crossed the border into Northern Ireland before returning to mainland Britain.

**8 November**     Ritz Cinema, Fisherwick Place, Belfast, Northern Ireland

Note : Back in England, this day's edition of the TV programme *Ready Steady Go!* carried the Beatles singing 'She Loves You' in a repeat of the 4 October appearance.

**9 November**     Granada Cinema, East Ham

Before the show George Martin, with news hot from EMI, announced to the Beatles that their forthcoming single, 'I Want to Hold your Hand', had sold almost one million copies in advance of release. Later on, still before the release date, sales did actually top the one-million mark – the first time this feat had ever been achieved in Britain.

**10 November**     Hippodrome Theatre, Birmingham

**12 November**     Guildhall, Portsmouth
CANCELLED

Hampshire's teenage population mourned *en masse* as a gastric flu virus hit Paul McCartney and caused cancellation of the Beatles' Portsmouth gig. It was re-scheduled for 3 December. Also cancelled was the planned Beatles appearance on the Southern Television's *Day by Day*.

**13 November**     ABC Cinema, George Street, Plymouth, Devon

**14 November**     ABC Cinema, Exeter

**15 November**     Colston Hall, Bristol

155

| | |
|---|---|
| **16 November** | Winter Gardens Theatre, Exeter Road, Bournemouth, Hampshire |

The news of Beatlemania was beginning to spread far and wide. Three different camera teams from the major North American television networks – ABC, NBC and CBS – filmed parts of this Beatles performance. Brief excerpts were shown on US television a week later, and a longer clip, of the Beatles singing 'She Loves You', was aired on NBC's *Jack Paar Show* on 3 January 1964.

| | |
|---|---|
| **17 November** | Coventry Theatre, Coventry |
| **19 November** | Gaumont Cinema, Wolverhampton |

Note: Monday 18 November had not been a day of rest for the Beatles as it was for the other artistes on the tour. Instead the group attended a ceremony at EMI House in Manchester Square, London, where they received a clutch of presentation discs: silver LPs for *Please Please Me* and *With the Beatles* (the latter in advance of release) from Sir Joseph Lockwood, chairman of EMI Limited; a miniature silver EP each for 'Twist and Shout' from George Martin; and a silver EP and single for 'Twist and Shout' and 'She Loves You' respectively from Gerald Marks, editor of *Disc*.

| | |
|---|---|
| **20 November** | ABC Cinema, Stockport Road, Ardwick Green, Ardwick, Manchester, Lancashire |

Pathé News cameras filmed three songs from the first Beatles house on this evening, 'From Me to You', 'She Loves You' and 'Twist and Shout', which, together with various backstage sequences, hysterical audience scenes and typically lofty, pun-filled commentary, combined to make an eight-minute colour newsreel film, *The Beatles Come to Town*, distributed around selected British cinemas from 22 December.

| | |
|---|---|
| **21 November** | ABC Cinema, Carlisle |
| **22 November** | Globe Cinema, High Street, Stockton-on-Tees, Durham |
| **23 November** | City Hall, Newcastle-upon-Tyne |
| **24 November** | ABC Cinema, Ferensway, Hull, Yorkshire |
| **26 November** | Regal Cinema, Cambridge |
| **27 November** | Rialto Theatre, York |

Note: Prior to this show the Beatles appeared on the Granada Television programme *Scene at 6.30*.

| | |
|---|---|
| **28 November** | ABC Cinema, Saltergate, Lincoln, Lincolnshire |
| **29 November** | ABC Cinema, Market Street, Huddersfield, Yorkshire |
| **30 November** | Empire Theatre, Sunderland |
| **1 December** | De Montfort Hall, Leicester |

BREAK IN TOUR

| | |
|---|---|
| **2 December** | Ballroom, Grosvenor House Hotel, Park Lane, London |

A most unusual live booking during the Beatles' one-day respite from the tour – a charity floor show in aid of spastics at the prestigious London hotel, the Grosvenor House. Rather more upmarket than the Beatles' old, similarly-named haunt, the Grosvenor Ballroom in Liscard, Wallasey!
  Earlier in the day, at ATV's Boreham Wood, Hertfordshire, studios, the Beatles taped a performance and a comedy sketch for the *Morecambe and Wise Show*. It was transmitted on 18 April 1964.

**THE BEATLES' AUTUMN TOUR CONTINUED**

| | |
|---|---|
| **3 December** | Guildhall, Portsmouth |

The show re-arranged from 12 November. After this gig, from 4 to 6 December, the Beatles enjoyed a clear break.

BREAK IN TOUR

| | |
|---|---|
| **7 December**
Afternoon | Empire Theatre, Liverpool |

**THE BEATLES' AUTUMN TOUR CONTINUED**

| | |
|---|---|
| Night | Odeon Cinema, London Road, Liverpool |

The Beatles' first home-town concerts in four months were part of this exceedingly hectic day. The afternoon was a special affair, a concert at the

*Top: An all-Epstein, all-Liverpool bill with the exception of the Barron Knights and Rolf Harris, all at the peak of their popularity. Above: An entry ticket to the special Beatles' Juke Box Jury.*

Empire Theatre before 2500 members of the Beatles' Northern Area Fan Club, though the rest of Britain had a chance to view the action when BBC television, in an unprecedented move, showed 30 minutes of the gig later the same evening in a special programme called *It's the Beatles!*
  Earlier the same afternoon at the Empire, utilizing the same fan-club audience, the BBC also filmed a very special version of their weekly *Juke Box Jury*, with the panel comprising all four Beatles. This too was transmitted that same day, with a staggeringly high audience of 23 million people tuning in. Not for nothing were sceptics moaning that the BBC really stood for Beatles Broadcasting Corporation! On the programme the Beatles voted six

ents THE BEATLES CHRISTMAS SHOW

PETER YOLLAND INTRODUCED BY ROLF HARRIS

MY KLY    THE FOURMOST    BILLY J. KRAMER with THE DAKOTAS

NTERVAL

CK    ROLF HARRIS    THE BEATLES

PROGRAMME SUBJECT TO ALTERATION

cidental music by EITHNE CUDDIGH, Additional material by IRELAND CUTTER and DAVID
TUDIOS LIMITED, GREENWICH, Mobile rostra by HALL STAGE EQUIPMENT LIMITED.

songs as Hits (by the Chants, Elvis Presley, the Swinging Blue Jeans, Steve and Eydie, Billy Fury and the Merseybeats) and four as Misses (by Paul Anka, Shirley Ellis, Bobby Vinton and the Orchids). Unfortunately for the BBC vast technical difficulties, compounded by the complete lack of rehearsal time and, worse still, the constant ear-perforating screams from the audience, all but ruined both programmes.

After their activities at the Empire were over, the Beatles dashed the 50 yards down a specially closed and police-reinforced Pudsey Street to the Odeon Cinema. Here they gave two more performances as part of the continuing Beatles' Autumn Tour.

Note: The Odeon date was added to the tour itinerary after the initial press announcement, and therefore does not appear in the tour advertisement illustrated on page 139.

**8 December**    Odeon Cinema, Lewisham

Note: The Beatles flew from Liverpool Airport back to London early in the morning.

**9 December**    Odeon Cinema, Southend-on-Sea

**10 December**    Gaumont Cinema, Doncaster

**11 December**    Futurist Theatre, Foreshore Road, South Bay, Scarborough, Yorkshire

**12 December**    Odeon Cinema, Nottingham

**13 December**    Gaumont Cinema, Southampton

END OF TOUR

**14 December**    Ballroom, Wimbledon Palais, High Street Merton, Wimbledon, London

The Beatles' Southern Area Fan Club's equivalent to the Liverpool festivities of the previous week. In addition to their live performance the Beatles also lined up behind the Palais' bar and shook hands with all 3000 ecstatic fans who slowly filed past them, often in less than orderly fashion.

The management of the Palais Ballroom, fearing their precious stage

might be damaged by an onslaught of rampaging Beatlemaniacs, created a makeshift platform for the Beatles and then erected an enormous cage around it to keep the frantic hordes at bay. Though safe, the Beatles, and their fans, were far from happy.

Note: On 15 December the Beatles filmed 'All my Loving', 'Twist and Shout', 'She Loves You' and 'I Want to Hold your Hand' for a second special all-Liverpool edition of ABC's *Thank your Lucky Stars*, transmitted on 21 December. On 17 December the group recorded another session for the BBC radio programme *Saturday Club*, while on the following day, 18 December, they recorded their own two-hour BBC radio special, *From Us to You*, broadcast on 26 December. On 20 December the Beatles again appeared on Granada Television's *Scene at 6.30*. And somehow, in between all this, the group crammed in as many rehearsals as possible for the upcoming *Beatles' Christmas Show*.

### THE BEATLES' CHRISTMAS SHOW

**21 December**    Gaumont Cinema, Bradford

The first of two special northern previews of the show, though in concert form only – without the elaborate costumes and comedy sketches, and the extravagant stage sets which were being assembled in London.

**22 December**    Empire Theatre, Liverpool

Another preview of the Christmas show, though again in concert form only.

**24–31 December** (excluding 25 and 29 December) (6 nights)    Astoria Cinema, Seven Sisters Road, Finsbury Park, London

This typically-Brian Epstein-conceived stage extravaganza, encompassing comedy, pantomime and music, settled in at the Astoria for 16 nights in all, with two performances each evening except for 24 and 31 December when there was only one. One hundred thousand tickets for the 30 shows went on sale on 21 October. By 16 November they were all sold.

During the run the Beatles' repertoire comprised 'Roll over Beethoven', 'All my Loving', 'This Boy', 'I Wanna Be your Man', 'She Loves You', 'Till there Was You', 'I Want to Hold your Hand', 'Money' and 'Twist and Shout'.

Note: All the northern-based members of the huge cast, most of whom were members of the NEMS stable, including the Beatles, flew home to Liverpool late on Christmas Eve to spend the following day with their families. They all returned to London early on Boxing Day.

**Other engagements played**

None.

**Engagements not played**

The Beatles did not play at the Majestic Ballroom, Birkenhead, on 7 January, as stated in several books. A simple misprint in *Mersey Beat* in an article on the Beatles' *17* January appearance there is the cause of the misconception.

The Beatles' provisional, and cancelled, booking at the Town Hall, Congleton, Cheshire, on 19 January, was never re-arranged. That did not stop local rumours circulating to the contrary, witness the following article, reproduced verbatim from the 1 February 1963 edition of the *Congleton Chronicle*: 'Rumours that the "Beatles", the group who recorded "Please Please Me", are appearing at the Town Hall in a Congleton and District Youth Council dance on 9th February are unfounded. Sorry.'

In late January 1963 the promoters of Saturday-night beat music dances at the Clipstone Welfare Hall in Mansfield, Nottinghamshire, included the Beatles' name in a newspaper advertisement listing their forthcoming attractions. They were probably a little premature with their announcement since a contract had yet to be signed and the Beatles never did fulfil a booking there.

When the Beatles' February/March 1963 tour with Helen Shapiro was first announced, in November 1962, it included visits to the Gaumont cinema in Hanley on 9 February, and the De Montfort Hall, Leicester, on 10 February. The Hanley Concert was later re-arranged for 3 March, with the Empire Theatre, Sunderland, slotted in its place, while the plan for a Leicester concert was dropped altogether in favour of a show at the Embassy cinema in promoter Arthur Howes' home town of Peterborough. (The Beatles didn't play at this concert anyway.)

An agreement that the Beatles would play at the May Ball of Christ College, Oxford University, was scrapped when it was realized that it would interfere with the Beatles' holiday plans, which started on 28 April.

The Beatles did not play at the Royal Albert Hall, London, on 9 May in a concert broadcast live by BBC radio, despite claims to the contrary in numerous books. They did perform in a similar show on 18 April however.

When the Beatles' May/June 1963 tour with Roy Orbison (originally slated for Duane Eddy) was first announced at the beginning of March it included visits to the Granada cinema in Harrow, Middlesex, on 24 May and the Granada cinema in Kingston-upon-Thames, Surrey, on 30 May. Neither of these appearances actually took place, and the tour visited Walthamstow and Manchester on those dates. The Walthamstow booking had initially been scheduled for 3 June, the date eventually chosen for the concert at the Granada cinema in Woolwich.

The Beatles did not appear in Margate, Kent, on 18 June, contrary to claims made in several books about the group. Nor did they appear at the Princess Theatre in Torquay, Devon, on 14 July, as first announced in the music press in February. This was changed to 18 August to allow the Beatles to appear in Blackpool on that day, while Gerry and the Pacemakers fulfilled the Torquay date.

The 21 June concert at the Odeon cinema, Guildford, was originally planned for the Dome Theatre, Brighton, Sussex.

There is a general belief that the Beatles played a gig in Southport, Lancashire, on 1 August 1963. This isn't true. The misconception arises from Allan Williams' book *The Man who Gave the Beatles Away*, in which he states that he promoted a massive outdoor beat music festival in Liverpool on that date but the Beatles couldn't be there as they had an engagement in Southport. In fact, Williams' show – the *Daily Herald* Beat Festival 1963 – took place on Saturday *31* August which duly explains the Southport connection. The Beatles appeared on *that* day at the town's Odeon cinema.

A concert tentatively set for the ABC cinema, Great Yarmouth, Norfolk on 1 September was cancelled several weeks beforehand to enable the Beatles to tele-record an appearance on ABC's *Big Night Out* at Teddington Studios, Middlesex. (It was transmitted on 7 September.)

The 7 September gig at the Fairfield Hall, Croydon, was originally to have taken place at the Broadway cinema in Letchworth, Hertfordshire. Brian Epstein objected.

The Beatles' appearance at the (Victory) Memorial Hall in Northwich, Cheshire, on 14 September is often erroneously credited to the Civic Hall, Nantwich, Cheshire.

In February 1963, when promoter Arthur Howes first announced the Beatles' series of summer dates at seaside resorts, they included three optional Sunday-night appearances at the Queen's Theatre in Blackpool, Lancashire, on 15, 22 and 29 September. These were later cancelled to make way for a holiday period, although Brian Epstein did later accept an afternoon booking for the Beatles in London on 15 September.

A Beatles appearance planned for the Music Hall in Shrewsbury, Shropshire, on 18 October was cancelled soon after it was announced, in August.

The author could find evidence of only one Beatles appearance at the Wimbledon Palais Ballroom, London, although one former patron of the Palais recalls them playing there twice.

The Beatles did *not* appear in the following towns/venues in 1963, contrary to claims made in various books or magazines: Cannock, Staffordshire; the RAF base at Finningley, Yorkshire; Reading, Berkshire; the Odeon cinema in Streatham, London; and in Accrington, Lancashire.

This is an attempt to detail the live performance repertoire of the Beatles in 1963, showing – where possible – the group's vocalist, the composer(s) of the song and the name of the artist/group who recorded the version which influenced the group. It is, in all likelihood, an incomplete guide.

| Song title | Main vocalist(s) | Composer(s) | Influential version (year) |
|---|---|---|---|
| All my Loving | Paul | Lennon/McCARTNEY | — |
| Anna (Go to Him) | John | Alexander | Arthur Alexander (1962) |
| Ask Me Why | John | LENNON/McCartney | — |
| Baby It's You | John | M. David/Bacharach/Williams | The Shirelles (1961) |
| Beautiful Dreamer | Paul | Foster | Slim Whitman (1954) |
| Boys | Ringo | Dixon/Farrell | The Shirelles (1960) |
| Chains | John/Paul/George | Goffin/King | The Cookies (1962) |
| (There's a) Devil in her Heart[1] | George | Drapkin | The Donays (1962) |
| Do You Want to Know a Secret | George | LENNON/McCartney | — |
| From Me to You | John/Paul | Lennon/McCartney | — |
| The Hippy Hippy Shake | Paul | Romero | Chan Romero (1959) |
| Hold Me Tight | Paul | Lennon/McCARTNEY | — |
| Honey Don't[2] | John or Ringo | Perkins | Carl Perkins (1956) |
| I Saw Her Standing There | Paul | Lennon/McCARTNEY | — |
| I Wanna Be your Man | Ringo | Lennon/McCartney | — |
| I Want to Hold your Hand | John/Paul | Lennon/McCartney | — |
| Keep your Hands off my Baby | John | Goffin/King | Little Eva (1963) |
| Little Queenie | Paul | Berry | Chuck Berry (1959) |
| Long Tall Sally | Paul | Johnson/Penniman/Blackwell | Little Richard (1956) |
| Love Me Do | Paul | LENNON/McCARTNEY | — |
| Misery | John/Paul | Lennon/McCartney | — |
| Money (That's What I Want) | John | Gordy/Bradford | Barret Strong (1959) |
| Mr Moonlight | John | Johnson | Dr Feelgood and the Interns (1962) |
| Please Please Me | John/Paul | LENNON/McCartney | — |

1 The Donays were an all-girl group so this was originally titled '(There's a) Devil in his Heart'.

2 John Lennon sang lead vocals on this song until approximately August 1963, after which Ringo Starr took over.

| Song title | Main vocalist(s) | Composer(s) | Influential version (year) |
|---|---|---|---|
| P.S. I Love You | Paul | Lennon/MᶜCARTNEY | — |
| Rock and Roll Music | John | Berry | Chuck Berry (1957) |
| Roll over Beethoven | George | Berry | Chuck Berry (1956) |
| She Loves You | John/Paul | Lennon/McCartney | — |
| Sheila | George | Roe | Tommy Roe (1962) |
| Some other Guy | John/Paul | Leiber/Stoller/Barrett | Ritchie Barrett (1962) |
| A Taste of Honey | Paul | Marlow/Scott | Lenny Welch (1962) |
| Thank You Girl | John/Paul | Lennon/McCartney | — |
| There's a Place | John/Paul | LENNON/McCartney | — |
| This Boy | John | LENNON/McCartney | — |
| Till There Was You | Paul | Willson | Peggy Lee (1961) |
| Twist and Shout | John | Russell/Medley | The Isley Brothers (1962) |
| You Really Got a Hold on Me | John | Robinson | [Smokey Robinson and] The Miracles (1962) |

# BRIAN EPSTEIN Presents

# ANOTHER BEATLES CHRISTMAS SHOW

AN IN...

THURSDA...
Copyright © 1964 by Tria...

## Jiggling Mob

# ...les Thrill 13,000 Girls

...LF
...Staff
...atles in
...ed them
...decorated
candy,
bracelets
gifts.
...tered with
...aide later
...d jewelry.
...jelly beans

...BY
...with shrieks
...inting spells
...and waving
...of exquisite
...n . . . John

on Page 33

...John." John
...ee!"
...Beatle signs
...." and Beatle
...atle hats and
...nd, even British

...ll was one huge
...gling, jiggling,
...down humanity
...type humanity)
...ght. There were
...phia's finest plus
...guards scattered
...wd to keep order.

The Beatles — (seated, from left) George Harrison, ... Lennon and (standing, from left) ... hold a press ...

agers, get them back on their feet.

There were 13,000 youngsters in the hall. Thirteen thousand voices raised in a mighty scream that would shatter glass.

This was the Beatles' show but there were other performers. But 'tis sad to play second fiddle to a fluffy-head. In the midst of every act, someone would shout "It's them."

And all throats would scream, all heads would turn, all hands would point. But it was nothing, only someone with a long crew cut.

There were binoculars. Little eyes peered in every corner, into the wings of the stage. Maybe "they" would appear.

Just before the mop-tops came on stage the police were given ham and cheese sandwiches. They needed the energy.

### GRAND ENTRANCE

And then "they" appeared. And, aieeeeee, delirium, rapture, ectasy, and of course, lots of noise.

The Beatles had arrived in Philadelphia shortly before 4 P. M. Wednesday and sneaked into Convention Hall unnoticed while thousands of their admirers waited in the streets chanting "We want the Beatles."

A half-hour passed before the hysterical crowd was notified that the barber-shy quartet had arrived unnoticed.

It was the s e c o n d time Wednesday t h a t screaming young Beatle fans had been de-

## SNEAK OUT OF SHORE

The shaggy foursome, ... antined in the Lafayette ... at Atlantic City for the last ... days, rode through thron... unsuspecting admirers at... P. M. Wednesday in the b... a fish truck.

Six miles west of Atlanti... the Beatles were transfer... the bus that carried th... Convention Hall.

After gaining sanctuar... hall, the Beatles let dow... tresses as they conducted... stick press conference f... porters, 25 VIPs and 5... men in a meeting room ... main auditorium.

For almost an hour ... little rich boys from ... joked, clowned and j... and down as they par... tions put to them by ... serious press.

## MODEST LODGINGS

When asked what ... do if they could ... hotel that would let ... overnight, spokesma... said, "Some humble... somewhere, would ... you know."

Ringo suggested ... stay in a national ... where.

Outside the h... continued to mo... hundreds of pol... screaming teen... barricades. They... disappointed at ... Beatles' arrival ... happy to know th... was behind the ... distance away.

# 1964 COMMENTARY

On 14 January 1964, after the final ten nights of *The Beatles' Christmas Show* at the Astoria Cinema, Finsbury Park, and a return spot on the live ATV show *Val Parnell's Sunday Night at the London Palladium*, the Beatles – minus Ringo who, it was said, was fogbound in Liverpool – set out for Paris and a marathon season at the Olympia Theatre. Ringo, accompanied by Neil Aspinall, followed a day later and, in publicity-stunt fashion, was sped from Le Bourget airport to the Beatles' plush suite at the George V hotel by champion rally navigator Stuart Turner in a car still warm from the recent Monte Carlo rally. He arrived just in time for the first French Beatles show, a dress rehearsal for the Olympia run, held at the Cinèma Cyrano in Versailles. The night was not a success, and the Beatles were far from satisfied with the French organization and also with their own performance. The opening night at the Olympia, on 16 January, was no better. The Beatles' amplification equipment broke down three times and George Harrison, for one, suspected sabotage. The audience at this opening Olympia show was largely comprised of the Paris society set, in full evening regalia, and there was clearly little mutual affection between them and the four Liverpudlians. The Beatles received a decidedly cool reception and as this was also the show attended by most of the French press, the reviews and stories of the group in the newspapers the next day were similarly frosty. Brian Somerville, the Beatles' press agent, even had to create a ham-fisted rumpus backstage in order to generate extra publicity for the group. There was to be no love affair between the French public and the Beatles for a while yet.

Although somewhat slighted by this first hiatus in their overwhelming climb to success, the Beatles – truth be told – couldn't much care. For after returning to their suite at the George V after coming off stage that first night at the Olympia, they received a telegram carrying news that 'I Want to Hold your Hand', rush-released by Capitol on 26 December 1963, had jumped straight from position 43 to number one in the following week's singles chart in *Cashbox*, the American record-industry journal. This, above all, was the big breakthrough Brian Epstein

and the Beatles had been waiting for. *No* British artist or group had ever broken through in the USA before, apart from occasional freak hits. And this, clearly, was no freak. After just three days, 'I Want to Hold your Hand' had sold 250,000 copies across the States. By 10 January it had topped the million mark. By 13 January the disc was selling 10,000 copies every hour in New York City alone. Soon all of the Beatles' singles, and their two albums, were crashing on to the American charts at an incredible rate. And all this was happening just *days* before the Beatles' visit to New York, set up three months previously, to appear on nationwide television via *The Ed Sullivan Show*. The coincidence – for it was nothing more – was quite simply remarkable.[1]

While the British press was busy filing daft stories about the 'new kings of the pop scene', London group the Dave Clark Five, who had 'sensationally knocked the Beatles' "I Want to Hold your Hand" off the top of the charts' (the Beatles, after all, had only been lodged there for six weeks . . .), the American press was insatiable for news of this strange British phenomenon which had taken an apparently effortless and fast grip on the American youth. A stream of reporters flocked to Paris to see the Beatles at the George V, from *Life* magazine, the *New York Times* and *Washington Post*, and the Associated Press and United Press International agencies. Brian Epstein had a visitor too, a New York theatrical agent called Norman Weiss. Weiss was employed by the company General Artists Corporation (GAC) and was present in Paris as the manager of Trini Lopez, an American

---

1 Speaking 20 years on, in 1984, Paul McCartney repeatedly attributed the Beatles' great, unprecedented success in the USA to the fact that they religiously kept to their cheeky affirmation made in 1963 that they would not visit America until they had a number-one record there. I believe this to be open to debate since the Beatles' visit for February 1964 had been booked long before 'I Want to Hold your Hand' was even released in the USA – when no one could have remotely guessed that they would ever top the American charts, let alone do so right at the time of the visit. McCartney, however, still contends that the tour, although discussed at length, was the Beatles' own decision, and that they *did* wait until they were number one in the charts.

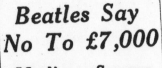

## Beatles Say No To £7,000

### Madison Square Offer Refused

The Beatles have turned down a £7,000 offer to appear at Madison Square Garden during their New York tour.

Their manager, Brian Epstein, told an *Echo* reporter in London last night that it would take the edge off the Carnegie Hall concert the group are giving on the same night, February 12

"It would be a risky business and I don't want to over-expose the boys nor to over-work them," he said.

The promoters had said they could fill the 19,000 capacity Madison Square Garden within 48 hours of opening bookings, but Mr. Epstein felt that another factor was whether satisfactory sound could be achieved in a hall of that size.

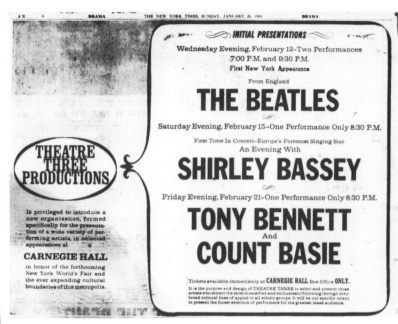

*North America beckons. Left: Brian's rejection of the Madison Square Garden offer. Above: The New York Times advert for the Carnegie Hall shows.*

singer who was also on the bill with the Beatles at the Olympia. An associate of Weiss at GAC, Sid Bernstein, had, for some time, been keen to book the Beatles – as an independent promoter under his company Theatre Three Productions – into the prestigious New York Carnegie Hall. He had even tentatively reserved a date, 12 February, but Epstein had been loath to commit the Beatles to the booking until the time was right. Now it was right, and Weiss, on Bernstein's behalf, concluded the arrangements with Epstein in Paris. The Beatles were booked for two shows for a total fee of $7000. Under the GAC umbrella Weiss also signed them for one appearance in Washington DC on 11 February. Epstein was particularly keen to arrange both of these dates in order to offset the expenses of the forthcoming American trip not covered by the television deal with Ed Sullivan. On 3 February, shortly before the end of a largely uneventful three weeks at the Olympia, the four Beatles visited the United States Embassy in Paris and obtained the visas and work permits necessary to visit, and work, in America. On 5 February they returned to England.

Two days later, 7 February, at 1:20 p.m. local time, the Pan American jet flight Boeing 707, PA 101, carrying among its passengers the four celebrated young men from Liverpool, touched down at the newly re-named John F. Kennedy International Airport in New York. Their reception was startling –

even by the exaggerated standards of Beatlemania. Three thousand lusty screams rained down on the four Beatles, each of whom was wrestling with the question of why – when America had her own stars aplenty, and when she had created the very music which had prompted the formation of the Beatles in the first place – they were being so well received. What they didn't realize was that America, in her post-Kennedy assassination gloom, needed the Beatles quite desperately. The entire country – as preposterous as it may now seem – succumbed to the Beatles almost wholly, and in a typically uncompromising, all-enthusiastic manner.

Besieged in their suite at the Plaza Hotel in Manhattan, the Beatles were fêted like kings, but again felt like prisoners. Let there be no doubt that the hysteria, the uncontrollable, unexplainable, and almost indescribable mayhem which surrounded them was highly dangerous. Should a Beatle have become submerged in such a (paradoxically well-meaning) crowd – and there were many instances on this and future occasions when that was quite possible – he would not have come out alive. The delirium was not just inexplicable but very, very frightening.

On 9 February, before an extremely live audience of 728 frantic New York teenagers, the Beatles gave their first performance on *The Ed Sullivan Show*. As much as these things can accurately be measured, it is estimated that 73 million people across the continent tuned in and saw them. Certainly the programme smashed the existing world record for the largest-ever TV audience for an entertainments show. Two days after that, on 11 February, the Beatles stepped on stage at the Washington Coliseum in the nation's capital and gave their first live concert performance in the United States. The scenes of utter pandemonium, together with the Beatles' clearly evident enthusiasm on finally playing live in the USA, were captured on film by CBS and shown on closed-circuit cinema screens in March. It makes fine viewing even now, more than 20 years on. Twenty-four hours after the Washington gig a similarly wild reception greeted the two Beatles shows at the famous Carnegie Hall – staging a rock concert for the very first time. To ensure that the Beatles remained physically unscathed, 362 policemen had to be employed. After the show promoter Sid Bernstein and Brian Epstein walked in the cold New York night across to the huge, world-famous Madison Square Garden indoor arena. The Garden management badly wanted the Beatles and were prepared to print tickets and have them on sale within hours. Bernstein offered $25,000 for one show but Brian, who had already turned down one offer a few days previously, still could not be tempted. 'Let's leave it for next time, Sid,' he said.

When the Beatles eventually departed the shores of America on 21 February they left behind them a nation truly besotted – a fact as inexplicable as it was improbable. But Brian Epstein, who had conceived the visit in his own inimitable fashion – weighing up, as no other pop-group manager would, the value of a cut-price television appearance against the great promotional value obtained – moved swiftly to refuse the flood of offers for an immediate return visit. Fearing over-exposure, he ensured that, despite enormous demand, the Beatles did not return to North America until August.

If 1963 had been the year in which the Beatles conquered Britain, then 1964 can be seen as the year they conquered the world. With immortality at home already assured, the Beatles had begun to move further afield with visits to France and the USA. On 9 March, sitting at his desk on the first day at NEMS' brand-new London location – situated, not unintentionally, next door to the prestigious London Palladium – Brian Epstein surveyed offers for the Beatles from Australasia, the Netherlands, Belgium, Denmark, Finland, Israel, Hong Kong, South Africa (a second offer, following the one made in November 1963) and Sweden. Arthur Howes was pestering for another British tour, and Epstein also wanted to stage a second Beatles Christmas extravaganza.

Somehow almost all of this was accomplished, the only exceptions being the vists to Belgium, Finland, Israel (at one stage set for the end of September 1964) and South Africa (provisionally scheduled for November 1964 but later scrapped). On top of this, just nine days after their return from the USA, the Beatles started work on their first feature film, untitled at that stage but eventually christened *A Hard Day's Night*. Throughout all this time the pace of the Beatles' work – filming, writing music, recording, press, radio and TV appearances, and live concerts – was frightening, but never was the quality allowed to suffer, at least not noticeably so.

On 20 March a new Beatles single was released, 'Can't Buy Me Love' backed with 'You Can't Do That'. Three days previously, at midday on 17 March, EMI had proudly announced that, once again, they had received advance orders of over one million copies in Britain alone. In America the advance sales were 2,100,000. These figures guaranteed another lengthy spell at number one for the Beatles on both sides of the Atlantic. In the States it only served to augment the Beatles' total domination of the charts until so recently impenetrable to British artists. The *Billboard* (another record-industry journal) 'Hot 100' singles listing for 4 April 1964 had the Beatles at positions 1, 2, 3, 4, 5, 31, 41, 46, 58, 65, 68 and 79. A week later two more Beatles singles entered the fray, while in the album charts they held numbers one and two. Of equal importance perhaps was the fact that a number of other British groups were also now making headway in the USA, after the Beatles had made the American audience look to Britain in a new light. But the Beatles' chart dominance was by no means restricted to the UK or USA. In Australia, for example, the group occupied every one of the top *six* placings on the Sydney singles chart on 3 April 1964, and it was there that the Beatles headed after quickly completing the movie *A Hard Day's Night*, and the album of the same name.

The Australasian trip, in retrospect, was not a particularly happy one for the group, and it got off to a lurching start which certainly boded ill for the rest of the tour. The Beatles were due to give concerts in Denmark, the Netherlands and Hong Kong as a prelude to the antipodean trip, and were set to fly out for Copenhagen on 4 June.

On the morning of 3 June Ringo Starr collapsed during a Beatles photographic session at Barnes, London, with tonsillitis and pharyngitis. The group and Brian Epstein were momentarily thrown into a quandary. It was certainly too late to cancel the tour so there was really only one alternative: to hire a temporary replacement drummer. George Harrison,

*The front page of the* Hong Kong Tiger Standard, *10 June 1964.*

in particular, was set against such an idea and assumed a truculent stance in his insistence that if Ringo couldn't go then neither would he. Eventually Brian Epstein and George Martin were able to persuade him otherwise. But Brian realized the importance of bringing in a drummer who would be relatively inconspicuous, and sufficiently unknown to prevent a rash of rumours about his employment being anything other than temporary. He and George Martin immediately thought of Jimmy Nicol, who led his own group, the Shubdubs, assigned to the Pye label. Nicol had been around for several years, beginning his career as a drum repairer for Boosey and Hawkes and then playing with the Swedish group the Spotnicks, and with Georgie Fame's Blue Flames, among others. And as an anonymous session musician he had recently backed Epstein-protégé Tommy Quickly, and had also played on an eminently forgettable anonymous cover version LP called *Beatlemania*, released on the budget label Top Six. At least he would be familiar with the Beatles' material.

Later that morning on 3 June George Martin telephoned Nicol and summoned him to Abbey Road

studios for a 3:00 p.m. session with the Beatles. They rehearsed six numbers – 'I Want to Hold your Hand', 'She Loves You', 'I Saw Her Standing There', 'This Boy', 'Can't Buy Me Love' and 'Long Tall Sally' – before everyone went home to pack. Eighteen hours later John, Paul, George and a stunned Jimmy were on their way to Denmark, and then on to the Netherlands, Hong Kong and Down Under.

The Beatles' reception in Australia was, if anything, more riotous than their American welcome four months previously. Manic scenes preceded, then accompanied, the Beatles' every move throughout the tour. Many people were hurt in the 24-hour-a-day chaos, and the Beatles, caged like animals in a zoo and ritually paraded before a seemingly endless procession of mayors, civic dignitaries, airport receptions, press conferences, street receptions and shrieking audiences, were pulled and pushed, shoved, grabbed and screamed at from close proximity throughout the entire trip. Despite the occasional fun moments they were beginning to loath the whole charade. In Adelaide a crowd estimated at 300,000 congregated outside the Beatles' hotel in the hope of

*North America succumbs. Bottom: Playing to 14,720 in Seattle. Left: Running for cover after 20,261 had witnessed the group's nifty 29-minute show in Vancouver Canada. Below: A rare poster for the tour, complete with numerous mistakes in the spelling of venue names. Even 'Capital' has been mis-spelt.*

RUNNING FOR THEIR LIVES, George Harrison, John ... and Ringe Starr, sprint for their car after police ordered sudden end to performance at Empire Stadium Saturday night. At signal from police official, Beatles dropped instruments and bo... stage to waiting limousine with police es...

## 20,000 Beatlemaniacs Pay So Much — for So Little

By WILLIAM LITTLER

Seldom in Vancouver's entertainment history have so many (20,261) paid so much ($5.25 top price) for so little (27 minutes) as did the audience which screamed at The Beatles in Empire Stadium Saturday night.

As music critic I have had to subject my eardrums to more than a little of the cacophony which currently dominates the hit parade but the efforts shouted by these Liverpudlian tonsorial horrors left me particularly unimpressed.

That is, what portion of it I could hear between choruses of deafening screams left me ...

**GOOD THING GOING**

John Lennon, Paul McCartney, George Harrison and Ringo Starr seemed to have a good thing going for themselves. They looked anthropologically interesting, appeared to be having fun and performed with great gusto.

Moreover, with drummer Starr enthroned high at the back of the stage, bobbing his head as he smashed at the snares and crashed at the cymbals, they had the big beat necessary for hard driving rock 'n roll and rhythm and blues.

But aside from their haircuts (or lack of them) and Mersey-side accents, I perceived nothing that made them ...

**'RINGO JUST BOBS'**

Perhaps their personalities set them apart. Paul is quite set them apart to his audience with assorted gestures; he and John shout with great energy in close harmony; George plays an especially vigorous guitar and is more restrained otherwise.

Ringo just bobs and bashes away.

As for their "singing," what little of it penetrated the audience-produced pandemonium—seemed to be concerned with twisting and shouting. Long Tall Sally, A Hard Day's Night and She Loves You, yeah, yeah, yeah.

Fortunately or unfortunately, depending on one's point of view. The Beatles performed for less than a half hour, leaving ...

to a collection of mediocre talents of deservedly lesser note.

First among them in order came the Bill Black Combo, a dull-sounding big beat rock ensemble composed of sax, guitar, drums and tambourine. They were followed by a quartet called the Exciters, who offered bluesy gospel type rock 'n' roll vocals accompanied by loose-jointed, twist-inspired contortions.

When they had concluded their pelvic and vocal meanderings, the Righteous Brothers bounced on stage to show that they were even more mobile-jointed, and that they could screech higher, shout louder and wiggle lower than their predecessors.

**AUDIENCE TOLERANCE**

Obviously they had not an...

for this blond songbr... seemed to activate ... cords by stamping, y... hips and urging th... to shout with her...the stadium shaki...

The audience te... of these acts in... of what was ... needless to say ...all the way fr...

I do not kno... why it came ... go away. B... Beatle phen... with it will... The day ha... it does, m... where can ... yeah.

'HERE THEY COME THE FABULOUS'

# BEATLES

## American Tour 1964

| | |
|---|---|
| Aug 19 San Francisco Cow Palace | Sept 4 Milwaukee Auditorium |
| Aug 20 Las Vegas Convention Hall | Sept 5 Chicago International Amphitheater |
| Aug 21 Seattle Municiple Stadium | Sept 6 Detroit Olympia Stadium |
| Aug 22 Vancouver Empire Stadium | Sept 7 Toronto Maple Leaf Gardens |
| Aug 23 Hollywood Bowl | Sept 8 Montreal Forum |
| Aug 26 Denver Red Rock Stadium | Sept 11 Jacksonville Gaiter Bowl - Florida |
| Aug 27 Cincinatti Gardens | Sept 12 Boston Gardens |
| Aug 28 New York Forest Hills Tennis Stadium | Sept 13 Baltimore Civic Center |
| Aug 29 New York Forest Hills Tennis Stadium | Sept 14 Pittsburgh Civic Arena |
| Aug 30 Atlantic City Convention Hall N.J. | Sept 15 Cleveland Public Auditorium |
| Sept 2 Philadelphia Convention Hall | Sept 16 New Orleans City Park Stadium |
| Sept 3 Indianapolis State Fair Coliseum | Sept 18 Dallas Memorial Coliseum |

HEAR THE BEATLES GREATEST HITS ON CAPITAL RECORDS

a balcony appearance akin to the royal wave at Buckingham Palace, while in Melbourne there was a
gathering of 250,000. The Beatles viewed these scenes
as potential Nazi-type rallies in Germany during the
Third Reich era, so John, in particular, regularly *Sieg
Heil*ed to the crowd, using a black comb to parody
Hitler's toothbrush moustache.

It was in Melbourne, on 14 June, that Ringo Starr
was reunited with the Beatles, having left his London
hospital temporarily cured of tonsillitis on the morning of 11 June. (On 2 December 1964 he was to go
back and have his tonsils removed.) He flew out of
London Airport for San Francisco on 12 June,
switching planes there for Sydney – via brief stops
in Honolulu and Fiji – and eventually Melbourne.
The reunion marked the end of Jimmy Nicol's short
stint with the Beatles. Today, Nicol is firmly of the
unlikely opinion that, on his return to London,
Epstein had him unofficially blacklisted in some way
since he did not find employment as easily as a one-
time Beatle should.[2] After another brief flirtation
with stardom on 20 June 1964 when he and the Shubdubs were called upon to deputize for the Dave Clark
Five – out of action because Clark was in hospital
– at the Winter Gardens in Blackpool, little was ever
heard of Nicol again. He lived in South America for
a number of years and returned to Britain at the
beginning of the eighties. Apart from immortality,
Nicol's short innings with the group brought him a
fee of £500, plus expenses, and a gold Eternamatic
wrist-watch inscribed 'From the Beatles and Brian
Epstein to Jimmy – with appreciation and gratitude'.

The concerts of the Australasian tour grossed over
£200,000, smashed several concert-attendance
records, and were seen by almost two hundred
thousand people. But the Beatles never went back.
They returned to London on 2 July and temporarily
switched their attention from the stage to the cinema
screen. *A Hard Day's Night* received its world
premiere, in aid of charity, at the London Pavilion
cinema on 6 July before Princess Margaret and the
Earl of Snowdon (Tony Armstrong-Jones) while outside the streets around Piccadilly Circus were closed
by police in anticipation of the 12,000 screaming
crowd. The film drew universally ecstatic reviews,
even from the 'serious newspapers', whose critics
were pleasantly surprised by the movie after eight
years of dirge-like B-rated pop films made on only
slightly less munificent budgets. Four days later, on
10 June, the Beatles travelled to Liverpool for the

---

**2** A ridiculous suggestion, according to Derek Taylor,
Beatles press officer and Epstein assistant at the time of
the tour.

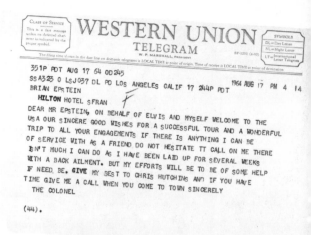

*From one top impresario to another :*
*Colonel Tom Parker's telegram to Brian*
*Epstein. Chris Hutchins was an NME man.*

northern premiere at the city's Odeon cinema. Prior
to the screening they were afforded a civic reception
at the Town Hall, and before that they were driven
into the city centre from Speke Airport along a pre-
arranged route. Some 200,000 people, more than one
in four of all Liverpudlians, were packed along every
inch of the route, welcoming home the city's famous
sons, while outside the Town Hall 20,000 more were
gathered. This was the reception the Beatles valued
more than any other.

With the film, of course, came the album of the
same name, comprising the seven new songs from the
movie soundtrack and six other new compositions.
All 13 tracks had somehow been conceived from the
prolific pens of Lennon and McCartney during the
incessant madness of Beatlemania and touring – a
truly remarkable achievement and testimony to their
inestimable songwriting talent. The album, and
accompanying single, effortlessly topped the charts
all over the world.

Following a handful of British stage appearances
in July and August, and their second trip to Sweden,
the Beatles were heading back to the United States
of America for their first nationwide trek. A trek it
certainly was, 32 shows at 26 concerts in 24 cities in
34 days. That sort of itinerary, while commonplace
in Britain, was absurd in a land the size of America
and was plainly too much. The Beatles spent almost
the entire trip on aeroplanes, in limousines, at one-a-
city press conferences, and being smuggled in and out
of hotels, towns and stadiums. It earned them a veritable fortune (and, therefore, the close attention of
the Internal Revenue Service) but, as they reasoned,
what use was the money when they were imprisoned?
Half the time they wouldn't even know which city
they were in. The scenes of rampaging Beatlemania

throughout the tour were stultifying, and it would be pointless, not to mention impossible, to detail every incidence of it here. There are, however, a few anecdotes which perfectly encapsulate the mayhem endemic around the Beatles during those 34 days in America.

They arrived in the States in San Francisco on 18 August to a frenzied airport reception from 9000 delirious fans. Still on the tarmac the group was herded into a limousine and driven 50 yards into a protective fenced enclosure which would allow the press photographers their required pictures. Suddenly the 9000 clamouring fans pressed all around the fencing started to push in unison, many fainting in the terrible crush. The Beatles, horrified, managed to escape split seconds before the assemblage collapsed under the feet of shrieking fans. From there, visibly shaken, the Beatles zoomed to their 15th-floor refuge at the city's Hilton Hotel, once again under siege. With them safely – but miserably – ensconced there, the hotel was positively crawling with armed policemen and security guards. Yet, at the same time, nine floors below on the sixth level, a middle-aged woman was slugged unconscious and robbed, her screams for help going ignored in the mistaken belief that she was another ululating Beatles fan.

During the course of the Beatles' show in San Francisco the next day Brian Epstein had a visit from one Charles O. Finley, the millionaire owner and President of the Kansas City Athletics baseball team.

Finley was disappointed that Kansas City had not been included in the Beatles' tour itinerary, and before he flew to San Francisco he had said that he would somehow get the group to play there, further vowing that he would not return without a contract. He offered Brian Epstein first $50,000 and then $100,000 for one gig but was refused both times. The only day it could possibly be arranged for was 17 September, designated as a rest day to enable the Beatles to visit New Orleans. But Finley was nothing if not persistent, and eventually, in Los Angeles, came the breakthrough he wanted. After Brian had reiterated that 'The Boys dearly want to explore the traditional home of jazz and I do not feel I can disappoint them,' Finley promptly tore up the $100,000 cheque, tossed it into an ashtray and wrote out another for $150,000, at that time the record fee paid to an artist or group in America for one show. Epstein told Finley to wait a moment while he talked it over with 'the boys'. The boys, trapped in their hotel room by adoring fans, were in the middle of another interminable card game when Epstein walked in and showed them the cheque. 'What do you want to do about it?' he said. With the other three nodding in agreement, John Lennon, hardly bothering to look up, simply shrugged his shoulders and blurted, 'We'll do whatever you want.' Epstein then relieved himself of the guilt in forfeiting the Beatles' one day off by assuring them of the enor-

*On the road yet again . . . the Beatles' 1964 tour of the UK. The group often had first choice of support artists and on this occasion plumped for Mary Wells, diminutive but soulful singer from the quickly booming Tamla Motown label, of which the Beatles were public supporters.*

mous prestige value in accepting the magnanimous offer before going back to Finley and accepting. For that one night the reluctant Beatles earned $4838 per minute. It was, remember, just 13 months after the group had last played at the Cavern Club.[3]

After the Beatles left Kansas City the manager of their hotel, the Muehlebach, sold all of the bed linen – 16 sheets and eight pillow-cases – to two Chicago businessmen for $750. The linen, unlaundered, was then cut into three-inch squares, mounted on a card, and sold with a legal affidavit at $10 a time. The towel used by the Beatles to mop their faces immediately after coming off stage at their Hollywood Bowl concert on 23 August was similarly cut into portions and sold. In New York City cans of 'Beatle Breath' were on sale and there were requests received for the Beatles' bathwater and used shaving foam. Meanwhile, backstage at several concerts, disabled people would be wheeled into the Beatles' dressing rooms to meet the group and receive a Messianic healing touch from the hand of one of the four Liverpudlians. The Beatles were appalled.

On 1 September, after the Beatles' show in Atlantic City – a town described by the group as a larger version of Blackpool – the group had a two-day break before their next gig, in Philadelphia on the 3rd. In those two days the Beatles were never once able to leave their hotel suite due to the incredible scenes of pandemonium outside. The tension *inside* was electric. Before the second of their two shows at the Convention Center in Las Vegas the management received an anonymous bomb scare. The Beatles had to play their second spot in the knowledge that at any second they could be killed. And one kindly and previously not unsuccessful woman astrologer then hit the headlines when she predicted that the Beatles' chartered aeroplane, hired by Brian Epstein for the entire tour at a cost of $37,950.50, would crash *en route* from Philadelphia to Indianapolis with no survivors.

Eventually the tour ended on 20 September with a charity performance in New York City in which tempers frayed in the audience as elegantly dressed socialites mingled with, and were upset by, the *hoi polloi*, young screaming teenagers. On stage too, the Beatles were disgusted – by probably the worst amplification system they ever had the misfortune to use.

---

**3** The forecast of heavy rain and thunder kept the Kansas City crowd down to 20,208 in a 40,957-seater outdoor stadium. Finley lost $40,000 on the deal but still wrote out a personal cheque for $25,000 to a local children's hospital to which he had promised to donate any profits. As Finley unashamedly said on the back of each ticket, 'Today's Beatles fan is tomorrow's baseball fan.'

*Fame, and the tiresome, endless meetings with mayors and holding of children. John Lennon's face says it all.*

The next day they flew home to London, having spent over 63 hours travelling 22,621 miles since 18 August (22,441 in the air, 180 on the road). Never again would they undertake such a tour.

Nineteen days later, on 9 October, the Beatles were off again – this time on their first and only British tour of 1964. Announced back in April to appease the home-based fans, it consisted of 54 shows at 27 concerts in 25 cities in 33 days. The Beatlemania was, of course, the same – only on a smaller scale than it had been in America. The Beatles' sense of 'imprisonment' though was as great. The tour, once again, visited most major British towns and cities, playing the Gaumonts, ABCs and Granada cinemas. If the American problem had been that the Beatles' concert venues were too big, the very opposite applied to Britain. A cinema rarely held more than 3000 people, often fewer, and the group would need to have played every night for a whole year in order to be seen by all their fans. By now, it seems, the Beatles weren't pleasing anyone bar the bank manager and the taxman, not their fans, and most certainly not themselves.

The tumultuous year of 1964 ended with the Beatles atop the worldwide singles charts with the double-A-sided 'I Feel Fine' and 'She's a Woman' and at number one in the LP charts with yet another new offering, *Beatles for Sale*. (In America, where Capitol unashamedly contrived to release 18 Beatles albums from 1964 to 1970 in place of the 12 in Britain – without using any extra tracks – it was titled *Beatles '65*.) On stage at the Odeon cinema in Hammersmith, London, the Beatles were involved in *Another Beatles' Christmas Show*, again conceived by Brian Epstein. On 7 September 132,240 tickets had gone on sale at the box-office, and £15,000 changed hands within one week. By the time of the show almost every seat was sold. It had been quite a year.

**1–11 January**  Astoria Cinema,
(excluding  Finsbury Park, London
5 January)
(10 nights)

The last ten nights of the 1963 *Beatles Christmas Show*.
  On the afternoon of 7 January the Beatles recorded a session for the radio programme *Saturday Club* at the BBC Playhouse Theatre in London.

END OF THE BEATLES' CHRISTMAS SHOW

**12 January**  London Palladium
  Theatre,
  London

A celebrated return spot on the live television show *Val Parnell's Sunday Night at the London Palladium*, following the Beatles' auspicious debut on 13 October 1963. The other star artistes on this show were singer Alma Cogan, of whom the Beatles were very fond, and Irish comedian Dave Allen, who had first met the Beatles when he compered their tour with Helen Shapiro.

**VISIT TO FRANCE**

**15 January**  Cinéma Cyrano,
  Versailles

The Beatles' first night in France, and a warm-up for all the artistes for the forthcoming three-week season at the Olympia in Paris, performed before 2000 people.
  A rare day off for the Beatles came on 13 January, and on the night of 14 January they had flown out of London Airport for Le Bourget Airport, Paris, and a welcome from 60 French teenagers.

**16 January–**  Olympia Theatre,
**4 February**  Boulevard des
(20 days and  Capucines,
nights)  Paris

A marathon season at the Olympia – 20 days of two, sometimes three, shows each, on an enormous bill of ten artistes. At no time was it ever made clear who was headlining: the Beatles, French *chanteuse* Sylvie Vartan, or Trini Lopez, the 25-year-old Texas-born singer famous for 'If I Had a Hammer'.
  The Beatles' repertoire for this season comprised 'From Me to You', 'Roll over Beethoven', 'She Loves You',

'This Boy', 'Boys', 'I Want to Hold your Hand', 'Twist and Shout' and 'Long Tall Sally'. One of the 19 January shows was recorded for transmission by ORTF-radio. On 22 January a camera crew from ORTF-tv filmed a show.
  During the day of 29 January the Beatles congregated at EMI's Pathé-Marconi recording studios in Paris and recorded German-language versions of 'She Loves You' ('Sie Liebt Dich') and 'I Want to Hold your Hand' ('Komm, Gib Mir Deine Hand'). These were released in West Germany on 5 March 1964, in lieu of a clamoured-for concert tour by the Beatles there, impossible to fulfil because of the complex legalities surrounding a paternity suit involving one of the group arising from the Star-Club days. At the same Paris recording session the Beatles also taped their next single, the newly-written 'Can't Buy Me Love'. (They did not record the B-side 'You Can't Do That' here, as reported in a great many Beatles books.)
  At 1:00 p.m. on 5 February the Beatles returned to London Airport from Le Bourget to a boisterous reception from 100 schoolgirls well versed in the art of truancy.

RETURN TO UK

**VISIT TO THE USA**

**11 February**  Washington Coliseum,
  Washington DC,

At 8:31 p.m. the Beatles stepped on stage to give their first-ever concert in North America, at the 8092-seat Coliseum. The entire concert, coupled

with the rampant scenes of Beatlemania, was captured on film by CBS and shown in cinemas as a closed-circuit telecast on 14 and 15 March. The Beatles' repertoire comprised 'Roll over Beethoven', 'From Me to You', 'I Saw Her Standing There', 'This Boy', 'All my Loving', 'I Wanna Be your Man', 'Please Please Me', 'Till there Was You', 'She Loves You', 'I Want to Hold your Hand', 'Twist and Shout' and 'Long Tall Sally'.
  After the Beatles' frenzied New York arrival on 7 February, the group had rehearsed their appearance for the CBS television programme *The Ed Sullivan Show* on 8 February, and again on the morning of 9 February (without George Harrison who was ill). That same afternoon, with George, they taped the appearance to be shown after their departure from America, on 23 February. On the night of 9 February the Beatles gave the first of their two live transmissions on *Sullivan*, performed in front of an audience of 728 persons in the CBS-TV studio at Broadway and West 53rd Street, and an estimated 73 million people in homes across the United States. They performed five songs altogether, three at the beginning of the show, 'All my Loving', 'Till there Was You' and 'She Loves You', followed by two in the second half of the programme, 'I Saw Her Standing There' and 'I Want to Hold your Hand'.
  The Beatles and their entourage had travelled down to Washington DC in an old Richmond, Fredericksburg and Potomac Railroad train called *King George* from New York's Penn Station on 11 February. They were unable to fly down, as scheduled, due to heavy snow. On 12 February Abraham Lincoln's birthdate and an American national holiday, they took the train back to New York.
  Note: Films of the three *Sullivan* appearances were repeated later in the year, on 12 July, 23 August and 20 September.

**12 February**  Carnegie Hall,
  New York City,
  New York

Two 34-minute stage appearances at the famed Carnegie Hall, at 7:45 p.m. and 11:15 p.m. with a capacity house of 2900 people at each one. The box-office for these two performances had opened on 27 January. All tickets were sold by 28 January.
  A plan by Capitol Records to record the two Beatles stage spots was

# YOU AIN'T SEEN *or heard* NOTHIN' YET!

## IN FULL CONCERT...
## A GREAT *NEW* SHOW!
## CLOSED CIRCUIT-
## BIG SCREEN!

NATIONAL GENERAL CORPORATION
PRESENTS

# THE BEATLES
(CAPITOL RECORDING ARTISTS)
DIRECT FROM THEIR

## FIRST AMERICAN CONCERT
IN
## WASHINGTON D.C., COLISEUM!

thwarted by the American Federation of Musicians.

On 13 February the Beatles flew down to Miami, Florida, arriving at 3:55 p.m., supposedly to enjoy a few days of rest at the Deauville Hotel in Miami Beach – an evident impossibility with the manic scenes which accompanied their every move. After a brief rehearsal on 14 February, a full rehearsal on 15 February and a dress rehearsal on the afternoon of the 16th, the Beatles' second live appearance on *The Ed Sullivan Show* took place on the night of 16 February, the group's segment coming direct from the hotel. They performed 'I Saw Her Standing There', 'I Want to Hold your Hand', 'From Me To You', 'Twist and Shout', 'Please Please Me' and 'She Loves You'.

Following several more days of 'rest' the Beatles, on board Pan Am PA 121, flew home to England from Miami, via a short stopover in New York, arriving at London Airport at 8:10 (half an hour after the scheduled touchdown) in the morning on Saturday 22 February.

RETURN TO UK

**26 April**  *New Musical Express* 1963–64 Annual Poll-Winners' All-star Concert, Empire Pool, Wembley

A bill-topping return to the British concert platform – the Beatles' first in 15 weeks – at the annual *New Musical Express* concert. The group

performed 'She Loves You', 'You Can't Do That', 'Twist and Shout', 'Long Tall Sally' and 'Can't Buy Me Love'.

Highlights of the entire show were broadcast on two mammoth TV specials entitled *Big Beat '64*. The Beatles' segment was in the second one, transmitted by ABC (British) television on 10 May and repeated on 8 November.

The Beatles were certainly not inactive – as it may appear – from their return from the USA to this date. Far from it, for in that time they began, and completed, all the filming for their first full-length movie, to be titled *A Hard Day's Night*, they recorded all of the six new film songs (plus 'You Can't Do That' and two other tracks for the imminent *Long Tall Sally* EP) in five sessions at EMI's Abbey Road studios, they made three television appearances, recorded two long sessions for BBC radio, recorded songs – and had five days of rehearsal – for a forthcoming TV special (tentatively titled *John, Paul, George and Ringo* though later changed to *Around the Beatles*), received top-rated awards at

*Advert for the closed-circuit screening of the Beatles' USA debut.*

two gala luncheons, from Harold Wilson and His Royal Highness Prince Philip respectively, and enjoyed a reunion party with Tony Sheridan at Brian Epstein's new London flat. On top of all this, John Lennon's first book, *In his own Write*, was published and was topping the list of best sellers.

**29 April**  ABC Cinema, Lothian Road, Edinburgh, Midlothian, Scotland

The first of two hugely successful nights in Scotland, promoted jointly by Albert Bonici and Brian Epstein.

On 28 April the Beatles filmed the Rediffusion TV special *Around the Beatles* before an audience at Wembley studios. The show encompassed music and a spoof-Shakespeare comedy sketch and was transmitted on 6 May.

**30 April**  Odeon Cinema, Glasgow, Scotland

Note: After this show the group rested for four weeks, resuming active work on 31 May. In the meantime the four Beatles went on holidays, John and George to Papeete in Tahiti, Paul and Ringo to St Thomas, one of the Virgin Islands. Both groups returned to London Airport on 26 May.

**31 May** — Prince of Wales Theatre, London

A return visit to the site of the Beatles' Royal Command triumph the previous November. This gig was the fifth in a series of seven consecutive Sunday-night pop concerts at this theatre, presented by Brian Epstein, under the title *Pops Alive!* There were six support acts: Kenny Lynch, Cliff Bennett and the Rebel Rousers, the Vernons Girls, the Lorne Gibson Trio, the Chants and the Harlems.

The Beatles' repertoire comprised 'Can't Buy Me Love', 'All my Loving', 'This Boy', 'Roll over Beethoven', 'Till there Was You', 'Twist and Shout' and 'Long Tall Sally'.

## THE BEATLES' WORLD TOUR

**4 June** — K.B. Hallen, Copenhagen, Denmark

Two shows, at 6:00 p.m. and 9:30 p.m., attended by 4400 people each, kicked off the Beatles' 25-day world tour which included visits to Denmark, the Netherlands, Hong Kong, Australia and New Zealand.

For the two Copenhagen shows, and the following ten concerts until Wellington, New Zealand, the Beatles' repertoire comprised 'I Saw Her Standing There', 'I Want to Hold your Hand', 'You Can't Do That', 'All my Loving', 'She Loves You', 'Till there Was You', 'Roll over Beethoven', 'Can't Buy Me Love', 'This Boy' and 'Long Tall Sally'. Occasionally 'Twist and Shout' would replace 'Long Tall Sally' as the closing number while just once – on the very first show of the Copenhagen gig – the Beatles opened their set with 'I Want to Hold your Hand' and switched 'I Saw Her Standing There' to the second song.

For the first five dates of the tour, encompassing Copenhagen to Adelaide, Australia, the Beatles employed a substitute drummer, 24-year-old Jimmy Nicol, in place of the hospitalized Ringo Starr.

Note: Before leaving England, on 1 and 2 June, the Beatles completed the recording sessions for the album *A Hard Day's Night*, taping all of the five new non-film songs, and also recording 'Matchbox' and 'Slow Down' for the *Long Tall Sally* EP.

**6 June** — Veilinghal, Blokker, The Netherlands

Two shows in Blokker, a matinee for which many seats remained unoccupied, and an evening gig for which all of the 7000 seats were sold.

The Beatles had arrived in Holland at Schiphol airport, Amsterdam, straight from Copenhagen on 5 June. That night they taped a television appearance for VARA-tv at their Treslong studios in Hillegom, 26 miles out of Amsterdam. It was transmitted on 10 June.

**9 June** — Princess Theatre, Kowloon, Hong Kong

Two shows at the 1700-seater Princess Theatre in Kowloon. Beatlemania was even evident here in the Orient, though predominantly among the English-speaking population. Nevertheless, neither performance here was sold out, principally because of the inordinately high ticket price, 75 Hong Kong dollars, set by the local promoter without the knowledge of Brian Epstein. The price, equivalent to £4 10s at the time, was then the average working man's weekly wage in Hong Kong.

The Beatles had left Amsterdam on 7 June and flown back to London where they took a connecting flight, conveniently delayed to allow for the Beatles' switch-over, and set out for Hong Kong. The plane made scheduled re-fuelling stops at Zurich, Beirut, Karachi, Calcutta and Bangkok. At each airport terminal, at any time of day or night, and irrespective of whether one or more of the Beatles actually left the plane, Beatlemania erupted. When the plane eventually landed at Kaitak Airport, Hong Kong, over 1000 fans were on hand to greet them.

CENTENNIAL HALL

JOHN MARTIN'S AZTEC AND STADIUMS Present

THE BEATLES

STALLS

ROW **LL** SEAT **6**

Sat. 13th June — **8.45**

**12 and 13 June** (2 nights) — Centennial Hall, Adelaide, South Australia, Australia

The Beatles' first four Australian shows, the repertoire comprising the same songs as in Denmark. Applications for 50,000 tickets arrived for the 12,000 available seats.

The Beatles arrived in Australia on 11 June, straight from Kaitak Airport, Hong Kong, except for a stop in Manila to refuel. But since this was deemed impossible by the Philippine airport authorities because of the extreme heat, an unscheduled refuelling stop was made at Darwin in the Northern Territory of Australia. Even at 2:35 in the morning 400 fans materialized at the remote Darwin airport, symbolic, by ratio, of the reception the group would receive on reaching the major Australian cities. From the brief stop in Darwin the Beatles flew on to Sydney, arriving at Mascot International Airport

172

# BEATLES ARE ANNOYED BY JELLY-BABY BARRAGE

## It Doesn't Give Us A Chance, Paul Complains

## RINGO: THEY ALL HIT ME

SYDNEY, Saturday.

Liverpool's usually cheerful Beatles are feeling annoyed to-day with the Sydney fans.

Despite all the appeals they've made to the huge audiences here not to throw jelly-babies during performances because of the danger to their eyes, girls are persisting in flinging handfuls of these sweets at John, Paul, George, and Ringo as the stage in the centre of the enormous Sydney Stadium revolves slowly, making them targets in turn to each section of the audience.

Paul McCartney said bitterly: " I keep asking them

### Beatles Done In The Eye

Monocled Sir Bernard Fergusson, New Zealand's Governor - General, has done the Beatles in the eye.

The Cathedral Grammar School at Christchurch has been swept by a Beatle-wig craze, but Sir Bernard recently visited Christchurch—and now the wigs have been replaced by a rash of imitation monocles.

not to chuck those damned things, but they don't seem to have the sense to realise we hate being the target for sweets coming like bullets from all directions.

### DUCKING

" How can we concentrate on our jobs on the stage when we are having all the time to keep ducking to avoid sweets, streamers and the other stuff they keep throwing at us."

John Lennon said: " It's ridiculous. They even throw miniature koala bears and gift wrapped packages while we are going round on the revolving stage. We haven't a chance to get out of the way."

Twice during the show, Paul McCartney has stopped singing in the middle numbers and said to the audience: " Please don't throw those sweets as us. They get in our eyes."

Each time his request has been greeted by screams and another shower of sweets, so Paul has finally shugged his shoulders and said: " Well, I asked you, anyway."

### NONSENSE

This nonsense about the Beatles liking jelly-beans began many months ago, with a much-regretted publicity yarn saying these were their favourite sweets.

" Wherever we've been since then — America, Europe and now Australia — that stupid story has gone ahead with the result that we get jelly-babies chucked at us until we're really fed up," said George Harrison.

Ringo Starr chipped in to say; " It's all right for you lot. You can jump aside and dodge them, but I'm stuck at the drums and can't move, so they all seem to hit me."

Apart from these reasonable grouses, our popular chamber music quartet rate Sydney audiences as among the noisiest they've ever experienced.

Said young George: " We can't hear ourselves singing, so how can they hear us? There's never a pause in their

Stadium has never kn anything like it.

More than 10,000 fans every performance, h according to official s ments by an acoustics ex of New South Wales Un sity. Mrs. Anita Lawre made more noise than Boeing 707 jet in full scr ing flight.

Said Mrs. Lawrence, last night took a sound-meter with her to check pitch of audience n "Normally, noise reaching ground from a Boeing plane 2,000 feet up is bet 90 and 100 decibels.

"When the Bea appeared, the pure scr alone showed 112 decibe the recording apparatus the next half-hour the n never fell below 100 and times leapt higher."

The decibel meter sh Paul McCartney the popular of the Be Whenever he bobbed his and grinned the needle up as high at 114 dec which is more than noise given out by an ele saw three feet away your ears.

### HYSTERIA

During the last coup nights here, more th hundred young girls received first aid ambu treatment after colla during the Beatles' formance.

Most of these were of hysteria and nobody injured.

To-night's two show our Sydney visit. To-m morning we leave Au for a week in New Ze where they tell us ment has been buildi for months in anticipat our arrival.

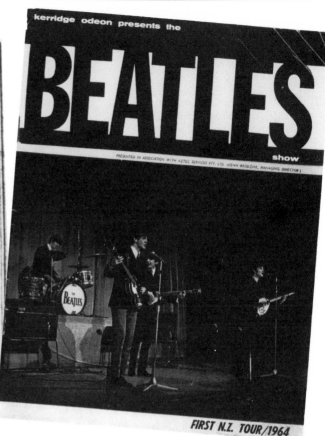

FIRST N.Z. TOUR/1964

*Mementos of the world tour and, opposite, some unusually honest reporting of the Beatles' misery at their treatment by Australian fans.*

| | |
|---|---|
| **18–20 June** (3 nights) | Stadium, Sydney, New South Wales, Australia |

A return to Sydney for six clamorous shows, with 12,000 fans, the biggest-ever pop concert audience in Sydney at that time, packing into the Stadium on each occasion.

| | |
|---|---|
| **22 and 23 June** (2 nights) | Town Hall, Wellington, North Island, New Zealand |

Four shows in Wellington at the 2500-seat Town Hall kicked off the Beatles' seven-day visit to New Zealand, they having flown in from Sydney on 21 June.

Ringo, his vocal cords recovered from their bout of tonsillitis, resumed his one-vocal-per-performance quota with 'Boys' at the first of the Wellington gigs, bringing the Beatles' repertoire back to a total of 11 songs.

| | |
|---|---|
| **24 and 25 June** (2 nights) | Town Hall, Auckland, North Island, New Zealand |

Four more shows, seen by 10,000 people altogether.

in the most torrential rainstorm imaginable, particularly felt by the four Beatles who had to parade before the packed airport enclosures in an open-top truck. Once in Sydney city centre the Beatles were, as usual, trapped inside their hotel suite by a massive following of fans.

The Beatles did not play any concerts in Sydney at this stage, and the entourage flew on to Adelaide on the morning of 12 June.

| | |
|---|---|
| **15–17 June** (3 nights) | Festival Hall, Melbourne, Victoria, Australia |

Three nights in Melbourne, two shows per night. A total of 45,000 people saw the six gigs. Ringo Starr re-joined the Beatles for the first of the shows and Jimmy Nicol made his way back to Britain.

The Beatles had arrived at Essendon Airport in Melbourne on 14 June. They left for Sydney on 18 June.

| | |
|---|---|
| **26 June** | Town Hall, Dunedin, South Island, New Zealand |

Two shows in this 4000-seater town hall.

The flight from Auckland to Dunedin had been an anxious one following an anonymous threat that a 'germ bomb' had been placed somewhere on board the plane.

| | |
|---|---|
| **27 June** | Majestic Theatre, Christchurch, South Island, New Zealand |

Note : On 28 June the Beatles flew out of Christchurch for Sydney, Australia, switching planes in Auckland. From Sydney they changed planes again, landing in Brisbane just after midnight on 29 June.

| | |
|---|---|
| **29 and 30 June** (2 nights) | Festival Hall, Brisbane, Queensland, Australia |

Four more shows, before 5500 people each, closed the Beatles' hectic tour of the antipodes. Early in the morning of 1 July they flew out of Brisbane, changing planes again at Sydney. At 11:10 a.m. on 2 July, after refuelling stops in Singapore and Frankfurt, the Qantas 735 touched down at London Airport.

END OF TOUR

**12 July**        Hippodrome Theatre,
                   Brighton

After the tour Down Under the Beatles returned to the British concert stage with the first of six scheduled gigs at seaside holiday resorts, a far cry from the 47 played in 1963.

One of the support acts on this evening was erstwhile temporary Beatles drummer Jimmy Nicol, together with his group the Shubdubs. Despite being on the same bill, the paths of Nicol and the Beatles somehow failed to cross during the entire night and the reunion was averted.

On 11 July the Beatles had appeared on *Lucky Stars (Summer Spin)*, unusually transmitted live from the ABC studios in Teddington, Middlesex, after a technicians' strike had precluded the pre-recording from taking place on 5 July.

**19 July**        ABC Theatre,
                   Blackpool

An evening organized by ABC television and transmitted live in their series *Blackpool Night Out*. The Beatles had earlier spent the day rehearsing for the show, having flown up to Squires Gate Airport, Blackpool, on 18 July.

On 14 July the Beatles recorded seven songs for the first edition of a new BBC radio programme, *Top Gear*. It was transmitted two days later, on 16 July. On 17 July they recorded their

fourth BBC radio bank holiday special, *From Us to You*, broadcast on 3 August.

**23 July**        The Night of a
                   Hundred Stars,
                   London Palladium
                   Theatre,
                   London

A special midnight revue, in aid of the Combined Theatrical Charities Appeals Council, featuring a glittering array of illustrious names from all walks of show business. The Beatles, representing 'pop music', performed a flying ballet sketch, 'I'm Flying', in part one of the show, and a short musical set in part two.

**26 July**        Opera House,
                   Church Street,
                   Blackpool, Lancashire

Note: On 25 July George Harrison had appeared live on the BBC-TV programme *Juke Box Jury* from the Television Theatre, Shepherds Bush, London, while – on the same day – Ringo recorded an appearance for the following week's (1 August) transmission.

### SHORT TRIP TO SWEDEN

**28 and 29 July**     Johanneshovs
(2 nights)             Isstadion,
                       Stockholm

The Beatles' second visit to Sweden

inside ten months saw them give four performances over two nights at the 8500-seater ice hockey arena. On two occasions they played to less than capacity audiences, 6500 for the first gig and just 3000 for the second. During that first show Paul received a mild electric shock from an unearthed microphone. John, too, suffered a jolt.

The Beatles had flown out of London Airport at 10:10 a.m. on 28 July, returning at 3:45 p.m. on 30 July.

RETURN TO UK

*Below left: A Lennon illustration served as the cover for the 23 July London Palladium charity programme. Below: Even one-night gigs now had a programme.*

| | |
|---|---|
| **2 August** | Gaumont Cinema, Bournemouth |

Also on the bill with the Beatles were the Kinks, a new and unknown London group, Mike Berry and Adrienne Poster (later Posta).

| | |
|---|---|
| **9 August** | Futurist Theatre, Scarborough |

Note: on 11 and 14 August the Beatles recorded five songs at Abbey Road studios in London for inclusion on their next album.

| | |
|---|---|
| **16 August** | Opera House, Blackpool |

One of the support acts on this bill was the High Numbers – 'a new R&B group' – shortly to change their name to the Who.

## THE BEATLES' FIRST US TOUR

| | |
|---|---|
| **19 August** | Cow Palace, San Francisco, California |

The first of 25 concerts in *The Beatles' First American Tour* – something of a misnomer since, though it was the group's first jaunt around the continent, it was actually their second visit to the USA, and the tour also ventured north into Canada for three gigs.

The Beatles performed just 12 songs in every show on this tour, usually 'Twist and Shout', 'You Can't Do That', 'All my Loving', 'She Loves You', 'Things We Said Today', 'Roll over Beethoven', 'Can't Buy Me Love', 'If I Fell', 'I Want to Hold your Hand', 'Boys', 'A Hard Day's Night' and 'Long Tall Sally'. Occasionally the Beatles would drop 'She Loves You', open with 'I Saw Her Standing There' and close with 'Twist and Shout'. At one show, in Las Vegas, they added 'Till there Was You'.

All 17,130 seats for this one gig were sold out, the gate receipts totalling $91,670 (then the equivalent of £32,740). The Beatles' gross share of this was $47,600 (£17,000).

The Beatles had left London at noon on 18 August and arrived (after brief stops in Winnipeg and Los Angeles, where 2000 fans gathered to greet them) at San Francisco International Airport at 6:24 p.m. to a reception from 9000 screaming teenagers. That night John and Ringo, with press officer Derek Taylor, managed to elude their heavy police guard and slip away from the Hilton Hotel to a night club in the Chinatown area of the city run by Billy Preston, the former keyboard player with Little Richard whom they had met in Hamburg, and in Liverpool in October 1962 when Brian Epstein brought Little Richard to Merseyside for two concerts. The paths of Preston and the Beatles were to cross again in 1969 when Billy performed with them

on the *Let It Be* project, and was signed to Apple Records.

| | |
|---|---|
| **20 August** | Convention Center, Las Vegas, Nevada |

The Beatles flew to Las Vegas immediately after the Cow Palace performance, arriving at 1:00 a.m. Here they gave two shows, at 4:00 p.m. and 9:00 p.m., before a combined total of 16,000 fans.

| | |
|---|---|
| **21 August** | Coliseum, Seattle, Washington |

Fans totalling 14,720 saw this one 29-minute Beatles performance.

| | |
|---|---|
| **22 August** | Empire Stadium, Vancouver, British Columbia, Canada |

Attendance at this one show was 20,261. Immediately afterwards the Beatles flew to Los Angeles, arriving at 3:55 a.m.

FOR their appearance at the Hollywood Bowl in the United States later this year, the Beatles have ordered some powerful amplifiers—100 watt.

Jennings Musical Industries, who make the amplification equipment the Beatles use, fitted the group out with 50 watt amplifiers for their last American tour.

But next time it has to be even louder . . .

| | |
|---|---|
| **23 August** | Hollywood Bowl, Los Angeles, California |

The Beatles' one gig at this magnificent venue was seen by 18,700 fans and recorded by Capitol Records – with the permission of the American Federation of Musicians – for 'future release'. It was eventually issued well into the future, in May 1977.

After the show, and for the next two days, the Beatles rested at a private house in Bel Air, venturing outside only for a star-studded private party in Hollywood, held in their honour and in aid of charity, on the afternoon of 24 August.

| | |
|---|---|
| **26 August** | Red Rocks Amphitheatre, Denver, Colorado |

Only 7000 fans turned up to see the

Beatles' one show in this natural amphitheatre, leaving 2000 seats unoccupied. It was reported that the stadium's location – 20 miles out of Denver with no public transport service – was to blame for the unsold tickets.

| | |
|---|---|
| **27 August** | Cincinnati Gardens, Cincinnati, Ohio |

Once again thieves broke into a Beatles dressing room during a performance, stealing various personal effects and money. The Beatles played one show here, before 14,000 people, and immediately afterwards flew on to New York City, landing at 2:55 a.m. to a reception from 2000 fans.

| | |
|---|---|
| **28 and 29 August** (2 nights) | Forest Hills Tennis Stadium, Queens, New York City, New York |

Two nights, one show each, performed before 16,000 fans on each occasion.

| | |
|---|---|
| **30 August** | Convention Hall (Center), Atlantic City, New Jersey |

For this one show 18,000 teenagers packed the Convention Hall. The Democratic Party National Convention had been held here the week previous to the gig and, the newspapers happily reported, the Beatles received a more boisterous reception than had been afforded the speech by President Lyndon B. Johnson.

| | |
|---|---|
| **2 September** | Convention Hall, Philadelphia, Pennsylvania |

Following riots in the city of Philadelphia a few days prior to this gig, the Beatles were disgusted to see a suspiciously all-white audience of 13,000 for this one show.

| | |
|---|---|
| **3 September** | Indiana State Fair Coliseum, State Fairgrounds, Indianapolis, Indiana |

Two shows, seen by a total of 29,337 people, and netting $85,232 (£30,440) in the process.

| | |
|---|---|
| **4 September** | Arena, Milwaukee, Wisconsin |

One performance.

| | |
|---|---|
| **5 September** | International Amphitheatre, Chicago, Illinois |

One performance.

## 6 September 1964

*Breathless reportage of the Beatles
hurricane that sent North America
spinning. The writers add a fair sprinkling
of genuine bewilderment to their stories of
sobbing, screaming girls.*

**6 September**    Olympia Stadium,
Detroit, Michigan

Two shows in the Motor City, famous in
music circles as the home of Tamla
Motown records, the Beatles' favourite
music at this time.

**7 September**    Maple Leaf Gardens,
Toronto, Ontario,
Canada

Two shows in one evening, seen by
35,522 people altogether. Road
manager Neil Aspinall had to miss this
night due to illness so Mal Evans was
temporarily promoted.

**8 September**    Forum, Montreal,
Quebec, Canada

Two gigs at the Forum, seen by 21,000
people. After the show, the Beatles'
flight to Jacksonville, Florida, was
diverted to Key West, on the southern
tip of Florida, because of Hurricane
Dora which was heading straight for
Jacksonville. The plane touched down
at Key West airfield, unannounced, at
3:30 in the morning of 9 September to
a reception from hundreds of
seemingly prescient screaming
teenagers. Hurricane Dora duly
reached Jacksonville as predicted,
causing immense damage so the
Beatles didn't fly there until mid-
afternoon on 11 September.

**11 September**    Gator Bowl,
Jacksonville, Florida

The Beatles had refused to play this
one gig until they had received an
assurance from the promoter that the
audience would not be colour
segregated.
    Because of the extensive damage
caused by Hurricane Dora, 9000 of the
32,000 ticket holders were unable to
get to the Gator Bowl.

**12 September**    Boston Garden,
Boston, Massachusetts

One performance.

**13 September**    Civic Center,
Baltimore, Maryland

Two gigs, seen by 28,000 fans
altogether.

**14 September**    Civic Arena,
Pittsburgh,
Pennsylvania

One performance, before 12,603
screaming spectators.

Those Four Chaps From Britain

## Don't Blame Us For 'Revolt,' Pleads Paul

By FREMONT POWER

If teen-age girls scream at the Beatles because
they are, in effect, revolting against their...

### THE CINCINNATI ENQUIRER

FRIDAY MORNING, AUGUST 28, 1964

George Harrison    Paul McCartney    Ringo Starr    John Lennon

## What's Future For Beatles? 'Count Money'

BY DAVID BRACEY
Of The Enquirer Staff

THE INDIANAPOLIS N

Friday, September 4, 1964

### Beatles
### $85,000
### Bomb TI

By FREMONT POWER

**15 September**   Public Auditorium,
Cleveland, Ohio

During this one performance a gaggle of Beatles fans managed to break through the police cordon and invade the stage. The police ordered the Beatles off the stage mid-song until, after an impassioned plea from Derek Taylor, and a police threat that the rest of the concert would be cancelled, some semblance of order was restored.

**16 September**   City Park Stadium,
New Orleans,
Louisiana

One performance, in front of 12,000 fans.

**17 September**   Municipal Stadium,
Kansas City, Kansas

The famous 'extra' concert. For this one occasion the Beatles opened their show with the Little Richard medley 'Kansas City/Hey-Hey-Hey-Hey!', to an uproarious reception. Once again, the Beatles had to leave the stage during the show until the audience calmed down a little in the face of a cancellation threat.

**18 September**   Memorial Auditorium,
Dallas, Texas

Note: After this one show, on 19 September, the Beatles rested at a remote ranch in Missouri.

**20 September**   Paramount Theatre,
New York City,
New York

Sub-titled 'An Evening with the Beatles', this special charity concert, in aid of the United Cerebral Palsy of New York City and Retarded Infants' Services, rounded off the Beatles' exhausting American tour. Paying up to $100 a ticket, 3682 people attended the show. The Beatles and the other artistes on the bill gave their services free.

The group flew back to England on 21 September, arriving at London Airport on the BOAC Boeing 707 jet, BA 510, at 9:35 p.m.

END OF TOUR

## TOUR OF THE UNITED KINGDOM

**9 October**   Gaumont Cinema,
Bradford

The eagerly awaited British tour, the Beatles' first and only one in 1964, got under way in Bradford, the same place as the first night of the Beatles' tour with Helen Shapiro back in February 1963, and also the venue where *The Beatles' Christmas Show* had made its bow in December 1963. On this tour the Beatles' repertoire comprised

# The night the Beatles came to town

## MANAGER'S B-PLAN A BIG HIT

The Beatles — the highest paid, most popular group of entertainers in the world today — made their long-awaited personal appearance at Wigan's ABC Cinema on Tuesday.

Behind that simple statement of fact, embodying a high-speed entry through the stage door, two 25 minute sessions on stage, and a lightning dash to a waiting police car at the end of the show, lies the story of weeks of careful planning.

Most of the intricate arrangements for the Beatles' visit, down to the ordering of a meal for hasty consumption between shows, and the installation of a television set in the Beatles' dressing room, were made by ABC Manager Neville Ward, who is fast becoming an expert in the skilful art of handling pop stars.

### CONTROLLED FURY

A cinema manager for 17 years, Mr. Ward was handling his fifth pop package show, and none could have exploded—that is the only way to describe these volcanoes of sound—with such controlled fury as this.

The smallest detail, including every possible reaction from the audience, was anticipated weeks ago.

— had already done their duty, and 40 St. John Ambulance Brigade members hovered, smelling salts at the ready.

Behind the scenes, the ABC's chief projectionist, John Ellwood, having 'long since "flown" the cinema's huge screen 85 feet into the air, issued last minute instructions to the six members of his staff and to the six volunteers from Wigan Amateur Operatic Society who acted as stage hands.

Finally, the curtain opened. The Rustiks, Michael Haslam, Sounds Incorporated, Mary Wells, Tommy Quickly and compere Bob Bain went through their acts, generously applauded by an audience secretly willing the hands of the clock to a quicker pace.

And then—The Beatles.

### BEDLAM

A deafening scream, hurled towards the stage from 2,000 throats, pierced both air and eardrums and, with no let-up in the din, the Beatles played and sang for 25 bedlam-like minutes.

The screaming did not worry Mr. Ward or his five dinner-suited assistants who patrolled the aisles, calming over-enthusiastic teenage girls who were ready to rush the stage given the slightest opportunity. Only one fan risked it. She dashed from the second row and was hauled back from the six-foot deep orchestra pit.

'Twist and Shout', 'Money', 'Can't Buy Me Love', 'Things We Said Today', 'I'm Happy Just to Dance with You', 'I Should Have Known Better', 'If I Fell', 'I Wanna Be your Man', 'A Hard Day's Night' and 'Long Tall Sally'.

Between the Beatles' return from the USA and the beginning of the UK tour, the group spent four days at Abbey Road studios taping five more songs for release on their next album and one song for their next single. On 3 October they were filmed singing three songs: 'Kansas City/Hey-Hey-Hey-Hey!', 'I'm a Loser' and 'Boys', at the Granville Theatre in Fulham, London, for transmission in the USA on Jack Good's *Shindig* programme on 20 January 1965. It was never shown in Britain. During this period the group also made several British radio and television appearances.

*Back home to more mayhem, even if the reportage was more sober and British.*

| | |
|---|---|
| 10 October | De Montfort Hall, Leicester |
| 11 October | Odeon Cinema, New Street, Birmingham, Warwickshire |
| 13 October | ABC Cinema, Station Road, Wigan, Lancashire |
| 14 October | ABC Cinema, Ardwick, Manchester |

Note: Before this show the Beatles filmed an appearance on *Scene at 6.30* at the Granada Television studios. It was transmitted on 16 October.

| | |
|---|---|
| 15 October | Globe Cinema, Stockton-on-Tees |
| 16 October | ABC Cinema, Hull |
| 19 October | ABC Cinema, Edinburgh, Scotland |

Note: The Beatles spent 18 October at Abbey Road studios recording eight songs and the 1964 Christmas message for their fan-club members.

| | |
|---|---|
| 20 October | Caird Hall, Dundee, Scotland |
| 21 October | Odeon Cinema, Glasgow, Scotland |
| 22 October | Odeon Cinema, Leeds |
| 23 October | Gaumont State Cinema, Kilburn, London |
| 24 October | Granada Cinema, Walthamstow, London |
| 25 October | Hippodrome Theatre, Brighton |
| 28 October | ABC Cinema, Exeter |

Note: On 26 October the Beatles completed the sessions for their next LP, taping the final two tracks, 'Honey Don't' and 'What You're Doing'.

| | |
|---|---|
| 29 October | ABC Cinema, Plymouth |
| 30 October | Gaumont Cinema, Bournemouth |
| 31 October | Gaumont Cinema, Ipswich |
| 1 November | Astoria Cinema, Finsbury Park, London |
| 2 November | King's Hall, Showgrounds, Balmoral, Belfast, Northern Ireland |

The second of November had originally been assigned as a rest day but promoter Arthur Howes squeezed in a late booking for Belfast. The entourage flew into Aldergrove Airport from London during the afternoon.

| | |
|---|---|
| 4 November | Ritz Cinema, Gordon Street, Luton, Bedfordshire |
| 5 November | Odeon Cinema, Nottingham |
| 6 November | Gaumont Cinema, Southampton |
| 7 November | Capitol Cinema, Cardiff, Wales |
| 8 November | Empire Theatre, Liverpool |

The Beatles' first home-town concert since 22 December 1963.

*Another Lennon drawing, this time for the cover of the Christmas programme.*

**9 November**     City Hall, Sheffield

This date was included in the tour after Peter Stringfellow and his brother Jeff had petitioned Brian Epstein in his London office. Epstein was so impressed by the boys' professionalism that he not only saw that the date was added to the tour but also handed the compere's job on this one night to the brothers, relieving the contracted Bob Bain.

**10 November**     Colston Hall, Bristol

END OF TOUR

### ANOTHER BEATLES CHRISTMAS SHOW

**24–31 December** (excluding 25 and 27 December) (6 nights)     Odeon Cinema, Queen Caroline Street, Hammersmith, London

Following the previous year's seasonal extravaganza, Brian Epstein presented *Another Beatles Christmas Show* at the Hammersmith Odeon, across town from Finsbury Park. The venue may have changed but the formula was much the same: music, pantomime, comedy and, of course, a constant barrage of screaming from the youthful audience. The Beatles appeared in two sketches, one with Freddie Garrity (of Dreamers fame) and the other with disc jockey Jimmy Savile, and sang 11 songs, 'Twist and Shout', 'I'm a Loser', 'Baby's in Black', 'Everybody's Trying to Be my Baby', 'Can't Buy Me Love', 'Honey Don't', 'I Feel Fine', 'She's a Woman', 'A Hard Day's Night', 'Rock and Roll Music' and 'Long Tall Sally'. Rehearsals for the show began on 21 December.

The show ran for 20 nights, two shows each, except for 24 and 29 December where there was only one. A total, therefore, of thirty-eight performances. The box-office receipts for the show on 29 December were donated to the Brady Clubs and Settlement Charity in London's East End.

---

**Other engagements played**
None.

**Engagements not played**
The Beatles did not appear live at the Empire Theatre, Liverpool, for a week's residency between 30 March and 6 April 1964. This engagement was cancelled soon after the initial press announcement in late 1963. Had any Beatles fan have gone to the Empire that week he would have seen Frank Ifield.

The Beatles did not appear at the Futurist Theatre in Scarborough on 12 July. That date was switched to the Hippodrome Theatre in Brighton while the Scarborough booking was re-arranged for 9 August.

When the Beatles' August/September American tour was first planned it did not include the concerts in Indiana, Boston, Pittsburgh, Cleveland, and – of course – Kansas City. The Coliseum, Seattle gig on 21 August was, at that time, set for the Municipal Stadium; the Olympia Stadium, Detroit gig was planned for Cobo Hall; the Jacksonville concert on 11 September was lined up for either Gator Bowl or the Coliseum (the former was finally selected); and the charity show at the Paramount Theatre, New York, was – at that early planning stage – down to take place at the Metropolitan Opera. One show was scrapped altogether: a Beatles concert set for Colt Stadium, Houston, Texas, on 19 September. This date was eventually selected for rest at a remote ranch in Missouri.

When the Beatles' October/November British tour was first announced, at the end of April, it included visits to the Odeon cinemas in Hammersmith on 23 October, in Lewisham on 24 October and in Southend-on-Sea on 31 October. In mid-June these dates were re-arranged for Kilburn, Walthamstow and Ipswich respectively. The New Victoria Theatre in London had also been erroneously mooted as the venue for the 23 October show.

# THE MUSIC

Here is the complete live-performance repertoire of the Beatles in 1964, showing the group's vocalist, the composer(s) of the song and the name of the artist/group who recorded the influential version.

| Song title | Main vocalist(s) | Composer(s) | Influential version (year) |
|---|---|---|---|
| All my Loving | Paul | Lennon/McCARTNEY | — |
| Baby's in Black | John/Paul | Lennon/McCartney | — |
| Boys | Ringo | Dixon/Farrell | The Shirelles (1960) |
| Can't Buy Me Love | Paul | Lennon/McCARTNEY | — |
| Everybody's Trying to Be my Baby | George | Perkins | Carl Perkins (1958) |
| From Me to You | John/Paul | Lennon/McCartney | — |
| A Hard Day's Night | John | LENNON/McCartney | — |
| Honey Don't | Ringo | Perkins | Carl Perkins (1956) |
| I Feel Fine | John | LENNON/McCartney | — |
| I Saw Her Standing There | Paul | Lennon/McCARTNEY | — |
| I Should Have Known Better | John | LENNON/McCartney | — |
| I Wanna Be your Man | Ringo | Lennon/McCartney | — |
| I Want to Hold your Hand | John/Paul | Lennon/McCartney | — |
| If I Fell | John/Paul | LENNON/McCartney | — |
| I'm a Loser | John | LENNON/McCartney | — |
| I'm Happy Just to Dance with You | George | LENNON/McCartney | — |
| Kansas City/Hey-Hey-Hey-Hey![1] | Paul | Leiber/Stoller/Penniman | Little Richard (1959) |
| Long Tall Sally | Paul | Johnson/Penniman/Blackwell | Little Richard (1956) |
| Money (That's What I Want) | John | Gordy/Bradford | Barret Strong (1959) |
| Please Please Me | John/Paul | LENNON/McCartney | — |
| Rock and Roll Music | John | Berry | Chuck Berry (1957) |
| Roll over Beethoven | George | Berry | Chuck Berry (1956) |
| She Loves You | John/Paul | Lennon/McCartney | — |
| She's a Woman | Paul | Lennon/McCARTNEY | — |
| Things We Said Today | Paul | Lennon/McCARTNEY | — |
| This Boy | John | LENNON/McCartney | — |
| Till there Was You | Paul | Willson | Peggy Lee (1961) |
| Twist and Shout | John | Russell/Medley | The Isley Brothers (1962) |
| You Can't Do That | John | LENNON/McCartney | — |

**1** This medley of two songs recorded separately by Little Richard in 1959 was not the Beatles' idea. Richard himself recorded the same medley in 1959 and it is this version which the Beatles cover.

This was a curious year for the Beatles, one in which they consolidated all the successes and excesses of 1964 by virtually repeating everything already achieved. They made a second feature film, *Help!*, generally regarded as inferior to *A Hard Day's Night*. They toured America again, where Beatlemania continued to rage on a Gargantuan scale. And then they toured Britain again – though it was only a short tour. John Lennon even had a second book published, *A Spaniard in the Works*, which was – if anything – too similar to his first book, *In his own Write*, to achieve the same, startling, runaway success.

But there was one new development. As the Beatles became increasingly suffocated by the unceasing adulation around them they began to divert their attention to pleasing themselves rather than the public. The result of this switch in direction was a significant, further leap forward in their always innovative recordings, culminating – in 1965 at least – with the group's most progressive album yet, *Rubber Soul*. A chronological summary of the events of 1965, principally through their concert tours, shows just why this new phase of the Beatles' career began to assume the shape it did.

Like the previous year, 1965 kicked off with the group involved in the remains of a Christmas production, *Another Beatles Christmas Show* at the Odeon cinema in Hammersmith, London. A few weeks later, after a holiday period, the group flew off to the Bahamas to begin the shooting of *Help!*[1] As with most films of the day – a full decade before the excesses of film productions began to necessitate setting aside up to a whole year to complete a movie – the entire film was shot in under three months and was on general release within just two further months. With the film came the album of the same name, a superb collection of 14 new songs which, once again, shot to number one all over the world.

On 12 June, seven weeks before the film premiere, it was announced from Buckingham Palace that the four Beatles had been awarded Membership of the

Most Excellent Order of the British Empire in the Queen's Birthday Honours list. While it crowned the Beatles' acceptance by the Establishment, a great many previous recipients – notably battle-scarred veterans – of this and other awards, were livid to see their own honours cheapened by the granting of MBEs to four Liverpool pop stars. The Beatles, for their part, were bemused by the award but accepted it none the less. (John Lennon, who never felt easy about receiving the decoration, actually returned his medal – though not the actual award which cannot be revoked once given – to Buckingham Palace in November 1969.) The group assumed that they had received the honour for services to the British export drive, 'not for playing rock and roll music' as George Harrison acidly observed. In fact, Prime Minister Harold Wilson was the force behind the granting of the Beatles' MBEs with what, in hindsight, has been interpreted as an attempt to woo the youth of Britain to the Labour Party. Although hardly enough to raise a glimmer of controversy these days, where the MBE is even given to television puppeteers, the public

---

**1** Not an obvious location, the Bahamas was chosen simply to show the island's authorities the Beatles' goodwill in their intent to set up a business concern there.

ramifications and angry remonstrations continued unabated for quite some time in, and after, June 1965.

With the controversy still ringing loudly, the Beatles set off for Paris to begin their first concert tour of the year, a quick two-week saunter around France, Italy and Spain. Mostly the tour was remarkable for what it *didn't* produce – sell-out concert halls. Maybe once or twice over the previous two years a Beatles gig had not been seen by capacity houses, but now it was a regular occurrence. Far fewer people, too, were on hand at airports to wave the Beatles a fond farewell or to greet them on their arrival. There were still quite vast hordes of fans following the group's every move, and causing chaos at every juncture, but, nevertheless, the fan following was diminishing and the Beatles themselves were by no means ignorant of the fact. Perhaps the fans were at last realizing the futility of paying money to see the Beatles perform an inaudible 25-minute stage set from up to 500 yards away. The Beatles themselves had realized it long ago.

They realized too that touring was probably never going to return to the sanity of pre-1963, when they could enjoy playing a gig as much as their audience could enjoy the spectacle. The Beatles began to hanker for those long-lost days of lunchtime Cavern Club sessions where their musical prowess could blossom and not be stifled by enveloping screams, where no one would make a grab for them except to thrust a piece of paper carrying a song request into a Beatle's hand. The very antithesis of this lamented era was a 1965 Beatles concert tour of North America.

Brian Epstein had flown to the USA as early as 19 January to fix the dates of the Beatles' August 1965 American gigs. It was to be a hit-and-run tour, typified by the selection of large, and still larger, outdoor stadiums capable of satisfying the biggest ticket demands, arrival in these stadiums in armoured cars, a swift sub-30 minutes on stage and a fast getaway to an airport or besieged hotel, usually in the same armoured vehicle – the engine of which would be left running throughout the concert, by the stage, in case of a pitch invasion by lunging fans. It was a military-style operation that attempted to mix spectacle with safety but which, on occasions, lost on both counts. The tour opened in fine style with the *pièce de résistance*, a concert before a massive, record-breaking, screaming and swooning crowd of 55,600 fans at Shea Stadium in New York. Perhaps the most famous of all Beatles concerts, it was heralded as the apogee of the group's live career and was duly captured on film for a later television special. Even the Beatles seemed to be inspired by the vast crowd

*Opposite: These girls in Portland, Oregon, show that in 1965 American fans were as wild as ever. But in Europe (below) the Beatles experienced the start of dwindling audiences.*

## No Full Houses Yet For The Beatles

### Heat Wave's Effect On Italian Tour

Rome newspapers to-day showed mixed reactions to the Beatles' concert there last night. Il Messaggero said they sang well and had good rhythm. It went on: "No more than four ugly faces, four long heads of hair, four sublime idiots, four barefoot bums—but they succeeded in creating a spectacle that one can only admire."

Il Tempo said: "The real show was by the fans, and for this reason it was not a good show."

**ELEMENT OF TRIUMPH**

Some Italian newspapers said the Beatles' visit had the elements of a triumph, even without the capacity audiences the organisers had predicted.

Paese Sera, pro-Communist Rome daily, noted that the Adriano Cinema was not air-conditioned and said: " Whoever succeeds in half-filling a cinema in mid-afternoon with the temperature at 37 (98 Fahrenheit) can well be satisfied."

The Beatles are coming to the end of their Italian tour with something of a record for them—they have not played to a 'full house yet.

Making their Italian debut in Milan last week in the 22.000 - seat Vigorelli Velodrome, they attracted 7,000 fans. A second performance was better, with 20,000.

Two Genoa performances failed to fill the 25,000-seat Lido Sports Palace there. At one show the audience barely reached 5.000, including 1,000 police on hand to keep order. They proved unnecessary.

**TO SPAIN NEXT**

In Rome yesterday, at two performances in the Adriano Cinema, there were empty seats in the 2.000-seat theatre. The organisers had claimed that all the seats had been sold. The Adriano Cinema advertised that seats were available for the two final performances to-day.

From here the Beatles go on to Spain.

Rome newspapers suggested that high prices was one reason for the lack of spectators. Seats for the Rome performances ranged from 11s 6d to £4. The cheapest and most expensive seats were selling best—the cheapest to teenagers, the expensive ones to such Beatle fans as actor Marcel Mastroianni and actress Ursula Andress, who attended last night's show.

The heat wave may have kept the crowds down.—Associated Press.

## Man Escape From Hospit

### Armed With Ri And Shotgun

A man who esca police custody and armed with an autom rifle, a 16-bore shot and between 70 and rounds of ammuni was to day believed t in the London area.

Anthony John Stevenson, aged 22, was treated in the North bridgeshire Hospital, W when he escaped on nght.

He was wearing pyjamas and white so police believe he may dressed in a charcoal is described as dark, eght inches tall, with moustache and extens and abrasions to the

Superintendent Calvert, of King' (Norfolk) police, sai "If anyone attempts him, he is likely to determined effort to

*Mentor and manager Brian Epstein
surveying his charges during arguably their
greatest show, Shea Stadium, 15 August.*

before them and put some semblance of effort into their playing.

For the rest of the tour, however, this temporarily renewed sparkle all but disappeared once more as the group's old contempt for Beatlemania surfaced anew. Their musicianship at some of these gigs was not far short of abysmal, and hardly the sort of sound one would have expected from the world's undisputed number-one band. Not that the Beatles were entirely to blame for this sad state of affairs. Two years of playing to audiences who could not hear a single note, indeed who would not have cared even if they *had* heard sloppy instrumentation and off-key singing, had instilled in the Beatles an enormous grudge and – hardly surprisingly – not inconsiderable laziness. They had, by now, all but ceased rehearsals before a show or even, incredibly, before a tour. Ringo Starr has since said that, on occasions, all four Beatles might suddenly stop playing and no one in the audience would notice. John Lennon, who – for over a year – had audibly been shouting at the screaming fans to 'Shurrup' during his between-songs patter, now began to release his pent-up hatred of touring by screaming obscenities at the Beatles' concert audiences during songs handled by Paul, George or Ringo.

Another aspect of this military-style tour was the Beatles' new procedure at airports. Just as the fans had finally begun to realize how crazy it was to spend hours, even days, camped out on airport viewing towers, or gamely hanging on to balustrades, in all manner of weather, day or night, when – if anything – all they would catch was a two-minute glimpse of the Beatles as they sped through to the airport terminal building, the Beatles themselves had decided that they would no longer tempt fate by landing so publicly. Several hundred fans were on duty at Kennedy International Airport on 13 August to greet the Beatles' plane from London when – 'for public safety reasons' it was said – it touched down on a remote landing strip completely out of sight from the heavily fan-laden terminal building. All but the briefest immigration formalities were forsaken before a waiting limousine scudded the group to their hotel.

The wisdom of this airport policy was amply illustrated a few days later in Houston, Texas, when the Beatles' pilot had no alternative but to land on a normal runway in front of the terminal. It was two o'clock in the morning on 19 August 1965 when their chartered Electra plane came to a halt on the airstrip, yet 5000 screaming fans were there to greet the group's arrival. Within seconds every one of the 5000 broke through the airport barricades and inadequate police lines and invaded the plane. It was a nightmare situation. The Beatles were trapped, the police were helpless to quell the seething, adoring crowd, and the pilot was unable to taxi the plane to safety because teenage fans had surrounded it and were even underneath it. Many had even climbed on to the wings to press their faces up to the windows in the hope of seeing a Beatle. Forty minutes of this claustrophobic mayhem passed before a small pathway was cleared and the Beatles were 'sprung' from a nine-feet-high emergency exit at the rear of the plane into a service truck, and made their getaway. Their two shows that night at the Sam Houston Coliseum were little more than a continuation of the earlier airport scenes, and the Beatles' armoured car, which ferried them from

New York, August 1965. Yet another press conference, Brian Epstein in dark glasses. The man with the microphone, conducting the proceedings, is Tony Barrow. From initially enjoying these occasions and planting their own man in the audience to ask 'When will the bubble burst?' the Beatles soon grew tired of what soon became farcical affairs.

their hotel to the Coliseum and back, was never more necessary than on this night. Had the brokers from Lloyd's of London witnessed the day's events they would have been nervous wrecks. Before the tour each Beatle was personally insured against injury to the tune of $5.5 million. Should the entire group have been seriously hurt or maimed Lloyd's would have faced a $22 million pay-out.

For the American Beatles fans, just plain glad to have the group back on their soil, the tour was as exciting and memorable as the previous year's visit had been. They could have no perception of the growing unhappiness within the Beatles' camp over their dread of going back on the road to perform inaudible music to a sea of far-off Beatlemaniacs. Existing records of the group's one-a-day press conferences

– marked by the staggering inanity of the proffered questions – and of their concerts from this tour, portray a noticeably irritable, bored and frustrated, no longer 'happy-go-lucky Fab Four'. For the Beatles the best part of this American tour was their six-day break in a rented millionaire's house, secluded high in the Hollywood Hills. Trapped they still were, but at least they had the mobility denied them in hotels, and were afforded at least an outside chance of resting.

The Beatles flew home to England on 1 September 1965, collectively one million dollars the richer but with the embryo of a plan in their minds. The touring had to stop. They had said as much to Brian Epstein when he had put forward his plan for an autumn/winter concert tour of the United Kingdom, a second

*The Beatles and touring party for the American jaunt. Neil Aspinall is seated on Ringo's left. The front row is, left to right, Alf Bicknell, the group's chauffeur, Tony Barrow, and Mal Evans, Aspinall's assistant.*

appearance at the Royal Command Performance, and a third successive Christmas spectacular. Both of the latter plans were unanimously vetoed by the group, now beginning to flex their not inconsiderable collective muscle over the vain wishes of their manager. They didn't want to do a yuletide show so they wouldn't. And as for the Royal Command appearance, that was dismissed as a retrogressive step. They were going to Buckingham Palace on 26 October to be invested with their MBEs, and that was enough.

Brian Epstein's dogged persistence in encouraging the Beatles to tour Britain did eventually get through, though it certainly took some time, as can be seen by a sequence of NEMS press releases from that period. On 2 August they announced, with all certainty, that 'the Beatles will not be undertaking a tour of Britain this year'. Then, on 1 September, a reverse statement was issued, quoting Brian Epstein as saying that the group would tour the UK after all. Six weeks of protracted haggling then took place between the Beatles, Brian Epstein and Arthur Howes, the promoter, over the precise logistics of the tour. On this point the group was adamant: if they had to tour at all it should be a very short one. Eventually a token nine-night December itinerary was drawn up and announced to the press on 11 October. The box-offices opened for business on 31 October.

Those nine concerts constituted the last-ever Beatles tour of their homeland. It wasn't announced as such, of course, because – at this time – it was a secret realization shared by just four people. That something was then definitely amiss in the Beatles' attitude is – in retrospect – transparently obvious. The first date on the tour, Glasgow on 3 December, coincided to the very day with the release of the Beatles' new album, the enterprising *Rubber Soul*. In the becalmed confines of the recording studio the Beatles had poured all the energy which was once devoted to endless touring into making better music and, above all, experimentation with sound. This was their new escape and future direction. The *Please Please Me* LP was recorded in one long February 1963 session. *Rubber Soul* took 13 sessions over a four-week period. The disc housed 14 more new songs, lyrically and instrumentally the group's most ambitious project at that time. Yet, on the tour, the Beatles performed just one number from the LP, 'Nowhere Man'. Certainly it would have been difficult in those days of primitive pop concerts, and equally primitive equipment, to reproduce on stage the ever progressive complexity of sounds one could make inside a recording studio. But, nevertheless, it was not an impossibility. The Beatles didn't bother. After all, what was the point? No one wanted to listen, only to scream.

**1–16 January**    Odeon Cinema,
(excluding 3    Hammersmith, London
and 10 January)
(14 nights)

The last 14 nights of the 1964
production *Another Beatles Christmas
Show*.

END OF ANOTHER BEATLES
CHRISTMAS SHOW

---

**11 April**    *New Musical
Express* 1964–65
Annual Poll-winners'
All-star Concert,
Empire Pool,
Wembley

The Beatles' third consecutive
appearance at this annual afternoon
gala. They performed 'I Feel Fine',
'She's a Woman', 'Baby's in Black',
'Ticket to Ride' and 'Long Tall Sally'.
Highlights of the entire show were
again broadcast on two 85-minute TV
specials, *Big Beat '65*, the one including
the Beatles' appearance transmitted on
18 April.
    After their stage spot the Beatles
dashed to the ABC Television studios at
Teddington, Middlesex, for a live
appearance on *The Eamonn Andrews
Show*. They sang two songs and also
featured in a lengthy interview with
Andrews.
    The interlude between the final night
of the 1964 Christmas show and the
*NME* concert saw much Beatles
activity. Most of the filming for their
second feature film *Eight Arms to Hold
You*, later to be re-titled *Help!*, was
shot in this period – in the Bahamas
from 22 February to 10 March, in
Austria from 13 March to 22 March, and
latterly at, and around, the film studios
in Twickenham, Middlesex (where the
shooting was eventually completed on
12 May). Six days of recording sessions
at EMI from 15 to 20 February had seen
the taping of half of the *Help!*
soundtrack and album material, and
numerous television appearances had
also been made. The actual song *Help!*
was recorded on 13 April.

---

**THE BEATLES' EUROPEAN TOUR**

**20 June**    Palais des Sports,
Porte de Versailles,
Paris, France

Two shows, at 3:00 p.m. and 9:00 p.m.,
at the Palais des Sports got the Beatles'
short European tour under way. Six
thousand people saw each Paris gig,
the second of which was broadcast live
on the radio station Europe 1. French
television cameras also captured the
event for posterity. The relationship
between the French audiences and the
Beatles on this visit was far warmer
than the relatively cold reception
which greeted the group on their
January 1964 season at the Olympia.
    The Beatles' repertoire throughout
this fourteen-day European tour
comprised 'Twist and Shout' (truncated
version), 'She's a Woman', 'I'm a
Loser', 'Can't Buy Me Love', 'Baby's in
Black', 'I Wanna Be your Man', 'A Hard
Day's Night', 'Everybody's Trying to
Be my Baby', 'Rock and Roll Music',
'I Feel Fine', 'Ticket to Ride' and 'Long
Tall Sally'.
    The Beatles flew into Orly Airport,
Paris, at 9:55 a.m. on 20 June and
stayed in the city until the afternoon of
22 June when they flew on to Lyon.

---

**22 June**    Palais d'Hiver,
Boulevard de
Stalingrad,
Lyon, France

Two shows, seen by 3500 people each.
From Lyon to Rome the Beatles
travelled by road and rail.

---

**24 June**    Velodromo
Vigorelli,
Milan, Italy

The Beatles' first and only visit to Italy,
at three venues. The group performed
two shows at the Velodromo Vigorelli,
a 22,000-seater open-air arena. Neither
was a sell-out, the afternoon show
attracting just 7000 spectators while the
evening gig was seen by 20,000. At
both shows 700 policemen, 400 civilian
guards and 30 firemen were on hand to
quell any overt Beatlemania.

---

**25 June**    Palazzo dello Sport,
Piazza Kennedy,
Genoa, Italy

Two performances in this 25,000-
capacity arena. The first show, in the
afternoon, was seen by just 5000 fans.

---

**27 and 28 June**    Teatro Adriano,
(2 nights)    Rome, Italy

A total of four shows in Rome, at
4:30 p.m. and 9:30 p.m. on each of the
two days. It was originally scheduled
as one date but the 28 June
performances were added later, an

odd decision since the Adriano was
never more than half filled for any
Beatles gig.

---

**30 June**    Palais des Fêtes,
Nice, France

---

**2 July**    Plaza de Toros de
Madrid,
Madrid, Spain

One show, at 8:30 p.m.

**3 July**     Plaza de Toros
Monumental,
Barcelona, Spain

The last date on the tour. The Beatles'
two-hour Iberia IB 424 flight back from
Barcelona to London Airport on 4 July
touched down at noon.

END OF TOUR

**1 August**     ABC Theatre,
Blackpool

Another live performance as part of
the ABC Television transmission
*Blackpool Night Out*. On the bill with
the Beatles on this occasion were
Teddy Johnson and Pearl Carr, Johnny
Hart, and the Lionel Blair Dancers.
Mike and Bernie Winters compered
the show as usual.

## TOUR OF NORTH AMERICA

**15 August**     Shea Stadium,
Flushing, Queens,
New York City,
New York

The Beatles' one show at this massive
outdoor stadium, home of the New
York Mets baseball team, was seen by
55,600 screaming fans, creating a new
world record for a pop concert. The
Beatles' share of the $304,000 takings
was also a world record – $160,000
(then approximately £57,000).
A planned spectacular entry into the
stadium by helicopter, landing on the
baseball playing area, was vetoed by
the New York City authorities. Instead
the group travelled by limousine from
their Manhattan hotel, the Warwick, at
West 54th Street and the Avenue of the
Americas, to a waterfront heliport.
From there they flew over New York
City to the roof of the World's Fair
building and made the final 100-yard
journey into Shea Stadium in a Wells
Fargo armoured truck.
The show, together with the
helicopter ride and backstage
sequences, was filmed by (Ed) Sullivan
Productions Inc., in association with
NEMS Enterprises Ltd and Subafilms Ltd
(directors: Brian Epstein, John Lennon,
Paul McCartney, George Harrison and
Richard Starkey) for a 50-minute colour
television special, premiered on 1
March 1966 by the BBC. (And repeated
on 27 August 1966.)
The Beatles' repertoire for this
concert, and the remainder of the tour,
comprised 'Twist and Shout' (truncated
version), 'She's a Woman', 'I Feel
Fine', 'Dizzy Miss Lizzy', 'Ticket to

*Mementos from the Beatles' record-
breaking concert at Shea Stadium, New
York, 15 August 1965.*

Ride', 'Everybody's Trying to
Be my Baby', 'Can't Buy Me Love',
'Baby's in Black', 'Act Naturally' (or,
occasionally, 'I Wanna Be your Man'),
'A Hard Day's Night', 'Help!' and 'I'm
Down'.
Notes: The Beatles had left England
for New York, with another vociferous
send-off from 1000 fans at London
Airport, at noon on 13 August
(TWA 703). Once in New York,
besieged – as usual – in their hotel, and
unable to go out, the Beatles received
a succession of visiting contemporary
musicians, including Bob Dylan and the
Supremes. Rolling Stones Mick Jagger
and Keith Richard were also among the
55,600 crowd at the Shea concert.
On the afternoon of 14 August the
Beatles taped another appearance on
*The Ed Sullivan Show*, performing 'I'm
Down', 'Ticket to Ride', 'I Feel Fine',
'Yesterday' (performed by Paul with
three violinists), 'Act Naturally' and
'Help!' The segment was transmitted
on 12 September.

**17 August**     Maple Leaf Gardens,
Toronto, Canada

Two 27-minute performances at this
indoor arena, seen by 18,000 people
each. The Beatles flew to Toronto from
New York on the morning of the gigs.

**18 August**     Atlanta Stadium,
Atlanta, Georgia

One show seen by 30,000 fans, in this
new 55,000-seater baseball park.

**19 August**     Sam Houston
Coliseum,
Houston, Texas

Two shows at this 12,000-capacity
arena. The Beatles arrived in Houston
at 2:00 a.m. The riots at the airport, and
during the concert, were probably the
worst yet in the epidemic called
Beatlemania. Despite this, the Beatles
collected $85,000 for their two gigs.

**20 August**     White Sox Park,
Chicago, Illinois

Two shows in Chicago, at 3:00 p.m.
and 8:00 p.m., with 25,000 fans
attending the first and 37,000 the
second. The Beatles' share of the
overall gate receipts was $155,000,
comparing rather favourably with the
paltry $30,000 reaped from the group's
1964 visit to Chicago.

**21 August**     Twin Cities'
Metropolitan Stadium,
Minneapolis,
Minnesota

One show, seen by 25,000 people in
this 45,000-seater stadium.

**22 August**     Memorial Coliseum,
Portland, Oregon

Two gigs, before a total of 20,000 fans.
In between shows the Beatles were
visited in their dressing room by Carl

# 350 Ready To Guard 4

## Beatles To Get Security Force

The Beatles, who will appear in Portland for performances atat 3:30 and 8 p.m. Sunday will have the protection of up to 350 security officers to insure their safety while guests in the City of Roses.

Wilson and Mike Love of the Beach Boys.

**28 August**    Balboa Stadium, San Diego, California

Notes: Between the morning of 23 August, when they flew into Los Angeles, and this gig, the Beatles enjoyed a clear break, resting in a massive house, amid tight security, in Benedict Canyon, North Hollywood. Late in the evening of 27 August the group trooped across to Perugia Way, Beverly Hills, to meet their one-time idol Elvis Presley, a summit conference carefully orchestrated by Presley's manager, 'Colonel' Tom Parker, and greatly anticipated by the four Beatles and Brian Epstein. The meeting was not a great success, though Elvis and the Beatles did have a brief jam session, poor quality tapes of which are rumoured – but not confirmed – to exist.

One Beatle, Paul McCartney, had already spoken with Presley – and perceived the sixties' normality of the fifties' legend – during a telephone conversation from the group's Atlantic City hotel to Memphis on 31 August 1964.

**29 and 30 August**    Hollywood Bowl, Los Angeles
(2 nights)

Two concerts, one each night, at this splendid outdoor arena set against the picturesque Hollywood hills. The second of the two, on 30 August, was recorded by Capitol Records following their taping of the Beatles' 23 August 1964 concert at the same venue. A segué performance of both gigs was released on the album *The Beatles at the Hollywood Bowl* in May 1977.

The Beatles' share of the $156,000 gate receipts over the two nights was $90,000.

**31 August**    Cow Palace, San Francisco

The 10th and final concert of the tour, at the same venue which had opened the Beatles' 1964 bash a year previously. There were two shows, a matinee seen by 11,700 fans and an evening one seen by 17,000.

END OF TOUR

## TOUR OF THE UNITED KINGDOM

**3 December**    Odeon Cinema, Glasgow, Scotland

What was to become the Beatles' last-ever tour of their homeland was a small affair compared to previous British excursions – visiting nine venues (eight cities) in ten days, with two shows each time. The Beatles' repertoire on this outing comprised 'I Feel Fine', 'She's a Woman', 'If I Needed Someone', 'Act Naturally', 'Nowhere Man', 'Baby's in Black', 'Help!', 'We Can Work It Out', 'Yesterday', 'Day Tripper' and 'I'm Down'.

Between the end of the American tour and this British jaunt the Beatles had recorded their next album, *Rubber Soul*, released on 3 December.

**4 December**    City Hall, Newcastle-upon-Tyne

**5 December**    Empire Theatre, Liverpool

The Beatles' last-ever Liverpool gig; 40,000 ticket applications were received for the two shows.

**7 December**    ABC Cinema, Ardwick, Manchester

**8 December**    Gaumont Cinema, Barker's Pool, Sheffield, Yorkshire

**9 December**    Odeon Cinema, Birmingham

**10 December**    Odeon Cinema, Hammersmith, London

**11 December**    Astoria Cinema, Finsbury Park, London

**12 December**    Capitol Cinema, Cardiff, Wales

END OF TOUR

---

## Other engagements played
None.

## Engagements not played
The Beatles did not play a concert in Jerez de la Frontera, Spain, on 1 July 1965, contrary to reports in several Beatles books.

When the Beatles' August 1965 American tour was first announced, at the beginning of February, the venue for the concert on 20 August was still undecided – Detroit or Chicago. The latter city was eventually chosen. That first draft of the tour itinerary also included a concert in Mexico City, Mexico, on 28 August, later switched to the southern California town of San Diego.

The Beatles only played one night at Shea Stadium, New York – on 15 August. Common belief that they gave a second gig there, on 16 August, is incorrect.

The Beatles' two London concerts, on 10 and 11 December, were – at one time – mooted for the Royal Albert Hall and the Empire Pool, Wembley. Eventually the Odeon, Hammersmith and the Astoria, Finsbury Park were selected instead. The date of 6 December was kept free but tentatively set aside for a concert in either Leicester, Bristol or Leeds should promoter Arthur Howes have persuaded the Beatles to relent and perform that day. The Beatles didn't relent. The Gaumont Cinema, Sheffield, concert on 8 December was originally scheduled for the nearby City Hall but later switched.

# THE MUSIC

Here is the complete live performance repertoire of the Beatles in 1965, showing the group's vocalist, the composer(s) of the song and the name of the artist/group who recorded the influential version

| Song title | Main vocalist(s) | Composer(s) | Influential version (year) |
|---|---|---|---|
| Act Naturally | Ringo | Russell/Morrison | Buck Owens (1963) |
| Baby's in Black | John/Paul | Lennon/McCartney | — |
| Can't Buy Me Love | Paul | Lennon/McCartney | — |
| Day Tripper | John/Paul | Lennon/McCartney | — |
| Dizzy Miss Lizzy | John | Williams | Larry Williams (1958) |
| Everybody's Trying to Be my Baby | George | Perkins | Carl Perkins (1958) |
| A Hard Day's Night | John | Lennon/McCartney | — |
| Help! | John | Lennon/McCartney | — |
| Honey Don't | Ringo | Perkins | Carl Perkins (1956) |
| I Feel Fine | John | Lennon/McCartney | — |
| I Wanna Be your Man | Ringo | Lennon/McCartney | — |
| If I Needed Someone | George | Harrison | — |
| I'm a Loser | John | Lennon/McCartney | — |
| I'm Down | Paul | Lennon/McCartney | — |
| Long Tall Sally | Paul | Johnson/Penniman/Blackwell | Little Richard (1956) |
| Nowhere Man | John | Lennon/McCartney | — |
| Rock and Roll Music | John | Berry | Chuck Berry (1957) |
| She's a Woman | Paul | Lennon/McCartney | — |
| Ticket to Ride | John | Lennon/McCartney | — |
| Twist and Shout | John | Russell/Medley | The Isley Brothers (1962) |
| We Can Work It Out | Paul | Lennon/McCartney | — |
| Yesterday | Paul | Lennon/McCartney | — |

'I reckon we could send out four waxwork dummies of ourselves and that would satisfy the crowds. Beatles concerts are nothing to do with music any more. They're just bloody tribal rites.'

So said John Lennon in 1966. The concerts really had to end. The Beatles knew that after their UK tour in December 1965. Eight months later, by August 1966, any remaining vestige of doubt had been thoroughly eradicated, for the sequence of events that accompanied the Beatles' overseas concert tours between June and that August was so utterly fantastic that it eclipsed even the worst horrors thrown up in the previous two years.

The Beatles did not give any live performances at all until 1 May, by far their longest break between engagements since Quarry Men days. The gig on 1 May, a 15-minute set at the *New Musical Express* Annual Poll-Winners' All-Star Concert at the Empire Pool, Wembley, was the last concert appearance the Beatles ever made in their homeland. It wasn't always going to be so. At the end of February NEMS issued a press statement announcing that 'the Beatles will tour Japan, the USA and West Germany in the summer and Britain at the end of the year'. After the events of the summer, the winter UK tour was put on ice. Permanently.

The first leg of the tour that later visited Japan and the Philippines found the Beatles making a return visit to West Germany, and to Hamburg, for the first time since 1962. This part of the tour, at least, proved uneventful except for the usual screaming mayhem and mania, some violent street riots, police arrests for ticket forgery, with a dose of nostalgia thrown in for good measure.

It was *en route* from London to Tokyo on 27 June that things started to go awry. (The Beatles flew back to London from Hamburg in order to catch a direct flight to Tokyo.) The approach of a typhoon – named, as is the peculiar custom, after a person, in this case Kit – forced the pilot to make a long stop in Anchorage, Alaska. The Beatles spent the entire afternoon and evening miserably holed up in their hotel suite while upwards of 400 Alaskan Beatles fans – no doubt rubbing their eyes in disbelief at having their idols in town – congregated outside the hotel,

screaming, cheering and, according to the press at least, rioting. Eventually, with the typhoon threat past, the plane was able to take off for Tokyo, landing at 3:40 in the morning of 29 June.

The Beatles' visit to Japan caused a storm that was certainly equal to the typhoon. Local promoter Tats Nagashima had booked the Beatles to give five shows – over three days – at the Nippon Budokan, a magnificent octagon-shaped hall deemed by many to be a sacred building, suitable only for the presentation of traditional, honourable, Japanese martial arts. Even the usage of the Nippon Budokan for judo during the 1964 Olympic Games had caused a furore. Now it was to be used as a venue for amplified Western pop music with its attendant screaming audiences. Opposition to the Beatles' concerts was bitter and there were angry demonstrations and marches.[1]

Police presence was intensely heavy throughout the Beatles' four-day stay on Japanese soil with, incredibly, a total of 35,000 security men used. At Tokyo International Airport on 29 June, despite the early-morning arrival, 1500 fans crowded the terminal to catch a glimpse of the group, only to be thwarted by squads of riot police blocking all the entrances. During the Beatles' five shows at the Nippon Budokan the police numbered 3000 among the 10,000 crowd per show, standing two abreast at strategic places in every aisle to quell any pandemonium. The Beatles' standard of live musicianship reached its nadir in this less-than-ideal situation. A surviving colour television film of the group's first Tokyo gig, on 30 June, shows a staggering degree of uncaring on the part of the Beatles as they murder, one by one, 11 brilliant compositions and studio recordings. George Harrison's rendition of his own 'If I Needed Someone' has to be heard to be believed, so out-of-tune and mistimed was its delivery.

From their police-festooned, heavily guarded

---

1 The Beatles' concerts at the Nippon Budokan were, in fact, simply breaking new ground. The hall has since been acknowledged as Tokyo's premier rock venue, frequently playing host to top British and American acts in the three decades since.

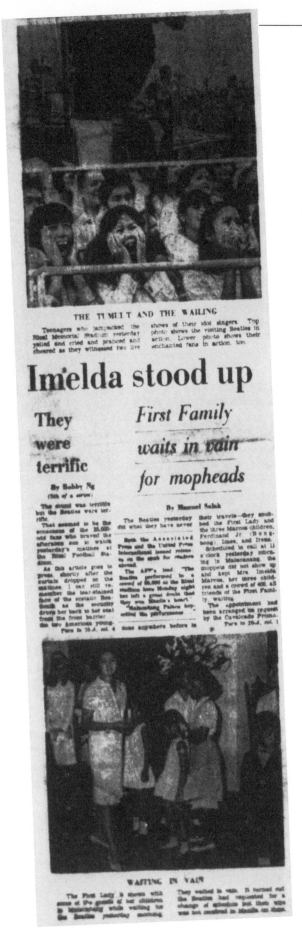

*In some countries it is not entirely advisable
to upset the authorities.*

Tokyo Hilton refuge the Beatles flew on to their next stop, the Philippines. The events in Tokyo, the anti-Beatles marches and public disputes, seemed like a garden party compared with what happened in Manila. Criticism of the Beatles was stoked up just three hours after they had landed, when the group held their seemingly obligatory press conference, at the Philippine Navy Headquarters.[2] The local media took a dislike to the group's flippant answers to their questions – always the same old questions like 'When are you getting married, Paul?' or 'When did you last have a haircut, George?' – and bore equal resentment over the Beatles' apparent ignorance of the Philippines itself. The group had long ceased to be interested in the history or topography of the country in which they were touring. What did it matter – they only saw airports, screaming crowds, limousines, screaming crowds, hotel rooms, screaming crowds, concert halls, screaming crowds, more limousines, more screaming crowds and finally another airport.

The *Manila Sunday Times* on 3 July, the day before the Beatles' two live shows, sowed the seeds of the story which would soon break into a giant-sized rumpus. Its article ran: 'President Marcos, the First Lady, and the three young Beatles fans in the family, have been invited as guests of honour at the concerts. The Beatles plan to personally follow up the invitation during a courtesy call on Mrs Imelda Marcos at Malacañang Palace tomorrow morning at 11 o'clock.' The Beatles, in fact, had received no such direct invitation. All they knew about the party was a vague mention of a swift afternoon (three o'clock) Palace drop-in, printed on their Philippine schedule drawn up by Ramon Ramos, the concert promoter. That suggestion had already been rejected by the group because their first show was scheduled to start at 4:00 p.m. and they wanted to arrive at the stadium at least two hours beforehand. Ramos, caught in the middle between the Palace and the Beatles, and anxious not to press the point with, or offend, either side, left the situation alone. The next morning a Palace official came to collect the Beatles. They were still in bed and Brian Epstein refused to rouse them.

---

2 An unusual venue, chosen because the Beatles spent the afternoon on a yacht in the harbour. The concert promoter's wish that the group also spend the night on the cramped vessel was soon dismissed by the Beatles who baulked at the idea and demanded to stay in a hotel. Many hasty phone calls ensued until a suitable hostelry – The Manila Hotel – was found.

BEATLES LEAVE WITH A KICK AND A WHIMPER

Beatles John Lennon, Ringo Starr and George Harrison take a last look at their fans and Manila after a wild rough and tumble sendoff at the international airport yesterday, (left photo), while at the terminal building, a member of the Beatles entourage is being helped up by customs and airport officials after he was reportedly shoved and kicked, (middle photo), and on the MIA deck, fans gave out a whimper to find their singing idols booed and jeered and humiliated. The Beatles' departure was delayed when the BIR slapped ₱74,000 tax on the net income.

# Beatles booed, roughed up on departure

*The Manila incident draws to its ugly conclusion, mentally – and almost physically – scarring the Beatles.*

After the group had failed to show at the Palace all hell was unleashed, the *Manila Times*, the next morning, under a bold-type headline screaming, 'Imelda Stood Up', accusing the Beatles of 'snubbing the First Lady and the three Marcos children ... [keeping them] and a crowd of 400, all friends of the First Family, waiting'. The ramifications were serious. Ramon Ramos refused to pay the Beatles their substantial cut of the gate receipts from the group's two shows. Bomb and death threats were telephoned through to the beleaguered British Embassy and to the Beatles' hotel suite. Brian Epstein was so stricken with personal guilt and grief over the mess that he arranged with Channel 5, one of the local television stations, for a film crew to visit the hotel and record a press statement and apology he had hastily written with Tony Barrow. But later in the evening, when the recording was transmitted, an unfortunate but hardly coincidental surge of static blighted every TV screen in the Philippines just as Epstein began speaking. It obliterated his every word until the speech finished, when the static mysteriously vanished.

The next day proved a watershed in the Beatles' career. Firstly, Misael Vera, a commissioner of the BIR (Philippine tax authority) insisted that the Beatles could not leave the country until they had paid income tax on their concert receipts (which Ramon Ramos was still withholding). A furious row developed until Brian Epstein, although correct in his insistence that Ramos was responsible for the tax levy, eventually capitulated and filed a bond for P. 74,450 to settle the matter. Arguing about contractual logistics was pointless. Paying the money just seemed the simplest way to get out of the country.

Secondly, after 'snubbing Imelda Marcos', all of the security forces protecting the Beatles were withdrawn. Kicked and jostled as they left their hotel, the Beatles and their entourage arrived at Manila International Airport in a harassed state. Worse was to follow. Airport manager Guillermo Jurado ordered that they be further left to fend for themselves, even to the extent of shutting down the power to the escalators so that the Beatles had to climb several flights of stairs with their baggage. An angry crowd of 200 Filipinos finally caught up with their prey on the second floor of the airport and, amid much scuffling, the Beatles were brutally manhandled. According to the *Manila Times*, 'Drummer Ringo Starr was floored by an uppercut. As he crawled away the mob kicked him. George Harrison and John Lennon received kicks and blows as they ran to the customs zone. Paul McCartney was relatively unhurt as he sprinted ahead. Manager Brian Epstein received the brunt of the mob's ire. He was kicked and thrown to the floor. As a result he suffered a sprained ankle and had to be helped to the customs area.'

In reality, the *Manila Times* was just as guilty as, say, the *Bootle Times* back home in exaggerating a local story to suit local taste, since all four Beatles actually remained physically unscathed during the ordeal, although they certainly were pushed and shoved. But Brian Epstein was indeed injured, as was the group's assistant road manager, burly Mal Evans, who received several hefty kicks to his ribs after being felled to the floor. The Beatles' chauffeur, Alf Bicknell, actually suffered a fractured rib in addition to a spinal injury. And they were not out of danger yet. As the Beatles' haggard party proceeded through immigration they were greeted by a barrage of cat-

194

calls and boos, and an angry mob baying, *Beatles Alis Diyan!* ('Beatles Go Home!') Acutely conscious of the possibility of being shot by a sniper, the Beatles' entourage virtually flew across the tarmac and up the steps to the shelter of their KLM flight to New Delhi via Bangkok.

The Filipinos had two more carefully orchestrated pieces left to play. Shortly before take-off the pilot of the plane received and put over the Tannoy an instruction from the airport that Mal Evans and Tony Barrow were to return to the terminal. Both nervously made their way back across the tarmac, Barrow in the belief that they were going to be framed and detained for a crime they hadn't committed. Instead they were told that *no one* could leave. Due to a convenient bureaucratic bungle, there was no record of the Beatles' arrival in the Philippines two days previously. Since, technically, they hadn't arrived, they couldn't leave either, being – in effect – illegal immigrants. The Beatles spent forty-four nail-biting minutes on board the plane, unaware of the reason for the delay, before Evans and Barrow returned with the necessary paperwork and the plane took off.

The second move was a press statement issued by President Marcos. It read: 'There was no intention on the part of the Beatles to slight the First Lady or the Government of the Republic of the Philippines.' In a remarkable feat of good timing, the statement was issued to the press minutes *after* the Beatles' departure from Philippine soil.

On board their plane the Beatles were nothing less than livid about the whole ghastly affair, and with Brian Epstein specifically and concert tours generally. Brian was distraught with sorrow.

What was intended as a peaceful post-Philippines rest in New Delhi was all but ruined too by – amazingly – vast screaming crowds of Indian Beatlemaniacs. The Beatles were rapidly approaching the end of their tether. After two days (during which they bought three sitars for use on future recordings – Paul even commissioned a hand-made left-handed model to be flown to the UK) the group flew home to England. Still angry. At London Airport on 8 July a reporter asked George Harrison what was next on the Beatles' schedule. The acidic reply, although George could hardly have known it then, was a painfully accurate prediction. 'We're going to have a couple of weeks to recuperate before we go and get beaten up by the Americans.' Portentous words indeed.

High up on the 27th floor of the Astor Towers Hotel, in beautiful lakeside Chicago, John Lennon faced the

worst situation in his 25 action-packed years to that time. It was 11 August, five months and seven days after an interview had been published in the London *Evening Standard* in which Lennon The Intellectual Young Man had told writer Maureen Cleave that he was reading extensively about religion (paying, although he didn't actually say it, particular attention to Hugh J. Schonfield's best seller *The Passover Plot*), adding, 'Christianity will go. It will vanish and shrink. I needn't argue with that; I'm right and I will be proved right. We're more popular than Jesus now . . . .' Lennon *was* right. All over the world, but in Britain especially, church attendances and the role of religion in society had dwindled dramatically. More people *did* buy Beatles records than go to church: more people than ever *were* turning their backs on religion in pursuit of ungodly aims and interests. Tucked midway through the whole-page interview, John's quote – in which, if anything, he was deploring the situation – went unnoticed. People were used to Lennon's caustic comments and, besides, most agreed with his opinion.

On 29 July, long after the article had been published – and forgotten – in London, the American teenage magazine *Datebook* reproduced the interview under a syndication arrangement, trailering the item with a front-page banner which paraphrased Lennon, totally out of context, saying that the Beatles were greater than Jesus. Within days the furore of the nation, or at least of the southern Bible Belt, had been raised to American fever pitch. Ignominiously led by WAQY in Birmingham, Alabama, a total of 22 radio stations banned Beatles music indefinitely from their airwaves.[3] Several even went so far as to organize, and broadcast live, public burning of Beatles memorabilia, where people were invited to ritually toss records, books and Beatles merchandise into a blazing bonfire while smiling at conveniently situated press and television cameramen.

For a while the situation was so nasty that Brian Epstein seriously considered cancelling the Beatles' impending US tour – due to start within days, with a Chicago concert on 12 August. His worst fear of all was that one of the Beatles would be shot. On 6 August Epstein travelled alone to New York and held a solo press conference in an attempt to stem the rising anti-Beatles tide and, at the same time, qualify Lennon's remarks. He was only partially successful. The tour, however, was to go ahead.

The Beatles' opening press conference, at the Astor Towers in Chicago, was dominated by the 'Jesus

---

3 Some never broadcast Beatles music anyway, but were keen to jump on the pro-Jesus anti-Beatles bandwagon.

incident'. For once there were no shallow 'teen' questions, and no irrelevant egotistical bonhomie from ingratiating local disc jockeys. Lennon was placed firmly under the spotlight and grilled by American newsmen over his so-called blasphemous remarks. Before the press conference, in his hotel room, Lennon had actually broken down and wept – as, literally, never before – under the pressure. Now the assembled journalists were demanding the second impossible Lennon concession: an apology. Before the eyes and ears of the world John twisted and wriggled his reply every which way, in true politician style, rather than actually utter the word Sorry. He reasoned, he qualified, he explained once and then a second time what he had really meant. But one hack wanted his pound of flesh: the magic word. Lennon gave in, said Sorry, and almost immediately the whole trumped-up incident was over. Lennon had apologized. The Beatles had learned their lesson.[4]

The entire episode seemed ridiculous then; in the eighties it is almost impossible to comprehend how so many people could have become so agitated over the purely personal opinion of a pop musician.

The tour that followed was a chronicle of ineptitude and bad experiences. On 14 August the Beatles' gig at a Cleveland baseball stadium was interrupted for half an hour while 2500 screaming Beatles fans invaded the pitch. On 15 August five Prince George's County Ku Klux Klansmen, led by the Imperial Wizard of the Maryland clan, and clad in red, white and green robes, paraded outside the DC Stadium in Washington before the Beatles' concert there. On 19 August the Beatles received an anonymous phone call that one or all of them would be assassinated at some time during the group's two shows that day in Memphis. Mid-way through the second show somebody threw a firecracker on to the stage which promptly exploded. All of the Beatles – and Brian Epstein watching from the side of the stage – fully believed that one of them had been shot. On 20 August the promoter of the Beatles' gig in Cincinnati tried to cut costs and failed to provide a canopy cover for the group in the open-air stadium. Whereas on 16 August in Philadelphia rain had miraculously held off until ten minutes after the concert had ended, in Cincinnati a downpour just as the Beatles were due on stage promised certain electrocution if they

played. With 35,000 fans already inside the stadium the gig was cancelled and re-scheduled for lunchtime the following day. The Beatles were nervous wrecks backstage, Paul actually vomiting with fear. After the re-scheduled gig, the Beatles flew straight to St Louis for their evening concert. It poured there too, but there was, at least, a tarpaulin cover.

The Beatles were playing the huge open-air stadiums in order to satisfy as many fans as possible in the least possible time, with the least possible effort, while maximizing their income. In Los Angeles, for example, instead of playing one or two shows at the 18,700-capacity Hollywood Bowl, as in 1964 and 1965, the group played one gig at the Dodger Stadium before 45,000 fans. Unfortunately,

---

4 Later on in the tour, by no means chastened by the bad experience, John Lennon gave vent to his true feelings over the affair. 'In England they take what we say with a pinch of salt,' he said, caustically adding that the anti-Beatles protesters were 'middle-aged DJs and 12-year-olds burning a pile of LP covers'.

# Epstein checks on U.S. "holy war" against Beatles

The Beatles' manager, Mr. Brian Epstein, to-day weighed the prospects of a U.S. tour by his mop-haired quartet in the face of a 'holy war" against them in America.

The furore was caused by Beatle John Lennon's reported remark that the Beatles are more popular than Jesus Christ.

As a result, fans in several U.S. cities have been urged to make bonfires of their Beatle records, and radio stations across the nation have banned Beatles records.

Mr. Epstein, who cut short a holiday to fly to New York last night from London, said he hoped that the Beatles' four-week tour would go ahead. It was to start on August 12.

He said no decision would be made until he had talked with the General Artists' Corporation, the agency which booked the Beatles for their 14-city tour.

"MISINTERPRETED"

The "holy war" against the Beatles started in America's "Bible Belt" and quickly spread across the nation.

In Mississippi an imperial wizard of a Ku Klux Klan group said he believed the Beatles had been "brainwashed" by the Communist Party."

On arrival in New York Mr.

Epstein was asked whether he thought the Beatles were more popular than Christianity. "Of course not," he said.

He said: "John Lennon's views have been misinterpreted," but he declined to say whether he meant that he had been misreported.

"The whole thing." he added, "Is a typical Beatles furore."

Mr. Epstein, who has managed the Beatles since their earliest days, will be keeping a close watch on the pop record charts for any reaction by the buying public.

A readio station which has never before played a Beatles record started playing one every 30 minutes last night, preceding the records with a statement denouncing the "hypocrisy" of banning the group's music.

Station W.S.A.C. said in a commentary: "his is the best way we can think of t show our contempt fo hypocrisy personified."

Some of the stations whic have banned the Beatle records play other songs tha are "the most pornograph melodies since Elizabetha times," the station said.

"Perhaps the Beatles cou become more popular tha Jesus," as Beatle Joh Lennon allegedly said.

"Perhaps that is what wrong with scoiety, and the they are, dear friend. Y made them so, not Jesus, John Lennon, and not t Beatles."

W.S.A.C. plans to contir broadcasting the commenta and playing a Beatles rec indefinitely. a spokesman sa

## POST OFFICE SITE

No decision yet on offer by Birkenhead Council

*The fine line between enthusiastic hysteria and violence, which had somehow remained intact between 1963 and 1965, started to disappear in 1966. The end had to follow.*

## Beatles 'escape' in an armoured car

The Beatles fled in an armoured car from thousands of screaming fans after their concert in the Dodgers baseball stadium at Los Angeles last night.

As the quartet tried to leave by the main gates scores of delirious teenagers climbed all over the limousine and it was forced to turn back.

The Beatles then fled to offices under the grandstand as crowds charged the 151 foot high entrance gates.

Time and again, police were forced to hit out with their clubs, to keep the fans' off the gates.

Youths then charged the gates with wooden barricades which had been set up to keep the crowds back.

They hurled sticks and bottles at police until they were finally turned away with a shoulder-to-shoulder charge by officers who cleared a sort of no - man's - land between the crowds and the exit gates.

### DOZENS HURT

Meanwhile, the Beatles, virtually imprisoned beneath the grandstand by fans stampeding from one spot to another in the vast outdoor stadium, made good their escape by armoured car at the opposite end of the field.

Police said dozens of people among the 45,000 attending suffered minor injuries in the clashes between fans and police and in the crush of the stampeding crowds.

Debris littered the area around the exit gates and crowds milled around for about an hour after the performance ended.

detained by his police. It had not been decided whether to make formal charges against them.

Two of the Beatles, Paul McCartney and George Harrison, are planning to present and promote modern plays and other theatrical productions such as musicals.

With the Beatles in the scheme are pop singers Donovan and Eric Burdon, of the Animals group.

the Beatles could no longer sell out this type of venue and few of the group's concerts in this final tour played to capacity audiences. The show-business newspaper *Variety* wrote that the box-office success of the tour was 'solid ... if not as spectacular or hysterical as in previous years'. It certainly wasn't. The 55,600-capacity Shea Stadium in New York was left with 11,000 unsold tickets for the Beatles' 23 August concert. The previous year it had sold out within hours.

If box-office sales weren't, as *Variety* reported, 'hysterical', the fans certainly were. Still. The Beatles had grown up very quickly between 1963 and 1966 but their fans just couldn't match the pace. They still screamed and sobbed and demanded 'She loves you, yeah yeah yeah' which, to the Beatles in 1966, was little more than a children's nursery rhyme. They had progressed in dramatic – and ridiculously fast – fashion from 'She Loves You' to the jangling and mysterious, experimental and highly innovative *Revolver* album – recorded through April, May and June 1966 and released just before the August US tour. It was a time for the lyrical 'Eleanor Rigby', for the ruthless wit of 'Taxman', for the nonsense primitive psychedelia of 'Tomorrow Never Knows', for backwards tapes and for Eastern musical instruments. The Beatles did not perform a single song from *Revolver* at any time during their American tour. It was almost as if two entirely separate personalities had evolved – the Beatles as recording artists and the Beatles as concert performers. And ne'er the twain re-met.

Amid the never-ending Beatlemania, the group churning out songs they did better not to hear, even if it was possible above the incessant screams, and running humourlessly through 33-minute concerts they now hated with a passion so intense that they didn't even bother to rehearse before the tour, the group came to 29 August and the last show. On a bracing San Francisco night, the wind whipping in from the north California coast, the Beatles stood at second base in the airy open spaces of Candlestick Park, on a stage elevated five feet above the ground. They were fully caged in by a six-foot-high fence, in front of which stood a human wall of 200 private and city police. An armoured car stood by, its engine running. They played from 9:27 p.m. until precisely 10:00 p.m. when, after nostalgically closing with 'Long Tall Sally' for the only time on the tour, they stepped off the stage for ever.

After nine years and over 1400 concert appearances the Beatles had given their last show.

1 May     *New Musical Express* 1965–66 Annual Poll-winners' All-star Concert, Empire Pool, Wembley

The Beatles' last-ever live concert performance in the United Kingdom. Though it wasn't announced as such, the group knew that there would be no more British tours or concerts after this, their fourth consecutive appearance at the annual Sunday-afternoon *NME* event.

The Beatles performed 'I Feel Fine', 'Nowhere Man', 'Day Tripper', 'If I Needed Someone' and 'I'm Down'. Once again the proceedings were filmed by ABC Television but the cameras were switched off for both the Beatles' and the Rolling Stones' performances because of contractual disagreements between ABC and the respective group managements.

Between January and April 1966 the Beatles had enjoyed a comparatively restful time after five years of continuously strenuous activity. Mostly the four months were taken up by holidays, a honeymoon (George married on 21 January) and recording sessions for the group's most ambitious album yet, a project eventually to be titled *Revolver*.

### TOUR OF WEST GERMANY, JAPAN AND THE PHILIPPINES

24 June     Circus-Krone-Bau, Marsstrasse, Munich, West Germany

Two shows in Munich, at 5:15 p.m. and 9:00 p.m., got this short tour under way. With hindsight it was somewhat apt that the Beatles should return to West Germany before the cessation of their live-concert career, just as they had travelled to Hamburg in August 1960 immediately after their inauguration as a professional group.

The Beatles' repertoire for this mini-tour comprised 'Rock and Roll Music', 'She's a Woman', 'If I Needed Someone', 'Day Tripper', 'Baby's in Black', 'I Feel Fine', 'Yesterday', 'I Wanna Be your Man', 'Nowhere Man', 'Paperback Writer' and 'I'm Down'.

The second of the two concerts here was filmed by the national TV station, ZDF, while the entire West German leg of the tour was dubbed the Bravo Blitztournee after the name of the country's leading entertainments magazine *Bravo*, which sponsored the

*Above: Two tickets for the Beatles' second show in Munich, one forged, one genuine. But which is which? Below: From the English-language* Japan Times.

visit. Soon after the Beatles had flown into Munich from London Airport, at noon on 23 June, police arrested five men for forging and distributing 125 tickets for the two shows in the city.

25 June     Grugahalle, Essen, Nordrhein-Westfalen, West Germany

The Beatles travelled from Munich to Essen in a special train which, one year previously, had been the mode of transport employed by Queen Elizabeth II during her royal visit to West Germany. The four Beatles, plus accompanying entourage of five, all had their own suite of rooms on board.

The Beatles gave two shows at the Grugahalle, after which they immediately returned to the station and continued their railway journey across the country. Next stop: Hamburg.

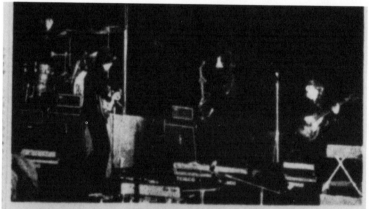

## Beatlemania Hits the Budokan
#### By MAX E. LASH

The Beatles' debut in Tokyo Thursday before an audience of about 10,000 was a howling screaming success.

It could have been more than that but Tokyo's finest had things quite well organized, thank you. Just before the Beatles were announced on the stage of the Nippon Budokan in Kudan, Tokyo, in MC F. H. Eric, rows of gray-clad, white-capped policemen moved down into the aisles and sat down.

The kiddies could scream and wave their hankies, many with tears streaming down their faces and swoon, practically, when one of their bushy-haired heros (not really bushy, mind you, but then neither are they "mop hair" ed) looked in their direction, waved, did a little dance, smiled (oh, bliss), or even shrugged.

It was all over in 30 minutes flat. Warm up music was furnished by three Beatle imitator groups from Japan. But the imitators out gyrate the genuine Beatles, in fact, they exaggerated everything

*Thousands of fans packed the Nippon Budokan in Tokyo Thursday evening to hear the Beatles with policemen sitting in the aisles.*

the Beatles, said, "We're not good musicians . . . just adequate." I wish someone would drop that adequacy on me.

McCartney did much of on-stage emceeing, too. In fact the only time the whole half hour the crowd quieted down enough to hear an image-orthicon TV camera drop to the floor was when Paul sang "Yesterday."

future this guy was a complete bust.

About losing touch . . . I'm sure the Beatles wouldn't mind a touch now and then from their little fans. But being torn apart is something else. No one has to put up with that. And I'm in favor of protecting them as long as they care to sing, write songs

**26 June**  Ernst Merck Halle,
Hamburg,
West Germany

The Beatles' train pulled into the
Central Station in Hamburg a little after
6:00 a.m. on 26 June. It was the first
time any member of the group had set
foot in the city since 1 January 1963,
three and a half incident-filled years
earlier, when – as relative nobodies –
they had completed their fortnight's
Christmas stint at the Star-Club.

On hand at the station, and backstage
before the Beatles' two shows at the
Ernst Merck Halle, were many faces
from the past, ranging from friend
Astrid Kirchherr to Bert Kaempfert, the
producer who, in 1961, had been the
first man to record the Beatles. Even
Bettina Derlien, the buxom, blonde
barmaid from the Star-Club, was there.

After the two shows, each performed
before 5600 people, 44 Hamburg
youths were arrested for rioting inside
and outside the concert venue. Despite
this, both John and Paul managed to
take a discreet, nostalgic midnight
stroll down the Reeperbahn, visiting
old haunts and friends.

---

**30 June–2 July**  Nippon Budokan Hall,
(3 nights)  Daikan-cho,
Chiyoda-ku,
Tokyo, Japan

Five concerts in the Nippon Budokan,
one on 30 June and two each on 1 July
and 2 July, before 10,000 fans on each
occasion.

Although the concerts were
massively successful (and the Beatles
legend is enormous in Japan to this
day) it was here that the tour started to
go badly wrong, and where began the
sequence of events which would finally
turn the Beatles off the idea of touring
for ever.

The first Nippon Budokan concert,
on 30 June, was filmed in colour by NTV
(Japanese television) and shown on 1
July.

From Tokyo, at 10:40 a.m. on 3 July,
the Beatles took off for the Philippines,
via a 70-minute stop-over in the VIP
lounge at Kaitak Airport, Hong Kong.

---

**4 July**  Rizal Memorial
Football Stadium,
Manila, Luzon,
Philippines

The calm before the storm . . . that is,
if two performances before a total of
80,000 fans, 30,000 at the afternoon
show and 50,000 in the evening, can be
called calm.

The Beatles left Manila International
Airport at 4:45 p.m. on 5 July and
headed for New Delhi, India (via a
brief re-fuelling stop in Bangkok), for a
few days of peaceful rest and
exploration of Indian music. Instead,
totally surprising and further
depressing the four harassed
musicians, 600 Beatles fans were on
hand to greet them at the airport and
besiege their hotel. Eventually the

*Left: Advert for the two Manila shows.
Above: Just three days before the Beatles'
Washington DC show there were 'good seats
still available'.*

---

group returned to England, touching
down at London Airport at 6:00 a.m. on
8 July.

END OF TOUR

---

**TOUR OF NORTH AMERICA**

**12 August**  International
Amphitheatre,
Chicago

The start of the last-ever Beatles tour.
Not bothering to rehearse any new
songs for live work, the Beatles
employed the same musical repertoire
as for the West Germany/Japan/
Philippines concerts. There were two
shows on this first date, with 13,000 fans
attending each one, a little short of full
capacity.

The Beatles had flown into the United
States from London Airport on 11
August, landing at Boston and
switching planes there within minutes
for Chicago.

---

**13 August**  Olympia Stadium,
Detroit

Two shows, before a total of 28,000 fans
at this indoor arena, though neither
concert was a complete sell-out.

---

**14 August**  Cleveland Stadium,
Cleveland, Ohio

This concert, like the Cleveland gig on
15 September 1964, was held up for 30
minutes after 2500 of the 20,000 fans
invaded the Cleveland Indians'
baseball pitch, from which the Beatles
were playing, during the fourth song,
'Day Tripper'.

---

**15 August**  DC Stadium,
Washington DC

One show, seen by 32,164 fans, after
which the Beatles' entourage moved
straight on to Philadelphia by coach.

---

**16 August**  Philadelphia Stadium,
Philadelphia,
Pennsylvania

This one show, seen by 21,000 people,
was held at the 60,000-seater open-air
Philadelphia Stadium. The concert was
marred by almost constant lightning,
but the potentially lethal rain held off
until ten minutes after the show had
finished.

---

**17 August**  Maple Leaf Gardens,
Toronto, Canada

Two shows at this 18,000-capacity
arena. The first, in the afternoon, was
seen by 15,000, the second, in the
evening, by 17,000.

---

**18 August**  Suffolk Downs
Racetrack,
Boston, Massachusetts

Twenty-five thousand people saw this
one show, held in one of the most
unlikely Beatles concert venues mid-
centre green on a horse-racing course.

---

**19 August**  Mid-South Coliseum,
Memphis, Tennessee

Two shows in this 13,300-seater venue:
10,000 attended the afternoon gig and
12,500 the evening performance. It was

during the second show that the famous firecracker episode took place. The Beatles effected their escape from the Coliseum back to their hotel in a Greyhound Bus while their limousine was sent out as a decoy.

**20 August**  Crosley Field, Cincinnati, Ohio

This open-air gig was cancelled owing to heavy rain and re-scheduled for noon on the following day.

**21 August**
Lunchtime
Crosley Field,
Cincinnati, Ohio

Night
Busch Stadium,
St Louis, Missouri

The re-arrangement of the Cincinnati gig meant that the Beatles had to give two concerts in one day, in cities 341 miles apart, reminiscent of the 1961–3 era. The open-air St Louis show, seen by 23,000 fans, still took place in heavy rain, despite grave risks of the Beatles being electrocuted.

After these shows, on 22 August the Beatles had a free day in New York City.

**23 August**
Shea Stadium,
New York City,
New York

Although 2000 fans had been in the queue long before the box-office for this one gig had even opened, on 31 May, the concert failed to sell out, with 11,000 of the 55,600 seats remaining unsold. This only partly explained the lack of excitement in the stadium compared to the heady success of the exuberant, record-breaking 1965 show.

The show grossed $292,000 – of which the Beatles received 65 per cent ($189,000).

Immediately after the concert the Beatles flew to Los Angeles, arriving early in the morning of 24 August, for

25,000 watched the Beatle happenings at Candlestick Park

# Bedlam at the Ball Park

a 24-hour rest in a rented house in Beverly Hills. On the morning of 25 August the group flew north to Seattle.

**25 August**
Coliseum,
Seattle, Washington

Two shows in this 15,000-seater arena. Only 8,000 tickets were sold for the afternoon performance while the evening gig was sold out.

**28 August**
Dodger Stadium,
Los Angeles,
California

After three more days of rest at their Beverly Hills mansion the Beatles returned to the concert stage with this one show, seen by 45,000, largely uncontrollable, fans.

*The end of an era, played out before 25,000 fans and surrounded by 200 policemen. It was little over nine years since John Lennon had formed his amateur skiffle outfit.*

**29 August**
Candlestick Park,
San Francisco,
California

The last-ever Beatles concert. A crowd of 25,000 saw the event, and a surprisingly good-quality cassette recording of the show was made, for posterity, by NEMS press officer Tony Barrow, at the insistence of Paul McCartney.

After the show the Beatles flew down the California coast back to their rented home in Beverly Hills. They eventually arrived back at London Airport on the morning of 31 August.

**Other engagements played**
None.

**Engagements not played**
The Beatles' two live shows in Manila, the Philippines, on 4 July 1966, before a total attendance of 80,000 at the Rizal Memorial Football Stadium, have – somewhat inexplicably – been detailed in every book on the Beatles as one solitary show in front of a 100,000 crowd at the Araneta Coliseum. Clearly another example of the 'Give a lie . . .' proverb explored in the introduction of this book. There is indeed a place called the Araneta Coliseum in Manila and many top rock groups

played there in 1966 and beyond. The Beatles were not one of them.

When the Beatles' August 1966 American tour was first announced, in April, the 14 August gig was set for the State Fairgrounds, Louisville, Kentucky. It was later switched to the Cleveland Stadium, Cleveland, Ohio. The group's 18 August Boston, Massachusetts, concert at the Suffolk Downs Racetrack was originally intended for the city's Fenway Park.

Once again, the Beatles played only one night at Shea Stadium, New York, on the tour – on 23 August. Widely published reports that they played a second concert there, on 24 August, are incorrect.

# THE MUSIC

Here is the complete live performance repertoire of the Beatles in 1966, showing the group's vocalist, the composer(s) of the song and the name of the artist/group who recorded the influential version

| Song title | Main vocalist(s) | Composer(s) | Influential version (year) |
|---|---|---|---|
| Baby's in Black | John/Paul | Lennon/McCartney | — |
| Day Tripper | John/Paul | LENNON/McCartney | — |
| I Feel Fine | John | LENNON/McCartney | — |
| I Wanna Be your Man | Ringo | Lennon/McCartney | — |
| If I Needed Someone | George | Harrison | — |
| I'm Down | Paul | Lennon/McCARTNEY | — |
| Long Tall Sally | Paul | Johnson/Penniman/Blackwell | Little Richard (1956) |
| Nowhere Man | John | LENNON/McCartney | — |
| Paperback Writer | Paul | Lennon/McCARTNEY | — |
| Rock and Roll Music | John | Berry | Chuck Berry (1957) |
| She's a Woman | Paul | Lennon/McCARTNEY | — |
| Yesterday | Paul | Lennon/McCARTNEY | — |

# CONCLUSION

## 'At that time I was just so sick of it... It was like four nervous wrecks getting flown around everywhere... It was just too much.'

GEORGE HARRISON

It was George Harrison, perhaps the most vehement among the Beatles that the concert charade had to stop, who first uttered the words that indicated that the end was nigh. Reclining in his seat as the Beatles' aeroplane left San Francisco on 29 August 1966, Harrison testily said, 'Well, that's it, I'm not a Beatle any more.'

He was nearly right. Within three more years the Beatles were effectively finished. Three highly productive years certainly, in which many people feel – the Beatles included – that they achieved far more than in the 1962–66 period. It is doubtful that *Sgt Pepper's Lonely Hearts Club Band* or *Abbey Road* could have come from the group if they were still touring.

It was hardly a coincidence that within one year of the Beatles' final concert Brian Epstein was dead from an accidental drug overdose. With his four young charges no longer so young, and with no more Beatles tours to organize – always the bread and butter work for a pop group manager – Brian's influence on the group fell away, and their dependence on him likewise. He was 32 years old.

In late 1968 Paul McCartney realized the dilemma facing the Beatles. Acrimony had invaded the ranks of the four members as never before. To Paul, ever the trooper and a real, driving showman to this day, the only hope for the Beatles was to return to their roots, their first love. Live performances. He was the only one to hold the view. John and George in particular flatly rejected the idea. Three comeback concerts mooted for the Roundhouse theatre in Chalk Farm, London, between 14 and 21 December 1968 were scrapped, as was a plan for a solitary show at the same venue on 18 January 1969. Plans to do the show from a Roman amphitheatre in North Africa – typical of the era when, it was believed, anything was possible – or from a stage in the Sahara desert, were also discarded. McCartney's final plea – that the group pile into a van and play anonymously in a church hall or pub or wherever the vehicle ended up was quashed without a second thought by the others. Hadn't they done all that before? Eventually, at lunchtime on 30 January 1969, the group compromised, and performed live – but unannounced – from the high rooftop of their Apple headquarters in Savile Row, London. (This impromptu gig is not regarded as a bona fide concert since it was not previously announced, no tickets were printed and no one could even see the group.) They were audible to the crowds quickly massing below, but invisible. That was as far as they would go.

# LIVE ENGAGEMENTS VENUE INDEX

This index refers to the Live engagements sections and Other engagements played sub-sections of the book only. Many venues have more than one entry per page reference. Performances marked as cancelled are included here, denoted by the letter c immediately after the page reference. You will find the full postal address of a venue, where known, under the first page reference.

# CREDITS

**Illustration credits**

Every effort has been made to acknowledge all those whose photographs and other illustrations have been used in this book, but if there have been any omissions in this respect I apologise and will be pleased to make the appropriate acknowledgement in any future editions.

Leslie Kearney – 11b, 18b, 20/21, 98a; Charles Roberts – 13a/b, 19b; Geoff Rhind – 14b; Beatle City – 15a, 115; David Hughes – 22a; Kressley – 27a; Sotheby Parke Bernet & Co – 27b, 28, 37a, 37b, 47b, 59b, 63, 97, 110a, 111b, 113a, 142b, 144c, 155, 167, 188b; Johnny 'Guitar' Byrne – 29b, 47a, 99, 108a; Kressley – 30a; Ken Beaton (supplied by John Askew) – 33a; Astrid Kirchherr – 40/41; The David J Smith Collection – 40a/b, 60a/b/c; Brian Kelly – 54a, 57b, 65a, 70b, 71c, 76b, 96b; Dick Matthews – front cover (a), 53a, 56, 59a/c, 61a, 62a, 66a/b, 67, 69a/b, 79 (supplied by the V & A Museum), 80a, 80c (V & A), 81a, 98c; Nigel Greenberg/Debbie Geoghegan – 57c, 114b; John Cochrane – 65c; Dave Forshaw – 71a, 72c, 107; Jurgen Vollmer – 74/5; Arthur Barry – 81b; Albert Marrion – 87b, 90b/c; Les Chadwick/The Peter Kaye Agency – 100, 104a; John Fallon – 102d; Bill Fraser Reid – 109a; Spencer Leigh – 116, 117; Tim Procter – 125a; *South Eastern Newspapers Ltd* (supplied by Terry Pratt) – 127a; Harry Hammond – 129a; Roger Howell – 129b; David Moores – 132/133; Dezo Hoffmann – 133; *Home Counties Newspapers plc* (supplied by Mark Richards) – 136/137, 137a, 160, 169; Mark Cousins – 140/141; Maurice Haigh – 144a; Peter Stringfellow – 145a; The *Reporter* Group (*South Lancashire Newspapers Ltd*) – 146b; John Smith – 149b; Liz and Jim Hughes – 156a; Unique Posters – 166b; Kathy Shaffer – 171a; The Graham Moyle Collection – 172a, 173b/c; *The San Francisco Chronicle* (photographer Art Frisch) – 181b; Tony Barrow – 185a/b, 186; Roger Scott – front cover (b), 191a, 202, back cover; Don Valentine – 208. All other illustrations are from the author's own collection.

**Newspaper credits**

The newspaper extracts in this book have been used from the following journals: *Liverpool Echo* – 11a, 20/a/b/c, 55c, 65d, 68a, 71b, 72a, 73b, 75a/b, 76a, 89a, 105, 106a, 113b, 143b, 152, 163a, 172b, 183, 196, 197; *South Liverpool Weekly News* – 14a, 16, 19a, 22c, 29a, 89b, 93a, 98b; *Liverpool Evening Express* – 15b; *West Derby Reporter* – 17b; *Manchester Evening News* – 18a, 106b; *Bootle Herald* – 22b; *Bootle Times* – 31, 43b, 44, 55a; *Alloa Advertiser* – 33b; *Inverness Courier* – 33c, 45a; *Heswall and Neston News and Advertiser* – 34a, 45b, 46a; *Wallasey News* 34b/c, 35, 43a, 45c, 46b, 48, 64, 72b, 77a/b; *Prescot and Huyton Reporter* – 38; *Maghull and Aintree Advertiser* – 38; *Maghull and Aintree Advertiser* 70a, 73a; *Walton Times* – 77c; *Crosby Herald* – 78; *Southport Visiter* – 87a, 106c; *Bebington News and Advertiser* – 90a; *Stroud News and Journal* – 91b; *Mersey Beat* (courtesy of Bill Harry) – 94, 104b, 120, 146a; *Record Retailer* (Spotlight Publications) – 101, 175; *Rhyl Journal and Advertiser* 112a; *Port Sunlight News* – 114a; *Peterborough Standard* – 118; *Runcorn Weekly News* – 119; *New Musical Express* – 128b, 139b, 168; *Kilburn Times* – 130; *Middleton Guardian* – 131; *Daily Herald* – 134/135, 136, 137b; *TV Times Magazine* – 138, 154; *Disc* – 139a; *Bridge of Allan Gazette* 143a; *Darwen Advertiser* – 144b; *The Star* (Sheffield) – 145b; *Nottingham Evening Post* 147a; *The Yorkshire Evening Press* – 147b/c, 150; *The Derbyshire Times* – 148a; *Evening Sentinel* (Stoke-on-Trent) – 149a; *Salisbury Journal* – 151b; *Guernsey Evening Press* – 153; *The Philadelphia Inquirer* – 161b; *The New York Times* – 163b; *Hong Kong Tiger Standard* – 165; *Seattle Post-Intelligencer* – 166a/c; *France-Soir* – 170; *The Sun-Herald* (Sydney) – 173a; *Svenska Dagbladet* – 174a; *San Francisco Examiner* – 176a; *The Cincinnati Enquirer* – 176b; *The Indianapolis News* – 176c; *The News-American* (Baltimore) – 177a; *Pittsburgh Post-Gazette* – 177b; *The Kansas City Star* – 177c; *The Dallas Morning News* – 177d; *Wigan Observer* – 178; *Il Giornale D'Italia* – 187; *Oregonian* (Portland) – 189a; *The Manila Times* – 191b, 193, 194, 199a; *Süddeutsche Zeitung* – 198a; *The Japan Times* – 198b; *The Washington Post* – 199b; *San Francisco Chronicle* – 200.

# NOTES ON THE FREE DISC

Unless you happened to be a patient in either Cleaver or Clatterbridge hospitals on the Wirral in England on 28 October 1962 it is unlikely that you will have heard the very rare interview featured on this free disc.

It was recorded by Monty Lister, who in those days regularly broadcast two shows, *Music with Monty* and *Sunday Spin*, at Cleaver and Clatterbridge. At 8.45 pm on 27 October 1962 Monty went to the Hulme Hall in Port Sunlight on the Wirral to interview the Beatles taking with him Malcolm Threadgill and Peter Smethurst to put questions from 'the teenage angle'.

The Beatles' first-ever radio interview is fascinating not just as an historical artefact, but because of its content. We hear Paul McCartney telling Monty that 'John Lennon is the leader of the group'. Ringo Starr, very much the new boy, is so pleased to be one of the Beatles that he is keeping a count of the number of weeks since he joined. They are making regular visits to Hamburg and telling of how these trips started, talking about the recording of their discs with Tony Sheridan in 1961 and about their first *official* record 'Love me Do'. (The group are even able to quote the disc's catalogue number – Parlophone R 4949 – in unison, proving how long they must have stared adoringly at the label.) They also mention, without naming it, a track to be recorded for their next single ('Please Please Me') and discuss their, albeit lowly, entry into the charts (or 'hit parade' to use the vernacular of the day ) and their television debut.

All this plus the group's characteristic humour – the reference to local places on the Wirral and in Cheshire are pure Beatles wit – encapsulates in a single seven-minute tape many of the ingredients which not long afterwards would gel into a musical and cultural phenomenon.